maps of the mind

The Unbalanced Mind

The Unbalanced
Mind

Julian Leff

Weidenfeld & Nicolson
LONDON

First published in Great Britain in 2001
by Weidenfeld & Nicolson

Copyright © Julian Leff 2001

A CIP catalogue record for this book is available
from the British Library.

ISBN 0 297 64640 0

Typeset by Selwood Systems, Midsomer Norton
Printed by Butler & Tanner Ltd, Frome and London

Weidenfeld & Nicolson
The Orion Publishing Group Ltd
Orion House
5 Upper Saint Martin's Lane
London, WC2H 9EA

Acknowledgements

I am grateful to my wife, Joan Raphael-Leff, for providing loving companionship during many hours of writing and for acting as a living thesaurus and a constructive critic. Thanks are also due to her mother, Fan Raphael, for researching Shabbetai Zvi, the false Messiah. The following friends and relatives read through various drafts of the book and provided me with invaluable guidance and comments: Michael Dorfman, Cheli Duran, Alex Leff, Jessa Leff, Andrew Szmidla. I am very grateful to Steven Rose for initiating this project and for steering it through to a successful conclusion.

Contents

Introduction

The so-called 'master plan' of the human genome has recently been unfolded in its entirety. Some hail this as the key that will unlock a complete understanding of the human mind and hence of human behaviour. This is a chilling vision, reminiscent of *A Clockwork Orange*, as it implies that substituting for, or transposing, the basic units of the master plan will alter human behaviour to suit the manipulator of the molecules. My purpose in writing this book is to temper this Orwellian view of the future.

I grew up in an environment of optimism that improving the environment, both physical and social, would change human behaviour for the better. My mother was a committed Marxist who believed that the establishment of communism in Russia and China heralded the dawn of Utopia. My father, also a Marxist, worked as a public health doctor, ensuring that drinking water and food were safe, that sewage was properly disposed of, that factories were safe for the workforce, and that there were sufficient day-nursery places for young children. So convinced was he of the eventual effectiveness of these kinds of environmental improvements that he tried to dissuade me from studying medicine, arguing that doctors who treated individuals would soon be redundant. The year 1956 was a disaster for the utopian vision of my parents, with Khrushchev's revelations of Stalin's enormities and the Soviet invasion of Hungary. Their activities for the

Party virtually ceased, although my father's deep commitment to the National Health Service, which he helped to establish, remained undiminished.

I had never shared my parents' illusions about Soviet communism, being turned off by any autocratic system, but their beliefs about the overriding importance of the social environment were in my bones – not my genes, since my grandfather, who lived with us throughout my childhood, was a staunch capitalist! It was not surprising, then, that when I qualified as a psychiatrist and was looking around for a job, I jumped at the offer of a position in the social psychiatry unit at the Institute of Psychiatry in London. Not only was I attracted by the intellectual challenge of a research career, but the focus of the unit and its director, John Wing, appeared entirely consonant with my own views of society. I was understandably surprised, therefore, when the first study John Wing directed me to design and conduct was a test of the value of medication to prevent repeated attacks of schizophrenia. It had already been proved that chlorpromazine (Largactil) and trifluoperazine (Stelazine) helped patients with delusions and hallucinations to recover from their illness, but it was unknown whether it was useful for them to continue to take these medicines once they were well. I tackled the problems of designing a trial of preventive medication with a will, but was determined to include some measure of the social environment. Reading the literature, I discovered that social stress in the form of sudden happenings, known as life events, provoked attacks of schizophrenia (more about this later), so I included measures of life events in the study.

My conclusion at the end of the trial was that continuing with medication following recovery did reduce the chance of a further attack of illness.[1] The inclusion of the life events measure added another dimension to our understanding of the results. A similar trial was being conducted by my colleague Steven Hirsch, who was testing the value of preventive medication given by long-acting injection.[2] We were able to pool the data from the two trials to look at the effects of life events in a reasonably large group of patients. We found that eighty-nine per cent of patients whose illness returned while they were taking medication had experienced a life event in the five weeks before the relapse, compared with only twenty-seven per cent of those on drugs who remained well throughout the trial.[3] This showed that unexpected events causing a high level of stress could break through the protective barrier built up by the medication.

My first experience of conducting research in the unit gave me an understanding of the importance of including both a biological and a social perspective on psychiatric problems. In this book I do not challenge the importance of the biological basis of mental activity, but as far as possible show how it can be integrated with our understanding of the impact of the social environment. A substantial amount of research has accumulated over many decades revealing the importance to mental wellbeing of the network of relationships that each of us experiences as centred on ourselves. It appears to radiate outwards from us, encompassing (with increasing distance) family, friends, workmates, shopkeepers and acquaintances. This is, of course, an illusion stemming from our egocentric view of the world. Seen from above, there would be a continuous network with no centre, but with areas of greater and lesser density, constituting an entire culture. In the course of the book I will focus on smaller and larger sections of the network, from the most intimate relationships to the whole culture.

I will also present material on different types of psychiatric conditions. Mental illness takes many forms ranging from emotional distress, affecting most of us at some time in our life, to psychotic illnesses such as manic-depression and schizophrenia, which appear in about one per cent of the population. It is important to appreciate a general distinction between neuroses and psychoses. Neuroses represent an intensification of emotions that all humans feel, such as depression and anxiety, to the point when they interfere with daily life. People with psychoses can also have high levels of depression and anxiety, but in addition they have experiences that are out of the ordinary, such as developing beliefs that are not shared by their own social group (delusions), or hearing voices and seeing visions that others do not hear or see (hallucinations). The main psychoses are schizophrenia and manic-depressive illness. Depression is awkward because it runs across the boundaries between neuroses and psychoses and hence has always faced psychiatrists with the challenge of knowing how to fit it into their systems of classification. The social, political and economic forces that influence psychiatrists' choice of pigeonholes will be explored later.

Both psychoses and neuroses feature several times in the story as they serve to advance my argument about the importance of the social environment for the whole range of psychiatric conditions. The sequence of the narrative is driven more by my exploration of different features of the social environment than by any particular classification of illnesses. Hence I will sometimes use schizophrenia to illustrate a point, and sometimes depression or another neurosis. When I began my research career in 1968 there were six research units supported by the Medical Research Council or the Department of Health, dedicated to investigating social issues in psychiatry. Today there is none. Biological research is generally seen to be the best bet for finding the answers to people's mental problems, and since the technical equipment and support needed are very expensive, there are few funds left over for social research. By the end of the book, I hope you will have gained an appreciation of the need for a balance between biological and social explanations for the vagaries of the human mind.

Chapter 1 | How Blue is Blue?

We all have times when we feel miserable, often for no apparent reason. We talk of feeling 'blue', of being 'down in the dumps', or 'under the weather'. We proffer explanations which have no plausibility, such as 'I got out of bed the wrong side this morning'. Sometimes a low mood is an obvious consequence of a major disruption in our life, such as the break-up of a relationship or the death of someone we love. Our friends and relatives would be concerned for us if we became sad following such an event, but would not think of us as ill.

Andrew held a responsible job in a wines and spirits firm in which he had worked for twenty years. He had another fifteen years before retirement and enjoyed his work. The firm was taken over by a large corporation and he was declared redundant without notice. He was shocked and could not believe it had happened to him. He lay awake at night experiencing a mixture of misery and rage. He went off his food and moped around all day doing nothing. His wife and friends rallied round and encouraged him to think of alternative jobs. After a few weeks of being paralysed by his situation, he began to look for a position and realised that there were a number of options open to him.

How intense does our misery have to become before a doctor would consider it to be an illness and diagnose depression?

Should Andrew have been treated with antidepressants? The problem facing the doctor is that there is no test that will reveal whether the person is suffering from a depressive illness. In fact this problem affects the whole of psychiatry. There are no distinctive abnormalities of the blood, the body chemistry, the electrical activity of the brain or its appearance that can serve to diagnose any of the common psychiatric disorders. Numerous studies have identified changes in the structure of the brain and in the form of the brain waves in people with schizophrenia, while depressed people have been found to have abnormalities in the amounts of certain chemical transmitters in the brain. However, many people with these illnesses do not differ from healthy people in their brain structure and function, while some people with no psychiatric symptoms show the same abnormalities as the patients. This large overlap between healthy and ill people makes it impossible for the psychiatrist to use these brain changes to make a diagnosis.

Exciting new methods continue to be developed to visualise the structure and function of the brain. Although beautiful pictures are produced by these techniques, they have not advanced to the stage where they can be used to back up a diagnosis. There is a widespread belief among psychiatrists and researchers that this goal is not far off, but no one can be sure that it will ever be achieved.

Serendipity and psychiatric treatments

We can ask how far depression might be explained by changes in the functioning of the brain. Our thoughts, feelings and actions are obviously the result of brain activity at one level; but it does not follow that depression can be explained by changes in the way the brain works, or that reversing these changes would necessarily cure the depression. Antidepressant drugs were introduced in the 1950s and have become one of the most widely prescribed class of psychiatric treatments. But they were not designer drugs, chemically crafted to correct a known abnormality in the brain. Far from it: one of the first groups of antidepressants was developed from isoniazid, an antibiotic used for tuberculosis, because it was noticed that patients treated with this medication appeared to gain relief from the depressing effects of their chronic ill-health. Many of the treatments introduced into psychiatry have their origins in serendipity, including another frequently prescribed group of drugs, the tricyclic anti-depressants. The first representative of this group, imi-pramine (UK trade name Tofranil), was synthesised in the 1940s as one of a series of antihistamines, sedatives and painkillers. It was recommended as a treatment to calm agi-tated psychotic patients, but in 1958 it was found to do little for these patients, but to have effects in relieving depression.

How the brain sends messages

A recent development in the drug treatment of depression is the introduction of a family of drugs called specific serotonin reuptake inhibitors (SSRIs). Signals are sent between brain cells (neurons) by chemicals known as transmitters. One of the most common chemical messengers in the brain is serotonin, the chemical name of which is 5-hydroxy-tryptamine. Serotonin is also found in the gut, and in bananas as well! One theory is that depression is caused by an inherited lack of serotonin in the brain.

The brain is an efficient organ and does not waste chem-icals. When a transmitter has been released and has activated a receptor on the adjacent brain cell, any excess is transferred back into the nerve ending ('reuptake'), to be recirculated later. There is a specific serotonin reuptake process which works through a transporter molecule. The use of an SSRI to prevent this molecule transporting the excess serotonin back into the nerve ending results in an increase in the amount of serotonin washing around the neurons. Since serotonin activates a particular class of brain cells, this increase is believed to counteract the sluggishness of these neurons in depression. The drug fluoxetine, better known as Prozac, is an SSRI, but is only one of a whole family of antidepressants with similar effects on the level of serotonin in the brain. Although these drugs specifically block the reuptake of serotonin, they are not like so-called 'smart' bombs which pinpoint targets, since they affect the chemical process wherever it occurs in the body. As there are many serotonin receptors in the gut, 'collateral damage' occurs in the form of unpleasant intestinal side-effects, such as nausea and diarrhoea.

Maternity blues

One of the pieces of evidence put forward for a biochemical origin for depression is the occurrence of 'maternity blues' in the mother immediately after the birth of a baby. Dramatic hormonal changes occur in the mother's body with the expulsion of the placenta and the onset of lactation. The mother's mood swings up and down for the first few days after the birth and bouts of tearfulness are common, the lowest point being between the third and fifth postnatal day. There is, however, a great deal of individual variation: some mothers do not experience a low mood, and most of those who do level out in a few days, while a small group go on to develop a full-blown depressive illness. The proportions at each stage have been determined by a group of researchers working in a maternity hospital in Paris in 1997.[4] They gave two questionnaires to 126 women who gave birth at their hospital. The first questionnaire was designed to detect maternity blues and was filled in by the mothers on the third or fourth day after delivery. The second was aimed at picking up depression of clinical severity and was completed eight months after the birth. The mothers were asked to respond to the questions according to their feelings in the previous eight days. Almost exactly half the women reported experiencing maternity blues: of those with moderate blues, sixteen per cent were diagnosed as depressed eight months later, whereas of those with severe blues, the proportion who became depressed reached twenty-eight per cent. Of the sixty-four women who escaped the blues, only one was rated as depressed at eight months. These figures establish a strong link between maternity blues and later depression, and suggest that there may be a common biochemical basis for the two conditions, but that is not the whole story.

In order to discover why some women were more likely than others to develop depression after a birth, in the 1980s Channi Kumar and Kay Robson in London investigated a number of factors that might be responsible.[5] One of their findings was unexpected: women who had had an induced abortion were more prone to postnatal depression than those without this history. This was true even if the abortion had been many years earlier. It is inconceivable that the hormonal changes following an abortion could linger for years, so that the most plausible explanation is that the psychological impact of the abortion was reactivated by the birth of a baby, intensifying the biochemical changes occurring at that time. This is not the only environmental factor to be implicated in the origin of postnatal depression. Other researchers have stressed the importance of difficult living conditions, socio-economic problems, and lack of emotional support from the child's father and the wider social network. These aspects of environmental stress have also been shown to contribute to the causation of depression unrelated to childbirth.

Genes and the mind

Research on the impact of the social environment on a person's feelings, thoughts and behaviour has been overshadowed in recent years by the conviction held by many brain scientists that all mental activity will sooner or later be explicable in terms of genes and molecules. It is undeniable that the infant science of molecular genetics has already led to huge leaps in our understanding of certain physical diseases, such as cystic fibrosis. Identification of the specific sequence of the particular gene that gives rise to the abnormality raises the exciting possibility of correcting the problem at source through genetic engineering. There have been extravagant claims to have found a gene for homosexuality and for child abuse, but these have not been replicated by other scientists. A number of different genes have been linked with schizophrenia, for which the evidence for an inherited basis is strong. However, no single gene has been identified as the prime cause of the illness and some research groups have failed to find the same links as others. It seems likely that a number of different genes acting in concert are risk factors for the brain problems underlying schizophrenia. The inheritance of height, for example, is known to depend on the interaction of a number of genes. We have to conclude that, so far, the bright promise of molecular genetics has failed to illuminate any psychiatric condition beyond identifying some genes as potential risk factors.

Public attitudes

It is intriguing that the scientists' love affair with biological determinism has not influenced the views of the public on the causes and treatment of mental illness. Numerous surveys of public opinion over the years have come up with the same finding: stress is held to be the prime cause of the entire range of psychiatric conditions from anxiety to schizophrenia. This belief has a long pedigree: Shakespeare in *The Comedy of Errors* has an abbess question the wife of a man deemed to be mad as follows: 'Hath he not lost much wealth by wrack of sea? Buried some dear friend? Hath not else his eye stray'd his affection in unlawful love, a sin prevailing much in youthful men, who give their eyes the liberty of gazing? Which of these sorrows is he subject to?' When asked about the treatment of mental illnesses, the public favour social support and talking therapies over physical treatments, and are generally very wary of antidepressants, which they view as addictive. This mistaken conviction may well have been implanted by the widely disseminated information on the addictive nature of the minor tranquillisers, such as chlordiazepoxide (Librium) and diazepam (Valium), which for a time were extensively prescribed to depressed patients by primary care doctors.

The term 'addiction' is used loosely by the public, as in 'addicted to shopping'. In medicine it covers both a psychological reliance on a drug, and also a physical need for it, which develops over time with certain drugs. Thus a person who is physically addicted to alcohol will develop the 'shakes' after a day or so of not drinking, or even start to see small animals crawling over the walls and floor (delirium tremens or 'the DTs'). The minor tranquillisers can produce a physical addiction even at small doses, so that a patient who stops taking them will experience very unpleasant sensations. Antidepressants never produce physical addiction, and most patients can stop them without ill effects, although a few find that their depression returns soon after. An educational campaign mounted recently in Britain by the Royal College of Psychiatrists and the Royal College of General Practitioners, which was partly aimed at lessening public prejudice against antidepressants, made only a small impact. We shall encounter this prejudice and its effects on compliance with drug prescriptions later, in our discussion of treatments for depression.

Measuring depression across cultures

Up to this point we have sidestepped the issue referred to in the title of this chapter, namely how miserable do you have to be before you cross the threshold into the domain of depression that requires treatment. We have to confront this question before discussing the social factors leading to depression, since it is fundamental to any comparison of results across studies. In 1988 I compiled a review of a large number of studies of the frequency of depression in the general population. These surveys had been carried out in many different countries, both developed, such as Britain, Greece and Argentina, and developing, such as Taiwan, India and Uganda. A variety of interview schedules and questionnaires had been used, making direct comparison of results very problematic. Imagine using a ruler marked in inches in one country and one marked in centimetres in another, and then attempting to compare the two sets of measurements without knowing how to convert from inches to centimetres. A more useful approach is to employ the same instrument for measuring depression in both countries, but unless the people speak the same language, it is necessary to translate it. This is not as straightforward as it might seem, since the accuracy of the translation has to be verified. The technique that has been developed for this purpose is called back-translation. One person translates the instrument from language A into language B. A second person, independent of the first, then translates the instrument back from language B to language A. The two versions in language A are then compared for discrepancies, revealing any faulty translations into B, which can then be corrected. Even this careful procedure is not foolproof, since it fails to detect problems with the usage of particular words. An example is provided by Lyn Gillis and his colleagues who translated a psychiatric assessment interview, the Present State Examination, from English into Xhosa, a South African language, in 1982.[6] The Xhosa term for emotion, *inimba*, appeared to be correct when back-translated into English, but when the Xhosa version was used it emerged that the term denoted a feeling state that can only be experienced by women.

Very few of the studies I reviewed had used the same instrument plus the technique of back-translation. The frequency of depression and other neuroses ranged from a low of 0.8 per 1000 people in an aboriginal population on the island of Taiwan to a high of 287 per 1000 for women in Buenos Aires. It is unlikely that human populations differ so remarkably in their liability to neuroses, so that much of the variation can be attributed to problems of measurement. In support of this interpretation are the findings from a study conducted in 1979 in Uganda by John Orley and John Wing.[7] John Orley has an unusual combination of training in both anthropology and psychiatry. He lived in a village in Uganda for eighteen months and learned the local language, Buganda. He then translated the Present State Examination interview into Buganda, following which his version was checked by back-translation. He surveyed two villages with this measuring instrument and then compared the rates of neuroses with those derived from a survey in London. The rate for Ugandan women was 269 per 1000 compared with 106 per 1000 for women in London. The rates for men were 174 and 58 per 1000 respectively. While the rates are two and a half to three times higher for Ugandan women and men, this is a credible difference compared with the 300-fold variation between the highest and lowest rates in my survey of the literature.

Measuring symptoms

We can learn a great deal about the measurement of depression by considering the construction of the Present State Examination (PSE). In the absence of laboratory tests, the only information available on which to base a diagnosis is the person's experiences and behaviour. Experience can be tapped only by questioning the person directly, while behaviour can be observed by the interviewer, supplemented by accounts given by people who know the person well (usually relatives). The techniques of exploring the person's experiences and classifying them derive from the science of phenomenology, and were applied definitively to psychiatry by the German psychiatrist, Karl Jaspers, whose textbook was published in 1913. The PSE provides the interviewer with a skeletal structure of questions which prompt a dialogue with the interviewee. The purpose of the dialogue is to explore and clarify the person's experiences in order to determine whether they fit the categories of symptoms built into the PSE.

Here is an example of a dialogue with a patient generated by the section of the PSE which covers anxiety:

Interviewer: Have there been times lately when you've been very anxious or frightened?
Patient: Yes, there have.
Interviewer: Have you tended to get very anxious in certain special situations, such as travelling, or crossing the road?
Patient: Yes, I find it hard to go out.
Interviewer: Does it bother you to cross open spaces like parks or squares, or do you get anxious in shops or on buses?
Patient: I can walk across a square if there aren't many people around, but I can't stand being in a shop with crowds of people.
Interviewer: Is it the same problem with a crowded bus?
Patient: Oh, yes. If a bus comes along that's full of people, I'll wait for the next one in the hope that it will be less crowded.
Interviewer: Do you find it easier to go out at night?
Patient: Yes, I do all my shopping at late-night supermarkets, because there aren't many other people around and I don't have to stand in a queue with other customers.

The interviewer's detective work establishes that the patient has anxiety that is provoked by being in crowds, which is classified as a phobia. The interview schedule is accompanied by a glossary which defines each symptom precisely and gives examples. People's experiences rarely fit neatly into predetermined categories, so the interviewer often has to judge whether an experience approximates closely enough to a definition to be rated as a symptom. In making this judgement, the interviewer needs to take into account both the intensity of the experience and its frequency. To take the pertinent example of depressed mood, the questions that need to be asked are: how often during the past month has the person felt depressed? Has it occurred every day or only once or twice a week? How long does it last? Does the person cry or feel like crying? Here I should comment that the interviewer must gauge the answer in the light of the person's gender and culture. It is more acceptable for women to cry than men, except on the football field, where the whole range of emotions gains much freer expression than in everyday life. Furthermore, people from northern Europe are less expressive than those from southern Europe.

Other questions that will help the interviewer decide on the degree of depression are: does the low mood fluctuate in intensity or remain at the same level? Can it be relieved by anything, for example, can a friend cheer the person up? Has all enjoyment of life ceased or are there still things that can be enjoyed? How bad is the feeling when it is at its worst? This last question differs in kind from the others as it is not factual, but requires the person to find their own words to describe their experience. Expressions such as 'it feels like a dark cloud', 'I feel paralysed by it', or, paradoxically, 'it is an indescribable feeling', indicate a severity of mood that is well beyond ordinary sadness.

Here are some other descriptions by patients from interviews with the PSE which convey the experience of depression:

'I just can't make myself do anything. My brain isn't working at all. My mind has gone dead. I've just become like this. I can't say to myself, "do this, do that". I'm just not how I used to be.'

'I'm fighting the tiredness and the depression. Trying to organise my life. Everything's been such a muddle. I spent days lying in bed. The tiredness was getting me down. I have been crying incessantly.'

'I get gloomy over anything I read in the newspapers. I dreamed about my father dying. I feel everyone would be better off without me.'

'Sometimes I feel low and I cry quite a lot. I can see no future and I feel completely trapped. There's an emptiness inside me. Nothing means anything. I feel as if I'm sinking.'

The presence of depressed mood is obviously essential for a diagnosis of a depressive illness, but there are other symptoms that often accompany it and that contribute to the diagnosis. These include poor appetite and weight loss, difficulty in sleeping, loss of interest in sex, slowness in thinking and moving about, lack of energy, and poor concentration. The PSE requires the interviewer to enquire about each symptom in some detail to establish its presence, as in the example above. Consequently the interview is long and demanding for both interviewer and subject. Various short cuts have been developed in the form of self-report questionnaires, which do not require the presence of a professional person and can even be sent by post or be filled in on a computer. They cannot achieve the same degree of accuracy as an interview like the PSE, but they are practical alternatives for large-scale surveys. Some attempt to cover a wide range of symptoms of neurosis, such as the General Health Questionnaire developed by David Goldberg in 1970 while he was in Manchester,[8] while others have a narrow focus on symptoms of depression and/or anxiety, such as the Hamilton Rating Scale for Depression and the Beck Depression Inventory. A couple of questions from the latter will convey the style of these questionnaires.

B. 0 I am not particularly pessimistic or discouraged about the future.

1 I feel discouraged about the future.

2a I feel I have nothing to look forward to.

2b I feel that I won't ever get over my troubles.

3 I feel that the future is hopeless and that things cannot improve.

H. o I don't feel I am any worse than anybody else.

　1 I am critical of myself for my weaknesses or mistakes.

　2 I blame myself for my faults.

　3 I blame myself for everything bad that happens.

Processing the data

There is a major difference between self-report questionnaires and interview-based instruments in the way a diagnosis is derived from the answers. The PSE data are processed by a computer program which incorporates an algorithm, or set of rules. These assign greater weight to some symptoms than to others and attempt to reproduce the decisions a clinician makes in arriving at a diagnosis. A program of this nature not only standardises the process of diagnosis, which varies considerably from one psychiatrist to another, it makes the rules open to examination. By comparing the diagnoses of individual psychiatrists with the output of the program and discussing the differences, the diagnostic rules used by clinicians (which often remain unformulated) can be brought into the open and studied. As we shall see later, the opportunity to make this comparison internationally revealed striking differences between the Russians, the Americans, and the rest of the world in the rules governing the diagnosis of schizophrenia.

The answers to self-report questionnaires are dealt with in a much simpler manner. The scores on each question are simply added up to give a total score, and if this exceeds a certain threshold, the person is deemed to be suffering from a psychiatric illness. We can ask whether it is legitimate to add a score of two on depression to a score of three on hopelessness and come up with a meaningful five. Are we not giving equal weight to pigs and cows? Although this objection cannot be dismissed and should give rise to a continual sense of unease about the summing of scores on such questionnaires, this has become the standard way of deciding who is suitable for a trial of treatments for depression. The use of a 'Hamilton score' of fourteen or above has been the criterion for selection of patients for many internationally recognised studies, funded by prestigious scientific bodies. Furthermore, changes in such total scores have been used regularly to decide whether one treatment is more effective than another. The expression of the patient's experience in numbers, however spurious in principle, has been forced on psychiatric researchers by the absence of laboratory measures of mental ill-health.

Measuring stress

If the measurement of psychiatric symptoms is contentious, how much more so are attempts to quantify stress in the person's environment. One of the first instruments was developed in 1967 by Thomas Holmes and Richard Rahe,[9] whose interest was aroused by the high proportion of men who developed a psychiatric illness shortly after joining the American navy. They compiled a list of what they called Life Events, which were sudden happenings in a person's life which would be expected to have a psychological impact. There are events that we would all think worthy of inclusion, such as losing your job or the birth of a baby, but then there are hard choices over less portentous happenings, such as finding that someone has scraped your parked car. Faced with the problem of determining the relative impact of their list of events, Holmes and Rahe decided to rely on the common sense of the ordinary citizen and asked a panel of nearly 400 non-professional people to rank forty-three events in order of severity. They were advised to base their judgement on the intensity of response and the time required to adjust one's accustomed pattern of life to the event. There was generally good agreement between the judges on the rank order, with death of spouse heading the list, followed by divorce, and with Christmas coming one from last.

Life events and schizophrenia

Ground-breaking as Holmes' and Rahe's innovation was, there are faults with the method that were picked up by George Brown, a British sociologist who has made many creative contributions to the field of social research in psychiatry.[10] Starting his research in the 1950s, he introduced three modifications which jacked up the technique to a much higher level of sophistication. Two of them aim to unravel the problem of cause and effect, which we shall encounter again and again in these pages. If a life event is to be a potential cause of a psychiatric illness, it is obvious that there has to be a time interval between its occurrence and the beginning of the illness. However few psychiatric illnesses develop abruptly over a few days, and some individuals experience a year or more of gradually deteriorating health before the illness declares itself with characteristic symptoms. Some people who eventually arrive at the clinic with schizophrenia have endured many months of poor concentration, sleeplessness and irritability, symptoms which in themselves are not diagnostic of any psychiatric illness. Nevertheless, these heralds of illness may so impair people's ability to work that they may be dismissed from their job.

William left school at eighteen and found a temporary office job in a software firm. He did well for the first six months and was being considered for a permanent position. However, he began to experience difficulty getting up in the morning and started arriving late. When he was reprimanded by his manager he argued fiercely, claiming that it was not his fault. He was given a warning and for a week or so his timekeeping improved. Then it was discovered that work he was supposed to have completed was left undone. He was dismissed and stayed at home, spending most of the day in bed. A few weeks later he started to complain that people were following him in the street and that his bedroom was bugged.

In this example, losing the job was not a cause of the illness but followed from the problems William experienced through its early manifestations. To clarify this confusion, Brown stipulated that in studies of life events only patients with a clear-cut onset of illness should be included, and furthermore that the onset should be dated conservatively, that is as far back in time as suggested by the history of its development. In addition he distinguished between events that had clearly been brought about by the patient's behaviour (dependent events), those that *might* have been so caused (possibly independent events), and events that could not be ascribed to any action of the patient (independent events). Returning to Shakespeare's list of events from *The Comedy of Errors*, the first two, loss of wealth through shipwreck and death of a friend, are obviously independent events, while the third, an extramarital affair, would be classified as a possibly independent event or a dependent event according to the nature of the illness. For instance, some patients who develop mania (a state of excitement) become promiscuous during the early phase of the illness. Brown excluded dependent events from consideration and conducted separate analyses for independent and possibly independent events. His first study to introduce these innovations was conducted on schizophrenia with the collaboration of Jim Birley, a psychiatrist. They used a sample of employees from a south London factory as a control group and found that fourteen per cent of them experienced an independent life event in any three-week period before the date of the interview. The patients had a similar rate in each three-week period covered by the interview except for the one immediately preceding the onset of an episode of schizophrenia, when the proportion with an independent event rose to forty-six per cent. This clustering of events in the three weeks before an attack of schizophrenia strongly suggests that a proportion of such attacks (nearly a third) are brought on by the stress of a life event.

Life events and depression

Brown next turned his attention to depression, but was still not entirely satisfied with the measurement technique he was using. From his research on schizophrenia he had learned that the same event could have a very different impact on people depending on their life circumstances. For example, the reaction to the death of a parent would depend on one's relationship with the deceased person, as well as their age at death, the nature of their terminal illness, and the time period over which they died. He was not convinced of the value of Holmes' and Rahe's panel of ordinary citizens for this purpose, and instead introduced a method of assessing what he termed the 'contextual threat' of particular events.[11] His data indicated that the events preceding a depressive illness represented the loss of a valued relationship, a cherished goal, or a material object of value. In order to assess the psychological implications of such an event for particular individuals, it is necessary to know a great deal about their life and the nature of their relationships with the significant people in their social ambit. In collaboration with Tirril Harris, Brown developed an interview schedule to collect this information; the Life Events and Difficulties Schedule (LEDS). Armed with these data, a group of researchers meet to discuss the meaning of each event in the context of the person's life circumstances and to reach a consensus on the level of severity it represents. After receiving training, researchers can reach a high degree of reliability in making these judgements.

The innovative nature of this technique needs to be seen against the tendency to collect increasingly larger samples of subjects, which is occurring throughout medical research. The greater the number of subjects, the higher the likelihood that the researcher will obtain a result that can be shown to be important by statistical tests. As sample sizes increase, it becomes more and more difficult to collect detailed information about each subject, so that researchers are always seeking short cuts to obtain data. Hence the popularity of self-report questionnaires over in-depth interviews. As a result of this trend, the uniqueness of the individual becomes submerged in the ocean of extensive, but not intensive, data. Brown has shown that it is possible to retain a focus on the individual subject even when collecting quite large population samples.

Vulnerable women

Brown's and Harris's research was focused on women, since population surveys regularly show that women are almost twice as likely as men to develop depression. They studied population samples in London and used the PSE to determine which women were currently suffering from depression. By comparing non-depressed with depressed women, they were able to show that the latter experienced an excess of moderately or severely threatening life events in the three months before the onset of their symptoms. Brown and Harris not only provided research evidence for the popular belief that stress can bring on depression, but went on to identify factors that made particular women more vulnerable to life events than others. Some women in their sample experienced threatening life events without developing depression during the next three months. By comparing these subjects with the depressed women, Brown and Harris picked out three factors making women particularly likely to develop depression following a stressful life event: loss of the woman's mother before she was eleven years old; three children under the age of five years; and the absence of an intimate relationship with a partner. Each of these vulnerability factors has different social and psychological implications, although they may be linked in interesting ways.

Michael Rutter,[12] a child psychiatrist who worked with George Brown in the 1960s, conducted a comprehensive review of the research on separation from one's mother and came to the conclusion that separation was not inevitably harmful to mental health. The effects depended on whether there was a reasonable mother substitute available in the form of other relatives or foster parents, or whether the child was consigned to the not-so-tender mercies of institutional care. Subsequent to Rutter's review, it has become known that physical and sexual abuse have been horrifyingly common in British children's homes. It is likely that girls who have lost their mother and have not experienced adequate substitute care, fail to value themselves as women. It is also known that abuse in childhood damages a person's self-image. Low self-esteem has been found to characterise people with depression, and could also lead to choosing a partner who fails to provide emotional support. Women who have been abused as children often form relationships with men who are likely to repeat the abuse. The stressful nature of caring for three children under the age of five is self-evident; however, we should take account of the influence of social class on this factor. Working-class women are less likely to be able to plan the interval between their children than middle-class women, while the latter have more resources to buy in help with child care. By an 'intimate' relationship, Brown and Harris meant one in which the woman could confide in her partner and receive emotional support. For most subjects intimate relationships were with male sexual partners, but some women achieved intimacy and received emotional support from other women in a non-sexual relationship.

Support for these findings came from a large-scale survey in the north west of England in 1998. Judy Harrison and her colleagues in Manchester sent out Goldberg's General Health Questionnaire to 61,000 adults and received completed forms back from sixty-three per cent, the usual level of response to postal surveys.[13] A high score on the questionnaire indicates that the person is suffering from depression or anxiety. The strongest association with a high score was not having someone to talk to about problems. Contact with a friend in the previous two weeks was linked with lower scores. I will return to the importance of these confiding friendships later.

The research of Brown and Harris has become justly famous for identifying social factors as making both remote and recent contributions to the causation of depression. How do these findings square with biochemical theories? They are, of course, not mutually contradictory. The fact that SSRIs, working on neurotransmitters in the brain, can relieve depression does not negate the influence of social factors in bringing about and perpetuating the condition. I will present research bringing together these disparate perspectives in Chapter 4.

Neurasthenia in China

A thorny problem affecting the clinical management of depression is the strong tendency for the symptoms to recur. For this reason, many experts recommend taking anti-depressant drugs for at least six months, and some stipulate one year. But what if the social circumstances contributing to the depression have not altered when the patient stops the medication? An intriguing study in China illuminates this question. Arthur Kleinman,[14] an American anthropologist and psychiatrist, became interested in the diagnosis of neurasthenia, regularly used in China but no longer found in the diagnostic vocabulary of psychiatrists in the rest of the world. He interviewed a consecutive series of one hundred patients who attended the psychiatric outpatient clinic of a hospital in Hunan for the first time, and who were given the diagnosis of neurasthenia. As he had anticipated, he found that ninety-three of the hundred patients satisfied the criteria of the American diagnostic system for a depressive illness, although only nine of these complained of depression. The great majority presented exclusively or predominantly with bodily symptoms, a phenomenon I will return to in Chapter 6. Kleinman then treated the depressed patients with antidepressants, following which sixty-five per cent reported that they were substantially improved six weeks later, and another seventeen per cent that they were slightly improved. However, thirty per cent considered their social impairment to be worse, and thirty-seven per cent sought further help from practitioners of traditional Chinese medicine and from Western-style doctors. Kleinman concluded, 'Medical treatment for chronic conditions without significant psychosocial intervention exerts only a limited effect on the overall illness.' He recommended that psychiatrists should direct their efforts to changing the patient's social environment, including interventions on a large scale. While psychiatrists' power is puny compared with the forces behind the Chinese Cultural Revolution, altering the patient's immediate social environment would be feasible. In Chapter 3 we describe the effects of such social engineering on a micro scale.

Manic-depressive illness

Depression varies considerably in severity, ranging from the relatively mild varieties that Brown and Harris studied in community samples, to a degree of intensity where people may be so slowed down in thought and action that they are unable to move or speak. At this severe end of the spectrum patients may develop delusions and hallucinations, symptoms that are commonly seen in schizophrenia and are described in detail in Chapter 2. The severe type of depression is also associated with mania, its opposite in terms of speedy thinking, talking and moving. There have been long and inconclusive arguments in the psychiatric literature as to whether the depression that is part of manic-depressive illness lies on a continuum with milder forms, common in the community, or whether it should be classified as a distinct condition. Once again, psychiatric diagnosis founders on the absence of characteristic laboratory findings. What has been established, however, is that manic-depressive illness runs in families and that it is strongly determined by heredity. It has been argued that psychiatric conditions with a strong inherited basis are largely attributable to biochemical changes in the brain. At its most extreme, this stance has been satirised as 'the crooked gene gives rise to the crooked thought'. The argument can be extended to propose that strongly inherited conditions are less influenced by factors in the social environment. Depression with delusions and hallucinations is one of the rarer psychotic illnesses, and so far the role of life events in determining its onset has not been established. Mania has been more extensively studied in this aspect and several researchers, including myself, have found that independent life events cluster in the few weeks before the first onset of this illness. Interestingly, one study found that there was no excess of life events preceding later episodes of mania. This suggests that life events play an important role in setting the illness in motion, but it then develops a momentum of its own, perhaps driven by biochemical changes in the brain, and uninfluenced by environmental stress.

One other aspect of manic-depressive illness marks it off from the milder form of depression, and that is the response of the symptoms to a naturally occurring salt, lithium chloride. Many patients find that their mood swings, both up and down, are controlled by taking lithium chloride. Once again this was a serendipitous discovery. Lithium chloride, which has a salty taste, was used as a substitute for table salt (sodium chloride) for patients with high blood pressure who needed to restrict their intake of sodium. It was noticed that hypertensive patients on lithium chloride were more stable in mood than those not using it, and it was tried out for patients with mania and found to be effective.

The measurement of depression

I have described the range of disturbances of mood from mild forms of emotional distress to manic-depressive illness and have shown how psychiatric researchers have attempted to identify when depression should be treated. This has been done by using a combination of a qualitative approach, exploring the person's experience of mood changes, and a quantitative approach, adding up scores on a list of symptoms. No doubt mistakes are made either side of the boundary between distress and depression, but in the present state of knowledge this is the best practical solution. To return to the example which opens this chapter, if Andrew had been given a questionnaire to fill in, his score could have been used to decide whether he was suffering from a depressive illness. However, although this would be the procedure for a research study, it would certainly not be used by his general practitioner, who would rely on clinical skills to make the decision. Unfortunately it has been well established that general practitioners miss one-third of the cases of depression that come to their clinics. This is not a trivial problem since even the milder forms of depression can disrupt the person's life and relationships, an issue to which I will return later.

At the end of this chapter I referred to manic-depressive illness, one of the psychoses. In the next chapter I will explore how psychiatrists distinguish between this illness and schizophrenia, the other major psychosis, and investigate the cultural and political forces that shape the process of diagnosis.

Chapter 2

Moscow and Washington versus the Rest of the World

Delusions and religious beliefs

In the previous chapter I emphasised the importance of thoroughly exploring the patient's experience in order to determine which types of symptoms are present. In no area of symptoms is this more important than those characterising the psychoses. The term 'psychosis' is used for conditions in which the patient loses touch with reality; these include manic-depressive illness and schizophrenia. Up to the end of the nineteenth century these were lumped together under a general category of 'madness'. It was the German psychiatrist Emil Kraepelin who separated off the two entities in 1896, naming them 'manic-depressive psychosis' and 'dementia praecox'. In 1911 Eugen Bleuler, a Swiss psychiatrist, coined the term 'schizophrenia', which has displaced Kraepelin's original label. The symptoms that the two psychotic conditions have in common are delusions and hallucinations. Delusions are defined as false beliefs, which are not shared by others from the person's cultural background, and which cannot be shaken by argument. The proviso about the cultural background is essential but gives rise to many difficulties in interpretation.

Particular problems arise in relation to religious beliefs. The beliefs of mainstream religions which have millions of adherents create no dilemmas, but small sects can raise the difficult issue of what constitutes an acceptable belief. Two recent examples are the sect headed by Jim Jones in Guyana and the Branch Davidian sect in Waco, Texas, led by David Koresh. Both ended tragically: Jim Jones' group of more than 700 followers committed suicide at his instigation, while most of Koresh's group died in a fire when their headquarters were stormed by federal troops. When a large group of people share a set of beliefs, however unusual they may seem to outsiders, they form a subculture which legitimises their convictions and invalidates their being labelled as delusions. An even more extreme example was the suicide of a small group of people in America and Switzerland as the comet Hale–Bopp passed close to the Earth. These people believed that they would be transported by aliens as the comet passed by and that they had to quit their earthly bodies in order to achieve this. This last example raises the question of how large a group has to be before it forms a recognisable subculture. The Hale–Bopp group of about two dozen people was probably close to the lower limit of size.

The complicating factor is that groups holding very unusual beliefs attract people who are deluded and who may find shelter in such a group, at least for a while. There is evidence that Jim Jones believed that he was the new saviour and that he had special powers of healing. He must have been convincing and plausible to have accumulated a large band of followers who accepted his claims, and were willing to die for him. There have been other historical figures who have claimed to be the Messiah: Shabbetai Zvi in Turkey during the seventeenth century persuaded a large number of his fellow Jews that he would lead them to Jerusalem to re-establish the land of Israel. When threatened with death by the sultan he converted to Islam. Since the eighteenth century no more false Messiahs have emerged from among the Jews, as western peoples have become increasingly sceptical about the religious claims of individuals. Joan of Arc would not be able to persuade the French army to follow her into battle today on the grounds that she heard angelic voices giving her commands. At the time, the English soldiers who captured her did not dispute that she heard spirit voices, but they identified their source as the Devil rather than God, and burned her as a witch. While we no longer deal with witches so barbarically, they have not disappeared from our culture. There are groups of people practising as witches in Britain today and following satanic rituals. It should be evident that in order to judge the status of a person's belief, it is necessary to be familiar with the convictions of any subculture to which the patient belongs. In the multicultural societies of today in which many small sects flourish, no individual could be expected to be familiar with all the subcultures likely to be encountered. In the absence of the necessary understanding of a subculture, it is essential to interview a person from the same cultural group as the patient, usually a relative, in order to learn about their shared beliefs.

Hallucinations and bereavement

Hallucinations, the other characteristic symptom of psychotic illnesses, are perceptions without a stimulus in the external world. The most common form is hearing voices in the absence of any person, but hallucinations can occur in any of the other senses – vision, touch, smell and taste. Hallucinations should not automatically be considered an indication of a mental illness. Half the people who have been recently bereaved see or feel the loved person after their death.

Betty's husband died suddenly after a brief illness. They had been married for over thirty years and she felt very lonely without him. Shortly after he died she began to see an image of him sitting in his favourite chair when she entered their lounge. He was dressed in his customary clothes and appeared to be watching television although the set was not on. She was about to say something to him when she remembered that he was dead, and the image vanished. She continued to see his image for a number of years and found it comforting rather than eerie.

Some bereaved people feel the warm body of their former partner lying beside them in bed. Occasionally people who have been very close to a pet animal see or hear it after it has died. One young woman told me that after her dog died she would hear it scratching at the door to be let in. So real was this sound to her that she was impelled to go to the door and open it. These experiences can persist for years, but are rarely recounted to other people because of the fear of being thought mad. Since such a high proportion of the population is affected, this type of hallucination cannot be taken as a sign of illness.

Hallucinations in healthy people

There exist traditional cultures in which it is considered a privilege to hear the voices of ancestors. A person who returns from the forest and tells other villagers about this experience is certainly not thought of as mad. There are also cultures where hallucinatory experiences are actively sought, usually as part of a religious ritual and often by eating hallucinogenic plants, for example the peyote cactus in South America. Where hallucinations are valued by the culture, it is possible that people are more likely to report them, or, more interestingly, have a lower threshold for experiencing them. Probably we all have the capacity to hallucinate under certain circumstances. In the 1960s there was a flurry of research into the effects of sensory deprivation following the 'brainwashing' of captured American soldiers during the Korean war. In fact my own research career began with an experiment on sensory deprivation. I did not have access to resources to fit out a sophisticated laboratory, so I improvised with bits and pieces of equipment. I used army surplus goggles with writing paper in front of the lenses to obscure any definite images. The subjects also wore headphones through which I played 'white noise' – the kind of hissing sound that a badly tuned radio makes – and gloves made from sheets of foam rubber, and during the experiment reclined in an adjustable chair in a quiet room. I used volunteer medical students for this experiment. Even with the crude equipment I had constructed, half of them developed hallucinations during the three hours in the room, some of them within a few minutes of starting. One subject reported the following experiences:

> I just got an image of a head and shoulders then, of a man. I think he's wearing a suit 'cos there's clean outlines to his shoulders ... I got a strange vision then. Someone with a white robe. Like a knight with a white coronet. It was very vivid ... Saw a hunchback then. Saw him then as an image as if he was standing twenty feet away ... It's like looking up at a ceiling now. I can see the join between the ceiling and the walls. It's a long box-like room, relatively very high.

In the 1970s Mary Schwab conducted a survey of the general population in northern Florida.[15] She asked respondents: 'How often do you see or hear things that other people don't think are there?' She found that young people were much more likely to report hallucinations than the middle-aged, but this could simply have been due to their use of street drugs. Black respondents were twice as likely as whites to report hallucinations, and there was also a link with religious affiliation. The highest proportion of reports were from black Baptists, black Methodists and members of the Church of God, while the lowest were from Lutherans, Presbyterians, white Methodists, Episcopalians and Jews. The top score was reached by members of the Church of God, twenty-one per cent of whom reported hallucinations. These findings strongly suggest that certain sects encourage and even reward visionary experiences.

If delusions and hallucinations overlap with the experiences of mentally healthy people, how do we recognise that a person is suffering from a psychotic illness? The answer lies partly in the duration of the experiences and partly in their quality. The hallucinations of bereaved people fade in a few seconds, while those of the subjects in my sensory deprivation experiment lasted for a matter of minutes. People with psychotic illnesses can experience delusions and hallucinations for weeks, months or even decades. Furthermore, in the course of a psychosis, a person usually has a large variety of both delusions and hallucinations. Some of the delusions are clearly attempts to explain what is happening: if you were to suddenly start hearing voices when there was no person present, what sense do you think you would make of it? You might think at first that you were mistaken, but if it went on for hours you would have to find a way of coming to terms with it. At the beginning of these experiences, patients often consider a variety of explanations, including the possibility that they are going mad. This is, of course, very frightening to contemplate, so they usually settle on an explanation that is tolerable. I once looked after a general practitioner who had developed a psychosis. Somehow he was able to retain a professional stance towards his symptoms at the same time as being immersed in the experience. He told me he was suffering from auditory hallucinations, then added in an agonising tone, 'but the voices are driving me mad'.

Explaining hallucinations

Patients need to come to an understanding of two kinds of problem: how are these unusual experiences produced, and why is it happening to them? The mode of production is chosen from the available knowledge about influences that operate over a distance. In developing cultures, spirits of the ancestors or magic are common choices, whereas in developed countries, radio waves, computers, satellites or even extra-terrestrials are cited as the origin of the voices. Even in developed countries spiritual forces still have credence, and God and the Devil feature in some patients' accounts. Explanations for why they should be chosen for these special communications tend to be either positive – they are the new Messiah, a member of the royal family, or recruited by MI5 – or negative – the IRA or the KGB are after them, or the Devil is trying to take over their mind.

Distinguishing schizophrenia from manic-depressive psychosis

We now need to return to Kraepelin's historical division of the psychoses into manic-depressive illness and the condition named by Bleuler as schizophrenia. Mania and depression are polar opposites of mood. The patient with mania is excited or even elated and feels on top of the world. Any delusions or hallucinations that develop are in keeping with this mood, so that patients believe they have been chosen by God to save the world, that they can heal the sick and foretell the future, and they hear the voices of angels praising them. Patients with a depressive psychosis believe they are the worst sinners in the world, that they have brought ruin on their families and are condemned to eternal punishment. They hear voices saying that they are evil and should die. While people with schizophrenia can become depressed or excited, their delusions and hallucinations are not in harmony with their mood. Whereas people with severe depression believe they deserve punishment, people with schizophrenia are indignant at the persecution directed at them.

In addition to this disjunction between the prevailing mood and the tenor of delusions and hallucinations, schizophrenia is characterised by a group of unusual experiences. Another German psychiatrist, Kurt Schneider, described these clearly in 1957 and proposed that they were cardinal signs of schizophrenia. He did not claim that they occurred exclusively in this condition, and studies of these first rank symptoms, as

Schneider termed them, have shown that they are occasionally shown by patients with severe depression or mania. But once again, the lack of a laboratory test for any of these conditions means that we cannot tell whether Schneider was correct in viewing his first rank symptoms as defining a central syndrome of schizophrenia. However, they are of the greatest importance to the story I am about to tell concerning international disagreements over diagnosis, so I will describe them in some detail.

One cluster of symptoms comprises four forms of interference with the normal process of thinking:

1. Patients feel that thoughts entering their mind do not belong to them and must have originated from outside.
2. Trains of thought terminate abruptly leaving nothing behind so that patients feel that their thoughts have been extracted by some outside agency.
3. The patient's thoughts seem to be transmitted to other people so that what we normally experience as a private experience becomes a public one.
4. Thoughts are immediately repeated in the same form but without the sense of volition and ownership that we take for granted. One patient described this to me as: 'I think something and then it rethinks it for me.'

A related symptom affects actions rather than thoughts. Patients no longer feel that they are in command of their own body. Movements occur without their willing them, the voice that issues from their mouth has been produced by someone else, even their feelings can seem to be imposed on them. These experiences can be so pervasive that the patient feels possessed by some other person or a spiritual entity.

One of the most common first rank symptoms is a particular form of auditory hallucination. It may take the form of a voice commenting on the patient's thoughts and actions in the third person, for example, 'He/she is going to the kitchen. He/she is sure to make a mess of things', or of two voices discussing the patient between themselves as though the person were not present.

Most of these distressing symptoms involve the disruption of a central function of the mind which is so essential to our sense of self that we take it for granted without question, namely that we are in the driving seat and have full control of our thoughts and actions. Although the workings of our unconscious reveal themselves in dreams, slips of the tongue, difficulties in recalling particular words or names, and other phenomena identified by Sigmund Freud, we never feel displaced from the centre of control to the extent to which patients with first rank symptoms do.

Theories of the causation of schizophrenia

Early in the twentieth century, clinical observers noticed that schizophrenia tended to run in families. This observation can be explained in at least two ways: there are genes that carry a susceptibility to schizophrenia; and disturbed parents drive their children mad. Theories that parents caused the illness by the way they treated their children were proposed in the USA by several groups of researchers in the 1950s and '60s, and by Ronnie Laing in Britain.[16] Steven Hirsch and I reviewed all the published work on this topic in 1975 and came to the conclusion that there was no solid evidence involving parents in the causation of schizophrenia.[17] On the other hand, research into the inheritance of schizophrenia has produced positive results. The closer the blood tie between an individual and a person with schizophrenia, the greater the risk of developing the same illness. People whose parents both suffer from schizophrenia have the highest risk, about fifty per cent. Strong evidence also comes from studies of one-egg (monozygotic) and two-egg (dizygotic) twins. For dizygotic twins, who share half their genes, if one twin has schizophrenia the other twin has a twenty per cent chance of developing the illness. For monozygotic twins, who share exactly the same genes, the equivalent risk is fifty per cent. This much higher risk for a monozygotic twin supports inheritance as a major contributor to the causes of schizophrenia. But – and this is a very big 'but' – half the twins who have the same genes as their affected twin do *not* fall ill. This proves that the environment must be playing a part in the causation of schizophrenia, although which particular aspects of the environment are involved remains uncertain, a theme that I will pick up again later.

While the evidence for a genetic contribution to schizophrenia is generally accepted, the nature of the brain problem that gives rise to the characteristic symptoms of the illness is still unknown despite increasingly sophisticated techniques of producing pictures of the brain at rest and during activity. A theory that has been popular for over forty years concerns a particular type of chemical transmitter in the brain. In Chapter 1, I described the theory that serotonin plays an important part in the origin of depression. The transmitter that was believed to be important for schizophrenia is dopamine. This chemical became the focus of interest with the introduction of the first drug that benefited patients with delusions and hallucinations, chlorpromazine (Largactil).

The story of the discovery of its value for psychiatry is yet again one of serendipity. Chlorpromazine was in use in the 1930s as an antihistamine and for clearing the urine of bacteria and the gut of worms (its trade name, Largactil, is an awful pun on 'large number of actions'). One of the standard tests of the safety of a drug is to find out what dose will kill fifty per cent of a group of laboratory mice. When it was tested in this way, the pharmacologist noticed that those mice that survived were very sleepy, and had the bright idea of trying it on psychiatric patients. It proved to be much better than a general sedative, in that it reduced the patients' delusions and hallucinations, and its use rapidly spread around the world. Chemical tests on the brain showed that it blocked the action of the transmitter dopamine on the nerve cells. Furthermore, when a whole range of similar drugs were eventually marketed, they were all found to have the same action on the brain, and their potency in improving patients' symptoms was closely related to the strength of their dopamine blocking effect. The resultant theory that an excess of dopamine in the brain was the basic problem in schizophrenia held sway for decades.

Many years ago the Wellcome Trust founded a unique club for active researchers in the field of schizophrenia, bringing together scientists from many different disciplines who would otherwise be unlikely to share ideas. At one meeting, an eminent biochemist stood up and announced that after more than ten years' work on the dopamine hypothesis, he had come to the conclusion that it was a blind alley. There was a shocked silence. It was as dramatic as if the Pope had announced that he no longer believed in God. No one commented, and this announcement had no perceptible impact on the psychiatric community's faith in the dopamine hypothesis. Since 1992, a new series of antipsychotic drugs has been introduced which are just as effective against the symptoms of schizophrenia as the older drugs but have little or no blocking action against dopamine. As a consequence the dopamine hypothesis was toppled from its pedestal, ten years after the agnostic biochemist's declaration, and as yet has not been replaced with an alternative theory.

American and British diagnoses

I described in Chapter 1 the construction of the Present State Examination (PSE), the semi-structured interview for assessing psychiatric symptoms. Schneider's first rank symptoms occupy a prominent position in the schedule because, in the set of rules used to process the PSE data, the presence of just one of them leads to a category of schizophrenia. One of the incentives to construct the PSE was the possibility of making international comparisons of diagnosis. At the end of the 1960s, Morton Kramer drew attention to the fact that the diagnosis of schizophrenia was being made twice as commonly for patients on their first admission to hospital in America as for their British equivalents.[18] If this was a true reflection of a difference in the frequency of appearance of schizophrenia, it would demand investigation of the possible causes, a situation we will encounter in the last chapter. Kramer's observation prompted a bilateral study using the PSE to assess patients on both sides of the Atlantic, and a team of psychiatrists who used the same method to make diagnoses.[19] Standardisation of these procedures eliminated the difference in frequency of the diagnosis of schizophrenia between the USA and the UK, showing that this was simply a consequence of transatlantic variations in psychiatrists' approaches to interviewing and diagnosis. The reasons for the difference revealed by this study lie in the training of the psychiatrists, in particular the domination of psychoanalysis in the USA at that time compared with its marginal position in the UK. The process by which a psychoanalytic training leads to a broad concept of schizophrenia is explained below.

An international study of diagnosis

At about the same time as this US–UK comparison began, the World Health Organisation (WHO) was planning a more ambitious study of the same nature but involving nine different countries. The aim was to collect at least a hundred patients in each centre who had been given a local diagnosis of schizophrenia and then to compare them in terms both of their symptoms as recorded with the PSE and the diagnostic categories produced by the associated computer program. Of course the set of rules incorporated in the algorithm of the computer program does not invest the resulting diagnostic categories with any absolute truth. The rules represent the consensus of the three psychiatrists who constructed the program in 1974, John Wing and John Cooper, both British, and Norman Sartorius, a Croatian.[20] They are as arbitrary as any other psychiatrists' diagnostic rules. However, the program possesses the advantage of always doing the same thing each time it is fed data from a patient, which cannot be claimed by any psychiatrist. Additionally, as stressed in the preceding chapter, because the rules are explicit they open up the possibility of studying the diagnostic procedures used by individual psychiatrists.

The centres chosen for the International Pilot Study of Schizophrenia (IPSS), as the WHO study was named, were deliberately sited in a mixture of developed and developing countries. The former comprised Aarhus (Denmark), London (UK), Moscow (then USSR), Prague (then Czechoslovakia) and Washington (USA). The developing centres were Agra (India), Cali (Colombia), Ibadan (Nigeria) and Taipei (Taiwan). I had just finished my study on sensory deprivation and had joined the Medical Research Council social psychiatry unit at the Institute of Psychiatry in London, which was one of the research centres of the IPSS. I had recently been trained by John Wing, director of the unit, to use the PSE, and I was asked to collect the cases for the London centre. Thus began my involvement with the WHO which still continues, and which took me all over the world, stimulating my interest in cultural issues as they relate to psychiatry.

Back-translation

The PSE was developed in English and had to be translated into the seven other languages used in the IPSS centres, and then back-translated. This procedure revealed some interesting problems: for instance, there was no equivalent word for 'depression' in Yoruba, the language used in Ibadan. In Chinese, only a single word could be found to stand for 'anxiety', 'tension' and 'worrying', which refer to different symptoms in the English version of the PSE. These dif-

ficulties in translation were much more common in the
section dealing with neurotic symptoms than in the psychotic
section, so did not impede the principal aim of comparing the
diagnosis of schizophrenia across the participating centres.

The consensus and the odd ones out

The psychiatrists in each centre were required to make their
own diagnosis on the patients collected by their team. They
could base this on the PSE ratings and any other information
they had gleaned about the patients. Their diagnoses were
then compared with the categories produced by the application of the computer program to the PSE ratings. The
surprising result, displayed in Table 1, was that there was
a high level of agreement between the computer-generated
categories and the diagnoses made by the psychiatrists in
seven of the centres. The two centres showing major discrepancies between the computer categories and the local
diagnoses were Moscow and Washington. If these two centres
are excluded, the overall agreement between the other seven
centres and the computer categories is ninety-six per cent on
schizophrenia and eighty-six per cent on manic-depressive
psychoses and the neuroses. Even in the two rogue centres,

Table 1 Discrepancies between computer-generated categories and
psychiatrists' diagnoses in the International Pilot Study of
Schizophrenia

Centre	Percentage discrepancy
Aarhus	13.8
Agra	13.1
Cali	7.0
Ibadan	9.8
London	3.9
Moscow	35.1
Prague	13.7
Taipei	4.6
Washington	21.5

there was a heavy reliance on Schneider's first rank symptoms as indicators of the diagnosis of schizophrenia. Across all nine centres, if any one of the first rank symptoms was rated as present, there was a likelihood of ninety-five per cent or greater that the psychiatrist would diagnose schizophrenia.

It is no surprise that the London psychiatrist, myself, was in closest agreement with the computerised categories, since I worked in the same institution as the main architect of these, John Wing. What does require an explanation is that the Taiwanese psychiatrists agreed almost as closely with the computer output as I did. The answer lies in some curious quirks of history. Japan occupied Taiwan following the Sino-Japanese war in 1895. Psychiatric training in Taiwan during the period of occupation was strongly influenced by the prevailing Japanese culture. Because of political and ideological links with Germany, Japanese psychiatry adopted the German approach to assessing symptoms, including Kurt Schneider's identification of first rank symptoms. In the opposite geographical direction, the German influence on British psychiatry was strengthened by refugees from Hitler's persecution. A number of Germans fled to the UK in the 1930s and became prominent and influential teachers in psychiatry and psychology. It is ironic that imperialism and persecution should have been largely responsible for the concordance reached between psychiatrists worldwide on diagnosis.

Psychoanalysis in the USA

Now we need to consider why the Washington and Muscovite psychiatrists were outliers in the international comparison. The disagreement between the Washington psychiatrists and the other centres echoed the findings of the US–UK comparison described above, but I have yet to explain the reasons behind it in detail. They lie in the domination of American psychiatry by psychoanalytic theory and practice up to the 1980s. Woody Allen's films capture the ethos of that era, when many Americans who considered themselves to be enlightened and could afford the fees, engaged in a personal analysis, regardless of whether or not they suffered from psychiatric symptoms. In response to this demand from clients for what was seen as a prestigious and health-promoting experience, the majority of psychiatrists underwent a training in psychoanalysis, involving a heavy expenditure of time and money. As a result, psychoanalytic theory dominated the assessment of patients' mental state and the diagnostic process.

Psychoanalysis places a great emphasis on unconscious mechanisms that are believed to underlie symptoms. These were proposed by Sigmund Freud and expanded by his daughter, Anna, a child psychoanalyst. They are considered to be ways in which the mind deals with threatening information and the basic drives of sex and aggression. These mechanisms include repression, pushing uncomfortable thoughts or experiences out of the mind so that they do not intrude on consciousness, and projection, attributing to other people our own characteristics that we find unacceptable. There is a relatively small number of these proposed mechanisms compared with the rich diversity of symptoms. Specific mechanisms such as projection are considered to be characteristic of psychoses. Analytically trained psychiatrists focus on identifying the unconscious mechanisms being employed by the patient rather than the precise nature of the symptoms, which are viewed as relatively superficial phenomena. This leads to a broad definition of schizophrenia, which includes most cases that would be diagnosed as mania by British psychiatrists, and a sizable proportion of those who would be identified as having a personality disorder. It must be emphasised that diagnostic practices in the USA have changed dramatically since the 1980s, partly in response to the striking findings of the US–UK comparison and the IPSS, and partly due to the spectacular decline in popularity of psychoanalysis among American psychiatrists.

The KGB and psychiatry

The reasons for the Muscovite psychiatrists being out on a limb are completely different and have sinister undertones. At the time of the IPSS, Moscow psychiatry was dominated by one man, Andrej Snezhnevsky, who was head of the Psychiatric Institute. The structure of the Institute reflected the strict hierarchical nature of Soviet society, so that all the psychiatrists employed there were constrained to use Snezhnevsky's diagnostic system. This was based, not on the nature of the symptoms, but on their time course. Any psychotic symptoms that were recurrent were taken as an indication that the illness was schizophrenia. The Muscovite psychiatrists were perfectly capable of identifying symptoms of mania and depression, but if more than one episode of any of these symptoms occurred, the diagnosis of schizophrenia was given. Thus a case history could read, 'The patient has had two episodes of mania and one of depression, and is suffering from schizophrenia.' To summarise this approach crudely, 'If you've had it before and you've got it again, it's schizophrenia.' The social adjustment of the person between episodes of illness was also given great diagnostic importance. If there were indications of difficulties in adjusting to society, this was taken as confirmatory evidence of schizophrenia. Incidentally this system had not spread to Leningrad, where the psychiatrists were making diagnoses in a similar way to the concordant IPSS centres. The Moscow approach to diagnosis led to a broad definition of schizophrenia, as in America, but for completely different reasons. It also opened the door to exploitation of psychiatry by the Soviet secret police, the KGB.

Individuals who openly protested against the Soviet system were diagnosed as harbouring 'reformist delusions'. As I have argued above, this is a misuse of the term 'delusion' since there were enough dissidents to form a substantial subculture sharing the same views. But the term was sufficient to allow the Moscow psychiatrists to make a diagnosis of psychosis (being out of touch with reality), and a person who protested on more than one occasion would inevitably be given the label of schizophrenia. This was a boon for the KGB who could then invalidate the political activity of the dissidents by locking them up in psychiatric hospitals and forcibly administering antipsychotic drugs which they did not need. It is difficult to determine whether many of the Moscow psychiatrists were actively collaborating with the KGB, but my opinion is that Snezhnevsky introduced his diagnostic system in good faith and it was then exploited politically. What is clear is that he failed to protest at what was happening to the dissidents. The Royal College of Psychiatrists of the UK, of which he was a corresponding member, initiated the process of expelling him, but before it could run its course, he resigned.

Soviet dissidents in Israel

Some years later the Soviet authorities relaxed their ban on the emigration of Soviet Jews to Israel, and among the immigrants were several dissidents who had been given a diagnosis of schizophrenia and had been incarcerated in psychiatric hospitals. I took the opportunity of a visit to Israel to interview three of these men with the PSE. They were all happy to cooperate with the procedure and to talk openly about their history. Two of the men were vigorous, high-achieving individuals who had no symptoms of psychosis when I saw them and, as far as I could determine, had never suffered from any psychiatric illness. The third man was a quiet academic of high moral principles, who had been deeply affected by the Soviet invasion of Czechoslovakia to suppress the resurgence of democracy. He resolved to commit suicide publicly as a protest and set fire to himself in a public place. His life was saved by some passers-by and he was given a diagnosis of schizophrenia and admitted to a psychiatric hospital. He had no symptoms when I interviewed him, and despite my careful questioning of him about the period before the suicide attempt, I could find no evidence of depression or any other psychiatric illness. I came to the conclusion that his action was what the sociologist Emile Durkheim identified as altruistic suicide, giving up your life for a higher cause.

Politics, economics and diagnosis in the USA

I do not want to give the impression that psychiatric diagnosis is influenced by political forces only in totalitarian countries. There have been two recent examples of this type of influence in the USA, one of which concerned the status of homosexuality. Following the revealing findings of the US–UK comparison and the IPSS, vigorous efforts were directed at compiling guidelines for diagnosis which would be accepted and used by all American psychiatrists. The resulting document is named the *Diagnostic and Statistical Manual of Mental Disorders*, and is now in its fourth edition (DSM-IV). During the preparation of a revised version of the third edition (DSM-III-R), the issue came up of whether homosexuality should remain in the *Manual* as a pathological condition. The political organisations in the United States that represent homosexual interests put pressure on the psychiatrists to end what they saw as an aspect of persecution. It is well to remember that the Nazis insisted that homosexual men wear a pink triangle, and that thousands were murdered alongside six million Jews and over 100,000 mentally ill people. The American Psychiatric Association put the matter to the vote and homosexuality ceased to be included as a disease by a majority decision.

The other example illustrates the power of commercial forces to alter diagnostic habits. In the absence of a national health service, American medicine is dominated by private health insurance agencies. These operate a system known as managed care, which gives them the power to withhold funding for treatments they consider to be ineffective. Thus they refuse to pay for days spent in hospital by patients with schizophrenia during which they receive no drug treatment. Personality disorders represent a difficult area for psychiatry, since there is no generally accepted treatment that is considered to work. This is a problem facing the current British government in attempting to formulate a new Mental Health Act. Personality disorders are excluded from compulsory admission under the existing Act of 1983 as they are not considered to be amenable to treatment. For the same reason, the health insurance agencies in the USA were unwilling to fund psychiatric care for people with a personality disorder.

Before the 1980s a diagnosis termed 'multiple personality disorder' was very rarely used. In 1973 an American psychiatrist, Cornelia Wilbur, published an account of a case of hers in a book titled *Sybil*, which was made into a successful film. The fame achieved by this single case study was followed by a great increase in the professional use of the diagnosis. In 1980 multiple personality disorder became an official diagnosis incorporated in the third edition of the *Diagnostic and Statistical Manual* (DSM-III), although the term was changed to 'dissociative identity disorder' for DSM-IV in 1994. Ian Hacking records that by 1992 there were hundreds of patients with multiple personality disorder in treatment in every sizable town in North America, and that entire private hospitals dedicated to the illness were being established all over the continent.[21] Hacking points out that doctors treating this condition must capture as much insurance coverage for non-drug treatments as possible. At the ninth meeting of the International Society for the Study of Multiple Personality and Dissociation in 1992, the conference theme was health insurance. The result of the official recognition of the condition by its inclusion in the DSM is that health dollars can now be claimed for the treatment of this personality disorder. It is striking that this diagnosis is rarely made in Europe, and it is not included in the European equivalent of the DSM, the

International Classification of Diseases (ICD-10), compiled
by the World Health Organisation.

The frequency of appearance of schizophrenia across cultures

Social, political and commercial forces could not influence
the diagnostic process if there were objective tests for diagnostic entities. In their absence, the reader could be excused
for taking a nihilistic view of the attempts by psychiatrists to
classify diseases. However, it is necessary to retain a sense of
perspective on the issue. Seven out of the nine centres in the
IPSS reached a close agreement on what symptoms constituted a schizophrenic illness. This engendered sufficient
confidence in the mental health division of WHO, directed
by Norman Sartorius, to proceed to the next step in their
ambitious programme, an international study of the frequency of appearance of schizophrenia.

Incidence and prevalence

Here I need to introduce two technical terms, incidence and
prevalence, and explain how they differ. *Incidence* refers to
the number of people who first develop an illness over a set
period of time, usually one year. *Prevalence* includes anyone
who is ill at the time of the head count, which is a mixture
of new cases and people who have been ill for some time.
Prevalence can be measured at a single point in time, the
point prevalence, or over a year, the annual prevalence. If
you are interested in studying the causes of illness, it is the
incidence rate that is important. When the incidence varies
between two populations, one can look for other differences
between the two groups that might explain this variation.
One of the first studies of this kind was carried out in London
during the nineteenth century by John Snow to investigate
the causes of a cholera epidemic. By plotting the number of

new cases (the incidence rate) on a map of London, he discovered that households supplied with water from one reach of the Thames, below a sewage outlet, were much more likely to develop cases of cholera than households that received their water from a reach of the Thames above the sewage outlet. By removing the handle from the Broad Street pump, distributing water from the lower reaches, he halted the epidemic.

The principal aim of the second WHO study was to measure the incidence of schizophrenia in centres that differed widely in their social, economic and cultural aspects, thus providing a greater opportunity to identify the possible causes of the illness. Twelve centres were chosen in developed and developing countries, and in urban and rural settings. The study was named the Determinants of Outcome of Severe Mental Disorders (DOSMD) since a second aim was to compare the outcome for patients in the various centres. This was prompted by the results of a follow-up of patients in the IPSS, which showed that patients in developing centres had a better outcome than those from developed centres. This was surprising because, of course, psychiatric facilities were much sparser in the developing centres so that patients received much less professional care. The interpretation of this finding was clouded by the fact that the IPSS sample contained both first-onset cases and patients who first became ill some years back, and that the mix of these was different between centres. To make a true comparison of outcome it was necessary to confine the samples to first-onset cases only.

Making contact with the services

It is actually almost impossible to pick up people at the first onset of symptoms of schizophrenia, because they do not immediately seek professional help. In fact the average time lag between onset of symptoms and making the first contact with medical services is well over a year, and is considerably longer for men than for women. In practical terms, then, the DOSMD study recorded first contact with medical services for psychotic symptoms. This is not too demanding an exercise when services are centralised in a hospital, but becomes increasingly difficult with the dispersion of services throughout the community. In a developing country there is the added complication of limited resources of Western type and the consequent flourishing of traditional forms of treatment. Hence, in the developing countries, the researchers had to identify all the traditional healers in the area of the survey, and gain their cooperation in notifying the research team when they saw suitable clients. The difficulties of this endeavour are such that in only one developing centre, Chandigarh in north India, was the finding of cases considered tight enough to provide a reasonably reliable estimate of the incidence of schizophrenia. This is a pity, since the greatest contrast in socio-economic conditions and culture was between developed and developing countries. At least Chandigarh included both an urban and a rural environment.

The centre in north India

The city of Chandigarh was built from scratch on an agricultural plain as the intended shared capital of two adjoining states, Punjab and Haryana. However, Punjab took it over exclusively, which remains a bone of contention between the two states. It was designed by the French architect, Le Corbusier, and contains many striking public buildings, including a Postgraduate Medical Institute. The city has attracted highly educated people to live there, so that during the period of the DOSMD study, the literacy rate was seventy per cent. There could hardly be a greater gulf between the lifestyles in the city and in the surrounding rural area, where people live in houses built of mud bricks and thatched with straw, the social unit is the extended family, and the literacy rate at the time was thirty per cent. Traditional healers were the main source of help for mental illnesses, but the psychiatry department at the Postgraduate Medical Institute, headed by Professor Narendra Wig, set up a mobile team which visited the villages in rotation to hold outpatient clinics and to facilitate the aims of the research.

Variations in incidence across centres

Twelve centres were originally included in the DOSMD study, but checks on the completeness of case-finding cast doubt on the procedures in four of the centres, which were consequently excluded from the analysis. The centres in which few patients were considered to have slipped through the net were Aarhus, Chandigarh (urban and rural), Dublin, Honolulu, Moscow, Nagasaki and Nottingham. As in the IPSS, the translated version of the PSE was used in each centre and the local psychiatrists were trained to interview patients and rate their symptoms reliably. The ratings from the PSE were processed using the associated computer program. In view of the central role played by Schneider's first rank symptoms in the diagnosis of schizophrenia across countries, incidence rates were calculated for two types of schizophrenia, with (S) or without (non-S) first rank symptoms. The number of cases of each type was divided by the number of people in the population studied who were between the ages of fifteen and fifty-four, since this was the age range of patients accepted into the study. The results are displayed in Figure 1.

It is evident that there is much less variation in the incidence of S schizophrenia than in the incidence of the non-S variety. The first contact rate for S schizophrenia ranged from 7 cases per 100,000 population per year in Aarhus to 14 per 100,000 in Nottingham. A statistical test showed that a difference this small could have occurred by chance, so that the rates from the eight centres should be treated as equal. This is an extraordinary result, since no other disease occurs

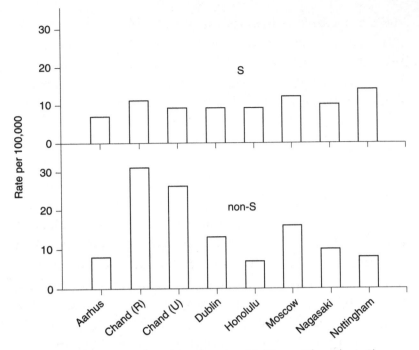

Figure 1 Incidence rates for schizophrenia with (S) or without (non-S)
Schneiderian first rank symptoms. Chand (R), rural area of Chandigarh;
Chand (U), urban area of Chandigarh

with the same frequency around the world. It suggests that
environmental factors play little part in the causation of S
schizophrenia, otherwise the contrasting social, economic
and cultural environments of the centres would have led to
large variations in the incidence.

Some critics have objected to the method used in this
international study, claiming that the PSE acts like a grid
imposed on the rich variety of unusual mental experiences
represented by the patients in the different cultural settings.
The psychiatrists using the PSE only pick up what is considered to be abnormal in the Western countries in which
it was developed. An appropriate analogy would be a chip
machine: whatever shape the potatoes are that go into the
machine, they all come out as chips. This argument has some
validity, but its force is weakened when we examine the
incidence rates of non-S schizophrenia. These provide a very

different picture, with a range from 7 per 100,000 in Honolulu to 31 per 100,000 in the rural area of Chandigarh. A more than fourfold difference of this magnitude must be taken seriously and points to the importance of environmental factors in the causation of this type of schizophrenia. The different balance of causative factors in S and non-S schizophrenia constitutes an argument for considering them to be distinct diseases. This is not a revolutionary idea: when Bleuler first introduced the term, he named the condition 'the group of schizophrenias', implying that it covered more than one disease. The resolution of this issue will have to await the discovery of underlying biological abnormalities which might distinguish the component diseases. In the meantime, the DOSMD findings illustrate how an epidemiological study can raise questions about accepted diagnostic concepts. Studies of this nature can also suggest possible causes of diseases but cannot prove a causal connection. This requires an intervention, such as John Snow's removal of the handle of the Broad Street pump to halt the cholera epidemic. In the next chapter I will describe how interventions can be used to establish causes of psychiatric conditions.

| **The Human Probe**

Cause and effect

When two events happen very closely together in time we tend to assume that the earlier event caused the later one. Whether assumptions of causality are based on previous experience or are 'hard-wired' into the brain is not known for certain, although Jean Piaget, a Swiss psychologist, demonstrated that children start to make these assumptions when they reach a certain age. While they prove to be correct most of the time, it is possible to make mistakes, as we saw in unfolding the story of life events. The point can be illustrated by the 'Spot the Ball' competition. Faced with a snapshot of footballers in a variety of positions and postures, from which the ball has been erased, the competitor has to guess the location of the ball. The fact that there are few winners shows how difficult this task is. If you were shown a videotape of the thirty seconds of preceding play, from which the ball had also been deleted, it would be much easier to locate the ball in the still image. Research into human behaviour faces the same problems. A cross-sectional study is equivalent to the snapshot: it can establish connections between events but cannot tell which is the cause and which the effect. A study conducted over a period of time contributes more to our understanding of causality, but there are strict limits to the length of time a study can take. These are partly imposed by the availability of funds and partly by the needs of researchers to obtain publishable results and move on to the next experiment. The longest study I have been involved in lasted thirteen years and was a five-year follow-up of nearly 700 patients who had been discharged from two psychiatric hospitals over the course of eight years. I had to seek renewal of my funding every three years and often did not know until the eleventh hour whether or not the study was going to continue. A major problem with psychiatric research is that the time period of interest is the lifespan of the patient. We would dearly like to know how experiences in childhood shape the susceptibility of the adult to psychiatric illnesses, and how this is affected by the changes in the life cycle all the way through to old age. No single researcher can encompass the entire life of his or her subjects, but there are ingenious short cuts. Lee Robins,[22] an American researcher, was interested to discover what happened in adult life to children who showed disturbed behaviour. In 1966 she looked backwards in time to records of children who had been referred to child guidance clinics in the 1930s. She was able to trace many of these children who had become adults by the time she began her study. This strategy enabled her to link disturbances in childhood, recorded by the staff of the clinics, with psychiatric problems in adulthood. Useful as this method of condensing time was, Robins was restricted to what the clinic staff thought important to record more than twenty years earlier.

Humans looking at humans

It is not only the dimension of time that is problematic for the researcher into human behaviour, it is also the fact that the experimenter and subjects occupy the same space. We have no difficulty in being objective about things that are astronomically bigger than us, such as stars, or microscopically smaller, like viruses. In fact we can only study them by using instruments which bring them closer to our own size. The problem with human beings as objects of study is that they are the same dimensions as the researcher, they occupy the same space, and we are biologically and culturally primed to react to people in specific ways. We have developed techniques that increase the distance between ourselves and the people we study. We can focus on a small part of the person; in the case of the brain, making records of its electrical activity or images of its structure. We can use audiotapes or videotapes, which we can stop and start at will, and play slower or faster than they were recorded, thereby altering our time relationship to the subjects. But however this distancing is achieved, eventually what has been learned has to be integrated into an understanding of the person as a whole living being. I write 'has to', but not all scientists feel this as an imperative. Many are more comfortable with visualising the person as a collection of chemical systems, or of strands of DNA. This has led to the charge of scientific reductionism: reducing the person to a series of formulae which maintain the distance between researcher and subject in the service of objectivity. What is lost by this manoeuvre is the exquisite sensitivity we possess to other people's feelings and behaviour, which is essential for the functioning of humans as social beings. I shall now describe one of the most innovative techniques in psychiatric research, which instead of rejecting our subjectivity, capitalises on this very sensitivity to other people in order to measure their feelings.

Out of the asylums

The spur to the development of this measurement technique was the change in attitude to the care of psychiatric patients in the old asylums. Patients who had spent many years of their life in a psychiatric hospital were discharged to live in the community. It has been claimed that this was a direct consequence of the introduction to psychiatry of chlorpromazine (Largactil, *see above*), which controlled delusions and hallucinations. However, chlorpromazine came into use for this purpose in 1955, whereas some hospitals, such as Mapperley in Nottingham, began to reduce their number of beds in the late 1940s. The first wave of patients to be resettled during the 1950s were in relatively good shape, and went to live with their families or in private accommodation with landlords or landladies. Sadly, after a time some of them had to return to the asylum when they fell ill again. This prompted George Brown and colleagues, working in the social psychiatry unit at the Institute of Psychiatry in London, to follow up a group of discharged patients to investigate what might account for their failure to remain in their new homes.[23] The unexpected finding was that patients who returned to live with their parents were more often readmitted than those who resided with brothers or sisters, or in private lodgings. George Brown followed a hunch that it was the emotional interaction between patients and their parents that led to a return of their illness. Before pursuing this line of enquiry he had to overcome a major obstacle: no measure of emotional interactions between people existed. To understand how this extraordinary deficiency persisted through more than fifty years of psychological studies, I need to make a brief excursion into history.

The split in psychology

From its beginnings, psychology developed along two paths which became increasingly divergent. The path beaten by Freud and his followers began with introspection, an attempt to establish the workings of the mind by reflecting on your own thoughts and feelings. Freud analysed his own dreams, and caught himself out in slips of the tongue and other actions he had not intended. In his writings he sometimes presented his discoveries as though they related to a patient of his, when they were actually a product of self-analysis. This was partly to protect the most intimate aspects of himself, but undoubtedly also to give a more 'objective' appearance to his discoveries. Following Freud, psychoanalysts use their own knowledge and experience of feelings and drives to understand the patient's emotions and behaviour. They convey their understanding to the patient in the form of an interpretation, which is a reformulation of the patient's speech, or silences, in terms of the patient's relationship with the analyst. This is based on the assumption that the patient behaves towards the analyst, an unknown stranger, as though the analyst were one of the salient figures in the patient's life – a process known as transference. Freud recognised that the analyst also develops emotional responses to the patient, referred to as countertransference, which he saw as an obstacle to the process of therapy. However, in 1950 Paula Heimann introduced the idea that analysts could use their feelings towards the patient to further their understanding of the patient's emotional state, since the patient made an important contribution to these feelings.[24] Her insight introduced greater reciprocity into what had been a somewhat one-sided relationship.

The other path was taken by psychologists who were determined to shape their discipline into a science. The stress was on objective measurement, large samples of subjects, and reproducible results. Many of the experiments were conducted on animals, usually rats, but occasionally monkeys, with very limited application to the understanding of human emotions. One school of psychologists, the behaviourists, was formed in the early part of the twentieth century. Led by Watson and Skinner in the USA, they rejected the idea of studying thoughts and feelings and strictly confined their observations to forms of behaviour. They decided to treat the human mind as a 'black box' with unknowable contents, and only attempted to measure the inputs and outputs. The barrenness of this approach led to a crisis in psychology in the 1960s, with a dawning realisation that the apparent objectivity might be alright for the study of rats, but was spurious for humans since the researcher could never be invisible to the subjects. Even if the experimenter were not present in the room, the subjects were well aware that someone had set up the experiment and would be evaluating the results. Hence their reactions were bound to be influenced by their emotional response to the testing situation and the absent researcher; which the psychoanalyst would recognise as transference. It was considered preferable to acknowledge these responses openly and to view them as contributing to the data yielded by the experiment. Psychologists began to appreciate the value of single-case experiments, which involved the intensive study of one subject, often using qualitative measures. While in this way experimental psychology began to approach psychoanalysis, there was very little prospect of a meeting of minds since psychoanalysts seemed unable to contemplate the measurement of the unconscious and dynamic forces with which they wrestled daily. At just this time the problem of integrating the subjective and the objective was solved by the development of a measurement technique which became known as 'expressed emotion'.

Measuring relatives' emotional responses

Measurement of expressed emotion was the brainchild of George Brown and Michael Rutter, both of whom we encountered in Chapter 1. It took them several years to finalise the technique, which centres on an interview with a relative who is caring for the sick person. Initially, in the 1960s, the research concerned people with schizophrenia, but it has now been successfully applied to a wide variety of psychiatric and physical illnesses. The interviewer asks the carer about the patient's symptoms and behaviour in the previous three months, a subject most carers will talk about eagerly. The interview, which occupies up to one and a half hours, is audiotaped. No ratings are attempted during the interview, but are made when the interviewer can listen to the recording at leisure. This entails going over a crucial sections several times in order to be confident of the assessment, so that rating can take up to twice as long as giving the interview and is obviously a painstaking procedure. The rater listens carefully not only to what the relative says, but also to the way in which the words are spoken. The rater treats the relative's voice as a channel of information about the relative's emotional attitude to the patient. To make this clear I am going to ask you to conduct a little experiment. Try saying as calmly as possible, 'My son lies in bed till the afternoon, and when he gets up he doesn't wash himself.' Now repeat exactly the same words, but convey as much anger with your voice as you can. If you think about how you changed the emotional tone of the sentence, you will find that the second time, you probably spoke louder and faster, and there were more ups and downs in the pitch of your voice. These clues from the voice, along with the content of speech, are used to identify the emotions expressed by the relative. In this example what is rated is termed a 'critical comment' and the number of such comments made in the course of the interview is counted.

The principle of the technique is that the rater's own emotional response to the relative's utterances is used to identify the emotion the relative is expressing. There is an obvious parallel with the psychoanalyst's use of countertransference, except that analysts do not discuss with each other the clues they use to identify particular emotions in their patients: this ability is taken for granted as common to all human beings. But in a research project it is essential that the experimenters are equally sensitive to these clues. Therefore they have to attend a two-week training course in interviewing and rating, during which the techniques are explicitly discussed and a number of master tapes are rated. Trainees have to reach a high level of agreement on rating the master tapes before they gain approval to do their own studies.

Criticism and hostility

Critical comments are the core element in the expressed emotion (EE) ratings, being the most commonly encountered. The number of such comments made in the interview is counted and indicates how angry the relative feels about the patient. In British studies, about one-third of relatives of patients with schizophrenia make no critical remarks, showing a high degree of tolerance for the difficulties of living with such a person. The average number of critical comments is around six, so this is used as the threshold to divide relatives into high- and low-criticism groups. At the extreme upper end of the range a few relatives manage a machine-gun rate of fifty to sixty in an hour. An extreme form of criticism is rated as 'hostility', which is recognised either as a bunching of critical comments or a critical attitude towards the patient as a person, rather than confining the remarks to the patient's behaviour. Comments such as, 'She's the laziest girl you've ever met' would rate as hostility.

Overinvolvement

The third component of EE is overinvolvement, which comprises a number of different behaviours and attitudes. Overprotectiveness is shown by relatives who behave towards the patients as though they were much younger than their actual age. Thus one mother would not let her daughter aged twenty cross the road on her own, while another bathed her son who was in his late teens. Some relatives become overemotional in the interview, weeping and making dramatic statements such as, 'I feel her illness has ruined my life.' In judging whether excessive emotion is being shown, the rater has to take account of the circumstances of the carer, including the cultural background. Women show their emotions more readily than men, and people from Mediterranean countries are more expressive than Scandinavians. I once asked a

Spanish colleague how he recognised overinvolved carers. He replied that he called them 'butcher relatives', and in response to my incomprehension explained that these were people who said, 'If it would make my son well, I would cut off my arm and leg.' Giving due consideration to the influence of the carers' culture is built into the training course, which often includes trainees from many different countries and cultures. The fact that sensitivity to cultural variations is integral to the measurement technique has enabled it to be used successfully in China, Japan and India as well as across Europe and America. Two additional aspects of overinvolvement are excessive self-sacrifice, when relatives devote too much of their time and emotional energy to the care of the patient at the expense of their own needs, and symbiosis. This term, borrowed from biology, refers to two organisms from different species which are mutually dependent on each other for survival, such as cleaner fish on the coral reef and their client fish whom they rid of parasites. The human pair also exhibit a lack of psychological boundaries, the carer believing that she or he understands the thoughts, feelings and needs of the patient without having to be told. While partners can be just as critical of patients as parents can, overinvolvement is rarely seen in partners and is much more common in mothers than in fathers.

Expressed emotion and the course of schizophrenia

When high levels of critical comments or overinvolvement are expressed, or hostility is present, the carer is denoted as 'high EE'. George Brown and his colleagues, Jim Birley and John Wing, first used this measure in 1972 in a study of patients with schizophrenia.[25] It proved to be remarkably successful in distinguishing patients who did well from those who did poorly. Relapse was defined as a return of the symptoms of schizophrenia in those who had completely recovered, or an intensification of symptoms in those who had never been completely free of them. More than half the patients who lived with high-EE relatives relapsed in the nine months after returning home from hospital, whereas only about one in six of those in low-EE homes did so.

A patient of mine, Sarah, lived with her elderly parents who were very conventional. Sarah was quite rebellious and upset her father who regarded himself as a pillar of the community. One day Sarah came home having dyed her brown hair bright red. Her father was appalled and had a furious row with her in which he criticised her appearance and behaviour, and called her a slut. She went to her room to escape his anger and within half an hour began to hear the critical voices which had been a feature of her previous attack of schizophrenia.

The dramatic difference in outcome between patients in high-EE and low-EE households appeared to explain the findings of the original study of patients discharged from the asylums; but was it a fluke? The essence of scientific experiments is replicability: can a different group of researchers in another place using a new sample of subjects produce the same results? There are so many extraneous factors that cannot be controlled, particularly when studying people, that replication is essential to prove that the original findings were not due to these uncontrolled factors. Consequently, at the beginning of the 1970s Christine Vaughn and I undertook a replication study.[26] Although we were working in the same unit in which the original study was done, George Brown and Jim Birley had left, and we collected a completely new sample of patients and their relatives. Both of us were trained to rate EE by the original researchers, and became highly reliable at doing this. The training has now been formalised as a course that is run regularly and is attended by trainees from all over the world. Almost all of them learn to make reliable ratings in two weeks, evidence of the applicability of the technique across languages and cultures.

Protection from a high-EE relative

In addition to repeating the design of the previous study, we decided to include a group of patients suffering from depression. The question we were addressing was whether the link between EE and course of illness was limited to schizophrenia, or whether it might apply to other psychiatric conditions. We chose to focus on depression because it provides such a contrast with schizophrenia, and for this reason we excluded any depressed people who were experiencing delusions or hallucinations. The part of our study dealing with schizophrenia turned out to be an almost perfect replication of the earlier research: exactly half of our patients in high-EE homes relapsed over nine months, compared with only twelve per cent of those living with low-EE relatives. The figures for the earlier study were fifty-eight per cent and sixteen per cent. Since we used the same measuring instruments for all aspects of our study as in the previous work, we felt justified in pooling the data from the two studies, which amounted to well over one hundred patients. This was a large enough group to carry out some more detailed analyses. We confirmed a finding from the earlier study that patients living in high-EE homes had two ways of protecting themselves from relapse: either by taking antipsychotic medication long-term, or by keeping out of the relative's way. Patients who spent little time with their high-EE relative were much less likely to relapse than those who were constantly with them. The protective effect of low social contact was as powerful as taking maintenance medication. If patients both took medication and kept a low profile there was an additive effect, resulting in a relapse rate of only fifteen per cent, which is close to that of patients in low-EE homes. The remarkable aspect of this finding is that a pharmacological agent and a form of social behaviour can act together to reduce the likelihood of another attack of schizophrenia. The challenge we faced was to formulate the susceptibility to schizophrenia in such a way that it could accommodate the influence of factors in two such different domains.

Expressed emotion and the course of depression

Before grappling with that problem we need to consider the findings for the depressed patients. Firstly they differed from the patients with schizophrenia in their living situations: whereas less than half of those with schizophrenia lived with a partner, virtually everyone with depression did so. As already mentioned, overinvolved attitudes are virtually confined to parents, so that they were not a feature of the relatives of the depressed patients. Among these carers, critical attitudes loomed large; in fact they turned out to be every bit as critical of their partners as were the relatives of the schizophrenic patients. However, when we applied the threshold of six critical comments that had worked with schizophrenia, it failed to separate patients who stayed well from those who suffered a return of depression. We looked carefully at the data and found that by lowering the threshold to two critical comments we could distinguish patients who did well from those who did poorly. This means that depressed people are even more sensitive to criticism from their relatives than are people with schizophrenia. This indication of the importance of the relationship with a partner in perpetuating depression accords with the identification by Brown and Harris of a lack of a supportive relationship as one of the vulnerability factors for developing depression in response to a life event (see Chapter 1).

Expressed emotion and schizophrenia: opposing models

It is tempting to interpret these results as proving that disturbed relationships make both schizophrenia and depression worse, but this inference cannot be made from snapshot studies of this kind, because of the problem of determining

Figure 2 Alternative models of the relationship between expressed emotion (EE) and relapse of schizophrenia

the direction of cause and effect, which I have already discussed. We can usefully examine the alternative interpretations of the link between EE and the course of schizophrenia.

In Figure 2, model A presents the 'common sense' interpretation that the relatives' critical and overinvolved attitudes have a direct psychological impact on the patient causing a return of schizophrenic symptoms. Model B, which is equally plausible, postulates that the patient's disturbed behaviour provokes the relatives to develop high-EE attitudes, and eventually develops into a full-blown schizophrenic attack. In this model there is no direct link between EE and relapse of the schizophrenic illness. In fact, in both the studies I have described, the degree of disturbed behaviour was measured with just this possible scenario in mind. In neither study was there any link between the level of disturbed behaviour and the relatives' EE rating. Low-EE relatives appeared to be able to tolerate quite a severe degree of disturbance without becoming critical or overinvolved. Unfortunately this does not resolve the issue. Any characteristic of the patient which may not even have been measured, could both provoke high-EE attitudes and render the patient more likely to relapse. It is here that a video film of the family recorded over a prolonged period would throw light on this problem. We could watch changes in the behaviour of the patient and the carers and decide which came first in time. But that strategy is impractical because we could never record family life unobtrusively, although it has been attempted for television programmes. Even more daunting is the prospect of analysing months of videotapes, considering that it takes many times as long to analyse such material as it does to record it. The answer lies elsewhere – in the form of the human probe.

Probing the family system

We can think of the family as a system. Observed from the outside, it is so complex that it is very difficult to appreciate the way it functions. Many attempts have been made to measure what goes on in families, but at best they capture only glimpses of the complexity. But suppose the observer enters the system and tries to change it from the inside. The family has to react to the presence of a foreign body in its midst and in doing so reveals many of the strategies it employs to maintain the integrity of the system. For example, various members of the family will try to form an exclusive alliance with the stranger in order to bolster their authority in any power struggle. Some may take advantage of the apparent safety guaranteed by the stranger to air grievances that have remained unspoken. Others may try to incorporate the intruder into the family and behave towards her or him in the way they would treat a particular family member.

In order to tackle the 'cause or effect' problem I have presented in respect to EE and the course of schizophrenia, I decided that the most telling strategy was to introduce a human probe into the families. I shall call this person the therapist, since the ultimate goal was to improve the outcome for people with schizophrenia. I certainly do not mean to imply that families caring for someone with this condition need therapy. When a family member develops schizophrenia, it taxes the resources of the family mightily. The remarkable fact is that half the families in Britain faced with this challenge respond with low-EE coping behaviours, managing to avoid becoming angry or overinvolved with the patient. High-

EE relatives are not sick and do not need treatment, but, for one reason or another, are using coping strategies that actually make things worse, and need to be helped to employ more effective ways of dealing with the daily problems that schizophrenia generates. The changes that the therapists were attempting to achieve were clearly definable: to reduce EE from high to low, or to reduce social contact between patient and high-EE relative from high to low. But how was this to be done?

Trials and placebos

In 1976 I assembled a team of colleagues to work out how to achieve these changes, and then to put the ideas into practice as therapists. They were Elizabeth Kuipers, a psychologist who already had experience of working with families with a behavioural approach, and two psychiatrists with a psychoanalytic approach, Rosemarie Eberlein-Fries and David Sturgeon. We spent some months deciding on the constituents of our intervention and then jumped in at the deep end. What we had put together was a combination of education about schizophrenia, teaching the family how to tackle problems and to improve communication, methods of decreasing anger and overinvolvement and of resolving conflicts, strategies for reducing contact, and a focus on developing realistic expectations for the patients. We did not have an overarching theory of family function but were like magpies, taking bits and pieces from different schools of therapy which we thought might help us succeed in our aims. To convey an idea of our approach, I will give an account of how we intended to reduce the output of critical comments. As I have already explained, critical comments are an expression of the relative's anger. Relatives get angry with patients because they care about them. If you didn't care for a person, their behaviour would be a matter of indifference to you. Therefore we bring out the caring attitude behind the anger. For example:

Mr Brown, referring to his son, Daniel, in an angry tone of voice: He's always wearing a dirty shirt.

Therapist: You really care about your son's appearance.

Mr Brown: Of course I do.

Therapist: Would you tell Daniel how you would like him to dress?

Mr Brown: Daniel, I'd like you to wear a clean shirt.

The last communication from Mr Brown is a positive request for change instead of an angry attack, and offers Daniel the opportunity to please his father.

In order to test the value of what we were about to do with families, we set up what is known as a randomised, controlled trial. This has become the standard experimental design for evaluating new drugs and other types of physical treatment, such as surgery. Patients are assigned to two or more different treatments by a random procedure. In the dark ages before computers this was achieved by tossing a coin. Nowadays computers are used to generate sequences of random numbers. Often, the treatment under investigation is tested against a placebo, since many medical conditions can improve, at least temporarily, in response to the attention received by patients taking part in a trial. This demonstrates the powerful effect of the person's state of mind on bodily ailments, and understandably an even greater influence can be observed on psychiatric conditions. For example, patients with depressive symptoms respond better to green pills, while patients with symptoms of anxiety show a greater improvement on yellow pills, even when they contain identical medication. A study conducted in Alabama found that responses to the colours of pills varied between ethnic groups. White subjects tended to assume that white capsules were painkillers, while black subjects saw them as stimulants.

An abortive trial of psychosurgery

In the case of a drug it is easy to prepare a placebo pill which looks exactly the same but contains an inactive substance like chalk, or a placebo injection which consists only of salt water. For social and psychological treatments it is impossible to invent a placebo. In any contact between two human beings, it is not possible for one of them, the therapist, to do nothing, and any interaction, however low-key, has the potential of being therapeutic. Therefore instead of using a placebo, it is necessary to include a comparison treatment which is considered to be the best therapy in current use. Even this design is not feasible for some procedures, for example psychosurgery. Many years ago I was asked by the Medical Research Council to work with two colleagues and a group of neurosurgeons to design a trial of psychosurgery. Lobotomy, as it was originally called, was introduced for the treatment of schizophrenia in the 1930s by Egaz Moniz, for which he received one of the only two Nobel prizes ever awarded in psychiatry. Psychosurgery is no longer used for schizophrenia but is seen as an 'end of the line' treatment for patients with severe depression or obsessions who have failed to respond to anything else. It would have been unethical to subject patients to the full sequence of neurosurgical procedures with the exception of the final cut into the brain, so a placebo control was rejected. We could not employ a comparison treatment because these patients had tried everything else that might have helped. The only practical design was to use a waiting-list control; that is, patients would be randomly assigned to receive psychosurgery immediately on referral or to wait a further six months, after which they would undergo the operation. The six-month period while waiting would then be compared with the six months following psychosurgery for the experimental group. Unfortunately the neurosurgeons would not accept this design, arguing that by the time patients were referred to them, they were desperate, so the operation could not be delayed since it undoubtedly helped them. Of course no one can state this with certainty, but so strong was their investment in the procedure that the trial was not carried out, and as far as I know never has been, so that the value of psychosurgery remains untested.

Evaluating the family intervention

The design we chose for our trial was to compare our newly constructed family intervention against the usual treatment given to patients with schizophrenia, which at that time did not involve any contact with family members. We realised that at the end of the trial if our intervention proved superior to the usual treatment, we would not know whether this was simply the response of relatives to the interest shown by the therapists rather than to the particular things we were doing with them. We would then have to design another trial to sort out that problem (which we did).

We decided to conduct the trial on the patients who were most likely to relapse, because that would give us the greatest leeway to show an effect of our intervention. We selected patients who were in high social contact with high-EE relatives, knowing that even on regular medication they would have a fifty per cent chance of relapsing over nine months. We aimed to establish them all on antipsychotic medication, since it was well established by my own drug trial and by many others subsequently, that medication gave at least partial protection against relapse. The question we wished to answer was whether changing the family environment could add any benefit over and above the effect of medication. Our previous research suggested that if we could lower EE or social contact, and these were not simply byproducts of the patient's behaviour, the expected relapse rate would be around fifteen per cent.

It took five years to complete the trial and we had to wait that long in suspense to discover the answer. The first result we were intensely curious about was whether our crafted intervention had succeeded in inducing changes in the families. To our surprise and delight we discovered that three-quarters of the experimental families had reduced their EE and/or social contact levels below the target thresholds. However, forty per cent of the control families, who had received no professional help, also achieved these changes, showing that some families possess a self-healing capacity. The next question was whether these changes in family attitudes and behaviour reduced the patients' susceptibility to relapse. Half the control patients relapsed over nine months, exactly the rate we had predicted from the earlier work. For the experimental patients, rather than the fifteen per cent we had optimistically aimed at, the rate was remarkably low at eight per cent. Thus the results support the model postulating that relatives' emotional attitudes and behaviour towards the patients have a direct impact on their liability to relapse, and if these are ameliorated the course of schizophrenia can be changed. In the process of trying to establish the direction of cause and effect, we had invented a new treatment for schizophrenia.

This result was not just a flash in the pan. Numerous similar trials by colleagues in Britain, America, China and Japan have produced the same findings: that working with the families of schizophrenic patients improves the outcome of the illness. Whatever the biological basis of schizophrenia turns out to be, this body of work demonstrates that patients with this condition are extremely sensitive to the emotional environment surrounding them. In this respect they are no different from the rest of humanity, but the popular stereotype of madness (of which more later in the book) has set them apart as alien beings.

Expressed emotion and psychiatric and bodily illnesses

Some relatives have reacted negatively to these findings, feeling that they are being blamed for causing the illness, but there are a number of considerations that should reconcile them to the results. Work on EE has developed in several different directions. The measure has been applied to a wide range of psychiatric and bodily illnesses, and high levels of EE have been found in almost all of them. However, while EE has been linked to the outcome of many psychiatric conditions, including manic-depressive psychosis, eating disorders, alcohol abuse and post-traumatic stress disorder, the only bodily illnesses this relationship has been found in so far are diabetes and epilepsy. A group of American researchers has shown that people with diabetes living with a critical relative have poorer control of their blood sugar levels than those in low-EE households. However, two British teams have failed to replicate this finding. A study of children with epilepsy carried out in Britain found that children with poorly controlled epilepsy were much more likely to live with high-EE parents than children whose epilepsy was well controlled. The pervasiveness of high-EE attitudes across such a variety of illnesses argues that they cannot be a specific cause of schizophrenia, even though they may aggravate the condition once it is established. Moving in another direction, EE has been measured in professional carers working in sheltered homes, many of which have been set up for patients discharged from the old psychiatric hospitals. These homes are often ordinary houses, and, unlike hospital wards, staff and patients spend much of the day in intimate social contact, sharing household chores. In this respect, the atmosphere is much more like that in a family home, and indeed the staff commonly develop high-EE attitudes towards their charges. Several studies, including one of our own, have detected highly critical attitudes from the staff, although they do not seem to become overinvolved with the residents. The commonality of high-EE attitudes in both unpaid and professional carers and across many different disorders suggests that they are by no means an abnormal response to the demands of coping with long-term or relapsing conditions. However, once a link is established between EE and the course of an illness, a window of opportunity opens for the development of an intervention which may improve the outcome for patients. In the next chapter I will recount how we exploited this opportunity for patients suffering from depression.

Chapter 4

A Couple of Pills or Couple Therapy?

Developing and testing the family interventions for schizo-phrenia absorbed the energies of the research team for well over ten years. But all along I had the nagging feeling that the work on depression was a loose end that had been left dangling. I was not confident that we had established the correct threshold for critical comments, since we had simply adjusted it down from six to two by eye (so to speak), to produce a significant difference in relapse rates between the two groups of depressed patients. Consequently I was relieved when I heard in 1983 that a young graduate psychologist from Oxford, Jill Hooley,[27] was keen to try to replicate our findings for her PhD thesis. As it turned out, her results were almost identical to ours, bolstering our confidence in the cut-off point of two critical comments that we had established. Further support came from a surprising source: in 1994 Ahmed Okasha,[28] professor of psychiatry in Cairo, repeated the work with a sample of Egyptian patients and their spouses. This time it appeared that a threshold of seven critical comments gave the best separation between depressed patients with a good and a poor outcome, but there was still a significant difference between the groups using our cut-off point. The accumulation of evidence for a relationship between the partner's critical attitude and the course of depression seemed to me sufficient to take the next step of designing an intervention study. We were well into the study by 1997 when we were informed of a failure to replicate this relationship by an experienced research group in Cambridge headed by Eugene Paykel.[29] The only possible explanation we could envisage for this divergent result was that the Cambridge sample, unlike the others, contained a high proportion of middle-class women. It is conceivable that their access to material resources enabled them to compensate for the deficiencies in their marital relationship. Whatever the correct explanation for this anomalous finding, even if it had come to our notice earlier, I don't think it would have deterred us from pushing ahead with the trial of intervention. In the body of work on EE and schizophrenia, there are also some studies which failed to replicate the association with outcome, but they constitute a small minority.

Research on people differs from experiments with inanimate matter in that it is possible to gain only partial control over the conditions of the experiment. Given a constant atmospheric pressure, water uncontaminated by other chemicals will always turn to steam at the same temperature, whereas individuals vary considerably over time in the amount of provocation needed before they lose their temper. Uncontrolled factors can produce differences in results that are beyond the ingenuity of the researchers to explain. Hence, in human research the scientist is always weighing up the balance of evidence for and against a proposition, and the most convincing conclusions can be drawn when the same study has been repeated by many different teams working in a variety of countries.

Self-esteem and cognitive therapy

In designing the trial we were mindful of two streams of research in addition to the work on EE. One was the line of enquiry that George Brown had continued to pursue since identifying the vulnerability factors for depressed women. He had reached the conclusion that the central problem in depression was low self-esteem, which led women (he did not include men in his samples) to feel bereft when events occurred that robbed them of relationships or roles which helped them to establish their worth. To investigate these ideas he had developed measures of both positive and negative self-esteem. The research on EE and depression seemed to fit neatly with these notions, since being faced with constant criticism from your partner must surely lower your self-esteem unless you are very resilient. The other area of relevance was the burgeoning of non-drug treatments for depression over the previous decade. The most rigorously tested was cognitive therapy, invented by Aaron Beck in Philadelphia. This embodies a psychological approach to improving a person's self-esteem by encouraging them to question their assumptions about themselves and their abilities relative to other people. It may sound simple-minded, but part of its effect is achieved through the relationship that develops between the therapist and the patient, as in all 'talking cures' (Freud's term for psychoanalysis). Seen from today's perspective, they might better be called 'relationship therapies' since the transference (see Chapter 3) of the patient to the therapist is a vital ingredient in them all. Cognitive therapy has been tested against antidepressant drugs in numerous randomised, controlled trials, and has generally been found to be equally effective in relieving depression, and in some studies in preventing relapses.

In addition we found that there had been a handful of trials of marital therapy, which were of particular interest to us since we were planning to involve the patients' partners in the treatment. These studies, although not as convincing as the body of evidence for the value of cognitive therapy, suggested that marital therapy could also achieve an improvement in depression equivalent to that conferred by medication. Not surprisingly, it appeared that marital therapy was better than drugs at improving the couple's relationship.

Systemic therapy

In order to stabilise people with schizophrenia, it is obvious
from a compendium of trials that it is essential to use antipsychotic medication as a foundation on which family interventions are built as an adjunct. The situation is completely
different with depression, since psychological treatments
such as cognitive therapy have proved to be at least as effective
as antidepressant drugs. Therefore we felt we could take the
risk of comparing couple therapy without any added medication against the best possible course of drugs. To be accepted
for the trial, patients had to be in a steady relationship with
a heterosexual partner, and the partner had to make two or
more critical comments when given the EE interview. Only
a handful of partners made just one critical remark or none
at all. In the previous studies, researchers also found that
low-EE partners constituted a small minority, so that most
depressed patients in a relationship are exposed to criticism
from their mates. For our studies of schizophrenia, my colleagues and I developed the intervention for families, but in
order to devise an intervention for depressed patients and
their partners we called on the expertise of two systemic
family therapists, Eia Asen and Elsa Jones. At this point I
need to explain the concept behind systemic therapy.

By now the term 'ecosystem' has become part of the language: it implies that all living things are dependent on one
another and on the non-living environment for their existence. The ecosystem is thought of as maintaining a har-
monious balance which humans are disturbing by their
'unnatural' activities. A system is recognised by virtue of
having defined boundaries and of maintaining its integrity
within those boundaries. This is achieved by the existence of
feedback loops which signal when a disturbance occurs in the
system, setting in motion some compensatory action. This
attempts to correct the disturbance and return the system
to its previous balanced state. Systemic therapists view the

family as just such a system. Each family has its own boundary, although in traditional cultures the boundary may
encompass several dozen people. Some years ago, during a
visit to India, I stayed with a Muslim family which comprised
thirty-five people living in the same household. Within its
boundary the family tries to maintain stability by com-
pensating for changes. Using as an example the reaction of
the family to a therapist coming to their home (*see* Chapter
3), they may try to neutralise the perturbation caused by the
therapist by socialising their relationship: asking personal
questions and offering food and drink. Alternatively, they may
close ranks and expel the therapist as being too threatening to
their system.

A colleague and I worked with a Greek Cypriot family: a mother and
her daughter who suffered from schizophrenia. The mother was very
grateful for our visits and each time baked us an orange cake. We
felt it would be churlish to refuse her hospitality, which also stemmed
from her cultural background, so after being given gargantuan por-
tions on our first visit, the next time we asked her to cut us each
one thin slice: an attempt to set limits on her generosity. However,
she was not to be confined in this way and, despite our protests,
wrapped up the rest of the cake for us to take home at the end of
the session.

The designated patient

Whereas doctors usually assume that any disturbance is
limited to the individual who comes to them for help, systemic therapists view the family system as selecting one of
its members as the 'patient' to convey a message to the source
of help that all is not well with the family. Hence they call
the person who presents to the doctor the 'designated patient'
and turn their attention to the whole family. There are clearly
limitations to this approach. When the presenting condition
has a strong basis in heredity, as with Huntington's disease,

it is worse than useless to treat the patient as a harbinger of the family's own disturbance, even though the relatives may well be very distressed by the appearance of the symptoms. The same considerations apply to schizophrenia, albeit that the role of inheritance is not nearly as pronounced as in Huntington's disease. The weaker the evidence for a biological determinant for the condition, the more likely it is that a systemic approach will achieve improvement in the symptoms. Thus behavioural problems in children, such as bed-wetting and school refusal, respond well to systemic family therapy.

Writing a treatment manual

We asked the two therapists who agreed to work with the couples in the trial to write down what techniques they were going to use, and to include an outline of how the therapy would proceed over the twelve to twenty sessions within which they would try to achieve their aims. They were not comfortable with this demand at first, since therapists like to feel free to follow their intuition. However, we needed them to produce a manual so that if their therapy proved to be successful, other researchers could put it to the test. I have emphasised several times the importance of replicating the findings of research on people. They did eventually provide what we wanted; a document that opens with a general statement of their approach to depression, from which it is worth quoting directly. 'Close relationships are regarded as both influencing and being influenced by the depressed patients and the symptoms. The responses of family members to the patient may be seen as helping to maintain, or contributing to the patient's distress and symptoms.' Their remedies for this situation include helping the couple to gain new perspectives on the presenting problem, to attach different meanings to the depressive behaviours, and to experiment with new ways of interacting with each other that do not include the depressive symptoms. Rather than teaching the couple how to improve their relationship, the therapists encourage them to find their own solutions so that they gain a sense of mastery over the problems.

The trial of couple therapy versus drug treatment

Preventing relapse

One of the most daunting problems posed by depression is that even when complete recovery has occurred there is a high risk of the symptoms returning. This has shaped the policy on prescribing antidepressant drugs, which is to maintain the patient on a moderate dose for at least six months after the illness has resolved. But if depression is a response to adverse social circumstances, including lack of support or constant criticism from a partner, unless these have improved, taking the person off the drugs exposes them to risk of a further relapse. I described in Chapter 1 the experience of Arthur Kleinman with victims of the Chinese Cultural Revolution, which perfectly illustrates this dilemma. Consequently, we were as interested in the potential of the treatments under study to prevent relapse as in their ability to remove the symptoms of depression. Patients were randomly assigned to couple therapy or to antidepressants. If they ended up in the latter group they were first prescribed one of the older type of drugs, known chemically as tricyclic antidepressants. If they did not respond in six weeks they were prescribed fluoxetine (Prozac). Medication was continued for one year and then stopped gradually. The patients were then followed up after a further year to test the preventive effect of the treatment. The couple therapy occupied the first nine months, following which no further treatment was offered in the period up to the two-year follow-up.

The depressed partner

During the initial assessment, not only did we measure the intensity of the patients' depression, but we asked the partners to fill in a questionnaire about their own mental health. To our surprise, one-third of the partners were suffering from depressive symptoms severe enough to need treatment. If these partners had approached us instead of the patients we would have included them in the trial as cases and considered the actual patients as partners. If both partners are equally depressed, what determines which of them presents their complaints to the doctor? The answer to this intriguing question will have to wait for a future study, but the systemic concept of the 'designated patient' appears to be entirely appropriate to at least one-third of our sample.

Dropping out of treatment

A researcher always hopes that the subjects will be well behaved in a trial, accepting the treatment to which they have been assigned and turning up for follow-up assessments. Unfortunately real life is not like that, and subjects often rebel against the artificial constraints of a controlled comparison of treatments. In this instance, even though the patients were clearly informed that the treatment they would receive was determined by chance, just over half of those randomly assigned to antidepressant drugs refused to take them or simply stopped coming to the clinic. This was not such a surprise since previous trials of antidepressants had also lost a high proportion of patients. Numerous surveys of public opinion about psychiatric treatments have shown that there is a strong feeling against antidepressant drugs, which most people believe are addictive, as explained in Chapter 1. Whatever the reason for rejecting drugs for depression, the great majority of the public favour talking cures for the whole range of psychiatric conditions. It was not unexpected, therefore, that only a small proportion (fifteen per cent) of patients dropped out of couple therapy.

Outcome of the trial

Following the period of treatment, patients were assessed again for the severity of depression. Both treatments gave considerable relief from the symptoms, but the improvement was greater for those receiving couple therapy. At the end of the second year, during which no treatment was given, the patients in the couple therapy group were still doing better than those who had been given drugs.[30] This shows that couple therapy was superior to drugs both for treating depression and for preventing the return of symptoms. This result gives support to the theory that depression is maintained by a problematic relationship between the two partners and that working to improve the relationship gives more lasting benefit than taking an antidepressant drug. It also backs up the view that depression in one partner signals a disturbance in the family system.

The value of a friend

During the mid-1990s, while our team was assessing the value of couple therapy, George Brown had arrived at a similar point in his research on the causes of depression in women. Having found that the absence of a confiding relationship increased the likelihood of a woman becoming depressed following a life event, he decide to test the effect of providing women with a befriender. Like our team, he also mounted a randomised, controlled trial to evaluate this intervention. For the study he chose women who had been depressed for at least a year, and randomly assigned them either to have a befriender immediately or to wait for one year before being offered this form of help. This type of design is known as a waiting-list control. Nearly two-thirds of the women were in a partnership, and the same proportion were experiencing severe difficulties in their personal relationships. The befrienders, all women, were recruited through advertisements in the local press, churches and health centres. They received three days' training in acting as a 'friend', listening, and 'being there' for the depressed woman.

How acceptable was the offer of a befriender? Of the forty-three women in the experimental group, twenty-five (fifty-eight per cent) engaged with the befriender, eight (nineteen per cent) refused after one meeting, and the remaining ten saw a social worker but not a befriender. It appears that the befriending service was not much more welcome than antidepressant drugs for this group of women with long-standing depression. However, at the end of a year sixty-three per cent of the women in the befriending group were relieved of their depression compared with only thirty-nine per cent of control women.[31] There was no comparison with drugs in this trial, but it shows that providing a supportive relationship for women who do not have one relieves depression. It is therefore an alternative approach to improving an existing relationship.

The biochemistry of depression

What do these trials tell us about the nature of depression? The success of these non-drug therapies impels us to reappraise purely biochemical theories of depression and the claims of the pharmaceutical industry for their products. As I explained in Chapter 1, the newest class of antidepressants, the SSRIs, increase the amount of serotonin in the brain and this is assumed to account for their effect on depression. Several other classes of drugs with actions on different neurotransmitters, such as the tricyclics, also increase serotonin activity in the brain, as does electroconvulsive therapy. However, the effect that treatment has on serotonin activity is not directly related to the improvement in depression. No single theory of the underlying biochemical disturbance in depression can explain the action of these different treatments, but since each of them outperforms placebo, the chemical and electrical events they produce in the brain are likely to be related to the biochemical basis of depression. It would be of great interest to know whether the non-drug treatments are influencing the same biochemical events through changes in the patient's psychological functioning. One study has attempted to bring together biochemical theories and the response to psychotherapy.

Steven Rose and Sarah Willis used an indirect method of measuring the level of serotonin in the brain, as it is very difficult to gain access to the chemistry of the brain in a living person. The measure they used was the amount of imipramine (a standard antidepressant) taken up by one of the constituents of the blood, the platelets, which reflects the serotonin level. They studied patients who had attended a walk-in clinic with emotional problems and had been offered psychotherapy. They matched the patients with healthy controls and carried out the same measures on both groups at the same points in time. The Hamilton Rating Scale for Depression gave an indication of the subject's intensity of depression. Before receiving psychotherapy, the patients' level of imipramine binding was about half that of the controls. As the patients' depression improved, the level rose to equal that of the control group. This result suggests that a non-drug treatment can have the same effect on brain chemistry as drugs specifically targeted on the serotonin system.

This study illustrates the difficulties of monitoring what is going on in the brain in response to environmental changes. Rose and Willis had to be content with an indirect measure of brain neurotransmitter levels. We encountered the same type of problem in trying to link environmental stress with the development of symptoms of schizophrenia. Our different approach to this knotty problem is described in the next chapter.

Chapter 5

I've Got You Under My Skin

Expressed emotion and life events

The research on how stress affects the brain to produce depression is in its infancy, whereas the same issue has been more extensively studied in schizophrenia. Before describing what has been discovered, I need to weave together the stories about life events and relatives' expressed emotion (EE). Life events happen over a short period, usually no more than a few days or a week or so. In contrast, exposure to a high-EE relative can continue over months or even years. How do these short-term and long-term stresses interact? In the study of EE and schizophrenia that Christine Vaughn and I worked on together in the 1970s we included the assessment of life events introduced by George Brown.[32] We found that patients living with low-EE relatives and not taking medication had a high rate of life events: over half of them had experienced an event in the few weeks before they fell ill. However, if they lived in a high-EE home they were no more likely to have a life event happen to them in the period before an attack of schizophrenia than a well person. Our interpretation of these results is that patients living in a high-EE environment are continually exposed to stress, which builds up to the point at which they suffer a relapse of their illness. Patients cared for by low-EE relatives do not experience stress in their daily lives until an event occurs which pushes them over the edge into a psychotic state. If this formulation is correct, one would expect patients in high-EE homes to have shorter intervals between relapses than those in low-EE homes, who stay well until a life event comes along. There is support for this from a long-term study of schizophrenia carried out in the 1980s by Robin McCreadie,[33] a psychiatrist working in Scotland. He followed patients for five years and found that those in high-EE homes relapsed about once a year, while those in low-EE homes relapsed only once every three years.

Is the laboratory neutral?

What is the impact of external stress on brain function that leads to the appearance of the symptoms of schizophrenia? Unfortunately we still understand very little about the way brain functioning in mental illness differs from that in healthy people. Modern methods of scanning the areas of the brain that are most active have shown that the frontal lobes and certain other regions of the brain show less activity in people with schizophrenia, particularly when they are suffering from an attack of the illness. But this is such a general finding, and varies so much from one individual to another, that it is of little help in answering the question I have posed. There is another, more technical problem arising from the mechanics of brain scanning. It requires the subjects to lie motionless on a couch with their head inside a large cylinder. Having gone through the procedure myself, I can confirm that it is quite stressful. Indeed, some people with even mild claustrophobia cannot tolerate it. People suffering from schizophrenia can sometimes incorporate the procedure in their delusions, fearing they are going to be electrocuted or to have their brain permanently altered. This illustrates the crucial fact for all experiments on humans that the laboratory is not the neutral place most researchers take it to be. It exerts a stressful influence which varies from person to person but is ignored in favour of the comforting myth that the laboratory is a standardised setting which affects every subject in the same way.

Measuring stress from the skin

Since the focus of our research was the stressful effect of the patient's environment, it seemed much more logical to make the measurements in a situation in which we knew the stress level, rather than in a laboratory in which we did not. Hence we took the bold step of conducting the experiments in the patients' own homes. But what could we measure of any interest using portable equipment? The answer was found in the lie detector. This piece of equipment, which has become famous through its portrayal in Hollywood films, is based on the changes in the electrical conductivity of the skin that result from sweating. The salt in sweat is a good conductor of electricity, whereas dry skin is not. Even small increases in sweating over brief periods of time can be detected quite sensitively by simple equipment. A rapid rise and fall in electrical conductivity is known as a spontaneous fluctuation (SF). The number of SFs recorded during a minute is termed the SF rate and is an indication of the level of excitation of the autonomic nervous system. This system is not under conscious control and reacts to perceived threats by preparing the individual for immediate action, traditionally summed up by the phrase 'fight or flight'. The heart races, breathing speeds up, blood is pumped to the muscles, and sweating increases, anticipating the need to lose heat generated by running or fighting.

It was not too difficult to rig up a portable machine to measure skin conductance and to take it in a van to subjects' homes. The experiments were run in 1977 by a PhD student, Nick Tarrier,[34] now professor of psychology in Manchester. Since we knew from the earlier studies that contact between the high-EE relative and the patient increased the risk of relapse, we decided to record the patient's skin conductance with only the researcher in the room for fifteen minutes and then to ask the relative to join them, and to continue recording for a further fifteen minutes. Three groups of subjects were involved; patients living in a high-EE home, patients in a low-EE home, and mentally healthy controls who lived with a relative. Nick Tarrier repeated the procedure on three occasions three months apart, and on each visit he asked the subject about life events that might have occurred in the period before the recording session.

The effect of a relative

The average SF rates for each of the groups of subjects during the thirty-minute period are shown as graphs in Figure 3 for the first occasion of testing. Looking at the control group you can see that they start out at quite a high SF rate, indicating that the novel experience of being wired up to a piece of equipment in their home was arousing. However, as nothing frightening happened after the experiment began, their SF rate descended steadily throughout the thirty minutes with a brief blip at the entry of their relative. This process of adaptation by the nervous system to something unusual happening is termed 'habituation'. If we did not habituate to new sights, sounds and other stimuli, we would be in a constant state of high arousal which would be very uncomfortable. As the author James Thurber remarked about an eccentric genius in one of his short stories, 'He constantly stimulated me to the pitch of a nervous breakdown.' The graph for patients in high-EE homes is a complete contrast to the graph of the control subjects, since their SF rate remains at a high level throughout the thirty minutes with no sign of habituation. They show a dramatic response to the entry of the high-EE relative, which is significantly greater than the equivalent response of the other group of patients to their low-EE relative. For the first fifteen minutes the graphs of the two groups of patients are indistinguishable, both remaining at high levels. However, the entry of the low-EE relative into the room causes something unexpected to happen. The patients immediately start to habituate and by the end of the second

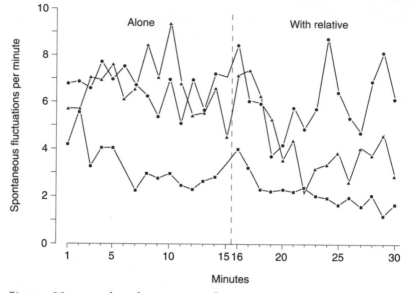

Figure 3 Mean number of spontaneous fluctuations per minute during the test period in eleven high-EE patients (triangles), ten low-EE patients (circles) and twenty-one control subjects (squares)

fifteen minutes are approaching the low level of the control subjects.

This surprising finding completely changed our way of thinking about low-EE relatives. It showed that their presence was reassuring for the patients, enabling them to come to terms with the psychologically disturbing effects of the experiment. Instead of viewing low-EE relatives as detached and neutral, we realised that they were playing an actively supportive role. We would never have made this important discovery if we had tested all the patients in a laboratory away from their home environment and their relatives. Indeed, Nick Tarrier did just that as one of his experiments. In the laboratory the patients from low-EE and high-EE homes produced skin conductance records that were indistinguishable.

The impact of life events

What about life events? Could we also detect their impact on the patients? Since events were relatively uncommon, we could not look at each occasion of testing separately. For example, only four patients reported a life event before the first recording session. Therefore we pooled the data for all the three sessions for the seven patients who had experienced a life event before at least one of the sessions. In effect we were using patients as their own controls, comparing their responses on occasions preceded by an event with event-free sessions. From the beginning of the session the patients show a reduction in SF rate whether or not a life event has occurred. Once the relative enters the room the two graphs diverge. When an event precedes the recording, the patients respond to the relative with a steep rise in the SF rate which then remains high for the rest of the session. This shows that there is an interaction between the arousing effects of a life event and the presence of the relative, which neither on their own produces (Figure 4). Most of these seven patients lived with a high-EE relative, but the numbers are too small to separate out the recordings for the different types of relative.

Symptoms and stress

This experiment succeeded in establishing a link between two kinds of environmental stress that we knew could provoke attacks of schizophrenia, and a bodily response indicating a state of arousal of the nervous system. There is, however, a problem with using the concept of arousal since it is common to a number of different emotional states experienced by normal people, including pleasurable excitement as well as fear and anger. It also applies to the whole range of psychiatric conditions, including depression, which can take an agitated form. The challenge, then, was to show that the general state of high arousal was linked with specific symptoms of schizophrenia. We could not use delusions for this purpose since they are relatively long-term symptoms which do not fluctuate in intensity over minutes or even hours. What we

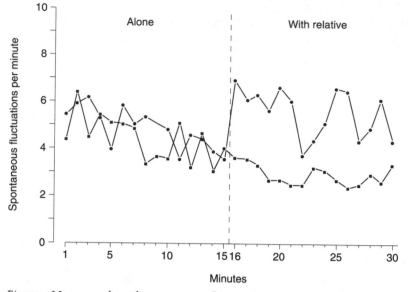

Figure 4 Mean number of spontaneous fluctuations per minute during the test period for seven patients on occasions preceded by a life event (circles) and the same patients on occasions when no life event had been experienced (squares). If a patient had two occasions succeeding a life event (or not), the mean of both was calculated. Patients who experienced (or did not experience) a life event on all three occasions are excluded from this graph

needed was an experience which came and went over a matter of minutes in order to look for associations with changes in the SF rate over the same period of time. The obvious choice was hearing voices, particularly as this is a common symptom in schizophrenia. The snag was how to determine when the patient was hearing voices. Of course we could simply ask the patient to tell us when this was occurring, but I had my doubts about relying on the patients to be accurate informants.

When I worked at Friern Hospital my research offices were adjacent to a house in the grounds in which lived twelve patients who were under my care. One of the men used to spend a lot of time sitting on the verandah, which was visible from my window. He often carried on a dialogue with invisible others, shouting and laughing at the top of his voice. Whenever I interviewed him to check on his progress I would ask him how much he was troubled by the voices. 'Voices, Doc?' he would query incredulously, 'I haven't heard voices for years.'

Charting 'voices'

As a result of several encounters of this kind I felt it was necessary to use a more objective and reliable indicator of auditory hallucinations. I had noticed that a number of patients who admitted to hearing voices showed characteristic eye movements. Their eyes would suddenly flick upwards and to one side, remain in that position for a few seconds, and then move back to a central position. If someone unexpectedly snapped their fingers next to one of your ears you would probably show the same response. With two colleagues, Ruth Cooklin and David Sturgeon,[35] I videotaped a few patients who showed these eye movements and we viewed the tapes independently. We found that we could agree most of the time on when the eye flicks began, although there was less consistency on when the eyes moved back to a central position again, presumably because the flick up and out was more abrupt than the shift back.

'Voices' and stress

We then set up an experiment in which a sample of patients who clearly showed these eye flicks had their skin conductance measured under two conditions: either sitting alone, or sitting with an experimenter who engaged them in conversation about neutral topics. We randomised the order of these two conditions so that some patients were alone first, while others started off sitting with the experimenter. The aim of introducing the experimenter was to see if the frequency of the voices would be reduced by interacting with a non-threatening person. We instructed the patients to raise their hand when they heard voices. The first thing we discovered in reviewing the videotapes was that the observers detected far more eye flicks than times when the patients raised their hand. Thus my reluctance to rely on the patients' reports was justified.

When we compared the time the patient was alone with the period spent talking to the experimenter we found that the number of eye flicks was significantly less during the sociable interaction. The importance of this observation is the practical advice that can be given to relatives and professional carers to attempt to engage the patient in conversation when they are obviously responding to auditory hallucinations. In order to test the hypothesis that had prompted the experiment, we superimposed the onset of eye flicks on the record of the SF rate. It was evident that most eye flicks coincided with an increasing SF rate. Thus we had established a link between a measure of arousal and one of the cardinal symptoms of schizophrenia. Unfortunately we were bedevilled by the ambiguity of the direction of cause and effect that we discussed in Chapter 3. We could not tell whether an increase in the patient's arousal triggered the voices or whether hearing the voices aroused the patient. And there our attempts to fill in the missing links in the chain of causality between environmental stress and episodes of schizophrenia have had to rest.

Visualising the brain in action

Since we halted our research into this difficult set of problems, the technology of functional brain imaging has developed. Unlike brain scans which produce a static picture of the structure of the brain, functional imaging generates information about the dynamics of the brain, allowing links to be made with transient phenomena like auditory hallucinations. Most methods of producing images of the functioning brain depend on the fact that when a region of the brain becomes more active the blood supply increases immediately to supply the brain cells with oxygen and glucose and to take away waste products. The technique used first to detect changes in the blood flow was to introduce a small amount of water tagged with radioactivity into the blood stream and to follow the pulse of radioactivity through the brain. More recently it was discovered that the magnetic properties of the hydrogen atoms in water distributed throughout the body and especially in the blood could be used to give more precise pictures of changes in blood flow. Functional magnetic resonance imaging (fMRI), as it is termed, is now the dominant technique in the imaging field.

Philip McGuire and his colleagues at the Institute of Psychiatry in London used a radioactive scanning technique in the early 1990s to measure blood flow through the brain in patients with schizophrenia. They chose patients who were hearing voices frequently and carried out a scan at this time and then repeated it five months later when the patients had improved as a result of treatment. This design uses patients as their own controls, comparing brain activity while hallucinating with that at a later time when the voices have faded or vanished. The main difference between the two sets of scans was that when the patients were hallucinating there was much more activity in the region of the brain on the left side that deals with the production of speech. In the vast majority of right-handed people the left side of the brain is concerned with speech, and nine of the twelve patients were right-handed. This result was a surprise since the expectation was that auditory hallucinations would be generated from the parts of the brain that deal with hearing and memory. The voices that patients hear are often those of familiar people repeating everyday phrases, so McGuire and colleagues expected that the region of the brain that stores what has been heard would be involved. The link with activity in the speech area, although not predicted by these researchers, fits with the observation that when words are accessed by a subject, blood flow increases to the front part of the brain and to the speech area. It also supports a theory proposed by several researchers that auditory hallucinations are actually a misinterpretation of the inner speech that continues in all of us just below the level of awareness. We can bring it into consciousness by making an effort to focus on it, a technique used by some writers such as James Joyce and known as tapping into the 'stream of consciousness'. Many children invent imaginary friends with whom they have conversations out loud, and some adults are aware of carrying on silent dialogues in their head when trying to make a decision. If auditory hallucinations and speech are indeed generated by the same region of the brain, there could be competition between them. This could explain the finding in our experiment that patients talking with another person showed less evidence of hearing voices than when they were alone.

These ideas were explored further by the group at the Institute of Psychiatry using the more recent technique of fMRI. They employed the same design of testing patients when they were hallucinating and then again three months later when they were much improved. This time they played a pre-recorded story to the patients while they were being scanned. This would be expected to activate the temporal lobe of the brain, the region which deals with memory for words. They found that the story produced less activity in the temporal lobe when the patients were hallucinating than when they had recovered. This result suggests that not only is there competition between auditory hallucinations and the patient's inner speech, but also with external speech produced by others. Many relatives complain that it is hard to get through to the patient at times, presumably because their attention is focused on the voices. Some patients learn to use a portable stereo recorder to compete with insistent voices and reduce their intensity, thus highlighting the practical value of such competition.

This work is promising but is still subject to the technical limitations of the measuring equipment: subjects have to remain lying down with their head inside a cylinder and fixed in place with a padded head restraint. The machinery is also quite noisy. Until the development of less cumbersome measuring techniques, the enormous advantage of recording the patient's responses to social situations of a known stress level will be beyond our reach.

Chapter 6

The People versus the Professionals

Untreated illness

I have already pointed out ways in which the public view of psychiatric illness differs from the professional view. In this chapter the discrepancies will be explored in greater depth. One of the reasons for the different perspectives was formulated in Britain by David Goldberg, a psychiatrist, and Peter Huxley, a social worker, in 1980.[36] They described a series of filters which intervene between the distressed person in the community and the patient in a psychiatric ward. The first filter operates between the person who feels miserable or anxious, and the general practitioner. By no means all people who develop a depression or anxiety state seek help from their general practitioner. Some may not recognise that they are suffering from a treatable illness. Others, from past experience, may expect their doctor to show little sympathy. Yet others may wait for some weeks in the hope that their symptoms will resolve without treatment, and they may be proved right. It is only when surveys are carried out on the general population that untreated neurotic illness comes to light. In 1995 the Australian Health Department funded a national survey of mental health and wellbeing. A random sample of the whole adult population was selected and these participants were interviewed with a standardised schedule designed to generate psychiatric diagnoses. It emerged that four per cent of men and seven per cent of women had suffered from depression within the previous year, seven per cent of men and twelve per cent of women suffered from anxiety, and eleven per cent of men and five per cent of women abused substances, including alcohol. The striking finding was that sixty-two per cent of people with a diagnosed psychiatric disorder did not seek any professional help for their mental health problems. The proportion of such untreated illness varies from country to country and place to place according to the psychological sophistication of the public and the availability and accessibility of a primary care doctor or other medical help.

Body language

The next filter in the sequence is the general practitioner, who operates a selection process which is both intentional and unintentional. The intentional filter allows only one in twenty of the patients the general practitioner recognises as suffering from a neurotic illness to be referred to a psychiatric specialist. The general practitioner can manage the great majority of patients presenting with neuroses. Referral to the next level is usually because the patient has not responded to the first-line treatments prescribed, or that the illness is more severe or more complicated than usual, or that there is a serious risk of suicide. The unintentional filter results from the fact that most general practitioners fail to recognise the presence of a neurotic illness in about one in three patients. One of the reasons is inadequate training, and David Goldberg has spent much of his professional life devising and testing training programmes to correct this deficiency. Contributing to the difficulty of diagnosis is the fact that many patients present their distress as bodily symptoms. In the previous chapter I described the way the autonomic nervous system prepares the body for fight or flight in the face of a threat. These changes occur when a person becomes anxious even when there is no obvious danger. As we shall see, anxiety and depression are often inextricably mixed, so that these bodily experiences are common to both states of mind. We can get an idea of how large they loom in public consciousness by a selection of phrases in common use: her heart sank, his skin crawled, her legs turned to jelly, it brought a lump to my throat, her heart was in her mouth, his head throbbed, it gave me goosepimples, he went white with fear, I've got butterflies in my stomach. Anxiety and depression are always accompanied by these bodily changes and the affected person may focus on these rather than the psychological symptoms. This creates a problem for the general practitioner who then has to distinguish between the bodily response to psychological distress and symptoms of physical disease. The general practitioner can sometimes feel impelled to embark on a prolonged and expensive series of laboratory investigations to exclude a physical cause for the patient's complaints. There is evidence that people in Western societies are becoming increasingly aware of psychological experiences. Agony aunts constantly give advice on how to deal with emotional problems, and television soaps captivate their viewers with the emotions thrown up by fraught relationships. The growing psychological sophistication of the public is not always matched by the sensitivity of general practitioners, some of whom have a blind spot for psychological problems and are only interested in dealing with bodily complaints. Patients learn to deal with this either by presenting their distress in the form of physical symptoms or by seeking out a doctor in the practice who is more responsive to psychological issues, assuming that they have a choice.

Traditional healers

The situation in developing countries is very different. The majority of the population are not psychologically minded and there are few primary care physicians. This role is filled by the traditional healer. Many traditional healers are rational and resourceful people operating within a culture which ascribes to them magical powers. But they are able to use their knowledge of the human condition to detect the emotional source of a problem even when, as is usual, it is presented as a physical complaint. Korean healers were described by Y. K. Harvey in 1976 as 'keenly intuitive and perceptive persons who make good use of their knowledge of people and human problems in helping their clients make the best of their situations. They give conservative advice, provide clients with outlets for potentially disruptive emotions, and get substantial help from the passage of time in solving clients' problems.'[37] No Western psychotherapist would feel slighted to be described in these terms.

There are a number of ways in which traditional healers are at an advantage compared with the general practitioner in the UK. They are usually much closer to their clients by virtue of living in a small community, and as a result know a great deal about the problematic relationships that exist. They also share the same world view as their clients, including beliefs about the causes and cures of diseases – which is not true of the general practitioner, whose medical explanation is almost always at variance with the popular views of causation. The traditional healer can assume that clients will understand the diagnosis and treatment without the necessity for long explanations. An account of a traditional healer in south India will illustrate these points. In the 1970s Mark Nichter studied Havik Brahmins in this region and found that women are expected to suppress the expression of emotion within the family.[38] They use bodily symptoms to signal distress, one in particular being known as *tale tirigutade*. This is translated as 'head turning' and is interpreted by most Western-trained doctors to mean giddiness or dizziness. However, traditional healers have another way of viewing the symptom. Nichter interviewed twenty-two clients of a traditional healer each of whom presented with this complaint. Among them were five individuals whose family was on the verge of breaking up, four people in economic crisis, four women aged over twenty-five who were anxiously awaiting marriage, two people experiencing adjustment problems following marriage, and one recently widowed woman who had two daughters but no sons. The common theme is that these problems induce uncertainty and disorientation, which the individuals expressed in bodily terms as dizziness. The healer would be very familiar with the family circumstances of these clients and would be able to make the link between these and the symptom with which they presented.

Mobilising social support

Whereas a Western psychotherapist would attempt to interpret the link between the patient's life circumstances and the symptom, a healer would avoid this kind of approach. Family relationships are not referred to explicitly in traditional societies, the subject being too sensitive; instead, the healer explains the symptom in terms of shared beliefs about the causes of illness, frequently within a spiritual context. For instance, in Taiwan the healer's interpretation of the client's complaints centres on a devil, a ghost or a god, which serves as a symbol of a significant person in the client's life. Instead of relationships with spouse, parents or neighbours being spoken of directly, which would be unacceptable, a deceased relative's spirit is identified as the source of the problem. In this way, the real-life drama is depicted using the insubstantial world of the spirits. Having formulated a diagnosis in acceptable terms, the healer will then prescribe a ritual which often has the effect of strengthening the bonds between the individual and the social group. For example, in Sri Lanka the healer might recommend an exorcism ceremony which involves a large group of participants, including musicians, dancers, and people who represent the spirits, and which continues from dusk till dawn. The cost of this production would be well beyond the means of an individual or even a single family, requiring cooperation between a large group of relatives. Another strategy was used by an Indian healer studied by Nichter: he focused the attention of the family on the patient by involving family members in the preparation of time-consuming medicines and special meals. By these means the social resources around the patient are mobilised, emphasising the emotional support that is available.

The healer is called upon to activate the patient's social supports at times of stress, but many cultures use such resources routinely to help a bereaved person deal with loss. I explained in Chapter 1 how George Brown's research established a link between events representing loss and the development of depression. Is it possible that cultures that have retained methods of supporting the individual experiencing loss reduce the risk of depression? A review of such cultures will help us to answer this question. Each account represents the fieldwork of an anthropologist at a particular time and with a specific group of the people being studied. We should be cautious about assuming that they are true of an entire culture and that they are unchanging over time. Nevertheless they have important lessons to teach us about cultural resources on which bereaved individuals can draw.

Reciprocity in New Guinea

The Kaluli are a forest people of New Guinea whose society is based on the principle of reciprocity. If a thief steals a pig, the owner may steal a pig from the thief or demand money in compensation. The same concept is applied to losses in the non-material area of human relationships. The expected emotional response is anger, the intensity of which is in proportion to the loss experienced. Grieving is a response to devastating loss and represents an appeal for retaliation and compensation, just as if it were a possession that had been taken away unjustly. Grief is expressed publicly and worked through in weeping and song, not only at funerals but on many other occasions in ceremonies in which social support

is offered. Of course the loss of an intimate personal relationship cannot be compensated for in any meaningful way,
but the public display of anger and grief focuses the attention
of the group on the bereaved person and ensures that he or
she receives emotional support.

Grief in Iran

Iranian culture and history are dominated by the themes of
tragedy, injustice and martyrdom. These colour both classical
Persian poetry and modern novels, which are pervaded with
melancholy and despair. The culture places a high value on
sadness, which is regarded as an indication of personal depth.
Individuals growing up in the culture are taught to express
sadness appropriately and in a socially acceptable manner.
Most children first learn to grieve in the context of ceremonies for Iranian martyrs. So from an early age experiences
of loss, sadness and grief are assimilated into the suffering of
the wider community. In this way personal losses are placed
in the perspective of national tragedy, and bereaved individuals are never left alone with their grief. In Iranian culture
the emotional response to individual loss is incorporated in
the communal consciousness of historical tragedy.

Meditation in Sri Lanka

In 1985 the anthropologist Gananath Obeyesekere described
the coping style used by Sri Lankan Buddhists to deal with
loss.[39] In Buddhist philosophy, hopelessness lies in the nature
of the world and salvation is achieved by understanding and
overcoming that hopelessness. To do so one needs to recognise
the illusory nature of the world of sense, pleasure and domes-
ticity. A particular form of meditation is practised to diminish
the experience of loss. This is meditation on revulsion, the
purpose of which is to induce a sense of disgust for sensory
pleasure and to heighten awareness of the transitoriness of

the corporeal body. The body is imagined as 'a clay pot, polished on the outside, but full of faeces'. This image is applied to people close to the meditator, such as parents, spouse and children, and eventually extended to the whole of humankind. By these means a sense of loss may be coped with by weakening the emotional bonds to people in one's immediate social circle. Obeyesekere writes that it is almost impossible for a Sinhalese person to use words expressing sorrow without invoking Buddhist concepts: 'words used for personal emotional states resonate with the hopeless dilemma of mankind.'

We can see that Kaluli and Iranian culture both help people come to terms with loss by providing a network of social and emotional support around the individual which takes action at a time of crisis. The Sri Lankan Buddhist method of coping with loss is quite different in nature and much less compatible with Western ideologies. However, the importance of these examples is that each of the cultures has developed active resources which are available to the individual at a time of loss. How effective they are in preventing the development of depression is unknown. To discover this would require a series of longitudinal studies of people suffering a loss in different cultures. What is clear, however, is that in the absence of such resources in Western cultures it has become necessary to substitute natural support networks by professional inputs. George Brown's befriending scheme and our own couple therapy (see Chapter 4) are examples of professional substitution for the lack of supportive relationships.

The ritual of mourning

It was not always the case that Western societies lacked cultural procedures for dealing with loss. During the Victorian era and extending into the beginning of the twentieth century elaborate mourning rituals were observed. The clothes that the bereaved family should wear were specified, as was the length of a period of full mourning, to be followed by a time of half-mourning. European children observed the correct rituals in the same way as adults. Children mourned the death of a parent for twelve months, in the first six wearing the dull black and heavy crêpe of deepest mourning. For the next three months of ordinary mourning they wore black silk without crêpe, while in the final three months they were dressed in half-mourning colours. The bereaved wife was expected to wear 'widow's weeds', and straw was laid down outside the house to muffle the sounds of passing horses and carriages. Among observant Jews today the bereaved family is expected to remain in the home for seven days, during which time the men do not shave. The family is visited daily by relatives, friends and neighbours who bring them food, so that they do not have to get involved in household activities. The period of mourning ends after one year when a stone is erected over the grave.

The value of these rituals is that they specify how bereaved people should behave, and they mark them out as needing special treatment by their social circle. They also set a clear limit to the length of the mourning period and indicate when the bereaved person should cease to grieve and should re-enter life fully. The disappearance of these practices has left people at a loss to know how to behave; both the bereaved and their well-wishers. It has also posed a problem to the professionals: when does a normal bereavement response become a depressive illness? In the current WHO ICD-10 Classification of Mental and Behavioural Disorders there is a diagnostic category termed 'prolonged depressive reaction', which is meant to be used for bereavement reactions that last longer than six months, but this is clearly an arbitrary limit.

Shifts in diagnosis

Obeyesekere presents the challenging view that the use of the term 'depression' in the West is a medicalisation of the response to loss. In the absence of culturally prescribed coping strategies, it has become necessary to deal with the emotions consequent on a loss as though they were an illness and to treat the distress with medication. This concept is not applicable to manic-depressive illness, which has a strong basis in inheritance, but could be seen as relevant to the less severe forms of depression common in the general population. Once antidepressant medication was introduced, the pharmaceutical companies seized the opportunity to make large profits out of a very common 'condition' and pushed their products with massive advertising campaigns. These of course were targeted at psychiatrists and particularly at general practitioners, who treat ninety-five per cent of patients with neuroses, as noted by David Goldberg and Peter Huxley. One surprising effect of this propaganda was detected by Edward Hare,[40] a psychiatrist at the Maudsley Hospital. He reviewed the diagnosis of neurotic conditions recorded in the hospital for the period 1949–69, during which the first antidepressant drug was made available. He found that after its introduction there was a major shift away from the diagnosis of anxiety, which was replaced by the diagnosis of depression. How could this have happened?

There are four factors that contributed to this abrupt change in the way psychiatrists diagnose their patients. I have emphasised the first throughout this book, namely that there are no laboratory tests to back up a psychiatric diagnosis, so that the boundaries between conditions can waver back and forth, swayed by the climate of opinion and by the idiosyncratic beliefs of individual psychiatrists. The second is the understandable need psychiatrists have to feel that they can offer effective treatments. When a new treatment becomes available it tends to be prescribed for a wide range of conditions in the hope that they will respond. It takes some years for psychiatrists to narrow down the range of a new treatment to the patients for whom it really works. The advent of the first antidepressant medication opened up exciting possibilities for psychiatrists, who, given the flexibility of the system, opted for a diagnosis that they thought they could treat. The third factor is the competition between the pharmaceutical companies for a very lucrative market. It is in the interest of a company to sell a product on the basis that it has specific advantages over its competitors. An instructive example is provided by the introduction of the first antipsychotic drugs.

Selling a product

I have already described the introduction into psychiatry of the first antipsychotic drug, chlorpromazine (Largactil), in 1955. It rapidly cornered the market worldwide and in the first ten years more than thirty million prescriptions were issued. A few years after its debut, a pharmaceutical chemist, Paul Janssen, synthesised a new drug, haloperidol, which belongs to a different chemical family. It had similar effects on psychotic illnesses but was not obviously superior to chlorpromazine. Currently it costs $200 million to bring a new drug to the market, and these costs have to be recouped. The spin doctors in Janssen's company came up with the idea of marketing haloperidol as a specific treatment for mania, hoping to replace chlorpromazine for this condition. In fact haloperidol is less sedative than chlorpromazine and is consequently less useful for manic patients, who are often physically and mentally overactive and need to be calmed down. Nevertheless, so successful was the marketing campaign, that haloperidol is still linked with mania in the minds of psychiatrists decades later, long after the patent on haloperidol ran out.

Overlapping diagnoses

The fourth factor is the substantial overlap in symptoms between depression and anxiety. This phenomenon is well recognised by researchers who survey samples of patients with standardised interviews. Yet you would not learn this by consulting textbooks of psychiatry, which present anxiety and depression as distinct, well-demarcated conditions. The different views of anxiety and depression held by psychiatrists and by the patients suffering from them were highlighted by a study I conducted in 1978.[41] It involved twenty patients suffering from neuroses and ten experienced psychiatrists. They were each asked to rate feelings of depression and anxiety on eleven psychological and eleven bodily symptoms. For instance, they were asked to state whether when depressed their heart beat fast (bodily symptom) and if they wanted to die (psychological symptom). The patients were asked to rate their own unpleasant feelings, while the psychiatrists were asked to respond as they expected a typical neurotic patient would do. The ratings were then analysed to see how much overlap there was between the symptoms of anxiety and depression. A correlation of 1 would mean complete overlap. For the patients the correlation between the two lists of symptoms was 0.62, which indicates that a great many symptoms were common to both conditions. For the psychiatrists the correlation was zero: no overlap between depression and anxiety whatsoever. These senior and experienced psychiatrists maintained idealised concepts of depression and anxiety as crystallised conditions, which bore little relation to the experiences of their patients.

The reality was revealed two years before my study by a survey conducted by Phillip Snaith and his colleagues in Leeds.[42] They asked patients suffering from anxiety or depression to fill in two questionnaires, one relating to symptoms of anxiety, the other to symptoms of depression. Of the patients diagnosed by the clinicians as suffering from anxiety neurosis, only twenty-four per cent had scores that did not overlap with those of the depressed patients. Similarly, only twenty-six per cent of the patients diagnosed with depression had scores that were distinct from those of the anxious patients. Of the total group, seventy-three per cent fell into the middle range of scores and were considered by Snaith and his colleagues to represent 'anxiety-depressions'.

Given that the majority of patients with neuroses experience an equal balance of symptoms of anxiety and depression, it is easy for the clinician to focus on one or other cluster of symptoms and impose a diagnosis of 'pure' anxiety or 'pure' depression. This explains how the psychiatrists at the Maudsley Hospital were able to shift their diagnoses from anxiety to depression over a few years in response to the availability of antidepressants. You may be wondering how it was that these astute clinicians failed to notice that their patients who would have been given a diagnosis of anxiety previously did not improve on an antidepressant. The answer is that most antidepressant drugs have sedative effects and reduce the symptoms of anxiety as well as those of depression. To call them antidepressants is therefore understating the range of symptoms they may affect beneficially. So even some patients with predominant anxiety can respond well to antidepressants.

Genes and environment

A study of twins by Kenneth Kendler and his colleagues in 1987 throws an interesting light on the relationship between anxiety and depression.[43] They used the strategy of comparing single-egg (monozygotic) twins with two-egg (dizygotic) twins to attempt to sort out genetic from environmental influences (see Chapter 2). Single-egg twins have exactly the same genetic make-up, whereas two-egg twins have only half their genes in common, as with any pair of siblings. Any characteristic that is more commonly shared by the single-egg than by the two-egg twins is likely to be largely inherited, while characteristics that are equally shared by the two types of twin pairs are more likely to be environmental in origin. I need to stress that the environment is a very broad concept that stretches from complications at birth, through parental styles of upbringing, and viral infections, to toxins such as lead in the atmosphere. Kendler and his group used the Australian Twin Register to send questionnaires on depression and anxiety to nearly 3000 twin pairs of the same sex. From their analysis of the responses to the questionnaire, they concluded that what is inherited is a general liability to psychological distress and that the genes do not determine whether the individual will become depressed or anxious. It is the environment that shapes the general distress into a predominantly anxious or depressed form.

Loss and danger events

In 1980 George Brown and Robert Finlay-Jones,[43] an Australian psychiatrist, had carried out research on precisely this issue: the features of the environment that determine whether a person will develop anxiety or depression. I presented in Chapter 1 the work of Brown and Harris which established that the onset of depression was associated with events that represented a loss of something or some person valued by the depressed individual. Following this they moved on to enquire into the relationship between life events and the onset of anxiety. Brown and Finlay-Jones interviewed 164 women who were attending a general practice in central London. Using the Present State Examination (*see* Chapter 1) they identified those women who had sufficient psychiatric symptoms to pass the threshold for someone to need treatment. They classified them into predominant depression, predominant anxiety, and a mixture of the two: approximately one-third fell into each category. They focused on the women whose symptoms had started within the previous year and compared them with women who were psychiatrically healthy. They gave each woman the Life Events interview that Brown and Harris had developed for the research on depression, but added a further dimension to it. They had previously rated events by the severity of loss they represented, characterising losses as those of a person by death or separation, of the individual's physical health, of jobs, career opportunities, material possessions, or of a cherished idea, for example, the partner's fidelity. They extended the description of events to include those that threatened danger. They found that women with depression had experienced an excess of loss events in the three months before their symptoms began, replicating their previous results. Women with anxiety had experienced an excess of danger events, while those with mixed symptoms reported both more loss and more danger events than the healthy women. It appears from the findings of the genetic research by Kendler and the social research by Brown that it is the character of happenings in our environment that determines whether we become depressed or anxious, and not our constitution.

What the public want

I have argued with respect to neurotic illnesses that the public experience of depression and anxiety differs from the professional concepts of these conditions. The treatment preferred by the public is talking therapy, which is appropriate given the link, established by research, between the lack of a confiding relationship and the development of neuroses. The majority of psychiatrists and general practitioners view medication as the first line of treatment, whereas the public are suspicious of drugs and often do not take them even when they are prescribed. A series of three surveys of public attitudes in Great Britain were conducted between 1991 and 1997 under the auspices of the Royal College of Psychiatrists and the Royal College of General Practitioners. During the six years covered by the surveys, over ninety per cent of the respondents thought counselling should be offered to people suffering from depression, compared with less than a quarter recommending antidepressants. This type of drug was considered to be addictive by three-quarters of the people surveyed. A public education campaign run jointly by the two Colleges increased the proportion of people endorsing antidepressants by fifty per cent but did not change the view of their addictive nature.

Madness and violence

Turning to the psychoses, schizophrenia and manic-depressive illness, there also exists a wide discrepancy between the public and professional views of these disorders. The lay image of psychosis is epitomised in the phrase 'mad axeman'. The stereotype of the unpredictably violent psychotic person is constantly reinforced by the media, with headlines such as 'Schizophrenic raped three' and films such as *Psycho*. How close is this image to the truth? Some patients with psychosis commit violent acts and a small number kill others, but they represent a tiny proportion of all those with schizophrenia or manic-depressive illness. It is not a simple matter to determine whether people with psychosis are more or less violent than the general population. This is because violent acts tend to occur in the early phase of these illnesses, and to be committed by young men. In the general population it is also young men who are the most violent. So a comparison with the general population has to take account of age and sex. This form of analysis was carried out in 1998 by two professors of forensic psychiatry in London, Pamela Taylor and John Gunn.[45] They calculated that people with mental illness were no more likely than members of the general public to commit homicide. Furthermore, most murders by the mentally ill are of members of their own family. Random killing of strangers is very rare, although it is blazoned in banner headlines when it happens.

I led a team in a study of nearly 700 patients discharged from long-term care in two psychiatric hospitals. We followed up these patients five years after they had moved into homes in the community, most of them having staff on the premises to supervise the patients. We found that nine patients had committed assaults on members of the public. Some of these were serious, but fortunately nobody died. To put this in perspective, the violence that the public most fears was shown by just over one per cent of the patients over the course of five years. Given that violence by the mentally ill is in reality quite rare, how can we explain the prominent position it occupies in the mind of the public? It is not only uncontrolled violence that colours the stereotype of the mentally ill person but also unbridled sexuality. In every culture a central aim of the upbringing of children is the control of aggression and sexuality. These drives are very powerful and though they may be driven underground by the process of socialisation, they remain a disturbing subterranean force. A common way of dealing with unacceptable impulses is to deny them in oneself and to impute them to others, a psychological defence known technically as 'projection'. A tiny minority of people with psychosis show aggressive or sexually inappropriate behaviour, but that is enough for the public to tar all the mentally ill with the same brush. Once unacceptable feelings have been projected onto the mentally ill, they can be dealt with by ejecting from society the people tainted with them.

This process of expulsion dominated psychiatry in nineteenth-century Europe and America. Hundreds of asylums were constructed: in Britain alone over one hundred. The Victorians were very proud of their asylum building programme, which they saw as a public service. The asylums were typically sited outside towns and cities, far enough away not to be in the sight of the public, but not too remote to make the transport of patients difficult. One of the asylums my team studied, Friern Hospital, was built on a green-field site to the north of London, and the railway was extended to reach the hospital. The pride taken in these institutions is reflected in their ornamentation: Friern is an Italianate Gothic building with a frontage that is protected by the Department of the Environment. Its prestige is also evident from the fact that its foundation stone was laid by Prince Albert in 1851.

The rise and fall of the asylum

These institutions became little worlds in themselves, surrounded by high walls enclosing large grounds, often including a farm which produced vegetables and bred livestock for consumption by the staff and patients. With the help of the unpaid labour of the patients, some even produced a surplus which was sold to outside buyers. So successful in its own terms was the Victorian asylum that it was exported to all parts of the British Empire. After planting the Union Jack, almost the next step in colonisation was to build a lunatic asylum. The first public mental hospital in Greece was built on Corfu in 1838, four years after the British occupation of the Ionian Sea islands. I have visited various parts of Africa, India and the British West Indies and have frequently been confronted by buildings of an uncanny familiarity which housed psychiatric patients. The asylums the British built around the Empire were mainly for their own people: the natives had to rely on their own resources. As we shall see, their own resources proved superior to what the colonials had to offer.

Once the usefulness of the asylums was appreciated, all manner of people rejected by society were admitted, often for life. Some unmarried women who became pregnant were sent into asylums and never returned to their homes. As a result the number of inmates rapidly exceeded the capacity of the buildings and extensions were added. Even this did not suffice; and dense overcrowding occurred. Patients had to climb over other people's beds to reach their own. Friern Hospital was originally designed for 1000 patients but by 1952, one hundred years after its opening, its population had reached 2400. With overcrowding came squalor; the staff could not cope with the mass of patients, and physical abuse became common, eventually leading to public scandals. In Britain the number of psychiatric beds reached a peak in 1954 and then began to decline.

This turnaround was due to a number of factors, in addition to the public scandals. During the Second World War, army psychiatrists treated numerous young men who developed neuroses after facing terrible dangers and harrowing sights. Conditions that had been labelled 'shell shock' in the First World War under the mistaken belief that they were the result of concussion to the brain, were now diagnosed more appropriately as 'battle neurosis'. Removed from the front line to Netley Hospital in England and treated sympathetically, many of these psychiatric casualties made a full recovery. The psychiatrists experienced an antidote to the pessimistic views regarding recovery that pervaded the asylums. With the ending of the war, these young army psychiatrists moved into the asylums, bringing with them a fresh optimism and novel ideas about treatment, including group therapy which had been instituted in the army. A few years later in 1955, the first antipsychotic drug, chlorpromazine (Largactil), was introduced, making it possible to discharge patients who had seemed incurable. Psychiatry advanced behind the banner of community care and successive governments of both the left and the right endorsed the policy of eliminating the old asylums. By the year 2000, only fourteen of the 130 asylums in England and Wales remained open. A similar policy is being pursued in the rest of western Europe and in America, although in the USA the ferment which activated the asylum staff was not principally army psychiatrists, even though it did stem from the war. Conscientious objectors in the United States were obliged to do public service in psychiatric hospitals, and introduced into these institutions humanitarian attitudes which had not been eroded by the hospital regimen.

Outcome of schizophrenia around the world

Of course the revolution in psychiatric care never happened in the developing countries, because they had not invested in building asylums, and the colonial legacy was limited to a few such institutions in any one country. The great majority of people with schizophrenia and manic-depressive illness were cared for by their families as they had always been. Was this better for the patients than the professional care provided in the psychiatric institutions? From the 1970s onwards studies began appearing of the outcome of schizophrenia in developing countries. Prime examples are a study in Sri Lanka by Nancy Waxler,[46] an American researcher, and a study by Henry Murphy and Abdul Raman on the island of Mauritius off the coast of Africa.[47] This research suggested that people with schizophrenia actually suffered from fewer relapses of their illness in developing countries than in the West, despite the lack of availability of professional care, including anti-psychotic drugs for both treatment and maintenance. Before it could be taken seriously, this provocative result needed to be replicated in an international study using the same methods of assessment in all the countries being compared. This was achieved in the International Pilot Study of Schizo-phrenia, the WHO study described in Chapter 2. The samples of patients in the participating centres were followed up after two years and then five years in order to compare the course of their illnesses. At both time points patients with schizo-phrenia did conspicuously better in centres in developing countries, particularly Agra in India and Ibadan in Nigeria, than patients in Western centres.

There was a problem in interpreting this finding since the patients in this study were not representative of all the people with psychoses in the catchment area of the centre. This difficulty was a spur to the initiation of the successor WHO study, the Determinants of Outcome of Severe Mental Disorders (DOSMD), which was based on catchment area populations (see Chapter 2). Once again a two-year follow-up revealed a better outcome for patients in developing countries than for those in the West. Prompted by the intriguing finding of the first WHO study, in which I was involved, a psychologist, Elizabeth Kuipers, and I decided to use the DOSMD study to test a hypothesis about the possible cause of the differences in outcome. Since the expressed emotion of relatives was a powerful influence on the outcome of schizophrenia (see Chapter 3), could it be that relatives in developing countries were less likely to show high-EE attitudes?

There was already a suggestion that this might be the case from a study conducted in the 1980s by Marvin Karno and Janis Jenkins of Mexican-American families in Los Angeles.[48] One-third of the population of this west-coast city is made up of Mexicans, many of them illegal immigrants. They have largely retained their traditional style of life, with large extended families living together or nearby. Expressed emotion was measured in the relatives of patients with schizophrenia, and it emerged that the proportion who rated high, forty-one per cent, was considerably smaller than the equivalent figure of sixty-seven per cent for Anglo-American relatives in the same city.

Expressed emotion in Indian relatives

Encouraged by this result, we incorporated in the DOSMD project a substudy of relatives' EE in the centre in Chandigarh, north India. We selected Chandigarh because it encompassed two contrasting cultural environments, a city and a surrounding rural area, the characteristics of which are described in Chapter 2. Training in rating EE was given to two local fieldworkers, Harminder Bedi, an anthropologist, and Keerti Menon, a social worker. The training was conducted in English, but the interviews had to be given in one of the local languages, Punjabi or Hindi. Therefore the schedule was translated into these languages and then back-translated into English as a check on the accuracy of the translation. Following the standard procedure, relatives were interviewed at the time the patients made contact with the psychiatric services. The patients were then followed up one year later and the course of their schizophrenia charted.

The EE ratings of the urban relatives were analysed separately from those of the rural relatives, and the two sets of figures were compared with those for a sample of relatives in London. The Chandigarh city dwellers were much less critical than their counterparts in London, but surprisingly showed a similar amount of hostility. They rated very low on overinvolvement, as did the rural relatives. The villagers expressed about half the amount of criticism compared with the urban relatives, and showed very little hostility. When these ratings were used to assign relatives to a high-EE category the differences between the three groups were striking: close to half of the London relatives were high-EE compared with thirty per cent of the Chandigarh urban relatives and only eight per cent of the villagers. This indicates a high level of tolerance by the rural relatives for the symptoms and behaviour associated with schizophrenia. Relatives living in the city of Chandigarh are about midway between the villagers and the London relatives for high-EE, suggesting that education and an urban lifestyle diminish tolerance for people with schizophrenia.

We compared the relapse rate for the Chandigarh patients with a group of patients with schizophrenia making first contact with the psychiatric services in London. The Indian patients had half the relapse rate of the London patients and their better outcome was largely accounted for by the low level of EE of their relatives. It seems that our hunch was right: the support relatives are able to give the patients is a major factor in producing a better outcome for schizophrenia in developing countries. Of course these results raise another question: what is it about life in rural settings that enables carers to maintain low-EE attitudes to the patients? To date no research has been directed at answering this question, but there are some educated guesses which are worth presenting.

Influences on EE

In traditional societies the causes of any illness are usually believed to lie outside the control of the patient. Illness is often ascribed to angered spirits, black magic worked by envious people against the patient, or simply fate. This type of explanation absolves the patient from any responsibility for falling ill. In contrast, in the West patients are increasingly held responsible for their illnesses. Patients with heart or lung disease are told they have brought it on themselves by choosing an unhealthy lifestyle. Mentally ill people are exhorted to 'pull yourself together'. Relatives become critical when they think the patients are in control of their actions and could behave properly if they really wanted to.

Another influential factor may be the extended family, in which a large number of relatives share the burden of caring for the patient. Hence no one individual is greatly stressed by the demands of being a carer. It is not uncommon in Western cities to find a middle-aged patient with long-standing schizophrenia being cared for by a single relative, often an elderly mother. It is hardly surprising that high levels of negative emotions develop in this situation. A further advantage of the extended family is the choice of relationships it offers the patient. If one relative has high-EE attitudes there are plenty of others with whom the patient can choose to spend time. Traditional families are also contrasted with the typical

Western nuclear family in restricting the expression of conflict within the family circle. Such families have ways of dealing with disagreements which avoid blow-ups and open dissension. They are probably aided in this by the acceptance of a hierarchy of authority based on seniority and gender, which has been eroded in the West.

While staying with a Muslim extended family in India I observed behaviour that puzzled me. The group of thirty-five people consisted of five brothers and their families living in a three-storey house. The women lived on the upper floors and never ventured into the rooms on the ground floor. I found that when one of the brothers was offered a cigarette, sometimes it was accepted and sometimes refused. I also noticed that the oldest brother would never give a command directly to one of the young boys, but would use one of the other brothers as an intermediary. I waited until I was alone with the most Westernised of the brothers and expressed my puzzlement to him. He seemed surprised that I was unaware of the convention that a man was not allowed to smoke in the presence of a senior male. The chain of command I had observed was a result of the rule that the senior male should not communicate directly with the most junior members of the hierarchy.

Finally, the nature of the work environment may play a part. In agrarian economies in developing countries there are still many unspecialised jobs available, such as minding the livestock, which do not demand a high level of skill. Thus even quite disabled people can do a useful job and feel that they are contributing to the family economy, since many enterprises are cooperatives run by the extended family. Furthermore there is not the insistence on time-keeping and productivity which are increasingly dominating the workplace in the West. It is obviously easier for a family to accept a member with schizophrenia who does something useful, however low-key, than one who sits around the home all day totally unoccupied.

Whatever the factors contributing to the development of high-EE attitudes may turn out to be, the evidence is strong that the urban environment in the West is inimical to people who have developed a schizophrenic illness. Could it also play a role in bringing it on in the first place? That question is addressed in the next chapter.

| # Do Cities Drive Us Mad?

The ecology of cities

The transition from hunter-gatherer to cultivator of the land anchored human communities in particular locations. As trade between communities flourished and central political control was established, villages grew into towns and towns into cities. Cities act as attractors to migrants from the countryside and inexorably increase in size. This process is still occurring: Mexico City is now one of the largest conurbations in the world, with 20 million inhabitants. While rural migrants in developing countries tend to build shanty towns from scrap materials on the periphery of cities, the pattern of settlement and growth is quite different in developed countries. One of the first descriptions of this process was written by Richard Faris and H. Warren Dunham in 1939 in relation to Chicago.[49] They saw the city as consisting of a series of concentric rings, each of which they called a zone. The central zone is dominated by businesses and places of entertainment, and few people live there. Western cities tend to expand from the centre outwards into the next zone, which is therefore known as the zone in transition. Since it is more profitable to build offices and shops than houses, domestic housing in the zone in transition is allowed to deteriorate structurally prior to its demolition. The rents are low, and affordable by the poorest sections of society. The surrounding zones increase in affluence as one moves further from the zone in transition, with a progressively greater proportion of owner-

occupiers until one reaches the outer zones constituting suburbia, where most people own their own homes. Most
Western cities fit into this pattern, although there are local
variations. For example, in London the many open spaces
are seen as desirable places to live near, which disrupts the
concentric zoning somewhat. Furthermore, after the Second
World War a Labour government restricted the expansion of
office building in the centre. This removed the threat hanging
over the zone in transition, which began to be recolonised by
the middle classes, who were becoming fed up with increasingly tedious commuting. This process, known as gen-
trification, only made sporadic inroads into the zone in
transition, which still retains much of its economically depressed character. As a consequence of the low rents, the zone in
transition is the first part of the city in which new immigrants
settle. Once they become economically well established, the
immigrants tend to move out to more salubrious zones. Thus
the Jews first settled in the East End of London in the sixteenth
century when Oliver Cromwell allowed them back into
England and later moved peripherally towards the northern
suburbs. Over time the East End has lost its Jewish character
as these immigrants were replaced by a wave of Bangladeshis
during the 1960s and '70s.

Distribution of illness in cities

Faris and Dunham studied the cases of schizophrenia and
manic-depressive psychosis admitted for the first time to
a central clinic in Chicago and to the state hospitals, and
calculated the incidence rates (see Chapter 2) for the different
districts. They found that the incidence of schizophrenia was
highest in the central zone and fell off peripherally in every
direction. They also looked specifically at the largest ethnic
minority group, the African-Americans. The rate for African-
Americans living among their own group was low, but those
living in predominantly white areas had a significantly higher

rate. As always with a cross-sectional study, these findings can be interpreted in two opposing ways. It is possible that the poor socio-economic conditions in inner-city areas produce a high rate of schizophrenia (the social breeder hypothesis). Alternatively, people predisposed to the illness may drift into the central zones of the city before the first appearance of the illness (the social drift hypothesis). Using similar arguments, African-Americans with little social support from their peers may be more likely to develop schizophrenia, or those with a susceptibility for the illness may shun their mates and seek isolation from their own group. I will return to these possibilities when considering African-Caribbean populations in the UK. In contrast with schizophrenia, admissions for manic-depressive psychosis were randomly scattered over the city, with no concentration in the central zones. Edward Hare,[50] a British psychiatrist, took the research a step further by studying the city of Bristol in 1955 and examining three main characteristics of the different districts, defined as electoral wards. He was interested in the proportion of single-person households (an index of social isolation), the mean rateable value (a measure of economic status) and the population density (relating to overcrowding). As in Faris and Dunham's study, the wards with the highest incidence of schizophrenia were all clustered together in the city centre, whereas other diagnostic groups, such as manic-depressive psychosis, neurosis and senile dementia, were distributed randomly throughout Bristol. The high rates of schizophrenia were not linked with economic status nor with overcrowding, but with the proportion of single-person households. This enabled Hare to formulate the opposing hypotheses more precisely: either social isolation predisposes to schizophrenia, or 'segregation' takes place and emotionally isolated people move into the lodging-house areas.

Social drift and social causation

Controversy over the interpretation of these results continued for some decades, but then died down when two further studies, one British, the other American, seemed to provide a conclusive answer. The British study was conducted in the 1960s by Tilda Goldberg and S. Morrison and concerned not geographical drift but social drift.[51] Not only is schizophrenia concentrated in the poorest locations in cities, but patients presenting with the illness for the first time are over-represented in the lowest social classes. Goldberg and Morrison argued that if this is due to a causative influence of low social class, then the patients' fathers should also show the same distribution. They focused on fathers rather than mothers since many women work in the home, which is hard to classify economically. Their approach was quite sophisticated: they argued that since people tend to improve their economic condition during their working life, it would be unfair to compare the patients at the beginning of their careers, when schizophrenia tends to first appear, with their fathers at the same point in time, when they would have been working for twenty years or more. A fairer comparison would be with their father's occupation at the time of the patient's birth, when the age of the father would be comparable with that of the patient on falling ill. This information was simple to obtain since father's occupation is recorded on all birth certificates. They found as expected that the patients showed the usual bulge in the lowest occupational classes at the time they fell ill. However, the social class distribution of their fathers did not differ from that of the general population. Their conclusion was that the patients drifted down the social scale from their fathers' position before the illness developed.

There is some support for this notion from anecdotal accounts of the school histories of people who go on to develop schizophrenia. Generally they keep up with their peers academically until adolescence. Then they often fail to fulfil

their earlier promise and leave school with few if any qualifications. Of course adolescence is a turbulent time for most
children, and many experience disruption to their studies
without it having any long-term effect on their careers. But
those with a predisposition to schizophrenia find it an uphill
struggle to make up for their lack of higher education and are
often forced into unskilled jobs. Thus they may not match up
to their family's level of social standing. Not all histories are
so dismal: some people manage to complete a university
degree before they fall ill. In general the earlier the illness
strikes, the more devastating is its effect on the person's
educational career and social development.

Mobility in Detroit

Twenty years after generating the original controversy,
Dunham returned to the problem.[52] This time he studied the
city of Detroit, an American centre of the car industry. He
identified two contrasting districts, one affluent – Connor-
Burbank – and the other working class – Cass. He monitored
all admissions for schizophrenia from these two districts over
a period of time, and found that the rate in Cass was three
times that in Connor-Burbank. He then divided the patients
into those who had lived in the district for more than five
years, and those who had moved into the district within the
past five years. The excess rate in Cass was almost entirely
due to the mobile patients. When these were excluded from
both groups the two rates became almost identical. Thus
Dunham felt he had shown that the high rate in impoverished
city areas is due to people moving in prior to the development
of a schizophrenic illness. When he looked at the places the
mobile patients had come from, they were not other parts of
Detroit but small towns outside the city.

   The Goldberg and Morrison study provided evidence that
poor socio-economic conditions do not directly contribute to
the causation of schizophrenia. Indeed if they did, one would

expect to see major variations in the incidence of schizophrenia with economic booms and busts, but the incidence
has been remarkably steady regardless of major international
upheavals such as the Great Depression and the two World
Wars. Hare demonstrated that the distribution of schizophrenia was linked with single-person households, and Dunham's second study suggested that people predisposed to
schizophrenia drifted into areas of the city where they could
find anonymity. And there the matter rested for over thirty
years, with a general feeling of satisfaction that the argument
had been settled.

Mobility in Nottingham

Then several papers were published which raised the dust.
One reported a small-scale study with a similar design to
Dunham's second survey in Detroit. This was carried out in
the British city of Nottingham, one of the centres taking part
in the WHO DOSMD study described in Chapter 2. Glynn
Harrison and his team collected sixty-seven patients with
schizophrenia presenting for the first time to the psychiatric
services during the two years 1978–80.[53] They charted the
areas of social deprivation in Nottingham and found as
expected that most of them were clustered in the centre of
the city, although there were scattered pockets of deprivation
in suburban zones. The incidence rate for schizophrenia in
the most deprived area was three times that in the most
affluent area, closely echoing Dunham's finding. High rates
were also found in the deprived areas situated in suburbia.
Harrison and his colleagues examined the mobility of the
patients in the five years before their first contact with the
services, just as Dunham had done. But here the similarities
between the two studies ended. Only eleven of the Nottingham patients had moved into the city in the preceding
five years, and they had settled randomly throughout the
various zones and did not account for the concentration of

cases in the deprived areas. Harrison's group took the argument one step further by looking at the place of birth of their patients. They found that a great excess of patients were born in areas of social deprivation. The Nottingham results directly contradict those from Detroit and suggest that social drift does not account for the link between social deprivation and high rates of schizophrenia. Could the discrepancy between the findings be due to the time lag of twenty years between the data collection in the two sites, or to different social conditions on either side of the Atlantic? We can only speculate about these possibilities, but fortunately the controversy has been overtaken by two large-scale studies which have employed a powerful method.

Linking records

There is a long tradition in northern European countries of keeping records on all their citizens. In Scandinavia it has been the responsibility of the parish priest for several hundred years to record significant events in the lives of his parishioners. These parish records are invaluable historical documents, chronicling changes in lifestyle over the centuries. National registers developed out of this tradition and because they cover the whole population, yield extremely useful data for research. Unfortunately national registers are also open to political exploitation, and the murder by the Nazis of over 100,000 mentally ill people naturally sensitised people to their dangers. So strong was public opposition in Germany that their national register was closed down some years ago, and this has been the fate of other European registers. The two studies that represent the greatest challenge to the social drift theory made use of national registers.

Swedish conscripts

In 1992 two British psychiatrists, Glyn Lewis and Anthony David, teamed up with two Swedish psychiatrists, Sven Andreasson and Peter Allebeck, to utilise data from a survey and a national register maintained in Sweden.[54] National service is still obligatory for Swedish men, and during 1969–70 a survey was conducted on all 50,456 young men called up for national service. The survey captured ninety-five per cent of the male population of Sweden in the age group eighteen to nineteen years. Among other questions, they were asked where they lived when they were growing up. Their place of upbringing was assigned to one of the following groups: the three biggest cities in Sweden, towns with more than 50,000 inhabitants, towns with fewer than 50,000 inhabitants, and the country. The data from the conscript survey were linked with the National Register of Psychiatric Care, which recorded admissions to psychiatric hospitals. This register was closed in 1983 so that it was possible to follow up the conscripts for fourteen years (1969–83) and identify those who were admitted for the first time with a diagnosis of schizophrenia. The highest incidence of schizophrenia was in the men brought up in one of the three cities (51.4 per 100,000), and was progressively lower for large towns, small towns, and the country, for which the rate was 31.2 per 100,000. This finding eliminates drift in the few years before the emergence of schizophrenia as an explanation for the concentration in cities. But the conscript survey did not ask where the men were born. The next study to exploit national registers did address this question.

Dutch registers

A study by Machteld Marcelis and his colleagues used two kinds of national register maintained in the Netherlands, which has experienced a great increase in urbanisation since the Second World War and is today one of the most densely populated countries in Europe. The Dutch Central Bureau for Statistics records all live births by sex. The Dutch National Psychiatric Case Register, like its equivalent in Sweden, records all admissions to psychiatric hospitals. First psychiatric admissions for psychosis between the years 1970 and 1992 were obtained from the Case Register and the place of birth of these patients was traced through the records of the Central Bureau for Statistics. Marcelis and his group found that people born in the most densely populated areas had the highest incidence of psychosis.[55] The strongest link with urban birth was found when they restricted the patients to those with narrowly defined schizophrenia. Applying this diagnosis, the incidence was twice as high for those born in the most urban areas as for those born in the least densely populated areas. These two studies have used the most sophisticated scientific methods available and have strongly supported the proposition that being born and brought up in cities increases the risk of developing schizophrenia in adult life. They have not been able to identify those aspects of city life that drive people crazy but they have provided a strong impetus for others to investigate this question. In the next chapter I will present the mental health problems of ethnic minority groups in the UK and discover what light they throw on the dangers of living in a city.

Chapter 8

A Black and White Issue

Immigration to the UK

Since the Second World War Britain has increasingly become a multicultural society. The influx of peoples from all parts of the globe has brought to the attention of psychiatrists the fact that some immigrant groups appear to be more prone to severe mental illnesses than others. This awareness has raised sensitive political issues, as well as reviving fears that cities may be mentally unhealthy places. The particular group around which the political storm has raged are the African-Caribbean immigrants. At the end of the Second World War there was a desperate shortage of labour affecting the infrastructure of the country, mainly transport and the health service, which was nationalised in 1948. Vigorous recruiting campaigns were held in the West Indies to attract men to work as bus and train drivers and conductors, and women as nurses. These were successful and shiploads of West Indians came to the UK during the next ten years until the Immigration Acts of the early 1960s halted the flow. During the same period there was a massive influx of people from the Indian subcontinent following partition and independence in 1947. As a form of shorthand I shall use the term 'Asian' to refer to people from the Indian subcontinent, while recognising that it includes groups with widely differing languages, religions and cultures. Similarly the term 'African-Caribbean' encompasses people from islands with different dominant languages, religions and histories, and – in the case of Trinidad – distinct ethnic groups.

Like the African-Caribbean population, the Asian migrants were attracted by the lure of economic betterment, but no recruiting campaigns were held in India or Pakistan. In London both groups settled in the zone in transition, but in different parts of it. The African-Caribbeans were concentrated in Brixton and Notting Hill Gate, while the Asians chose Southall and the East End, from which the Jewish community had already begun to relocate to the more affluent outer zones. Unlike India, which has succeeded in absorbing successive waves of conquerors, the British West Indies were strongly oriented towards the UK and British culture, albeit a version that existed in an Edwardian time warp. Most respectable African-Caribbean homes both in the West Indies and the UK maintain a front parlour, in which the best china is displayed in a cabinet and which is reserved for entertaining guests. Britain was viewed as the mother country and the expectation was of being welcomed by the British, particularly as many of the immigrants were recruited to leave their homes and settle in the UK. The shock of meeting almost uniformly racist attitudes ('NO COLOUREDS, NO INDIANS, NO DOGS') was therefore much greater for the African-Caribbean immigrants than for the Asians, who may never have expected to be treated as anything other than aliens.

Rates of mental illness among African-Caribbeans

From the 1960s onwards studies have been appearing regularly in the psychiatric press purporting to show that African-Caribbean people have a much higher incidence of schizophrenia than the white population. Alongside these alarming publications have been reports that African-Caribbeans are more likely to be admitted to psychiatric units against their will than whites, that they are over-represented among the population of forensic psychiatric units, and that they receive higher doses of medication and are less likely to be offered psychotherapy than the whites. It is hardly surprising that the black community has responded with accusations of racism against white psychiatrists acting in concert with the police, who become involved in compulsory admissions, and the criminal justice system, which commits patients to forensic psychiatric institutions. There is an added force and bitterness to these protestations, given the findings of several official enquiries of widespread racism in the British police force, manifested as tardiness and ineptitude in investigations of a number of blatantly racist murders of young black people.

Psychiatry and social control

The precedent of the Soviet abuse of psychiatry, discussed in Chapter 2, has been cited as evidence that mentally healthy people have been deliberately misdiagnosed as suffering from schizophrenia with the aim of exerting social control over dissident members of society. White British psychiatrists have been portrayed as 'thought police' stifling the legitimate protests of black people against an unjust and racist society. These political accusations were fuelled by a book published in 1982 by two British psychiatrists, Roland Littlewood and Maurice Lipsedge.[56] Littlewood trained both as an anthropologist and a psychiatrist. They studied a series of African-Caribbean patients with a diagnosis of schizophrenia and drew attention to the high proportion who expressed delusions of a religious nature. They considered that some of the religious beliefs were within the range of accepted ideas of the evangelical churches to which the patients belonged and hence should not have been identified as delusions. This issue has been extensively aired in Chapter 2 in the discussion on the nature of delusions. Littlewood and Lipsedge also noted that twice as many African-Caribbean patients had their diagnosis changed in the course of their contact with services than white patients. They suggested that either British doctors found it hard to come to a conclusion about their diagnosis, or that the patients did not fit easily into the standard pigeonholes. The message that politically minded people took from this book was that black people who were essentially in good mental health were being wrongly diagnosed as having schizophrenia.

Because of the absence of any objective tests to validate psychiatric diagnosis, the accusation of misdiagnosis is very difficult to counter. In 1998 an attempt was made to investigate this issue at the Maudsley Hospital in London. Robin Murray, professor of psychiatry there, brought over a black psychiatrist from Jamaica, Fred Hickling, who was himself politically active in the controversy.[57] Therefore if he had any bias, it would be to prove that white psychiatrists were making diagnostic errors on black patients. He interviewed a series of patients of the Maudsley Hospital using a standardised clinical examination, the Present State Examination (PSE). He made his own diagnoses in ignorance of the diagnoses made by the local white psychiatrists. The two sets of diagnoses were then compared. There were major discrepancies between the two lists, but these were not linked to the ethnicity of the patients. Disagreements between the Jamaican psychiatrist and the British psychiatrists were just as common for white patients as for black patients. These exemplify the well-known mismatch between research diagnoses and the diagnoses made by clinical psychiatrists, but do not reveal any ethnic bias. This one study will not put the controversy to rest since racism undoubtedly exists in psychiatry as in other British institutions, and the charge of misdiagnosis is difficult to counter. However, it obscures a question of crucial importance: if this difference in incidence rates is real, what does it tell us about the nature of schizophrenia? Epidemiologists the world over become very excited when they find that the incidence of a disease is significantly higher in one human group than in another, because one can then look for other differences between the groups that might give clues to the cause of the disease, just as John Snow did by mapping the cases of cholera in London.

Psychosis in the West Indies

Together with my colleagues, Rosemarie Mallett, a sociologist, and Dinesh Bhugra, a psychiatrist,[58] I wished to investigate one obvious possibility, namely that the incidence of schizophrenia was high in the West Indies, and that the immigrants to the UK were simply reflecting the susceptibility of the populations from which they had come. To answer this question we would need to mount a study of the incidence of schizophrenia in a Caribbean island, a venture that had never been attempted before. A small island is an ideal location for an epidemiological study as the population is contained within clear boundaries and it is feasible to cover a large section of it with a survey. We chose the island of Trinidad since there was a reasonable number of psychiatrists working there, we had already established good relationships with some of the key figures, and several of the psychiatrists were keen to be involved with the research. All the psychiatrists who took part were black Trinidadians, so the question of a racist bias in diagnosis should not intrude. Furthermore, at the start of the study in the early 1990s, Dinesh Bhugra trained all the participating psychiatrists to use the PSE. When wind of this study reached the UK during the planning stage, a group of psychiatric activists wrote to me expressing their disquiet at what they saw as a racist attempt to prove that black people were more likely to go mad than white people. I felt that by attempting to block our study the activists were spoiling their own case, as they were removing the impetus to investigate another possibility, that life in Britain including the experience of racial harassment, might be driving black people mad. Therefore I ignored their warnings and went ahead with the Trinidad study.

The result was clear-cut: the incidence of schizophrenia in Trinidad was no higher than among whites in the UK. This finding was confirmed in 1999 by a second study carried out in collaboration with us by George Mahy on the island of Barbados,[59] the home of Rosemarie Mallett, and a third study on Jamaica conducted in 1993 by Fred Hickling and Pamela Rodgers-Johnson.[60] Thus we could discount the explanation that black people were particularly susceptible to schizophrenia. But there were still several other theories that needed to be examined. One rather subtle idea is that of selective migration, which also capitalises on the inherited basis of psychosis. This postulates that people carrying the genes for schizophrenia are less attached to their family and friends and therefore more likely to migrate than those who do not share the genes. Thus if you were able to compare the migrants with the stay-at-homes, the former group of people would contain more of the genes for schizophrenia than the latter. The main problem with this theory is that it cannot be tested at present since we do not have biological markers for genes that may predispose to schizophrenia. There are other objections to this theory: since African-Caribbean people living in the UK also have a higher incidence of manic-depressive illness, one would have to postulate that the genes for manic-depressive illness also impel people to migrate. Furthermore, the process of selective migration cannot be specific to one group of people but must operate for all migrants who are making a free decision to leave their country of origin, as opposed to those who are forced to leave by racial or political persecution. If this is so, then it is crucial to study the incidence of schizophrenia in other migrant groups who chose to come to the UK. The obvious group for comparison is the Asian population, and that is why my colleagues and I included them in our study of the incidence of schizophrenia.

Asians and African-Caribbeans in London

As already noted, the main migration from India occurred over the same period as that from the West Indies and for the same reason of economic betterment. The Asian migrants also faced racial prejudice and harassment, but had no expectation of being integrated into the 'mother country'. If selective migration were operating one would expect the Asians to have as high an incidence of schizophrenia as the African-Caribbeans. In order to collect enough patients to make reliable calculations we needed to focus on areas of London containing large numbers of the groups in question. The region of south-east London around the Maudsley Hospital has a high proportion of African-Caribbean residents – as much as twenty per cent in some districts – but very few Asians. On the other hand, Southall has a large Asian population. Therefore we selected these two areas for our study, and collected all new cases of schizophrenia making contact with the psychiatric services over the two-year period 1991–3. The national census took place during our study and for the first time asked people to indicate which ethnic group they felt they belonged to. This was of great value to us in determining the sizes of the ethnic minority populations to calculate the incidence rates. Previously these had been estimated indirectly from other sources of information and could have been far from accurate.

Hopes and achievements

Our aim was more ambitious than simply comparing incidence rates between white, African-Caribbean and Asian groups, important though that was. We were also concerned to identify possible aspects of life in Britain for an ethnic minority group that might be stressful enough to provoke schizophrenia. We needed a measure of racial harassment, and Dinesh Bhugra developed one from the life events interview of

George Brown and Tirril Harris. Called the Racial Life Events Schedule, Bhugra translated it (and other instruments to be used) into the Asian languages current among the population of Southall. We also developed two other measures, one being an assessment of the gap between expectations and achievement on the basis of the following argument. The African-Caribbean immigrants were lured to the UK with the promise of good jobs, but their children have not done well. The boys in particular have failed to advance academically and have a high rate of unemployment. It was the second generation who were entering the period of risk for schizophrenia at the time of our study, and who might be expected to be bitterly disappointed by their poor prospects compared with the high hopes with which their parents arrived in the UK and which they presumably transmitted to their children. We built on an existing instrument created by Parker and Kleiner in the United States for a study of black Americans in the 1960s. Curiously this pioneering work had never been followed up. We covered five domains of life: academic achievement, employment, housing, finance, and social standing.

Who do you think you are?

The other area we wished to investigate was cultural identity. We considered that the African-Caribbean settlers in the UK aspired to be accepted by the white majority and that many would move away from their traditional lifestyle in the hope of becoming assimilated, but that this was doomed by the rejecting attitudes of the whites. Hence they would find themselves in the stressful situation of being between two cultures, to neither of which they fully belonged. In contrast, we postulated that the Asians would have less desire for assimilation and would prefer to remain immersed in their traditional way of life. We obviously needed a measure of cultural identity and we constructed one each for the Asian and the African-Caribbean groups with the help of anthropologists. When we

compared the two versions we found that there was considerable overlap and we were able to amalgamate them into
one schedule with minor variations for each ethnic group.
The items included covered such issues as preferred foods,
mode of dress, language, reading matter, television programmes and films, and admired figures in public life.

The design of the study needs some explanation. If we
simply compared the patients from the three ethnic groups
we would not know whether any differences between them
were attributable to their ethnic backgrounds or to the different rates of schizophrenia. Therefore we needed control
groups of healthy people from the same ethnic groups as the
patients. This is known as a case–control study and is a
standard epidemiological design for identifying risk factors
for diseases. We carried out random door-knocking to collect
healthy controls for the patients and interviewed them with
the same collection of schedules.

Ethnic minorities in The Netherlands

The first step in analysis was to calculate the incidence rates,
since if there was no difference between them, there would
be nothing to explain. In fact the rate of schizophrenia for
African-Caribbean participants was double that for whites,[61]
confirming the results of many previous studies. The rate
for Asians was slightly higher than that for whites, but the
difference could easily have occurred by chance. Therefore
the explanation of the high rate in African-Caribbeans in
terms of selective migration was most unlikely, since it did
not apply to the Asians. Just after the end of our study, in
1994, a paper was published by two Dutch researchers, Jean-
Paul Selten and Arno Sjiben.[62] They had studied the incidence
rates of schizophrenia among various immigrant groups in
The Netherlands and compared them with the rate for the
white Dutch population. They found high rates among Caribbean immigrants from Surinam and the Dutch Antilles, in

harmony with our results, but also among immigrants from Morocco. However, immigrant Turks did not have a high rate. These interesting results suggest that there are particular experiences, provoking the development of schizophrenia, which affect some ethnic minority groups but not others. They underline the importance of our comparisons between African-Caribbeans and Asians in the UK.

Social disadvantage

Our attempt to obtain information on racial harassment from the ethnic minority subjects was a failure. Very few respondents were able to report verifiable incidents that could be included as racial life events. Either such occurrences are actually rather rare or people were reluctant to reveal them to the interviewers at the time of our survey. The recent public enquiries into racism in the police force may have increased people's willingness to speak on such issues. Even if racist events are infrequent in any individual's experience, a single racist murder, such as that of Stephen Lawrence in London, can terrorise a community for years to come. We decided that it would be more important in future studies to assess the subjects' perception of the climate of racism, rather than restricting ourselves to objective evidence.

To our surprise, the enquiry into expectations and achievements yielded few significant findings. The unemployment rate was certainly appallingly high among the patients: about half the white and Asian patients were without a job at first contact with the psychiatric services, as were eighty-five per cent of the African-Caribbean patients. However, for each ethnic group the unemployment rate among the patients was about double that of the healthy controls. It is impossible to tell from this cross-sectional picture whether the personal difficulties leading up to the appearance of schizophrenia were responsible for the lack of a job, or whether unemployment contributes to the development of schizophrenia. What we found difficult to account for was that, despite the tiny minority of African-Caribbean patients in work, the patients did not depict a large gap between their expectations of employment and their achievements in the job market. Perhaps they had already adjusted their expectations to the reality of an unemployment situation which had existed for some decades. The only area in which the African-Caribbean patients differed from their controls was that of housing. The patients felt that their current housing situation was considerably worse than they had expected it to be, whereas this did not apply to their controls. We found that African-Caribbean patients were more likely to be living in council accommodation than white or Asian patients, but we did not collect information on the quality of housing so cannot corroborate the patients' perception. Could poor housing conditions contribute to schizophrenia? It would certainly explain the concentration of schizophrenia in the zone in transition, but the evidence for a direct effect is lacking.

Between two cultures

The Culture and Identity Schedule turned up trumps. The Asian patients were as adherent to their traditional culture as their controls, or in several areas even more so. The African-Caribbean patients showed a completely different pattern. In two areas, the question of which partner in a relationship should make the decisions, and in the use of patois, the patients were more traditional than their controls. But in four other areas they were significantly less traditional than their controls, indicating that they had moved away from their cultural roots. The areas were: preference for ethnic food, preference to live and work with members of your own ethnic group, leisure activities focused on your own ethnic group, and ethnicity of public figures you admire. In the last area, for example, the patients were more likely than their healthy controls to cite white celebrities as people they admired. It is

highly unlikely that they were accepted by the white community whose company they sought and whose values they
were beginning to adopt, so that we can assume that they
were in the uncomfortable position of having lost some of the
support from members of their community but with nothing
to replace it. The different pattern from the Asian patients
argues that this is not a result of developing schizophrenia,
but a possible contributor to the high rate among UK African-
Caribbeans. This is a unique finding as no previous study has
used a measure of cultural identity in relation to schizophrenia. The finding will have to be replicated in another
study before much weight is placed on it, but it is an exciting
prospect to have identified a candidate social factor in the
causation of schizophrenia.

Separation from parents

One unexpected finding emerged from our analysis. The
African-Caribbean patients had more often experienced four
or more years of separation from their mother and father in
childhood than their controls or than either of the other two
groups of patients. This pattern suggests that separation from
parents in childhood is specifically linked with the high rate
of schizophrenia in the UK African-Caribbean population.
But how could it operate to increase the risk of schizophrenia?
There are many possible reasons for children being separated
from one or both parents, including the development of
schizophrenia in a parent and their subsequent admission to
hospital. We were able to rule this out as a factor operating
in the lives of the patients in our study. We did not enquire
into other circumstances leading to separation, but it was
quite common for African-Caribbean parents migrating to
take up jobs in the UK to leave their children behind in the
care of female relatives. After some years, when they felt
financially secure and had established a permanent residence,
they would send for the children. By this time there were

often other siblings who had been born in the UK. Thus the children migrating belatedly would have to adapt to parents they might not have seen for many years and to a substantially new family. How they had fared in the meantime was also dependent on the quality of the substitute parenting they received. These major disruptions in family life and relationships could well have led to problems in forming attachments in adult life. In the previous chapter I quoted Edward Hare's research in Bristol which showed that the distribution of schizophrenia in the city was linked with the concentration of single-person households. It is possible to incorporate these two observations into a theory that childhood problems in forming relationships lead to social isolation as an adult which in turn increases the susceptibility to schizophrenia.

Leroy was born in Jamaica to parents who emigrated to England in search of jobs when he was three years old. They left him in the care of one of his mother's sisters who had no children of her own. She was a strict disciplinarian who discouraged him from playing with other local children, whom she viewed as too rough. Leroy's parents established themselves successfully in the Brixton area of London, his mother working in a local hospital as a nursing assistant while his father became a train driver. They had three more children and arranged for Leroy to come to England when he was twelve. He had great difficulty in making relationships with his brothers and sister, and became increasingly rebellious. He did not settle into schooling and regularly truanted on his own. He failed to make friends with any of his classmates and left school at age fifteen with no qualifications. After a series of stormy arguments with his father on account of his lack of occupation, he left home to live in a squat with a group of other youths who were part of a criminal subculture. During the next few years he was charged for a number of offences, mostly shoplifting and damage to property. At age eighteen he was caught by the police breaking into a store and was remanded in prison awaiting a trial. A few days later he began to behave strangely, taking off all his clothes and shouting. He was seen by a psychiatrist to whom Leroy complained that his cell was bugged and that he heard voices calling him a black bastard. The psychiatrist made a diagnosis of schizophrenia and admitted Leroy to a psychiatric unit.

A link between social networks in childhood and the later development of schizophrenia is supported by findings from longitudinal cohort studies. These are far-sighted endeavours in which all the children born in a particular period in one country are followed up at regular intervals for as many decades as possible. This strategy addresses the problem raised in Chapter 3 that the time unit of interest to the researcher is the lifespan of the subject. By engaging successive teams of researchers to follow up a birth cohort, between them they can keep passing on the Olympic torch, and eventually cover the whole lives of the subjects. This strategy has already thrown some surprising light on the origins of schizophrenia. Children who eventually develop schizophrenia as adults differ from those who do not by their level of sociability. Children with three or fewer friends are at much higher risk of later schizophrenia than those with a larger circle of friends. This has been interpreted as showing that the genes for schizophrenia already exert an influence in childhood by reducing sociability. But an alternative reading is that children who are unable to build a social support system for whatever reason are more vulnerable to the stresses that may provoke an attack of schizophrenia. Our findings for the African-Caribbean patients would fit with this interpretation.

Susceptibility of siblings

In 1994 a paper was published by two British researchers, Philip Sugarman, a psychiatrist, and David Craufurd, a geneticist,[63] which was of signal importance for the controversy between the genetic and environmental theories of schizophrenia in African-Caribbean patients. They conducted a family study of schizophrenia in African-Caribbean and white patients in Manchester. What they found was most surprising. Previous family studies had established that the risk of schizophrenia in the parents of people with schizophrenia is about 10 per cent compared with the general population risk of one per cent. They found the same increased risk in the parents of the patients of both ethnic groups, which is what a geneticist would predict. However, when they looked at the siblings of the patients a very different picture emerged. The siblings of the white patients had a risk of around two per cent, but the risk for the siblings of the African-Caribbean patients was very much higher. For those born in the West Indies the risk was four times that for the white siblings, while for African-Caribbean siblings born in the UK the risk was an astonishing twelve times greater. This finding could be explained by a combination of selective migration of people from the West Indies predisposed to schizophrenia, and assortative mating. The latter term accounts for a high incidence of a disease by postulating that people with a predisposition to it are attracted to each other, thereby passing on to their children a much higher risk of developing the disease. In this case, the fact that the parents of the white and African-Caribbean patients had a similar risk for schizophrenia argues against both selective migration and assortative mating, so that a pathogenic influence of the environment on second-generation African-Caribbeans is a more plausible explanation.

So challenging was the finding on family susceptibility that it demanded to be checked as soon as possible. The study was repeated in London in 1995 by an African-Caribbean colleague of ours, Gerard Hutchinson, and his associates.[64] They closely replicated Sugarman's and Craufurd's results. The parents of white and African-Caribbean patients with psychosis had a similar risk of developing the same illness. African-Caribbean siblings born in the West Indies had a slightly higher risk than white siblings, but African-Caribbean siblings born in the UK had a risk seven times that of white siblings. These startling results have focused attention on the environment in which African-Caribbeans in the UK live, but the physical environment is as much suspect as the social environment. Theories have been advanced that African-Caribbean women are more susceptible to virus infections than white women and that the spread of infections in crowded cities could lead to infections during pregnancy which might adversely affect the development of the brain. To date no evidence has been found to support this theory, or the suggestion that African-Caribbean women suffer more complications of pregnancy leading to lack of oxygen at birth. One explanation for our finding of a link between separation from parents and the later development of schizophrenia is that the patient was left behind in the Caribbean as a child. This would seem to conflict with the evidence for the deleterious influence of the living environment on African-Caribbeans born and brought up in the UK. However, just as geneticists now accept that several genes probably act together to produce the susceptibility to schizophrenia, there are likely to be multiple sources of environmental stress that influence the development of the illness.

A search for causative factors in the social environment does not negate the importance of an inherited component to schizophrenia, for which I find the evidence convincing. However, it does challenge the prevailing view of schizophrenia as a purely biological entity. The evidence that social factors influence the course of the disease is now generally accepted (see Chapter 3), so that it does not require a major act of faith to extend the concept of schizophrenia to encompass social causation. The strategy of studying schizophrenia in ethnic minority groups has not indicated for certain what it is about city life that increases the risk of schizophrenia. However, it has identified early separation from parents and uncertainty about cultural identity as possible contributors to the origin of schizophrenia. If indeed these experiences turn out to increase vulnerability to the disease, there is something that can be done about them, which could reduce the risk of developing schizophrenia and save some people from a lifetime of illness.

| **The Future**

There can be no doubt that techniques of monitoring the functioning of the living brain will increase rapidly in sophistication in the near future. It is equally certain that there will be major advances in the application of molecular biology to diseases of the mind. The complete map of the human genome is now available. However, I do not believe that it will ever be possible to explain human behaviour in terms of genes, neurotransmitters, or regional changes in activity of the brain. Human behaviour does not occur in a social vacuum. The psychoanalyst, Donald Winnicott, once made the challenging statement that 'there is no such thing as a baby'. He meant, of course, that a baby cannot survive on its own, but needs the nurture and care provided by other people. In this book I have presented many different studies which illustrate our interdependence as social beings with other people. Only a tiny fraction of the population live in total social isolation by choice. Even were we to consider a Robinson Crusoe, shipwrecked on a deserted island, he would carry with him the history of his relationships with all the important people in his life, with whom he would continue to carry on an internal dialogue. A complete knowledge of his genes would tell us nothing about his ongoing interaction with figures from the past who would people the island.

The complexity of the relationships we establish with other

Figure 5 Network of relationships between groups of two, three and five people

people should not be underestimated. While pondering this one day, I realised that there is a simple formula that enables us to calculate the number of relationships generated by the people who are close to us. It is: $n(n - 1)$. Two people have 2 × (2 − 1) = 2 relationships, that is, A's relationship with B, and B's relationship with A. If two people have a child together, n becomes 3, and the number of relationships increases to 3 × (3 − 1) = 6 relationships. A couple with three children and their partners have 56 relationships between them. No simple one-to-one correspondence between genes and behaviour could encompass the quantum leap necessary to understand the interactions in even a small social network of people (Figure 5).

The understanding achieved of one level of organisation of the physical world cannot simply be transferred to the next level of complexity. What we have learned about the behaviour of fundamental particles through the development of quantum mechanics does not help us to understand how atoms interact. The characteristic behaviour of atoms gives us no clues as to what to expect from a living cell. From the functional capacity of an individual nerve cell, we could not predict the abilities of the 100 billion neurons that make up the human brain, including the existence of consciousness, the origins of which remain obscure. By the same argument events in the brain – however clearly defined – throw only a dim light on social and emotional interactions between people. Although a group of people has been compared with an organism, the similarities are superficial. Group behaviour can only be understood by studying groups, not by extrapolating from what we know about the behaviour of individuals.

I could have introduced the book with this argument, but you would not then have been in possession of all the evidence presented here that our minds can be unbalanced by disturbances in our social environment, and that the balance can be restored by actively reshaping our relationships with the people who matter to us. I have shown that events in our early life and in recent months determine whether we will become depressed or anxious; that emotional relationships with family members influence the course of a wide range of psychiatric disorders; that skilled work directed at improving these relationships can reduce the risk of relapse for people with depression or schizophrenia; and that the better outcome for schizophrenia in developing countries is largely due to the attitudes of the family towards the patient.

My vision for the future of psychiatry is one that depends not on technical advances in making images of the brain or replacing bad genes with good ones, but on increasing our understanding of relationships between people. It has become starkly clear that industrialisation and urbanisation, those unstoppable forces of modern societies, destroy the extended family and bonds with neighbours which are the essence of traditional ways of life. With the loss of this natural support network, individuals are more vulnerable to psychiatric disorders and it becomes more difficult to restore their mental health. It is useless to issue pleas to retain the extended family, as do some pundits in developing countries. The changes that have already happened in the West are bound to sweep across the rest of the world. The best we can do is to help the reduced nuclear family to cope with psychiatric illness in one of their members by offering skilled professional help as early as possible in its course. This will require a considerable research effort to identify the disturbances in relationships that have contributed to specific psychiatric disorders and the most effective interventions to correct them. The pattern of research needed to do this has already been laid down. Progress will come from achieving the right balance between biological and social research into the complexities of the human mind.

References

1 Leff, J. P., and Wing, J. K. Trial of maintenance therapy in schizophrenia. *British Medical Journal* (1971) 3, 599–604.
2 Hirsch, S. R., Gaind, R., Rohde, P. D., Stevens, B. C., and Wing, J. K. Out-patient maintenance of chronic schizophrenic patients with long-acting fluphenazine: double-blind placebo trial. *British Medical Journal* (1973) 1, 633–7.
3 Leff, J. P., Hirsch, S. R., Gaind, R., Rohde, P. D., and Stevens, B. C. Life events and maintenance therapy in schizophrenic relapse. *British Journal of Psychiatry* (1973) 123, 659–60.
4 Fossey, L., Papiernik, E., and Bydlowski, M. Postpartum blues: a clinical syndrome and predictor of postnatal depression? *Journal of Psychosomatic Obstetrics and Gynaecology* (1997) 18, 17–21.
5 Kumar, R., and Robson, K. M. A prospective study of emotional disorders in childbearing women. *British Journal of Psychiatry* (1984) 144, 35–47.
6 Gillis, L. S., Elk, R., Ben-Arie, O., and Teggin, A. The Present State Examination: experiences with Xhosa-speaking patients. *British Journal of Psychiatry* (1982) 141, 143–7.
7 Orley, J. H., and Wing, J. K. Psychiatric disorders in two African villages. *Archives of General Psychiatry* (1979) 36, 513–20.
8 Goldberg, D., Cooper, B., Eastwood, M. R., Kedward, H. B., and Shepherd, M. A standardised psychiatric interview for use in community surveys. *British Journal of Social and Preventive Medicine* (1970) 24, 18–23.
9 Holmes, T. H., and Rahe, R. H. The social readjustment rating scale. *Journal of Psychosomatic Research* (1967) 11, 213–18.
10 Brown, G. W., and Birley, J. L. T. Crises and life changes and the onset of schizophrenia. *Journal of Health and Social Behaviour* (1968) 9, 203–14.
11 Brown, G. W., and Harris, T. *The Social Origins of Depression* (Tavistock, London, 1978).

12 Rutter, M. *Maternal Deprivation Reassessed*, 2nd edn. (Penguin, Harmondsworth, 1981).

13 Harrison, J., Barrow, S., Gask, L., and Creed, F. Social determinants of GHQ score by postal survey. *Journal of Public Health Medicine* (1999) **21**, 283–8.

14 Kleinman, A. *Social Origins of Distress and Disease: Depression, Neurasthenia and Pain in Modern China* (Yale University Press, New Haven, 1986).

15 Schwab, M. E. A study of reported hallucinations in a Southeastern County. *Mental Health and Society* (1977) **4**, 344–54.

16 Laing, R. D., and Esterson, A. *Sanity, Madness and the Family*, vol. I: *Families of Schizophrenics* (Tavistock, London, 1964).

17 Hirsch, S. R., and Leff, J. P. *Abnormalities in Parents of Schizophrenics*. Maudsley Monograph 22 (Oxford University Press, London, 1975).

18 Kramer, M. Cross-national study of diagnosis of the mental disorders: origin of the problem. *American Journal of Psychiatry* (1969) **125** (suppl.), 1–11.

19 Cooper, J. E., Kendall, R. E., Gurland, B. J., Sharpe, L., Copeland, J. R. M., and Simon, R. *Psychiatric Diagnosis in New York and London*. Maudsley Monograph 20 (Oxford University Press, London, 1972).

20 Wing, J. K., Cooper, J. E., and Sartorius, N. *The Description and Classification of Psychiatric Symptoms: An Instruction Manual for the PSE and CATEGO System* (Cambridge University Press, London, 1974).

21 Hacking, I. *Rewriting the Soul* (Princeton University Press, Princeton, 1995).

22 Robins, L. N. *Deviant Children Grown Up* (Williams & Wilkins, Baltimore, 1966).

23 Brown, G. W., Carstairs, G. M., and Topping, G. Post hospital adjustment of chronic mental patients. *Lancet* (1958) **ii**, 685–9.

24 Heimann, P. On countertransference. *International Journal of Psychoanalysis* (1950) **31**, 81–4.

25 Brown, G. W., Birley, J. L. T., and Wing, J. K. Influence of family life on the course of schizophrenic disorders: a replication. *British Journal of Psychiatry* (1972) **121**, 241–58.

26 Vaughn, C. E., and Leff, J. P. The influence of family and social factors on the course of psychiatric illness: a comparison of schizophrenic and depressed neurotic patients. *British Journal of Psychiatry* (1976) **129**, 125–37.

27 Hooley, J. M., Orley, J., and Teasdale, J. D. Levels of expressed emotion and relapse in depressed patients. *British Journal of Psychiatry* (1986) **148**, 642–7.

28 Okasha, A., El Akabawi, A. S., Snyder, A. S., Wilson, A. K., Youssef,

I., and El Dawla, A. S. Expressed emotion, perceived criticism, and relapse in depression: a replication in an Egyptian community. *American Journal of Psychiatry* (1994) **151**, 1001–5.

29 Hayhurst, H., Cooper, Z., Paykel, E. S., Vearnals, S., and Ramana, R. Expressed emotion and depression. A longitudinal study. *British Journal of Psychiatry* (1997) **171**, 439–43.

30 Leff, J., Vearnals, S., Brewin, C. R., Wolff, G., Alexander, B., Asen, E., Dayson, D., Jones, E., Chisholm, D., and Everitt, B. The London Depression Intervention Trial. *British Journal of Psychiatry* (2000) **177**, 95–100.

31 Harris, T., Brown, G. W., and Robinson, R. Befriending as an intervention for chronic depression in an inner city population. *British Journal of Psychiatry* (1999) **174**, 219–24.

32 Leff, J. P., and Vaughn, C. The interaction of life events and relatives, expressed emotion in schizophrenia and depressive neurosis. *British Journal of Psychiatry* (1980) **136**, 146–53.

33 McCreadie, R. G. The Nithsdale schizophrenia surveys. An overview. *Social Psychiatry and Psychiatric Epidemiology* (1992) **27**, 40–5.

34 Tarrier, N., Vaughn, C., Lader, M. N., and Leff, J. P. Bodily reactions to people and events in schizophrenics. *Archives of General Psychiatry* (1979) **36**, 311–15.

35 Cooklin, R., Sturgeon, D., and Leff, J. The relationship between auditory hallucinations and spontaneous fluctuations of skin conductance in schizophrenia. *British Journal of Psychiatry* (1983) **142**, 47–52.

36 Goldberg, D., and Huxley, P. *Mental Illness in the Community: The Pathway to Psychiatric Care* (Tavistock, London, 1980).

37 Harvey, Y. K. The Korean *Mudang* as a household therapist. In W. P. Lebra (ed.) *Culture-bound Syndromes, Ethnopsychiatry and Alternate Therapies* (University Press of Hawaii, Honolulu, 1976).

38 Nichter, M. Idioms of distress: alternatives in the expression of psycho-social distress: a case study from South India. *Culture, Medicine and Psychiatry* (1981) **5**, 379–408.

39 Obeyesekere, G. Depression, Buddhism and the work of culture in Sri Lanka. In A. Kleinman and B. Good (eds) *Studies in the Anthropology and Cross-Cultural Psychiatry of Affect and Disorder* (University of California Press, Berkeley, 1985).

40 Hare, E. H. The changing content of psychiatric illness. *Journal of Psychosomatic Research* (1974) **18**, 283–9.

41 Leff, J. P. Psychiatrists' vs. patients' concepts of unpleasant emotions. *British Journal of Psychiatry* (1978) **133**, 306–13.

42 Snaith, R. P., Bridge, J. W. K., and Hamilton, M. The Leeds scale for self-assessment of anxiety and depression. *British Journal of Psychiatry* (1976) **128**, 156–65.

43 Kendler, K. S., Heath, A. C., Martin, N. G., and Evans, L. G. Symptoms of anxiety and symptoms of depression: same genes, different environment? *Archives of General Psychiatry* (1987) **122**, 451–7.

44 Finlay-Jones, R., and Brown, G. W. Types of stressful life events and the onset of anxiety and depressive disorders. *Psychological Medicine* (1981) **11**, 803–15.

45 Taylor, P. J., and Gunn, J. Homicides by people with mental illness: myth and reality. *British Journal of Psychiatry* (1999) **174**, 9–14.

46 Waxler, N. E. Is outcome for schizophrenia better in non-industrial societies? The case of Sri Lanka. *Journal of Nervous and Mental Diseases* (1979) **167**, 144–58.

47 Murphy, H. B. M., and Raman, A. C. The chronicity of schizophrenia in indigenous tropical peoples. *British Journal of Psychiatry* (1971) **118**, 489–97.

48 Karno, M., Jenkins, J. H., De La Selva, A., Santana, F., Telles, C., Lopez, S., and Mintz, J. Expressed emotion and schizophrenic outcome among Mexican-American families. *Journal of Nervous and Mental Diseases* (1987) **175**, 143–51.

49 Faris, R. E. L., and Dunham, H. W. *Mental Disorders in Urban Areas* (Chicago University Press, Chicago, 1939).

50 Hare, E. H. Mental illness and social conditions in Bristol. *Journal of Mental Science* (1956) **102**, 349.

51 Goldberg, E. M., and Morrison, S. L. Schizophrenia and social class. *British Journal of Psychiatry* (1963) **109**, 785–802.

52 Dunham, H. W. *Community and Schizophrenia: An Epidemiological Analysis* (Wayne State University Press, Detroit, 1965).

53 Dauncey, K., Giggs, J., Baker, K., and Harrison, G. Schizophrenia in Nottingham: lifelong residential mobility of a cohort. *British Journal of Psychiatry* (1993) **163**, 613–19.

54 Lewis, G., David, A., Andreasson, S., and Allebek, P. Schizophrenia and city life. *Lancet* (1992) **340**, 137–40.

55 Marcelis, M., Navarro-Mateu, F., Murray, R., Selten, J. P., and van Os, J. Urbanization and psychosis: a study of 1942–1978 birth cohorts in The Netherlands. *Psychological Medicine* (1998) **28**, 871–9.

56 Littlewood, R., and Lipsedge, M. *Aliens and Alienists* (Penguin Books, Harmondsworth, 1982).

57 Hickling, F. W., McKenzie, K., Mullen, R., and Murray, R. A Jamaican psychiatrist evaluates diagnoses at a London psychiatric hospital. *British Journal of Psychiatry* (1999) **175**, 283–5.

58 Bhugra, D., Hilwig, M., Hossein, B., Marceau, H., Neehall, J., Leff, J., Mallett, R., and Der, G. First contact incidence rates in Trinidad and one year follow-up. *British Journal of Psychiatry* (1996) **169**, 587–92.

59 Mahy, G. E., Mallett, R., Leff, J., and Bhugra, D. First contact incidence rate of schizophrenia on Barbados. *British Journal of Psychiatry* (1999) **175**, 28–33.

60 Hickling, F. W., and Rodgers-Johnson, P. The incidence of first contact schizophrenia in Jamaica. *British Journal of Psychiatry* (1995) **167**, 193–6.

61 Bhugra, D., Leff, J., Mallett, R., Der, G., Corridan, B., and Rudge, S. Incidence and outcome of schizophrenia in Whites, African-Caribbeans and Asians in London. *Psychological Medicine* (1997) **27**, 791–8.

62 Selten, J. P., and Sjiben, A. E. S. First admission rates for schizophrenia in immigrants to the Netherlands. *Social Psychiatry and Psychiatric Epidemiology* (1994) **29**, 71–7.

63 Sugarman, P. A., and Craufurd, D. Schizophrenia and the Afro-Caribbean community. *British Journal of Psychiatry* (1994) **164**, 474–80.

64 Hutchinson, G., Takei, N., Fahy, T., Bhugra, D., Gilvarry, C., Moran, P., Mallett, R., Sham, P., Leff, J., and Murray, R. Morbid risk of schizophrenia in first degree relatives of White and African-Caribbean patients with psychosis. *British Journal of Psychiatry* (1996) **169**, 776–80.

Further Reading

Leff, J. *Psychiatry Around the Globe* (Gaskell, London, 1988).
Leff, J., and Vaughn, C. *Expressed Emotion in Families: Its Significance for Mental Illness* (Guilford, New York, 1985).
Parker, I. Qualitative research. In P. Banister, E. Burman, I. Parker, M. Taylor, and C. Tindall (eds) *Qualitative Methods in Psychology: A Research Guide* (Open University Press, Buckingham, 1994, pp. 1–16).
Rose, S. *Lifelines* (Allen Lane, London, 1997).
Warner, R. *Recovery from Schizophrenia: Psychiatry and Political Economy*, 2nd edn. (Routledge, London, 1994).
World Health Organisation. *The International Pilot Study of Schizophrenia*, vol. 1 (WHO, Geneva, 1973).

Index

maps of the mind

D0548179

THE
TRADE
SECRET

❖

Robert Newman

C

The Trade Secret
978-1908885173
Robert Newman
First Published 2013
Published by Cargo Publishing
SC376700
© Robert Newman 2013

Printed & bound by Bell & Bain Ltd., Glasgow
Cover design by Craig Lamont.
www.cargopublishing.com

For Vesi

Part One

1

As Nat Bramble searched the brilliantly lit Isfahan bazaar, he found an indoor city with a separate lane for each trade. Down one alley he passed all the clock-makers and down another the glassmakers, but when he came to a neighbourhood of metalworkers, he found a curious exception. For here, wedged between tinsmiths, was a narrow stall selling books, inks and paper, the very things that he'd been sent to buy.

Inside the stall, a burly young man about Nat's own age seemed entirely oblivious to the clanking. Could he not hear the loud stacking of samovar shells? The chank and tunk of tin being knocked into shape? Could he not smell the soldering irons? He dabbed at a silk page with a reed pen as peaceably as if he were in one of the sylvan scenes that hung across his stall like bunting. Perhaps he was deaf, or had no sense of smell? Just then, as if scenting Nat's presence, the young man sniffed and looked up.

'Why,' Nat asked him, 'does your master put you here among the tinsmiths and copper beaters?'

'Master? There's no master. This poor humble stall is my poor humble stall.'

'Yours? What are you? Eighteen?' Darius inclined his head. 'A year older than me and you've got your own stall,' said Nat enviously. He consoled himself that for all his independence this fellow was poor. He had surely been wearing that faded kameez a long time. Its floral print must once have been rows of blue flowers with yellow stamens, but now most of the petals had paled to invisibility, shaken by many winters.

Into the stall there stepped a young man as smartly dressed as the two of them were shabby, in an indigo tunic patterned with bright pink tulips. He was a couple of years older than they, with a horseshoe moustache to show for it. As Horseshoe Moustache reached up to unpeg an illustrated lyric from the line, an indigo sleeve fell back to reveal a forearm festooned with a motley of bandages and dotted with burns about the size of the brass coin with which he paid for his poem. The stallholder scrolled and beribboned the lyric. He handed it to Horseshoe Moustache and said,

'May this poem help you to win your true love's heart.'

After he'd gone, Nat asked about the burns and bandages.

'Marks of love,' came the grave reply. 'With us, the ardent suitor proves his love sincere by burning himself in front of his beloved. If she likes him, she gives him a bandage, dipped in healing salves and unguents, with which to bind his wounds. If she doesn't love him, she offers no poultice, no bandage and the spurned lover must walk away, the pain in his arm banishing the anguish in his heart. The more bandages you wear the more she loves you.'

'Are you a poet?'

'I am a silkworm. Here I sit in my narrow stall spinning out my silk, and I've just sold my finest poem for one single shahidi.'

'Have you no copy of the poem?'

'Here,' he replied, tapping his head and heart to show where his copy of the poem was lodged. Nat mistakenly thought he was doing the *salaam m'lakum* gesture and so touched heart, lips and head in return.

'Nat Bramble at your service. '

'Nat Bramble, I am Darius Nouredini. The poem goes like this.' He lifted his chin and recited:

I yearn for your touch
as silence before the final chord
aches for your fingers
upon copper and silver strings.
'Strum,' begs silence
after the last-but-one chord,
'for until the touch of your hand
the whole world hangs suspended,
like a frozen waterfall.'

'And what makes the poem exquisite,' he continued, 'is that the word *shor* means both to pour and to strum. My love, Gol, is a musician. She doesn't know I love her yet but I'll tell her very soon. What brings you here?'

When Nat told him his errand, Darius asked whether the ink and paper were for the writing of his letters or for drawing. Nat smiled at the very idea that he might be someone who entered into correspondence. He was a skink: the servant that other servants gave orders to, the dogsbody, potboy and errand-boy. Was the ink for his letters indeed! Or was Darius Nouredini mocking him? Nat cut him a look but found no trace of mockery in those dark brown eyes in their pure milk whites. The writing materials, he explained, were for the gentlemen of the Sherley party. Darius laid out his wares. The sealing wax was runnier than English and Venetian, the ink ordinary, but the quality of the smooth, strong cotton-blended paper was beyond compare.

Emerging from the bazaar's narrow covered alleys out onto the maidan, Nat was envious. There was a fellow his own age, a masterless man. Independent. What had Nat to look forward to when he crossed the maidan? What would he do today? More skinking. Polish more boots. Wash more clothes. Sharpen more swords and knives. Wait at table during more interminable suppers he could smell but never taste. Skink, skink, skink.

2

Sir Anthony Sherley stood on the Ali Qapu Palace's high veranda with one arm on the shoulder of the skink, and the other pointing across Isfahan's ten-acre city square.

'Over there. Those are the moneychangers, Bramble. On those steps on the far side of the square? There's two-hundred and fifty silver abbassi in this hawking bag. You will exchange these Persian coins for three-hundred Dutch lion dollars. Each Dutch dollar has a lion rampant on one side and is printed with the words *leeuwen daalder*. Dutch for lion dollar. Then you will come back, and place three-hundred dollars right here where the lines of good fortune cross long life.'

Nat was troubled. Why me? he thought. Why not send an upper servant? Why not send Angelo, the gentleman interpreter? What trick was Anthony pulling? Was he secretly planning to leave Isfahan, abandoning all the servants? Did he fear his gentlemen would want paying if they knew he had dollars in his purse? Clouds rolled off the veranda's mirrored pillars, and, dizzied by his commission, Nat's head spun with them.

'And if I cannot get three-hundred, Sir Anthony, then am I to bring the abbassi back?'

'Agh! Cock a' bones!' gasped Anthony, doubling over and clutching his side. When he slowly straightened up, his stone-blue bug eyes were blood shot and leaky with pain.

'Your stone, Sir Anthony?'

'Whoreson kidney stone! 'Tis gone. A spasm, a mere spasm. Cock a bones, that hurt! I'm quite well again. Now get thee gone, Bramble!'

❖

It was all transacted very quickly. Nat found a sarrafi offering three-hundred and three Dutch dollars for his silver abbassi. Three more than Sir Anthony had reckoned on! His master would be well pleased with that. The sarrafi poured the lion dollars straight from the scales into the hawking bag. Nat buckled the bag around his hips, pulled the skirts of his bumfreezer doublet down over it, and hurried back across the world's biggest city square to the Ali Qapu Palace.

In the lobby outside the Sherley brothers' second-floor chambers sat three gentlemen of the party, Parry, Pincon, and Angelo Corrai, the Venetian interpreter, who waved Nat away.

'Any business that *you* have can wait. Sir Anthony is sick with his stone. He will see no-one.'

'But he said he was well an hour ago, sir,' said Nat.

'And now he is ill, gnat's piss,' replied Parry. 'His stone has shifted.'

'When he's well again,' said Nat, 'please tell Sir Anthony that his order has been transacted at three-hundred and three.'

'What order?' asked Pincon, the Frenchman.

'Three-hundred and three what?' demanded Parry, the Englishman.

'If you have a letter you must give it to me to pass to him,' said Angelo.

'No letter, my masters. God give you good day,' said Nat.

Smiling to himself, he climbed the spiral staircase up to the fourth floor servants' quarters. He had reduced Signor Corrai, Monsieur Pincon and Mr Parry to mere go-betweens. Who's gnat's piss now?

3

Nat awoke at first light, hips and waist sore from sleeping on a belt full of coins. When he went down to the second floor he found everything pell-mell. The Shah's own physicians were within and he could hear Sir Anthony groaning in delirium. All the other servants were busy with hot water and cold compresses, passing in and out of the onion-shaped double doors of the Sherley brothers' chamber. The large and lumbering Eli Elkin handed Nat a steaming chamber pot of blood and piss, and said:

'Here's your breakfast, Bramble.'

Nat was extremely wary of Elkin, Sir Anthony's enforcer, his vicious master's vicious man. He knew that Elkin was looking for the slightest flicker of rebellion, the slightest excuse to crack his skull, and so he meekly took the pot of blood and piss from his hands. With his bunched eyes, turned-up nose and twisted leer, Elkin always looked as if he were halfway through pulling a tight collar off over his head. Nat never knew a man look so uncomfortable in his own skin. Perhaps that was why Elkin always had to make Nat and every other servant around him feel uncomfortable as well.

Returning the cleaned and polished chamber pot, he found a dozen of the Shah's bodyguards, the Tofangchi, posted outside Sir Anthony's chambers. Sir Robert Sherley, the weak-chinned, younger brother, came out.

'How does your noble brother, Sir Robert?' asked Nat.

'Why, Master Bramble, he recovers. Still abed, but better. The Shah attends him in person.'

'Just like Her Majesty at Lord Burghley's bedside, sir, when the Queen spoon-fed him with her own royal hand.'

'Let us hope not,' said Robert Sherley with asperity, 'for he died soon after.'

'Beg pardon, sir, I forgot.'

All Anthony's people, his upper servants and the gentlemen of the party, were gathering in the lobby. Such was the air of grave, muttered speculation that no-one thought to give Nat any more orders for the day. In a trice he skipped away to the bazaar.

As he emerged onto the broad expanse of the maidan he felt a surge of joy. Here was a whole day of liberty! He did not know when he would ever be so free again. Swinging his arms merrily, he sang snatches of the *Carman's Whistle*.

As I abroad was walking
By the breaking of the day
Into a pleasant meadow
A young man took his way.

He would show this Darius that a servant also had his free days, as much as any artisan stallholder. He would lounge and loiter. He would hum and haw. Let Darius see who had to work today and who had not. That's what a little visit would teach *him*.

Oh God a mercy, carman,
Thou art a lively lad
Thou hast as rare a whistle

As young man ever had.

Passing by the moneychangers, he allowed himself to dream. Ah, what if Anthony should die from his sickness! Then Nat might set himself up as independent as Darius Nouredini! Three-hundred and three lion dollars. He didn't know what that was in pounds sterling, but he could work it out from Spanish ducats. He enquired after the value of Spanish ducats at a succession of sarrafi stalls, and then it was that he made an astounding discovery: no two sarrafi agreed on their worth. Dutch dollars' value was consistent, but not so Spanish ducats. Was this an oversight, Nat wondered, due to the press of business?

The Isfahan sarrafi ran the greatest currency exchange in the world. Nowhere else were so many different currencies traded. Coins hammered from every metal ore ever mined out of the earth were traded in the open-air stalls. Coins from the east, west, north and south: Ottoman dinar, Indian rupee, Chinese liang, Malayan tael, Spanish ducat, Dutch dollar, Venetian zecchino, the Holy Roman escudo and dockatoon, and the home currency, the Persian gold toman, silver abbassi, and brass shahidi. All were exchanged on the maidan. Small wonder, then, that the value of a fringe currency such as Spanish ducats differed wildly from stall to stall. Small wonder that no two stalls agreed on how many abbassi a silver Spanish ducat might be worth. Perhaps they would spot their mistake as soon as he tried to act on it.

Nat drew three *leeuwen daalder* from the hawking bag around his waist and exchanged them for six Spanish ducats. Then he went to another sarrafi and converted his six ducats into six *leeuwen daalder*! He had now made Sir Anthony six more dollars. His master would be so delighted his thumb might even flip a spinning dollar Nat's way. For Anthony always preferred impulsive largesse to paying a servant the wages he was due. Largesse cost less.

4

Darius was enjoying the silence in his narrow stall. The metalworkers either side of him had not opened for lack of oil. He worked peacefully, delighting in sounds usually inaudible under the din, such as the swish of the smooth seashell with which he was shellacking cotton-rag paper for binding into an album.

Blank albums sold well. The fashion among young Isfahanis was for swapping artwork to paste into one another's albums. Lyrics and musical notation, meticulous full-colour illustrations of flowers and herbs, caricatures of friends or famous wrestlers, calligraphy samples, design motifs, proverbs, funny stories, bawdy verses and, more than all of these put together, illustrated poems, his main stock in trade.

As he worked, Darius weighed in his mind whether he dared yet give Gol a love poem to stick in her album. The last time they swapped keepsakes, he had come away kicking himself for his timidity in not giving her his lyrical *'I Yearn For Your Touch.'* But having had a day to think about it he was relieved. The hour was not yet ripe to declare his love.

His single lamp's filament made a contented pop and sigh. An oil shortage had all but closed the bazaar. Bandits raiding the Baku convoy, not for its oil but for money belts, silk turbans and horses had caused the shortage. And yet these deep country bandits, who'd probably dumped the oil in a ditch somewhere, dung burners that they were, would soon plunge a city they had never seen into darkness. No-one could imagine a life without oil. Soon he'd be no better than a beast in its cave.

At which point he smelt something exactly like a beast in its cave, looked up and saw the foreigner from yesterday. Nat Bramble had the look of a small nocturnal animal grown saucer-eyed in the dark as he asked,

'Why's the bazaar gone dark?'

After Darius explained, Nat went quiet for a long time, tipped his head this way and that, and then stuck out his arm and pointed at the lantern hanging on a hook.

'Do you mean to say there's oil in that lamp?' he asked.

Darius was flummoxed. It was like a toddler's question. Is there air in the sky? Is there light in the sun? He had no idea how to answer such a strange question – until it dawned on him that Nat might come from a land where oil was unknown.

'How do you heat your homes?' asked Darius. 'How do you cook?'

'Sea-coal, charcoal and wood.'

'And for light?'

'Wax for the rich, tallow for the poor.'

'Tallow?' asked Darius, but then didn't let Nat get more than a few words into his description of how animal fat was rendered before waving him to a stop. 'None of that at any time,' he said, screwing up his face with a shudder and blowing hard.

'What will you use when the oil runs out?' asked Nat.

'Thorn!'

'When does the next Baku oil convoy arrive?' asked Nat.

'Nobody knows. Today. Tomorrow. Next week. Next month. But I know of oil springs only a few days ride from here where you can get oil as simply as filling a bottle at a fountain.'

'Where?'

'The Temple of Mithras,' replied Darius. 'An old pagan shrine of

Zoroastrian fire-worshippers in Masjid-i Suleiman. My father took me there when I was a boy, before it became Ottoman territory. Any merchant who takes a dozen mules there and back before the Baku convoy arrives will be rich.'

'But it's Turkish oil,' said Nat.

'The Turks don't use oil any more than you Franks do. The oil is there for the taking. But to make money you need money. I've asked a few merchants to invest, but they said that the pagan fire-towers had all been extinguished and capped by the mullahs.'

'Have they?'

'Yes, but think for a moment. Eternal fire must be fed by eternal oil.'

'But if the oil is buried like coal in a mine, then you'll need miners and mining equipment, and that'll cost more than you'd ever earn from the oil.'

'You can no more bury oil than you can bury an acorn. It must rise. It seeps up everywhere.'

'I have seen it! For on our way here, we passed through a valley of pitch between Hit and Falluja where the oil comes boiling out of the ground incessantly and black smoke pours into the sky forever and ever and ever.'

Awestruck, Darius looked at his visitor in a whole new way.

'You have been to the Doors of Hell,' he said. 'That's what we call Hit's valley of pitch. What's it like?'

'A heaving swamp of tar under a noonday sky as black as night. One man stepped on a dark patch of pebbles and the oil bog closed upon him. A moment later there was no sign of him, just this tar pit bubbling away under the smoky sky. Then, one of the boiling ponds erupted, shooting rocks and petroleum into the sky. Sir Anthony Sherley, my master, and the gentlemen ran for cover, but commanded the rest of us to rescue the baggage while hot rocks and gravel rained down on our heads.'

'The Temple of Mithras's oil springs aren't like that,' said Darius. He pushed his scrappy brown turban back on his head, exposing tumbling black hair. 'There, the rock oil plays like a fountain. You'd just have to fill a few urns, I tell you, to come back a rich man. Oh, it is agony to have the solution to the whole city's crisis when you cannot put it into practice! It is agony to watch a fortune slip away! I wish the next Baku oil convoy would arrive today! At least then I'll no longer have to suffer my brilliant idea withering on the vine, because the moment will have passed. Come, let's go and see if there's any news of the convoy.'

It was a simple business to close the stall, merely dropping a black cloth over the front, and this very simplicity left Nat agog. This was what it meant to be an independent artisan with a stall of your own. Just flip down a cloth and leave when you like!

Nat and Darius emerged from the darkened bazaar onto the maidan. Stepping round stacks of melons and pomegranates, they passed an old woman just as she was spitting on the floor. Darius jerked his head as if she'd spat in his face.

'None of that at any time at all,' he muttered.

They had not gone much further before he put his hands over his eyes and stood stock still. An Uzbeg war veteran missing an eye walked by. It was a few moments before Darius deemed it safe to open his eyes again.

As they walked along, Nat stole a few glances at his curious new friend. Half the sights and sounds of the world seemed to put Darius quite beside himself, as if he had a skin too few. His soul and body, it seemed to Nat, were oil and water that did not mix. With his blunt jaw and broad shoulders, Darius had the body of a burly wrestler, into which frame had been poured the fine, sensitive soul of a poet. His splayfooted, galumphing walk was the poet giving a piggy back to the wrestler and struggling with the burden. His strong chin did not suggest resolve, nor his broad shoulders capability. They only made his lack of these virtues look calamitous, as if he did not know how to steer the big ship he found himself piloting. But when he spoke, his voice was a strong, assured oboe, softly honking in the roof of his mouth: 'Bring oil to Isfahan before the Baku convoy does and you will make your fortune. But here's where we'll find out when the convoy will come.'

Nat was confused. He thought they were going somewhere they could hear the news, but instead Darius brought him to a poultry fair. Boxes of doves were stacked as high as a man. The birds' cumulative cooing, burbling and trilling made such a tremendous noise that he had to raise his voice to ask Darius why he had brought him to this pet shop when what he wanted was news.

What Darius said next so astounded Nat that he began to wonder whether all those pamphlets he'd dismissed as 'traveller's tales' might have been true after all. Maybe Walter Raleigh wasn't lying about the Amazonian men whose head grew in the middle of their chests. Perhaps there really were winged horses in Guiana. There were certainly winged messengers here. For what Nat was looking at, Darius now explained, was the hub of a complex communications network that spanned an empire. Three thousand dovecots ringed Isfahan alone, sending and receiving information to and from distant cities, ports, ships at sea and generals in the field, and, with a bit of luck, the Baku oil convoy.

'Messages looped under the wings of doves hold the empire together,' said Darius. 'All the news comes here. The price of cloth of Khormanshah, the husband's apology to his wife, and the -.'

He broke off, and stared with his mouth wide open. Nat followed his gaze to a tall, gawky, raven-haired young woman approaching the pigeon stand. She handed a box of birds to the owner of the pigeon-post stand, together with a scrap of silk covered in tiny script for which she received a few brass coins. The woman then shouldered her stripy cotton bag, from which the headstock of a kind of lute or fiddle was showing, and turned to go.

'Gol,' whispered Darius. 'My beloved. Perhaps this is a sign that now is the time! I shall speak my heart! I shall tell my love! Farewell, Nat!' And with an air of great moment, he hurried after her, the oil quite forgot.

From a distance Nat watched Darius and Gol greet each other. They gabbled away, not with the clotted awkwardness of lovers, but the easy familiarity of friends. Far from declaring his love, whatever he was saying was making her smile and laugh. If that girl was Darius's beloved, she didn't know it. How could she, when he lacked the courage to tell her? His gestures as he spoke to her had all the empty bombast of a tumbril-stage player in a town square mystery play. Well, no doubt you could find a thousand things to say if you never said the one thing worth saying.

Watching Darius and Gol walk off together, Nat was seized by a terrible loneliness. Giving a servant a day off was like giving a sailor a horse, he thought. What was he to do with a day off? But there across the maidan was Ali Qapu palace, its tall stilted veranda a cobra's maw, the mirrored columns glistening teeth, ready to devour his time and thought and life and sweat. Instead of climbing back inside that cobra's mouth, he put off his return and loitered by the sarrafi.

The moneychangers' stalls were crowded. Travellers who were planning to leave with the Ottoman Embassy's caravan were changing abbassi to dinars. Voices were raised in a hubbub of business. Scales swung like jib-cranes, coins rose and fell. And the sarrafi were still out of kilter with each other on Spanish ducats.

Nat had six dollars Anthony didn't know about. What if he parlayed these half dozen dollars into a couple more that were his and his alone? He came upon a currency merchant who was offering to exchange lion dollars for ducats at one to two. For a moment he hesitated, but then he remembered Robert Sherley's words: 'Why, Master Bramble, he recovers,' and that decided him. Worse than struggling against temptation was the prospect of no temptation to struggle against. The chance might never come again.

He unbuckled the hawking belt. He exchanged all three-hundred and six lion dollars into six-hundred and twelve Spanish ducats. Once filled with so much Spanish coin, the belt weighed heavy on his hips as he marched down to the other end of the bleachers.

His luck was in. He found a sarrafi buying ducats for dollars at one to one. He unslung his belt and was just about to convert his six-hundred and twelve ducats into as many *leeuwen daalder*, when eight roughriders burst into the maidan from a nearby entrance. The shouting horsemen came galloping straight towards him. Nat clutched the hawking belt to his chest. They spurred their horses into a charge and bore down on him. He dived into the gap between two sarrafi stalls. The roughriders missed him narrowly. He expected them to wheel and come at him again, but by the time he dared raise his head, he found they had dismounted at the far end of the bleachers, ordered tea from the tea-caddies and were talking to a couple of older currency merchants.

The horsemen's arrival spooked the sarrafi, who refused to transact any more business of the day. And so Nat buckled the bulging hawking belt hard against his hips, and hurried back across the maidan. He could wait one more day to become a rich man. He would change the money tomorrow, as soon as he could get away.

Nat returned to Ali Qapu Palace. Behind the onion-shaped double-doors, the Shah's personal physicians were, he was told, by Anthony's bedside. Back in the servants' quarters, Nat turned in for the night. He pulled his blanket over him and clutched the money to his belly. Tomorrow these ducats would be dollars. Tomorrow he would hand Sir Anthony three hundred and three lion dollars. And keep all the rest! This was the making of him. He wouldn't always be a servant. One day he would be a merchant. His eyelids felt as heavy as the pennies on a dead man's eyes, and soon he was asleep.

5

O ne hundred!' exclaimed Nat. 'But this is six-hundred and twelve silver ducats here.'

'It's the best price you'll get,' said the sarrafi, half of whose teeth were silver. 'The Spanish have landed two ships full of silver at Ormuz.'

'Says who?'

'The *chopars.* They came in last night.'

'*Chopars?*' asked Nat.

'They are the Shah's couriers.'

'The horsemen with white sashes?'

'Yes, they brought the news. They overtook the Ormuz caravan only yesterday. Tomorrow all that Spanish loot comes here, and so everyone is dumping all their ducats as quick as they can.'

'But silver is silver. It is the same metal as it always was.'

'My friend, I don't want to melt it down to make a sword or a cup. I'm not a silversmith, I'm a sarrafi. And one hundred is the best price you will find anywhere today.'

'We shall see about that,' said Nat. But the next stall he came to offered only fifty *leuwe daalder* for his ducats, and the one after that wouldn't buy his Spanish coins at any price. So Nat returned to the first moneychanger. One hundred lion dollars were poured into the hawking bag, and he wandered away from the stall, dazed and grief-stricken. One part of his brain knew that his life was over and yet still his legs moved as he put one foot in front of the other, and still his ribcage rose and fell with every breath, and still he kept searching the currency exchange, long after he knew that he was never going to find any money merchant offering more than a hundred lion dollars. Once he gave up his search he would have to think about what happened next.

Into his mind there stole a memory from England, from the early days of the Datchworth famine. He remembered foraging for edible roots with a boy who died. Nat covered his body with his coat and found the boy's mother a few fields away. She must have guessed what news he brought, for she no sooner saw him coming than she dropped her spade and ran away. There she was, a grown woman, running from a boy. Boy that he was, he gave chase for a few paces, then stopped, for he suddenly understood that she was running away from the moment when she would be told her son was dead. For so long as she ran across the barren field, she could believe, in one part of her mind at least, that the truths of a few moments ago still held. So long as Nat hung around the sarrafi he could convince himself that his own life was not over.

He stayed by the moneychangers all day, until the setting sun tinted the scales red, and the lamps were lit. The oil dearth had reduced even the rich sarrafi to the use of inferior naphtha in their lanterns. Black smoke plumed from the sarrafi's cressets. The Doors of Hell were here.

'I am lost,' he told himself

Alone, he wandered the vast maidan. The biggest city square in the world now seemed to him a wilderness, a windy plain far from any human habitation. He was cold, hungry and tired. He passed a mosque, a synagogue, he sat in a cathedral, but the Armenians cast suspicious looks upon him, and so he left. There was nowhere in this whole city where he could rest. He found it hard to breathe. He pulled off his neckerchief and undid the hooks of his doublet. There was nowhere for him left on earth.

He sought out Darius in the bazaar.

6

A re these *chopars* really King's Messengers?'

'Yes, they are,' replied Darius.

'But they look like brigands!'

'They are brigands, too. Ha ha! In the Shah's name they are authorized to commandeer any man's horse to expedite the mail. That's the official function. But they are horse-thieves first and envoys second.'

'Then how can anyone trust the news these bandits bring?'

'What news? News about the Baku convoy? Is the oil coming?

'They're saying a ship full of Spanish silver has come in at Ormuz,' wailed Nat.

'What's wrong?'

'I have lost most of my master's money! What am I going to do now?'

'Oh, that is a heavy blow,' said Darius. 'Sit here! Sit down, yes, that's good. Don't worry, I can stand. Indeed I am sorry that such bad luck has hit you. But don't worry about this stolen silver, my friend.'

Nat cut him a look. How did he know?

'Stolen?'

'The Spanish steal their silver from the New World,' replied Darius equably. 'They have minted so many coins from their plunder that they have destroyed currencies all along the Silk Road from here to China.'

'But silver is silver,' said Nat.

'Too much and it's as cheap as tin.'

'But it's not tin, it's silver. There is the same amount in Isfahan today as there was yesterday, so why has the price changed? Why are Spanish ducats worth not one third of what they were worth yesterday on a few horse-thieves say so? Oh, I am in hell! What shall I do?'

'You were not to know. Your master will understand that you're not to blame for a caravan of Spanish loot arriving in Ormuz or here. Even the most experienced and venerable money changers could lose money to a sudden swarm of Spanish silver.'

Nat stuffed both hands into the hawking belt's meat pockets then scattered two fistfuls of silver ducats on the display table's black velvet.

'I happen to have saved this many coins from my wages. Let's set out for that pagan oil well. The Temple of Mithras.'

'No, no,' said Darius. 'It's too late.'

'Come on, I believe in your plan! Have the *chopars* said anything about a Baku oil convoy? No! No! We can bring back oil while the price is high and split the profits!'

'The moment has gone. It's too late now.'

'Too late? No, come on! Here, take it, invest it, let us leave at once, tonight or at first light!'

Darius stared hard at Nat.

'If you have all this money,' he asked, 'then why do you even need to attempt such a venture?'

Silence fell. Both men were still.

'I was speculating with my master's money,' Nat confessed, 'in the hope of earning myself a little profit. I had no authority to change the money into Spanish silver.'

'If the money is not yours then you have no right to try to drag me into your villainy. You are a man without honour!'

Nat scraped the ducats back into the hawking belt, buckled the meat pocket, and looked up.

'And what about you, Darius? You will never dare do anything in your whole life. You are all talk, all mouth. I saw you with Gol, I watched you with the woman you call your sweetheart. Sweetheart? Ha! Can you not see how your Gol sees you? You're her pet eunuch. You will never tell Gol you love her, never, not until you are eighty. You'll be an old man before your faint heart dare speak, and only then because your aged wits grow so feeble that you forget the fear in which you have wasted your little, little life, living only for independence!'

He left the stall with such speed that he heard the illuminated sheets flapping in his wake. As he searched for a way out of the dark labyrinth of the half-empty bazaar he feared that that, having lost his way in these dim passageways, he would stumble past Darius's stall again. But soon he was standing outside the bazaar in the night and staring across the maidan at Ali Qapu Palace. Now he had to face his fate.

All the way across the vast square he hoped for some accident to befall him. If only a runaway bullock cart would knock him spark out, then he could tell Sir Anthony that cutpurses had snatched the lion dollars. Everyone would pity him. If only a troop of horse-backed brigands would stab him and steal the hawking belt in full view of the palace guards.

With heavy tread, he climbed the narrow winding stairs to the second floor lobby. Robert Sherley stood outside the sealed double doors with Marshal, Parry and Pincon. Marshal laid a hand on Robert's shoulder. There were tears in Robert's eyes. New hope flared in Nat. Perhaps Anthony was dead!

'How does my master?' Nat asked.

'He mends,' replied Robert Sherley. 'He will be well again, after all! So we shall not be left here without him, God be praised!'

Nat began to cry. 'Hallelujah,' he sobbed.

On the fourth floor, he crept through the sleeping servants. He was the last to turn in. He rolled out his rug and lay on the mineral mosaic wishing the rock crystal were a deep cave into which he could plummet and vanish.

The following morning, Angelo said,

'Bramble, Sir Anthony summons you to attend on him in his chamber directly.'

'Thank-you, *signor*,' said Nat, sick to the pit of his stomach. The summons had come at last. He set down a bowl of hot water and laid a folded towel on its rim. His voice choking, he said: 'In faith, it is good to have our captain barking orders again. I must beg your leave in order to fetch him something which he requires me now to bring him, my masters.'

Nat stepped out of the palace into the hot morning. He crossed the giant, shadowless maidan like an ant under a schoolboy's burning-glass. Sir Anthony would have to wait just a little longer for his vengeance.

He went to the currency exchange hoping against hope, but today they wouldn't touch silver, not for any price.

So, today was his dying day.

But first Nat had one small duty: to apologise to Darius. He did not know whether Anthony would kill him with his own rapier, or turn him over to the Shah's bodyguards. Either way, even if he survived, Nat would be too degraded a wretch, once Anthony and Eli Elkin were finished torturing or branding him, for his apology to count for much. And so with brisk step Nat entered the bazaar in search of Darius, to make his apology while he was still a man.

But when he got to Darius's stall, the black cloth was down. Nat was just about to leave when he noticed broken books lying in the passageway, and an ink slick leaking out from under the cloth like blood from a slaughtered calf. On hands and knees he lifted up the bottom of the cloth and peeked inside. The stall had been ransacked - but someone or something was breathing inside, like a beast in a cave.

7

Earlier that morning, Darius had set out to formally declare his love to Gol Zarafshani. The nearer he got to her house, the more he realised how shabby and faded his clothes were. When had his peach kameez turned this tea-stain colour? When had it become so bobbled? He was sure those bobbles weren't there yesterday. They must have sprung up overnight like mushrooms. His kameez used to be loose and flowing, now it was tight like cloth wrapped around sweated cheese. How had he grown so flabby? When did his flesh start bulging?

He tried to focus on his good points. He twisted the curly black sidelocks which he wore fashionably long, a ringlet dangling by each ear. But then he caught sight of his reflection in a window and saw that parts of his old black velvet coat were worn as bald as a camel's knee. Still, neither dowdy clothes nor flabby body were going to make him turn back today. That much was certain. For just as on a breezy day, a man has only to turn into the wind for his ears to be filled with its roar, so if he turned tail now Nat Bramble's invective would fill his ears, and all be true.

On the corner opposite Gol's house lay a small vacant plot, site of a neighbour's abandoned building project that had never progressed beyond a white screed floor. On its waist-high clay wall there stood a straight-backed man with a horseshoe moustache who was dangling a burning taper over his exposed forearm. A rival! And such a rival! And such a rival in his fine new indigo tunic, patterned with pink tulips. Darius felt sure he knew that horseshoe moustache and indigo tunic from somewhere. So, Gol had another suitor. Why had she never mentioned it? Because it wasn't serious? Or because it was? Up on the roof, her shadow moved behind the elm screen. The rival raised his face to the elm screened roof garden and called out:

'Gol! Gol! Gol Zarafshani! You are beloved of Mani Babachoi, who will now prove to you and to your well-respected family that his love is pure as fire!'

This Mani Babachoi then lowered the flaming linen taper to his inner arm, and held flame to flesh for two long seconds, eyes streaming, body trembling, before he flung away the taper.

A poultice wrapped in vine leaves was thrown down from the roof terrace. Mani Babachoi snatched it up and pressed it to his lips. He anointed his fresh wound with the healing unguent Gol had tossed him, and bandaged his arm. Inspired by this latest love token from Gol, he then burned himself three more times in rapid succession, twice on the forearm, once on the neck. Darius turned away. None of that at any time at all.

What was Darius to do? Here was a rival who would walk through fire, crawl over broken glass and stand on hot coals for his beloved - as if he came from a fantastic land where all the mad, wild vows made in poems were actually done. He watched him pour water over his head, then heard him call up to Gol that he would read her a poem which spoke of what was in his heart, a poem which put into words the exact nature of his love for her.

Darius pitied him already. This Mani Babachoi would mouth some moth-eaten, musty old Hafiz, but Gol would not be won by that. Darius, on the other hand, had come armed with a poem which he had written especially for Gol, a poem expressing emotions he would never have dared read to her but for the stinging of that foreign hornet Nat Bramble. As his rival stepped forward, and raised a page of verse to his eyes, the wet bristles on the back of his shaven head glistened in the sunlight.

'Gol,' he declared:

'I yearn for your touch,
as silence before the final chord
aches for your fingers
upon copper and silver strings.

The ground reeled beneath Darius's feet. His guts twisted and writhed. At last he understood why that horseshoe moustache had nagged at him so. *'Strum,'* continued Mani Babachoi in his stentorian voice:

'Strum,' begs silence,
after the last-but-one chord,
'for until the touch of your hand
the whole world hangs suspended,
like a frozen waterfall.'

'How,' thought Darius, 'could I have known I was selling a poem I wrote about Gol to a man in love with her himself? How could I have known that he was buying for Gol a poem inspired by Gol? Oh, I am undone! I am punished for selling my heart for a shahidi!'

Mani Babachoi rolled up the poem, wound it in leather twine, and lobbed the scroll into the roof garden. Darius heard Gol clap her hands together. With delight? Or just to catch?

'But I wrote that poem for her,' said Darius.

'You sold it to me,' replied Mani, adjusting the fresh yellow bandage on his arm. 'Have you no poem for her? Quick now. The lady is waiting.

Speak your love.'

To his dismay, Darius discovered that he could not remember a single poem. Every last one had completely disappeared from his memory. Poetry had fled his brain.

At last, flying to the aid of a fellow poet in his moment of need, Jalal al-Din Rumi came winging across the ages to drop a pearl into a true lover's brain. Darius experienced the exultation of a man whose blazing house has been saved by a sudden downpour of rain. He threw a defiant, careless look at his rival and snapped his fingers in his face. He climbed onto the white clay wall opposite Gol's house. He stood on the wall, raised both hands in the air, and lifted his face to the elm screen. This rival could buy his leavings, but the true spirit, the living connection between himself and Gol would always flame into life. In a strong, clear voice, Darius began to recite.

> 'Should someone allude to the gracefulness of the night sky,
> climb on the roof and dance and say:
> Like this!

> If anyone wants to know what soul means,
> or the presence of God,
> lean your face towards them and hold it close:
> Like this!

> Should any wonder how Jesus raised the dead,
> don't try to explain the mystery,'
> just kiss me on the lips:
> Like this!

When someone quotes the old poetic fancy about
clouds disrobing the moon,
unknot the ties of your gown one by one,
let your loose gown fall open, and say -
OOUNGGMMFF!'

A shovel load of pigeon shit hit Darius. Hard as hail stones, dry as gravel, the crusty droppings stung his face. The filthy grit was in his mouth, eyes, and ears. His head rang. Gol's mother Roshanak was shouting at him.

How dare he come here and spout lewd brothel songs outside their house! How dare he, in full hearing of the neighbours, lie that he had seen her daughter Gol in the nude, and falsely pretend to know that her breasts looked like moons, which, by the way, they did not, and she should know, she was her mother. And while that slandered virgin's mother still breathed, he would never again see even so much as one of her ears!

Another load of hard, dry birdlime struck Darius full in the face, knocking him backwards off the wall. Half-blind, he stumbled from the house, spitting disgusting knobbly droppings from his mouth.

❖

At the wall-fountain by Sharestan Bridge, Darius washed his face, hair, neck and hands, and sluiced his eyes and ears of ashy, bitty filth. He returned to his narrow stall in a bazaar darkened for want of oil, and dropped the cloth behind him. He tore down the silk pages of illustrated lyrics that hung across his stall. He overturned the table, shattering ink bottles, sending blank albums and books sliding to the floor. Then he sat in darkness in the far corner of the wrecked stall, and crossed his legs under him.

'I must not let myself forget that despair is the one true state. Despair. All else, all other experiences are delusions and when I come back to this I know it is the one fixed truth. I must let my eyes get accustomed to this dark cave of despair, since it is the only proper dwelling-place. How stupid I was when I was out of my cave. What vanity was in my mind and soul. How shallow was my understanding.'

The one true state was despair. He must not lose this vision. Therefore he would live a simple dervish life, up in the hills, eating only rice and water, and that only so as to fortify himself for the study and practice of Ibn Senna, Aristotle, and Astarabadi, who held that severe asceticism must purify the soul until it was ready to receive true wisdom and illumination. He would train his body for *Muharram*: self-flagellation with chains, against which pain the stinging of a burning linen taper would be as petty as nothing. Chains with razors on, these would be.

He heard footsteps in the passageway outside his stall. All this useless coming and going. What purpose did it serve? Didn't people know that there was no point in anyone going anywhere for anything? If fools managed to delude themselves that there was, good luck to them. The footsteps stopped outside his stall. A splinter of weak light from the passageway crept across the debris of Darius's former life. Nat Bramble, his cheek pressed to the floor, poked his snout under the cloth.

'Darius? Is that you in there?'

A bull troubled by a gadfly, Darius slowly closed his eyes. This irritant would soon leave him be. Instead Nat crawled on his belly under the dropcloth and into the stall. 'Why are you sitting in the dark, Darius?'

Darius heard his name spoken, but he knew that the old self to whom that name once applied had been annihilated. Nothing of him survived the death he died outside Gol's house. His body would live on for a time, and then die. The foreigner would talk to the silence for a while and then go. His words would soon stop grouting his ears like dusty dove dung.

But grief calls unto grief.

'I have come to apologise,' said Nat. 'I had no right to try to drag you down with me. I just wanted company in hell. What I said of you I said in envy and malice. What I said about you and Gol, I mean. I know nothing about love and how to win a fair hand and so you are right to spurn every ignorant calumny that came from an envious mouth.'

'No,' replied Darius. 'What you accused me of was true. Everything about me is empty and false.'

A landslip of books broke the silence for a moment. Nat took a pace forward, crunching underfoot the rare shell Darius used for shellacking paper.

'I would have liked to have been your friend, Darius Nouredini. But my master's found me out. I will never be able to see you again. Well, not as I am, at least. Not as you should know me. So forgive me, and then we'll say farewell.'

Nat's voice wobbled. Darius said nothing for a time.

'How much money do you have left?' he asked at last.

'One hundred Spanish ducats.'

'It's a start,' said Darius.

'No,' said Nat, 'you have a life to lose. You are a masterless man. You are independent. You own your own stall.'

'To stay in this stall cursing our fate is one thing, to change our fate is another. Let us go to the oil springs and gushers surrounding the Fire Temple of Mithras, my friend! Come, let's away!'

8

Wee will go to my house,' said Darius. 'My mother and her husband Masghoud hold the key to the storeroom where my father's oil mining tools are stored. My mother claims the gear belongs to Masghoud by dint of marriage, but it's mine by blood.'

Hurrying down narrow unpaved streets, they passed the open door of a forge. Four men were holding down a sandy bay stallion while the farrier sliced a horny growth off the spur of his hocks with a razor. The stallion was thrashing his trussed legs wildly, his yoked hooves loudly clattering the wooden walls.

'Too much barley,' said Nat walking backwards so as not to miss a thing. 'When they eat too much barley then these chestnuts grow on the hocks and you have to chip them off. And you have to trim his lips, too. He'll do those next, you watch. Yes, there he goes...'

Darius tucked his own lips inside his mouth, and hurried away from the scene. When Nat caught up with him, he opened his lips just enough to hiss,

'None of that at anytime at all.'

His friend's extreme sensitivity and fastidiousness made Nat eager to see the home where Darius reposed after work, the place where he escaped the tinsmith's din, where all those sights and sounds of city life which so bruised and scalded his poet's soul were salved. Perhaps there would be a courtyard full of gillyflowers in fat earthenware pots, a caged nightingale, a loving mother swooping bowls of lamb stew down to the rug upon which her son sat, building up his strength for his next great poem. And maybe Darius's unmarried sisters would be asking who his friend was.

A few narrow streets later, he followed Darius down three steps and through a door. Lifting aside a tattered cloth, Darius said,

'Welcome to my home.'

The mean entrance opened into a cavernous basement. It was home both to the family and to the family's textile dyeing workshop. On a relay of washing lines, raised on pulleys to the crumbling ceiling, boiled clothes were drizzling fabric dye into a saffron-coloured puddle. Glass lanterns, strung on slanting ropes, dribbled black oil onto cracked tiles. The walls were so mouldy as almost to be alive.

Darius greeted his mother, who was stirring boiling linen with a brass ladle in a vat, her hairline oozing henna onto her forehead. She did not return his greeting. He greeted his sister, Pahnave, who was stirring rice. She ignored him too. He introduced Nat, but still they spoke not a word.

Darius handed Nat a bowl of rice. Hungry as he was, Nat swallowed only one mouthful, and then set down the bowl. Fabric dye had infused the broth. His head began to ache from the suffocating steam-heat, from the stench of perfumed laundry soaps and the clanging of steel ladles against boiling and bubbling metal vats. He couldn't understand why Darius did not say, 'None of that at anytime at all,' before pushing the bowl away from him. Instead Darius ate up every last grain of his fabric-dye rice, and then went back for seconds.

A man came in from a back room and laid a cold chisel on the table. Darius hailed Masghoud. His stepfather returned no greeting either, but Darius was not to be put off, and crossed the room.

'I would like to use my father's gear for an oil mining venture I am undertaking with my friend here, and I wonder if you would let me have the key to the storeroom where I can find what I need?'

'No chance,' his stepfather replied.

'But you never use the gear,' said Darius.

'I might do one day.'

'You just don't want me to have it.'

'I might sell it. I might use the tureens to freight wine.'

'When were you going to do this?' asked Darius.

'You show some respect,' Leila, his mother, told him. 'If you want your father's oil-mining gear, then you must, for once in your life, do something for us, for this family.'

'I contribute money,' said Darius. 'I pay rent.' Pahnave, his sister, snorted a dry derisive laugh.

'Have you any idea,' she asked, 'how much food costs?'

'But the rent is for feeding me.'

'Exactly,' said Pahnave, 'so you don't give anything to this family then!'

'What can I do beyond what I have done?' Darius asked his mother.

'You can,' she replied, 'help your stepfather's sister.'

All sounds of clanging and clanking ceased. Leila, Masghoud and Pahnave stopped their work. The only sound came from bubbles popping in the simmering vats of rice or clothes. Leila's last words had reignited The Great Family Controversy: the *sigheh.*

The law said that a woman could not divorce and remarry the same man three times in a row, unless she had married someone else in the interim, even if only for one day. This one-day marriage was called a *sigheh.* It was a lawful expedient to prevent sex outside of wedlock. Having divorced her husband twice, in order to earn a little money, Masghoud's sister wanted to marry him again so that they could resume living together in a respectable fashion. To that end Leila and Masghoud had decided that Darius should marry his step-aunt for a day.

'Don't worry, you won't have to do anything,' said Masghoud. 'In fact if you do I'll kill you.'

This was greeted by much laughter. Darius's mother placed a hand upon her copper pendants, and shook her finger at the rascally Masghoud.

'How can you ask your own son,' Darius asked his mother, 'to commit a crime against his very soul?'

'Just because you can read,' snapped Leila, 'you think you are better than everyone else. A *sigheh* is just a formality. It doesn't mean anything, and it is really nothing to do with you. You only have to stand there for an hour, just like the hangman's horse, while the mullah performs the ceremony.'

The hangman's horse has no inkling that a death sentence has been read out, but Darius knew a death sentence when he heard one. It was the death of who he was, of all he ever hoped to be.

'Just as your zinc-lined jugs will never be clean again,' he told them, 'if I marry for a day then neither will my soul ever be clean again.'

'No,' said his mother, 'your soul will be cleansed by having helped your family for once.'

Home was the place where Darius hardly knew himself. When he wasn't in this airless cavern he could clearly describe the full horror of this violation, but here he lost all his powers of persuasion. Even when he did place a solid gold argument in the family's crooked scales it somehow carried less weight than his mother's brassy rebuttal.

'You say the oil-mining tools are Masghoud's by right of marriage,' he said, 'even as you seek to defile the estate of marriage in the eyes of God and man!'

'Would you have Masghoud's sister live in sin?' she demanded.

'Good point, Leila,' said Masghoud.

'Yes,' said Pahnave. 'That's told you, Darius. Now do you understand?'

His head spun. He felt sick. If they had their way, he would never be able to present himself as a proper husband to Gol, because on Darius's wedding day the mullah would have to tell all the guests that he had been married once before. What gave Darius's life meaning was his vision of true love. This, and not a love of metre or cadence, was why he had committed whole passages of Rumi to memory. He had done so in the wish that he would one day live and feel like the poet of *Like This.* But he needed his dead father's oil-mining gear, and so once more he tried to get the storeroom key.

'I'll pay you twenty shahidi,' he suggested to howls of derision.

'Where will you ever get twenty shahidi from?' retorted Masghoud, his stepfather.

'From this oil venture,' replied Darius.

'Some things are more important than money, Darius,' said his mother. 'If you do your duty with this *sigheh* then your aunt will be able to return to respectable married life!'

'Twenty shahidi in advance.'

'Not if they were twenty solid silver abbassi,' she said, folding her arms.

Suddenly Nat broke in on the conversation.

'How about twenty-five, then?' He poured twenty-five solid-silver abbassi on the worktop.

'Give him the key, Masghoud,' said Darius's mother.

Together, Darius and Nat piled the old oil-mining gear onto a tarpaulin balanced between two broom handles. As they carried the equipment back through the house, Leila said:

'I suppose you're taking it to the old witch's barn.'

'We are going to my grandmother's,' replied Darius.

'All that big barn,' complained Pahnave, standing at a steaming dye vat, 'just for her and a few donkeys and chickens! The selfish old crone!'

'It is far too big for her,' agreed Masghoud.

'She's a mean old witch,' said Leila, 'and that's all there is to it. I've told her often enough how good this sale would be for the family, but all she thinks of is herself. What can she do with that barn? Nothing! But Masghoud is full of ideas for what we could do with her land. Full of them!'

❖

The mound of oil-mining gear clanked promisingly as they carried it along the narrow rutted street. They made way for a mule train bearing bundles of desert-thorn.

'Here's a good omen,' said Darius. 'Desert thorn is what everyone's been forced to use instead of oil.'

The young drover bringing up the rear of the mule train held his switch in a wooden hand, with which he waved his thanks to Darius for having given way. When the drover was out of earshot, Nat asked,

'Was he a veteran of the Uzbeg war, do you think?'

'Not like that at any time at all,' hissed Darius, who then performed an odd corkscrew shudder that travelled all the way up and down his spine, and twisted the features of his face.

They slept that night in his grandmother's barn.

9

The next morning, Darius rose early and went into town. He returned leading two mules and three donkeys, which he'd bought from Bachtiari nomads, and with boots, blankets, gloves and clothes.

Nat was well pleased with his mule. A strong-looking, sooty buckskin, the height of a good English hack, it had cream circles around its eyes, like the scoops in the chopars' grimy faces.

In the shade of a gnarly mulberry tree, whose ancient boughs zigzagged not just side to side but up and down as well, Darius handed Nat his Persian disguise.

'Where does it button?'

'There on the shoulder,' said Darius.

'The shoulder?'

'Only women wear shirts that fasten at the neck.' Nat belted a cambric sash around the cotton kameez which hung to the knees of his English breeches.

Kulsum, Darius's grandmother, joined them in the shade of the zigzag mulberry. Small, spry and nimble, her high-pitched speech sounded like an adolescent boy's breaking voice.

'Why the new clothes?' she asked.

'Nat-jan is in disguise,' replied Darius, sitting on a bough, 'so that he's not spotted by his master.'

'These boots might have been made for me!' said Nat, stamping about delightedly.

'Mine too,' said Darius, kicking his new boot heels through the dust. 'So many soldiers came back from the war with enemy boots that even an Uzbeg captain's boots like these are cheap.'

'If he's run away from service,' Kulsum began, but then broke off abruptly as she caught sight of her dead son's oil mining gear laid out on a blanket under the mulberry tree. She knelt in the dirt and ran her fingers over the equipment, over wooden-framed packsaddles, panniers, zinc-lined oil tureens, rope ladders, stacked buckets, block and tackle. 'All these stupid things came back,' she said at last, 'and he did not.'

She unwound a long skein of purple cotton from a hatchet's blade and ran her finger across the steel. 'Still sharp after so long. Do you remember any of these things, Darius?'

'The saddlecloth's fiery stag with the smoking hooves, I remember that.'

She spread the linen-backed saddlecloth on her lap. Its padded brocade was couched with a fire-breathing beast with hooves of smoke and antlers of fire, but what had once been vivid bronze flames had faded to the pale yellow of old butter.

'Chinese,' she said. 'Your father's love for things from faraway places,' she said, casting a look at Nat the foreigner. 'That's what took him to Baku. That's what killed him in the end, and why he died so faraway. Your father didn't want to be an agent for the oil merchants. He wanted to strike out on his own and so he fetched his own oil from Baku, and sold this Azeri oil in the bazaar, from the same stall where your bookstall is now - and that's why you are by the tinsmiths! On his first trip to Baku, I sent away your father as a boy and he came back a man. But the next trip he went away a young man and came back old.'

'Was that was the trip I went with him on?' asked Darius

piped up.

Kulsum nodded. Nat's heart sank to hear what happened to the last man to go with Darius on an oil expedition. Perhaps it wasn't the road but his son that did for the old man.

'Well, never fear,' Darius told his grandmother, 'we're not going nearly so far as Baku, only to Masjid-i Suleiman. Just a few days there and back. I've told Nat-jan all about the oil pools under the fire temples.'

'Be careful, Nat-jan,' said Kulsum. 'He sees what he wants to see, hears what he wants to hear.'

'Why didn't my father take me with him on his last trip? I could have looked after him.'

'He didn't want you to know how sick he was. He didn't want you to see him weak and struggling. And he wanted you to be schooled and to study so you wouldn't have to haul Azeri oil all your life. I told him he was too weak to go, but he wouldn't listen. I was so angry, I sent him away without my blessing. He died out on the road. Some dervishes buried him with all correct observance. Folk speak ill of the dervish but they buried your father right, remember that. They brought all this metal home, too. I keep friends with the dervishes. I always have victuals and a little drink for them when they pass here on their way up to the mountains. God knows there's enough people hate them already.'

'When we come back we will be rich, *mumuny*, rich enough to pay builders to throw up a house beside yours for Gol and I to live in.'

'Oh, my lamb, you do not know where the dream world ends and the real world begins.'

Over the next hour, she packed their provisions. She filled the young men's saddle pouches with parcels of cheese, flatbread and dried apricots. She slipped a raw mutton fillet under the saddle of the sooty buckskin. Tenderised under the saddle, she explained, salted and cured by the mule's sweaty back, this would be safe to eat without cooking should their tinder be lost or soaked, leaving them without the means to make a fire.

She lit a yard fire and set a bunch of rue to grill. When it began to smoke, she banged the flower heads in her hand. The rue at once disintegrated into ash in her palm. Cupping the pile of ash, she blew these flakes of rue first over Darius's head and face and then over Nat's.

'This is the blessing I never gave your father.' She whispered some lines of Hafiz:

> *Smoke of rue guard thee!*
> *A cloak of honour*
> *And a saddled steed I send thee,*
> *Constant comrade of my heart.*

Darius and Nat rode out of the gate and onto the road. Darius led the way on his chestnut mule, towing behind him the three panniered donkeys, looped together by the one long rope, and Nat brought up the rear on his sooty buckskin.

'We're doing it,' exclaimed Darius, 'we're really doing it!'

10

At the maidan, Nat and Darius dismounted and led their convoy past the hessian awnings of market stalls and livestock corrals. Before they saw the prisoner, they heard his screams.

The zealous red-sashed Qizilbash were parading a youth bound to the back of a mule through the maidan. Stripped to the waist, hands tied behind his back, the young prisoner had two flaming torches sticking out of the tops of his shoulders.

'Sweet Jesus, let the boy die quickly,' Nat prayed, wondering how deep the Qizilbash must have gouged to make the flaming brands stand up.

'What have you done to him?' cried a stallholder.

'A thief,' the captain of the Qizilbash declared. Half in delirium, the youth cried out:

'Help me, brothers! All I took was a little lamp oil and a lamp!'

Market traders rounded on the Qizilbash:

'A lamp?' cried one and all. *'You do this for a little lamp oil and a lamp? This torture for a lamp? A poor pilferer! Look at him! A boy so skinny deserves alms, not fire.'*

'What if it had been your lamps?' retorted the Qizilbash captain sagely. 'What then?'

A small object struck the ground with a clank. A tin lamp. A second clank was heard, then a third. One after another, the merchants began throwing lamps and lanterns at the red-fringed boots of the Qizilbash. More and more oil lanterns not worth a man's life crashed to the ground, some burst into flames on landing.

The Qizilbash put their hands on their dagger hilts. Once they had been the royal bodyguards - until ousted by the Tofangchi, orphan spawn of foreign slaves - and must they now endure pedlars' and traders' scorn? The next second merchants and Qizilbash were at daggers drawn. It looked like there would be blood. But then a hideous cry pierced the air, a cry so extreme that everyone stared at the prisoner.

The mule carrying the prisoner had bucked, dislodging from the torch's cup a burning gobbet of flaming pitch which landed on the open wound of the youth's shoulder. His scream of agony utterly silenced everyone who heard it. The Qizilbash seized the moment when everyone else was suspended in shock and horror to hurry the prisoner out of the maidan.

Nat turned to find Darius with both hands clamped over his eyes, the mule's reins in the dirt.

'You can open your eyes now,' he told him, but Darius did not move, or give any sign that he had even heard him speak. Nat placed the mule's reins in his palm, and said: 'You're facing the West Gate now, which is about five lengths away. Hold these reins and follow me.'

Nat led the convoy out of the maidan's bright sunlight into the dark archway of the city gatehouse. Too late he realised that they had walked straight into danger. As his eyes adjusted to the gatehouse gloom he saw that they were alone with the Qizilbash, who spun round at their approach. The lantern thief was hanging halfway up the wall. But not by his neck, the Qizilbash had ganched him on an iron hook which stuck out from his ribs. The torchlight from his shoulders illuminated the dark arch and cast flickering shadows on the dead boy. When Nat looked down he found a row of Qizilbash staring at him, their eyes aglow with reflected torchlight. In a voice that echoed round the vaulted stone, the Qizilbash captain declared:

'A warning to thieves!'

Nat stared in dumb terror at the Qizilbash. He couldn't reply. If he did they'd want to know why a foreigner was in disguise, and their great oil expedition would end right here at the city gates. Nat had led them into disaster and capture. But then he felt a hand on his shoulder and to his astonishment he heard Darius reply to the Qizilbash captain in a strong, clear voice:

'Let wrongdoers beware! None shall escape justice, for there is no hiding-place from God!'

The Qizilbash captain, grateful to be so vindicated, wished God's blessing upon their journey, before leading his men out of the gatehouse.

Long after the Qizilbash had gone, Nat and Darius were unable to move.

'Is he dead yet?' whispered Darius, looking at the stone paving between his new brown boots.

'Yes.'

'Thank God.'

Nat looked up. Molten pitch dripped onto the dead youth's naked chest, peeling his flesh into petal-shapes. For a long time, they stood there, heads bowed, pilgrims at a shrine, their packsaddles full of stolen money, below the body of the boy who had stolen a little oil and a lamp.

❖

The hooves of their mules and donkeys clattered and scraped slowly over the stone flags, as they emerged from the West Gate onto the broad, flat road. Nat felt exposed on this open road, and continually twisted in the packsaddle, sure that he would soon hear the thundering hooves of Sir Anthony's horse.

'This way,' said Darius, tapping his heel into the mule's right flank, leading them off the road into a lane of orchards. They rode a hidden track that ran parallel to the road through fig, apricot, almond and lemon orchards, and which opened out at last to waving barley fields under a great domed sky of duck-egg blue.

11

Three days' ride from Isfahan they came to a strange landscape where barren shale stretched either side of a thin ribbon of vegetation. An almost straight line divided the green ribbon from the bleak, rocky wilderness all around, the sudden snap between the living and the dead. The green ribbon, explained Darius, followed a subterranean stream. It seemed to Nat that the effects of an underground stream were more spectacular than an overground one. He was amazed to find such wild profusion, such colour against the grey rocks. Within this narrow ribbon were spiky, orange foxtail lilies as tall as his mule, crocuses the colour of peeled apples, lush purple vetches, and blue irises, all buzzing, clicking and chirping with bees, bugs and birds.

The subterranean stream put Nat in mind of the River Walbrook, and of its peculiar connection with where they were now headed.

'The Romans built a Temple of Mithras on the east bank of London's River Walbrook,' he told Darius as they rode along. 'The spot where the Temple once stood is marked by a foundation stone, a huge boulder called the London Stone. Hard to imagine there was ever Roman fire worship there, in fact it's hard even to imagine there was ever a river there. The Walbrook is either bricked over or else it's a stinking trench, or open sewer filled with -'

'None of that at any time at all.'

They heard a babbling sound where the underground stream

bubbled overground and ran as a bright, clear brook. As the mules dipped their heads in to drink, Nat turned in the saddle to ask Darius,

'Who was Mithras?'

'The Zoroastrians believed he was a Saviour sent to lead them out of darkness into light. Mithras's birth fulfiled a prophecy. Three Magi followed a star to where Mithras was born to a virgin on the day of the winter solstice.'

'That's December 25th, the same birthday as Christ!'

'Really? Mithras was about three hundred years earlier. There is no such thing as a virgin birth, of course, but the Zoroastrians believed that Mithras was the Son of God, and that his father, Ahura Mazda, was the God of Light, and that is why their day for worship is not Friday as with us, but Sunday, the day of the sun. At the end of his life, Mithras had a final supper with twelve of his disciples, each representing, you see, the twelve signs of the zodiac. This is the primitive way in which our ancestors thought. When Mithras died, they buried him in a *gurabe,* a tomb-dome, with a great rock blocking the entrance, but then the strangest thing happened -'

Nat interrupted:

'When after three days they came to roll the rock away there was nobody there.'

'Why, yes,' exclaimed Darius in surprise. 'That's exactly how the fable ends. Did I tell you the tale already?'

'No, not you.'

'Someone else, then?'

'You could say that. Yes. Someone else.'

Behind the sardonic reply, however, Nat was troubled. If Mithras lived and died three-hundred years before Jesus, where did that leave the Gospels? In the same way that playhouses might blow the dust off an old

Florentine play and set it on the Isle of Dogs instead, changing the hero from duke to shoemaker, had the gospellers just given an old story a new setting, shifting the scene from Persia to Palestine, changing the hero from sun god to carpenter? Nat began to fear Mithras. If this pagan godhead could strike at a man's faith, then could it not strike at his life?

He filled his water bottle at the stream, gulped half and offered the rest to Darius, who shook his head. Nat wiped the bottle mouth with the flat of his palm, and offered it again. Still no joy. Nat tried a third time, only this time, to accommodate his friend's fastidiousness, he made a great show of not just wiping his hands thoroughly under his own armpits, but then of drying them on a patch of turf that he had selected - and he hoped Darius appreciated this – for its being only very lightly covered in sheep and rabbit droppings. Having taken these elaborate pains, Nat then ran his finger round and round the bottle mouth until it was finally squeaky clean and ready for his lordship. Yet still, to Nat's amazement, Darius waved it away with one of his faces, then unwound the long strap on his own leather bottle and dropped it into the stream instead. There was no pleasing some people, thought Nat, and swigged the rest of his bottle himself. The water tasted pure to him at least.

❖

The green ribbon among shale gave way to forested slopes of larch, pine and cedar, as the winding path rose towards a nick between two peaks in the Zagros foothills. The mules' heads swayed as they climbed, and the nodding donkeys sent a ripple running up and down the single rope that bound them.

As they rounded a corner, they were suddenly able to see in vast panorama all the territory that they had covered over the last couple of days. Darius dismounted the better to look back at the way they had come. He wedged his hands into the coat pockets of his balding black velvet coat. This took a little time, since the pockets were too small for his hands. When he'd finally stuffed his hands in up to the wrists, he leaned his back against the twitching shoulder of his chestnut mule, which was chomping at a patch of arum thistles, and gazed out over the vast plain, where a silver river wound between unwalled villages, and where fields and woods lay open to the sky.

'Look at all that beauty and harmony,' he said. 'It takes a lot of work by some dedicated men to make this world unjust.'

The chestnut mule stepped away and he fell flat on his back. Lying among the thistles, Darius stared up at the sky, blinking away the spots in his eyes. He freed first one hand then the other from his coat pockets. He rolled onto his belly, and very slowly climbed to his feet. He yanked the chestnut mule away from a fresh patch of arum, and listened to the intensely irritating sound of Nat's laughter echoing down the mountain.

12

It was dusk when Nat and Darius crossed the snow line. The snow creaked under their boots as they led their mules and donkeys up the mountain. A recent snowfall had subtracted any scent of nature from the air. The only smells left in the world were dusty saddlecloth and the soupy odour that steamed from the mules' nostrils.

When the path curled round the dark side of the mountain, they ran headlong into a cruel cold wind. Hardier travellers might have pressed on and made the Zagros pass before nightfall, but the wind sliced like a razor's edge, their boots were wet, and their hide gloves were packed right at the bottom of their baggage. Their hearts leapt when they came upon the ramshackle lean-to of a shepherd's shelter.

Three walls of the shelter were the folds of the rock itself. The door and the sloping roof were made of mouldering timber covered with tarry sackcloth. Inside there was only enough room for the two of them plus the mules and packsaddles.

Nat led the donkeys behind a boulder out of the wind, and tethered them beside a red dogwood bush.

Nat and Darius stowed all the equipment save the packsaddles behind the boulder, and spread the tarpaulin that had served for their tent over their supplies. Nat used the other end of the donkeys' tether rope to secure the tarpaulin. He hammered a stake into the earth at every turn of the rope. When his fingers grew too cold to close over the hammer's shaft, he held its handle between the heels of both hands. He bashed the final stakes into the ground and at last the tarpaulin was lashed down over their gear and supplies, bound fast by the rope that crisscrossed over the mound as tight as a corset.

Emerging from behind the shelter of the rock, he fought the wind for breath as he ran back to the lean-to, where he held his hands to the yellow flames under the oil stove that Darius had got going.

Darius lit his father's oil lantern at the stove and set it on a natural shelf in the smooth, rippling rock wall. His grandmother had filled a jar with *ghormeh sabzi,* his favourite bean stew. He emptied the jar into the pot. As the stew popped and sputtered, the shack's odour of musty sackcloth and rotting timber was infused with delicious aromas of coriander, goat cheese, parsley, spinach and sorrel. He served their stew on two battered tin plates, and they sat down to their first hot meal of the expedition.

As the light flickered over three brass flames embossed on the lantern's bulbous reservoir bowl, Darius had a moment of perfect happiness. The next moment Nat began speaking with his mouth full.

'They look like three moneybags,' said Nat, pointing some half-chewed flatbread at the lantern's brass motif.

'Not money, flames. It's the Baku city symbol. Three flames. Baku is where my father showed me cold fire.'

'Cold fire?' asked Nat.

'Fire that's cold and harmless to the touch.'

'Then not fire.'

'You leave your hand there for a quarter of an hour and you'll think it fire, for it will slowly cook your hand.'

To cover the noise of Nat's eating, Darius decided to tell him the story of when he discovered the cold fire of Baku.

'We were in a field where my father dug down a knife's length, and held a live coal over the divot. A blue flame leapt from the earth, like a pike jumping for meat. The next thing I knew my father had put his hand into the blue fire, and was telling me to do the same.'

'Did it hurt?'

'No, it was like the flame of spirits of alcohol which you can extinguish with your hand because it never rises beyond a certain heat.'

'You have to dig down to get this cold fire?' asked Nat, as the buckskin mule's long, bristly lips snaffled flatbread from his palm.

'Not always. Once I saw tiny blue flames sprinkled all over the plain like gentians.'

'Then what's to stop the wild fire spreading and setting the whole country ablaze? Why isn't the plain burnt black? '

'This Baku fire is so cold and gentle that the Azeris balance their pots on hollow bamboo canes stuck in the soil. The pot boils but the canes don't catch fire. Listen to this, my father took me to the fire temple there, where they had two paper cylinders conducting fire-'

'*Paper?* Are you sure?'

'Paper - as I am sitting here now.'

'How old were you?'

'Nine or ten.'

'If this cold and gentle fire feeds only on itself, then put your hand in that flame.'

'What?'

'This lamp is from Baku, so open the glass and put your hand in the cold yellow flame.'

'No, no, no, I filled this lantern myself with plain old rock oil. If you want a lantern that burns cold fire, you can find men who have the skill of dissolving the sulphurous oil vapours of the plain into lanterns.'

Nat was halfway through licking his tin plate clean, when he heard the word sulphur.

'*Sulphur?* Why, Darius, this is marsh vapour, not fire! This is Will o' the Wisp, the Lantern Man!'

'Who?'

'In English marshes, fools see a man with a lantern beckoning them, when it's only sulphur flares. On dark nights, the Lantern Man leads these fools to their deaths in sinking sands or black ponds.'

'If I had not seen it for myself, I would not believe cold fire any more than -'

'Oh, God in heaven help us!' Nat burst out. 'Our saddles are packed with fishing-nets for the moon!'

He was angry. This was a fool's errand. He remembered Kulsum's words of warning about how her grandson only saw what he wanted to see, how he didn't know where the real world ended and his dream world began. Perhaps it wasn't too late to go back to Isfahan and throw himself on Sir Anthony's mercy and beg forgiveness?

'Calm yourself,' said Darius. 'We're not going to Baku for its cold fire, we're going to Masjid-i Suleiman for its oil.'

'How will we even know the fire temple when we see it?' raged Nat.

'The temple is a tower by a statue of Mithras, who has the head of a man and the body of a bird with outstretched wings.'

'But if the mullahs have defaced the icons then the fire temple will look like any old lime kiln and we'll ride right past it into oblivion.'

'Great fountains of oil gushing into the sky - that, my friend, is how we shall know the place! And look, we do not have fishing nets for moonshine - we have this gorgeous piece of engineering!'

Darius produced from the saddle-pouch a block and tackle. It was indeed gorgeous. The whole maple slab was the weight, shape and size of a Geneva Bible. A maple metal book with spinning parts! Nat clapped his palm voluptuously upon its cover. The steel wheel was grooved for rope. He spun the wheel and listened to its smooth, well-balanced whir. Maybe Darius did know what he was doing.

'All right, Darius. I suppose oil is in your blood, after all.'

Darius announced that they'd commemorate the return of Nat's faith in their oil venture with a pot of jasmine tea. He searched the saddle-pouch, found a cotton bag, opened it, sniffed and cried out in disgust.

'Oh no, she's given us these foul grinds of bitter beans! My grandmother drinks *qaveh*, this muddy bean drink the Arabs and Turks drink.'

Nat was curious, and so he prepared a pot and put it on the little oil-stove.

The charred odour the *qaveh* released as it came to the boil carried Nat back to the Sherley party's journey through the Ottoman Empire, when Nat had first smelt *qaveh* - or as the Turks called it *kaveh*. But he had yet to taste it. This would be his first time.

He poured a measure into a tin cup, and took a sip, and then another. Each swallow revealed new tastes: now earthy, now metallic, now nutty. He didn't know what Darius was on about: it wasn't bitter at all. Well, only the sandy lees were bitter, only on his last swig did he pull the face that Darius had pulled on his first.

'How much do we have?' he asked.

'Have it all,' said Darius, dropping torn orange peel into his cup to sweeten or disguise the foul taste.

Still in hats and coats, they wrapped themselves up in their blankets, set their necks comfortably on their saddlebags. Darius extinguished the Baku lantern, and they lay side by side in the pitch-black. Outside the wind howled and hooted, sending the odd shower of mud and stones clattering onto the roof. Darius asked:

'How did you first fall into Antonio's service?'

'I was living with my uncle,' replied Nat, 'a master tailor who was suiting two gentlemen of the Sherley party. They told him Sir Anthony needed a literate servant for his mission to Tuscany. I thought we were only going as far as Tuscany. Not Isfahan!'

'What was his mission?'

'To raise hell. His cousin the Earl of Essex, England's commander-in-chief, sent him to set Spain's Italian territories ablaze. The thinking was that the Spanish could not invade our island if they were busy fighting wars and putting down insurrections in Italy. Anthony was supposed to ally himself with Tuscan rebels, but by the time we got to Italy, they'd already surrendered to the Pope. Then a Venetian senator told Anthony that Shah Abbas needed a good soldier to help him liberate Ormuz from the Portuguese.'

'Why were you living with your uncle?'

'My father and mother died.'

'How did they die?'

'There was a famine in Datchworth, the village where we lived.'

'They starved to death?'

'Not exactly. They both died of the bloody flux, the dysentery which comes from eating nothing but boiled tussock grass and rotten barleycorn.'

'You buried them?'

'No. My parents sent me away from Datchworth in the middle of the second summer of rain, when the stewards and bailiffs were fencing in the woods and commons, and when my school classmates were dying. Seemed adults could survive on pigeon-pie, rye bread and rosehips, but not children.'

'Hard to believe a parent is dead and buried,' said Darius, 'if you

weren't there when they were dying, isn't it? If you never saw the body.
Never went to the funeral - if there even was one.'

'Yes. Hard. We have this in common, you and I. And the other
thing I found it hard to fathom was how there could be a famine only half
a day's ride from London, which is what Datchworth is. In London Bridge
corn mills, down on the meal floor, you have to walk to the water's edge
just to be free of the flour clouds. There I was under London Bridge choking from a superflux of grain, while out in the country the want of grain
was death. Down on the meal floor, lost in a wheat mist, I used to rage and
weep. Still, away from the corn mills I was content enough, because I was
learning.'

'Tailoring?'

'No, school. My uncle had sons enough, all trained to the craft, so
I wasn't needed to apprentice, which left me free to go to school almost
every day.'

The wind scattered more rocks or clods on the path outside. Nat
stilled his breathing. Reading his thoughts, Darius said:

'Antonio could not have followed you so far.'

'No,' said Nat, but even so he listened a few seconds more.

'What will he do if he catches you?'

'At least as bad as what he and Eli Elkin did to the Italian boy on
the ship we set sail in. They gave him the *bastinado,* broke both his arms.'

From Darius's sharp intake of breath, Nat could clearly imagine
the way he was wincing in the dark.

'But why did they do that?' asked Darius.

Nat told Darius how the Sherley party set sail from Venice for the
Levant on the *Nana e Ruzzina,* a ship they shared with seventy other paying
passengers, all of whom had packed three weeks' worth of food and drink
for the voyage. But not Sir Anthony. Oh no. He reckoned it was only a few

days' sail to Zakinthos, the ship's first port of call, and so ordered Nat and the other servants to pack only a few days' worth of food. First, Adriatic headwinds slowed the *Nana e Ruzzina*, and then the Mediterranean becalmed her. When they ran out of food, the gentlemen of the party devoured the servants' rations.

At the foot of the mast, under the flapping of the bark's only sail, Nat sat down and awaited the bloody flux. It had found him out. A man could wriggle and wriggle but never escape his fate. He had escaped Famine in Datchworth, only for Famine to find him in the Mediterranean. The bloody flux might have come, too, had it not been for one of the lower servants sharing food, and striking up friendships with Armenian servants from whom they cadged a little halva and kofte.

Soon even Sir Anthony himself was starving. Yet even when they were down to the last drops of stagnant rainwater from the butt, he still stood upon ceremony. He bid Nat pour the brackish dregs into a silver flask which was set upon a silver salver, before he stood up, proposed a toast to his cousin the Earl of Essex's victories against Papists, bowed to Robert Sherley, received his brother's bow in return, and together they knocked back the last of the rainwater. It was well done. But now even the water butt was empty. A mask of rage settled on Anthony's red-bearded face. And then the Neapolitans started mocking him.

There was a wood-burning stove against the wheel house, where some Neapolitans dined *al fresco* three times a day. They refused to sell a morsel to the English nobles, no matter how many jewelled rings the Sherleys pulled off their fingers. Mocking the Englishmen's hunger was too fine a sport to sell for any price. The Neapolitans wafted cooking odours towards the starving heretics, scraped leftovers into the sea for the birds, and threw sucked trotters at the starving Sherley retinue.

As the sun flared off the empty silver flask, Anthony heard from

Angelo that one of the Neapolitans had said that Queen Elizabeth was a man. That was all it took. Anthony prized open his parched and cracked lips and commanded Eli Elkin to find the slanderer. Elkin dragged the Neapolitan by the hair to the English end of the deck, where Anthony told him to administer the *bastinado*. Elkin set to work with his billy club. Anthony stood over him, as intent as a hunter signalling his dog into the brush, his pop-eyes rapt with the most terrible glee. Elkin broke both the Neapolitan's arms to stop him protecting his head. Then blood burst from his eyes, nose, mouth and ears. Once Elkin had begun flaying the slanderer he couldn't stop. He slathered at the mouth. All this fury even though he had no quarrel with the Neapolitan himself. But his dander was up. Eventually the English gentlemen themselves had to pull Elkin off him, and when they did, he thrashed his head like a dog pulled off a bear.

The young Neapolitan, his bones broken, howled so terribly that the crew and the passengers all came running. They squared up to the Sherley party. Anthony, Robert, and Angelo drew swords. A huge expanse of decking suddenly appeared. Into this gap stepped three Armenian merchants, entreating peace in a five-tongue pidgin: Farsi, Napolitano, English, Veneto, and Spanish, and offered food to the Sherley party. Everyone sheathed swords. There it might have ended. But the furious captain of the *Nana e Ruzzina* marched up to Sir Anthony, and demanded to know how any passenger dare meddle with his authority. Sir Anthony listened to Angelo's translation, nodding along, now and then asking his interpreter to clarify a nuance. When Angelo had satisfied him on all points, Anthony hauled off and punched the captain smack in the mouth. Eyes wide with disbelief, the captain spat out a tooth, and launched into a furious tirade, none of which Angelo translated.

While he was shouting, however, a wind arose, the sails filled and the ship creaked into life and made headway. Later that same day the

Nana anchored in the roadstead off Zakinthos harbour. The Sherley suite rowed ashore and went inland to stock up on food and drink for the next leg of the journey. But when they arrived back at the harbour they found their belongings stacked on the quayside, and the boat they'd rowed ashore in hanging from the side of the *Nana*. The captain had dumped them off his ship, bag and baggage. Well, Anthony wasn't going to stand for that, of course. It was an outrage. Breach of contract. Nat rowed a hired skiff back to the *Nana*, with Sir Anthony standing in the prow like a figurehead. As they drew near, the purple-mouthed captain trained two shiny black cannons upon the skiff. They could hear him shouting as he dangled a lit taper over one of the cannons' wicks.

'What does he want, Angelo?' asked Sir Anthony.

'He vows before God, Sir Anthony,' replied the Venetian, in as calm a voice as he could muster, 'that he will sink your boat before letting you on board his ship again.'

'Be pleased to remind him, that I have paid passage as far as the Levant, and we are not yet halfway there.'

The next thing Nat heard was a cannon boom. The cannonball sent a single high wave over their bows like the lick of a sea-monster's tongue. Nat let go of the oars in fright. The skiff rocked. Ears ringing, he ran his hands over his body, fearing he was drenched in blood, but it was only sea water. Sir Anthony's wet hair hung in a lank centre parting like a Puritan, and his beard shone with silver droplets. The blue jellyfish of his hat floated in the sea beside them. He told Nat to turn the boat round.

When the Sherley party finally arrived in the Levant, by way of another ship, there was more trouble, and it was this trouble which led to Nat being taught Persian. What happened was that Anthony's letter of complaint to the Ottoman governor about having to pay port charges was so high-handed that Angelo, its bearer, was clapped in irons for months.

That was when Anthony set Angelo's doomed manservant Hesam to teach Nat Persian.

'Sir Anthony wanted me to learn Persian in case Angelo was killed,' said Nat in the pitch black mountainside hut. 'But it was poor Hesam who was killed. He was always an anxious little fellow. The only time I ever saw him happy and at ease was when he was reunited with his family at the Shah's revels. Seconds later, the Shah noticed Hesam's Venetian doublet and stabbed him through its side-panel's laces. Thought he'd turned renegade. Hesam couldn't help how Angelo dressed him. He had no say in the matter. That's what comes of having no say. You end up dead. The worst of it, Darius, was when the Shah hung his arm around Anthony's neck - they were both a bit drunk - and said, "Sorry I killed your servant. Only I thought he'd turned Christian because of how he was dressed, do you see?"'

'And what did your master say?'

'"No, no, still one of your own. Can't be helped. No good crying over it."'

'God save us from powerful men.'

'Amen.'

'Good night, my friend.'

'Good night.'

13

A grey dawn strained through the sieve of the shelter's rotten wood and torn sacking. Darius stepped carefully over the sleeping mounds of man and beast, and out the door. The wind had dropped. The mountain air was cold and silent. He stood between the boulder and the dogwood bush. The equipment and the donkeys were gone. He walked to the ledge and looked down.

Strewn down the mountainside were three blood-soaked donkeys and all his father's gear. The sun, which had yet to reach him, glinted cruelly off the wreckage far below. There were the flattened zinc tureens. There were the smashed wicker panniers. There was the rope ladder, still coiled, yet utterly irretrievable since the drop was sheer. A long thin strip of purple cotton had snagged on an undershrub and unravelled its whole length, leaving the hatchet dangling like a bucket in a well. The hatchet's blade flashed in the sunlight as it twisted in the wind.

What had caused this tragedy? In seeking to escape the wind the donkeys must have burrowed into the clumpy red dogwood bush. But the dogwood hung over the cliff and the donkeys fell clean through. Bound by a single rope, each donkey had been tugged over the rocky ledge one by one, like worry beads. Their drop-weight had uprooted all the pegs, pulling all the oil-mining gear down the side of the mountain.

Darius looked at the surrounding mountain range with fear. The mountains wanted rid of them. The peak across the valley cast a chilly grey shadow upon him.

'That a donkey seeking shelter in a bush,' he thought, 'can destroy two men! What are we going to do now? What are we going to do now?'

He heard sobbing. Nat was squatting on his heels, hands in his hair, tears rolling down his face. Darius bit his tongue to keep from saying, 'Why did you use the same rope for everything?' But the sight of Nat's grief gave Darius the one thing he most needed at that moment, an answer to the unbearable questions going round and round his head. 'What are we going to do now? Where do we go from here?' Looking at his friend everything became very simple. Nat had no way back, so they must go forward. Darius pulled the mules out of the shelter and saddled up.

Riding on towards the Temple of Mithras at Masjid-i Suleiman, every creak of the packsaddle seemed to say, *You are doomed, you are doomed, you are doomed.* Each print of his mule's hooves called to Darius' mind the man Nat saw step into a tar bog at the Doors of Hell, each step sinking him deeper and deeper into the tar mire. Yet to turn tail now would only lead to bad, because it meant enjoining with negation, and only bad ever came of that. To ride on was to enjoin with good, and when you did that, then good might follow. It might not. But it might.

He remembered that Gol once told him the sparks produced by the clash of words and melody in Rumi's twelfth *ruba'ie* were almost magic in their power to steel the heart. Under his breath he began to growl its refrain,, *Afsous ke bi-gah shod-o ma tanha.*

> *Alas, we are lost upon a black sea!*
> *The stars be hid that led us to this woe.*
> *The coast has strayed, steering by clouds we sail,*
> *Only God's grace may bring us home again.*

Steering by clouds was better than turning back, and it was better than drifting around. So long as he rode on towards Masjid-i Suleiman, there was a rightness to the sound of the packsaddle creaking under the sway of his portly frame, and a rightness to the morning sunlight glinting off the bridle bits.

Over and over Darius growled Rumi's song of the lost sailors. With each round he hissed the lyrics a little less and sang them a little more. And soon Nat was riding alongside him, singing too.

14

By noon they reached the Karun River. The cable ferry, a small wooden platform, could not fit them all in one go, but could only carry the expedition in three batches: first Darius, then the two mules, and then Nat.

The barefoot, white-haired ferryman hauled Darius across the river. The cable ferry's wooden platform was buoyed by six inflated goatskins and wobbled with his weight. Darius was relieved to step off the platform onto the bank. A wooden cogwheel squeaked as the ferryman wound the cable ferry back across the river to the east bank, where Nat herded the mules onto the platform. With trepidation, Darius watched the mules cross the water. How small a slip might do for them just as it had done for the donkeys!

The platform wobbled each time the ferryman hauled on the cable. The chestnut and the buckskin hung their heads in the middle of the river. Powerlessness made the mules dejected. They knew that the weight of the packsaddles on their backs would drown them if their hooves slipped on the muddy planks.

The ferryman led the mules safely onto the bank. Before he wound the ferry back across the river, Darius had him haul the raft up onto the reeds and grasses of the riverbank, for a brilliant idea was forming in his brain, and he was curious to know more about the inflated goatskins.

'How do you get the air in?' he asked, running his hands all over the tough, tight hide. The ferryman showed him a leather-headed cork stopper under a tented flap of hide.

'Ingenious,' said Darius, slapping the side of a bulbous inflated goatskin. 'Most ingenious.' Hearing a shout from the far riverbank, he noticed Nat hopping up and down like a primitive barbarian on the coast of a savage island, but was too engrossed to pay him any mind. If the goatskins kept water out, he was thinking, running his fingers through the beginnings of a black beard, would they keep oil in?

'How much?' he asked the ferryman.

'What?'

'How much for all six?'

'No, I cannot sell them,' laughed the ferryman. 'If I sell them then how shall I ever live?'

'Twenty silver abbassi!'

'No,' said the ferryman, shaking his head at the exorbitant sum. 'I might eat like Shah Abbas for a month, but then my wife and I would starve. And all the good people who use the ferry would hate me as well.'

'Nails,' said Darius, coming back from a saddle pouch and unfolding before the ferryman a cotton square upon which lay brand new clout-head nails of shiny brass. 'With these nails you could widen your raft so much so that you wouldn't need the goatskins in the first place. All these nails for the six goatskins! '

Nails were another proposition altogether.

'Why, there's enough here to widen the raft *and* add another room on my house!' exclaimed the ferryman. 'But why do you need the goatskins so badly that you will offer a bag of nails for them?'

Darius told him about the disaster that had befallen them on the Zagros Mountains, and about their expedition to fetch oil from the tar pits of Masjid-i Suleiman.

'Is your friend all right?' asked the ferryman. Darius cast an eye over at the far bank, where Nat was jumping up and down.

'Yes, he's merry.'

'He looks angry.'

'He is from a distant land. I believe that's one of his native dances. These goatskins are perfect for transporting oil.'

The ferryman fetched out his wife.

'With this many nails,' he told her, 'I could build a raft as wide as the floor of a house and winch over a flock of sheep in one go as easy as wind a bobbin up.'

'Why a cable at all?' she replied. 'You'd have a punt so stable you could pole it across the Karun. You could do that until you're ninety!'

'I can show you better yet,' broke in Darius, 'if you'll help me drag this log out the reeds and allow me a couple of your new nails.'

Darius nailed the rotten log to two spars of cordwood so that it ran parallel to the raft.

'A book in my possession in Isfahan,' he explained, 'contains precise diagrams of the Catamarans of Tamil Nadu. This second hull -'

'The log?' asked the ferryman's wife.

'Just so. The log forms a second hull which is the very copy of the latest boats to ply the Bay of Bengal, living proof of Ibn Senna's law that the larger the surface area the greater the weight that may be carried.'

They carried the catamaran down to the river, and set it on the water. It floated a little higher on the raft side than the log-side. The ferryman and his wife hauled the cable, and the cogwheel turned, winding the catamaran across the river to the far bank. Darius watched Nat walk down to the water's edge and study the catamaran up close. He then appeared to be kicking up clouds of dust and stones, while shouting indistinctly.

'What's he doing?' asked the ferryman's wife.

'That is a dance his people do,' said Darius. 'It's called *Dance of*

Welcome for a New Boat.'

'But what's he shouting?' asked the ferryman.

'Song Of Joy For New Boat.'

'Why doesn't he step on?'

'He's just about to. Look, he's aboard. Let's heave away! Let's haul him ashore.'

Hand over hand they all three pulled the cable, drawing the catamaran from the far bank out into the river. When the catamaran reached the middle of the river it tipped sharply to one side. The waterlogged log was sinking and dragging the whole craft under. Nat climbed to the apex of the sinking ferry platform. In shame, Darius turned to the ferryman:

'I apologise with all my heart,' he told him, 'for sinking the cable ferry upon which your livelihood depends.'

'Can your friend swim?' asked the ferryman.

Nat was perched on the very last triangle of dry wood, which poked out of the water like a shark's fin. As they reeled him in, Nat wobbled at every pull of the rope, yet somehow kept his footing on the apex.

'Why, he's like a bird on a cherry twig!' exclaimed the ferryman.

Nat leapt from the raft - sinking it utterly with his leap - to land upon the bank on his ribs. He lay curled up and winded, gasping for breath. The ferryman pulled Nat to his feet.

'What balance!' he exclaimed. 'Your feet are not even wet, master! How did you do that? Even a slack-wire walker would have fallen into the river, but not you, master, not you! Heh-heh!'

Darius tried to help him up, but Nat snatched his arm away.

'I'm not talking to you,' he snarled.

The ferryman and his wife hauled on the cable, raising the wreck of the raft and dragging it up onto the grassy bank. The log had dropped off, but the two spars of cordwood to which the log had been attached still protruded from the side of the platform.

The expeditioners were invited inside for lemon tea and *pashmak,* a sweetmeat that looked and tasted like sugared wool.

'Now here's what I don't understand,' said the ferryman's wife. 'If you have money already then why choose this wild venture? Why put yourself through all this hard slog?'

Nat's jaw froze mid-chew, and Darius slowly set down his tea. The ferryman's wife had asked the one question that went right to the heart of their crooked endeavour, and which lay a hair's breadth away from exposing them both for the embezzlers they were. She and her husband awaited a reply, and were looking from Darius to Nat. At last Nat managed a reply:

'My friend Darius is performing this quest for the hand of a beautiful woman, a musician called Gol. She has set him the task of fetching oil from this fire temple so as to show all the world that he is not the fat, empty windbag, the great big hollow greasy sack of lies, cowardice and chicken farts that everyone thinks him to be.'

Touched by the romance of the story, the ferryman and his wife brought out a seventh goatskin, a little older than the rest, to add to the six.

When the ferryman learnt that the nails were to have been used for building a shadoof to hoist buckets of oil to the surface, he insisted that they take back half the shiny new nails they had given him.

'No,' said Darius, 'now we can just lower these goatskins down the well, and hoist them out full of oil.'

'Even with goatskins you'll still need to knock up a shadoof or little jib-crane. Take half the nails.'

'No,' said Darius. 'You will need every last nail if the ferry is not to sink again.'

'Not so many,' said the ferryman. 'Listen, you'll come this way on your return and you can bring back any nail which you can pull out of your shadoof when you're done.'

Feeling unworthy of such trust, Darius nodded his assent and finished his tea in silence.

Their venture rescued, and seven deflated goatskins folded upon their saddlebows, with half the nails back on loan, Nat and Darius made their farewells to the ferryman and his wife, and set off towards the border with the Ottoman Empire.

15

Two days' ride from the Karun River, Nat and Darius came to the River Oraxes, the border between the Ottoman and Persian Empires. The border was unguarded, deserted in fact, since garrisons were placed instead at city gates or crossroads.

The Pul-i-Shah, the Shah's Bridge, with its new style Isfahani architecture and tabletop-flat paving, appeared fantastically out of place in this valley in the middle of nowhere. It looked as if robbers had emptied it out of a bag. There was no other manmade structure in the valley. Just a few bees, oxeye daisies and scrub - and then this projection of political will spanning the River Oraxes. The mules' shod hooves rang upon Pul-I-Shah's paving slabs, before descending the ramp to the Turkish path. Resting a hand on the pommel to ease his saddle sores, Darius turned to Nat.

'Beware,' he said. 'We are entering territory where poetry is forbidden.'

'Why?'

'Sedition,' replied Darius. 'Too many poems by subject peoples seething against the Ottoman yoke. Too many satirical verses about the Sultan has made him ban poetry throughout his empire. And besides, to Turkish ears poetry is too Persian a thing. We are a nation of poets, they are not. Thus, at the River Oraxes, the whimsical thought, the flight of fancy, the heartfelt couplet must be left at the border, for we are in Ottoman territory now.'

The two muleteers ambled past a couple of open villages, and followed a road that skirted a walled town. Up ahead, on a long, straight, dusty road, sat a small stonewalled fort built on the roadside, from which emerged a dusty Turkish soldier about their own age, with a matchlock rifle slung across his back on a white crepe strap.

'Oh no,' said Darius, '*rhadar.*'

Rhadari outposts were placed along the road at strategic junctions. The bushy-haired Turkish *rhadar* walked round their mules and inspected their baggage. When he spoke, his voice was hoarse, probably from drinking and smoking late into the night in the lonely outpost

'Some mangy goatskins, a few coils of rope - where are you going?'

'Masjid-i-Suleiman.'

'What are you?' he asked.

'I am a poet,' said Darius with a grand gesture, 'and this is my companion.'

'Do you have any poetry in your possession now?' demanded the Turk in his cracked voice.

'One can no more own a poem than a snowflake,' said Darius. The Turk thought for a while.

'Was that a poem?' he demanded.

'No.'

'It sounded like a poem.'

'As does the babble of a river singing in the Zagros foothills,' said Darius. 'But we can never stop its song.'

'Yes, we can,' said the Turk.

'How?'

'What about a dam?'

'Yes, you are right. Yes, that will stop the song of the river sure enough.'

'Or ice,' said the Turk.

'How do you mean?'

'Ice silences the river's song.'

'Yes,' said Darius. 'Ice silences the river's song... Is that a poem?'

'No!'

'It sounded like a poem.'

'On your way!'

Tapping their heels on the mules, Darius and Nat rode away from the isolated *rhadar* garrison. They had not ridden far before they heard the Turk shouting after them. They reined their mules to a halt, and twisted round in their saddles.

Standing alone in the road, arms outstretched, the *rhadar*'s powerful hoarse voice called out:

'Listen to the reed flute!

'I beg your pardon?' called Darius.

'Listen to the reed flute! shouted the Turk:

'Grieving its exile, the reed flute says,
Since they cut me off from my bed of reeds,
The sound of my cry.
Tears to shreds,
The heart of any man or woman who hears my song
Far from home.
Hear the reed flute's song within all songs,
I long to return to my bed of reeds.
How shall we ever get home, my friend?
How shall we ever get home?'

The poem was finished but the Turk stayed rooted to the spot.

'*Tashakkur ederim!*' Darius cried out.

'*Dostum,*' bellowed the Turk, raising a hand in farewell.

'*Dostum!*'

'What does *dostum* mean?' asked Nat.

'Friend.'

'*Dostum,*' Nat called back.

They faced forward, tapped their heels on the mules, and rode away from the *rhadar*.

16

In the Ali Qapu Palace, Anthony awoke on his truckle bed. His fever had broken in the night. He listened to his breathing. Slow and steady. Except it had a kind of double sound. Not an echo, but an amplification like a heart murmur or a lung spot. He opened his eyes. The Shah was frowning down on him. In fury. With murder on his mind. Anthony's heart seemed to fall out of his body, and his head swam. The game was up. Queen Elizabeth must have written to the Shah disowning Anthony as an ambassador, exposing him as a fraud. In which case his life was over. He should have died in his sleep, or at the hands of the physicians who had administered strange potions and laid fetid compresses upon him. But then he realised that the Shah wasn't frowning but had shaved off his eyebrows and painted on a thick, menacing black pair. Only his forehead was angry, but the rest of his face was mild, as if it had yet to be told what the forehead had heard. A soft voice emerged from the Shah's small mouth.

'You live, Antonio.'

'Your Majesty has watched over me as he does all his people,' said Anthony.

'You are well again.'

The slow blink of Shah Abbas's hooded green eyes was eerie. He did not blink like a man so much as nictitate like a hawk - or perhaps Anthony still had a touch of fever. Sitting cross-legged on the tapestry cushion, he spoke softly.

'You must appear before my ministers in the *majlis,* my parliament, to tell them the true nature of your embassy.'

'As your majesty commands.'

'Within a very few days, the Turkish ambassador comes here, thinking he can renew the Peace League on the same terms as before. The *majlis* want to renew the Peace League. The army and I do not. The *majlis* will continue to oppose a Turkish war, but they may be swayed when they're convinced that we won't be fighting the Turk alone, but will have as our allies every Christian Prince in Europe.'

'What's it to you what your parliament says? Surely, so great a sovereign as Shah Abbas informs his parliament of his royal will and leaves them to see it done.'

'Merchants' gold is soldiers' pay. Good pay ever won more battles than good luck.'

'And parliament speaks for the merchants...?'

Tilting his head to one side, the Shah's face shone.

'It is incredible how you always know at once the true nature of the situation! Even when you have just come back from the dead you ask the one question that goes to the very heart of the matter.'

'I am pleased your majesty thinks so.'

The Shah beamed.

'You are very crafty, Antonio.'

Anthony attempted a crafty grin, but the truth was he had no idea what any of this was about. He was in the dark every bit as much as the bazaar which the Shah told him had been without oil for days. The merchants were learning that the oil supply wouldn't be safe while the Turk has Tabriz. This had brought a few of them round to supporting at least a limited war,

'Except it wasn't the Turks who raided the Baku convoy, was it?

Everyone says it was Arabs.'

'I believe you will find that not one single witness lived to tell the world just who it was who attacked and killed every last member of the Baku convoy and its escort when they were in a narrow gorge in the Zanjan hills.'

Anthony sensed he was being told something, but what? Was Shah Abbas saying that *he* had ordered the slaughter of the oil caravan? Was he saying that he had created the oil shortage on purpose as a way of convincing the merchants that they would be poorer without a war than with one? Anthony didn't know. He wasn't sure.

He wished he could ask his brother. Sit Robert here now, he'd twig the Shah's meaning in a trice. But to ask his brother to explain the Shah's parables and gnomic sayings would be to lose face. Anthony liked the fact that his brother believed he and the Shah were concocting grand stratagems together, and he liked giving Robert a sense that the time was approaching when he too would be initiated into these stratagems - only not just yet.

How he wished his politicking cousin and closest friend, Robert Devereux, Earl of Essex, whose gold was Anthony's pay, were here to advise him. What would Essex say? He'd say, Listen. Only listen, Anthony. That's what he'd say. Listen to the Shah and make his wants your study. When you become expert in what Shah Abbas desires then you will know what to do. For once, sweet cuz, you will not be my brave headlong soldier, but rather the patient fisherman careful to cast no shadow upon the water. Anthony sipped his little bowl of rose tea and listened to what Abbas was saying, hoping to understand what were the Shah's most pressing needs.

'The merchants' refusal to pay the army the funds it needs to fight the Turk, threatens the survival of my kingdom. I know this. You know this. My commander-in-chief, Allahvirdi Khan, he knows this as well. Only parliament does not.'

There's a pointer right there, whispered Essex. The commander-in-chief. He'll tell you straight out, soldier to soldier, the Shah's meaning. Anthony nodded so vigorously at Essex's wise words that the Shah paused and looked at him quizzically a moment - unless that was the eyebrows too.

'It was written in the stars that you would come to me, Antonio. Twelve years the war against the Uzbegs lasted, and the fact that you arrived in Isfahan on the very day of my victory parade shows the hand of Destiny.'

'I am honoured your majesty believes so,' said Anthony, who believed exactly the same. It was this belief that gave him confidence in his imposture. Providence sent him here. Anthony knew it was fate the moment they stumbled upon the victory parade outside Isfahan, as the glorious, vast, two-hundred-thousand-strong homecoming army flowed around stranded elms and oaks. Sunlight flared from brass instruments that looked like giant knotted trumpets, and sounded like the lowing of lonely sea-monsters, big beasts, just like Anthony and the Shah, whose very greatness made them lonely. Necklaces of hard, dried Uzbeg ears rattled on the breastplates of the royal bodyguard, and it was on this gruesome drumroll that Anthony and the Shah found each other at last.

Outside the windows of his sick room, Anthony heard again the lowing of the sea-monsters, those giant, knotted trumpets.

'What's that noise, great Shah?'

'Festivities to celebrate your return to health await you. I will now give the order for the great spectacle to begin! Come, get up and get dressed. Put this silver taj on your head. Sit on the veranda. Wait. Watch!'

17

Thousands had gathered along the edges of the maidan to behold the games and celebrations in honour of Antonio Mirza's return to the land of the living. Anthony was sat in state upon the palace's veranda, with its mirrored pillars. He was propped up on cushions between his brother Robert and Allahvirdi Khan, the Shah's *sipahsalar* or commander-in-chief, watching buffaloes wrestle. But he found his attention straying to a lone buffalo tethered on the other side of the maidan. Exempted from the wrestling, this garlanded bull was peaceably chewing cud. When the others were herded away, there he remained. Anthony didn't know why, but he couldn't look at this solitary buffalo in its floral headdress without his blood chilling.

A great cheer rose up from the crowd. Riders galloped into the square, every man carrying a long-handled mallet. There was Shah Abbas right in the thick of them, waving his mallet round his head. Fifty riders squared off against each other to play a game that looked to Anthony to be a sort of horsebacked pall-mall or shinty. With a long-handled mallet, each rider tried to whack a ball they called a *pulu* towards goals at either end of the maidan. Whenever Abbas was on the ball a line of trumpeters blew a fanfare. The Shah broke off from the game, galloped to the veranda and called up,

'Does the spectacle please you, Antonio?'

Anthony stood up and bowed. Each time the Shah scored a goal or gave the *pulu* a good crack, he galloped up to the veranda and asked how

Antonio liked the spectacle. Each successive visit left Anthony more full of trepidation. So much honour could not end well. His eyes drifted back to the lone buffalo, garlanded and doomed, tethered near the crowded bleachers.

The horsebacked pall-mall match ended, and the riders cleared the square. All bar one. Alone, Shah Abbas rode his white stallion to the veranda, and dismounted right below Anthony.

'Watch this!' he shouted up at him. 'Watch me!'

Kettledrums beat. Dressed all in white, a pageboy raced towards Shah Abbas to present him with a double recurve bow, and a silk quiver full of golden arrows flighted with eagle feathers. The Shah laid his royal back upon the dirt floor of the maidan. He pulled the bowstring taut, arrow pointing at sky. The ends of the bow bent until they almost touched. The kettledrums stopped. With astonishing agility, Abbas sprang up from his shoulders as if the earth were a bow and himself the arrow! While still in midair, he shot the golden arrow. On the far side of the maidan, the garlanded buffalo crumpled to the ground, its bellowing death throes subsumed in the cheering of the crowded bleachers. The pageboy raced across the empty maidan to retrieve an eagle-feathered golden arrow from its eye.

One moment the whole vast maidan was empty, save for the dead buffalo, and the next as many as one thousand cavalrymen, dressed in captured Uzbeg helmets, were cantering round the square to the boos, jeers and whistles of the crowd. Allahvirdi Khan leaned forward and said,

'Now comes the culmination of the festivities, Antonio Mirza, the grand battle re-enactment. Shah Abbas will take the part of Shah Abbas vanquishing the Uzbegs at Meshed.'

'Weren't you at that battle as well, Oliver?' asked Anthony, who found it comforting that the commander-in-chief had such a homely,

Norman-sounding name as Oliver de Cannes.

'Once is enough,' replied Allahvirdi Khan. 'It was a hot battle and a famous victory against a terrible foe. Shah Abbas was in the very heart of the fighting to the astonishment of the Uzbeg cavalry. This battle re-enactment, he hopes, will give the Christian princes, by your report, an idea of Persian arms, of the quality and the power of our cavalry.'

'Why does his majesty want me to speak to his parliament?'

'The Shah knows that you have been sent here by Queen Elizabeth on behalf of all the courts of Europe to orchestrate an alliance against the Turk. He hopes that when you tell this to the parliament they may be won round to supporting a war they now oppose. The *majlis* speak for the merchants, who all fear the havoc a long war will do the Levant trade.'

'Will it be a long war, Oliver?'

'Not with the Christian Princes attacking from the north and west, Antonio!'

Cheers broke out as Abbas led one hundred Tofangchi cavalry into the square. He raised his silver sword, and let out a high-pitched cry. Two lines of horse thundered towards each other, and then through each other, merging into a friendly squall of merry confusion in which it was impossible to descry any order of battle.

'Huh,' said Robert, 'we have swapped pall-mall for pell-mell! What squalid chaos! How poor a show!'

Robert was not the only one suffering from the sorry spectacle which the battle re-enactment had become. Down on the maidan, Shah Abbas was enraged by its dismal failure. Wheeling his great white horse, the Shah began hacking with his jewelled scimitar at his elite veterans in their captured Uzbeg helmets. At first none of the spectators realised what the Shah was doing. It was not until swathes began to open up around his white stallion that the spectators realised it was no longer a mock battle.

In quick succession three cavalrymen toppled from their saddles and lay bleeding on the ground. A gasp ran over the crowd. Shouting and whistling, they tried to warn the cavalry, most of who still had no idea what was happening, and were making merry in swordplay.

Right under the veranda, a Tofangchi captain in a captured Uzbeg helmet was tiptapping swords with an old comrade. They were both laughing because the Uzbeg helmet was too big, and kept slipping over one eye, every time it was dinked with a sword. Anthony saw Abbas charging his white horse straight at this cavorting pair. The enraged Shah was a black-whiskered panther running through a frightened herd of gazelle. Cavalrymen in Uzbeg and Persian attire dispersed in all directions, clearing the panther's path to his quarry.

The Tofangchi captain didn't see the Shah, until he was only a few lengths away. By chance he pushed up the Uzbeg helmet just in time to put spurs to his horse. He rode hard, trying to escape Shah Abbas. Standing up in the short stirrups, he looked for a way out of the square, but his mount was no match for the Shah's white stallion. The royal sword chopped him at the waist. The blade sank in so deep that the sword lodged in the Tofangchi's torso. Tofangchi, horse and sword galloped off together a little way, until the dead captain toppled off the saddle, and the horse stopped in its tracks. Abbas galloped out the square towards the Naqsh-i Jahan palace.

Crawling wounded littered the maidan. Corpses were carried away in sheets. The crowd buzzed in agitation. On the veranda, Robert Sherley said:

'Brother, if you have any money at all left from the silver he's given you, I beg you to purchase camels so we can quit this place at once. We could be home in a few months. Think of it, England in a few months! Wiston. Sussex. We must get out of here at once! Each day grows more oppressive. Sitting here with the king's two blind brothers right behind us... Do they not fill you with horror?'

'No. Why should they?'

'The Shah, their brother, ordered their eyes put out!'

'It was a mercy in Shah Abbas to spare his brothers' lives in this way.'

'By blinding them? Can you really think so?'

'It had been a mercy in King Henry only to have blinded and not slaughtered his wives. Our Queen, his daughter, chopped her cousin Mary's head off.'

'If a letter comes from the Queen, she will chop your head off too, with the Shah her axeman. I heard Oliver de Cannes say he believes the Queen has sent you here on a secret commission! And there were you stroking your beard and nodding away all the while as though it were true! What if a letter should come from Queen Elizabeth? Who knows what this Shah might do!'

At the far end of the maidan Anthony watched a group of men lug the dead buffalo from the square.

18

In the roof garden of the Zarafshani's one-storey house, Gol crouched behind the elm screen and squinted through its tightly woven mesh. There was Mani Babachoi yet again, standing in the vacant corner plot across the street. She watched his loose white sleeves fall back to the elbow revealing the coloured bandages that she had been throwing down to him day after day. He started his routine of pacing to and fro, flapping his white sleeves, building himself up for the act of burning his flesh to prove the ardour of his soul. He lit a dangling rag. Flame climbed the rag. Gol's heart sank. She once saw a white stork standing in a field of burning stubble, cooling itself with its wings, waiting to snap its beak upon any field mice that ran from the flames into its path. Mani Babachoi was the stork at the stubble burning. Trapped behind the dead twigs she was the crouching field mouse.

The field mouse crept to the other side of the roof garden and squinted through the elm screen hoping to see Darius walking up the road, but the road was empty. Where was he? Three days in a row he hadn't come. Had her mother destroyed him with her shovel of dung? Had Mani Babachoi scared him off?

The day after Darius's humiliation, Gol sought him out in the bazaar. She found his stall ransacked - by Mani Babachoi? - and spent an hour tidying it up. She put books back on the shelves, mopped black puddles of spilt ink, and tried to restore everything to how it used to be. As she did so, she found lots of drawings of a fiddle-playing woman who looked very much like herself embracing a man who looked exactly like Darius, only slimmer.

When Darius had appeared outside her house as Mani Babachoi's rival, Gol's first feeling was hurt that he should trade their friendship for mere wooing. But this pang had been succeeded by a much stronger feeling. Not love, not joyful reciprocation, not desire, but relief. That's what she felt. Relief from siege. Strange to say two suitors were less pressure than one. With Darius around, the stork had a clumsy bear to worry about. Two suitors had to pit their wits against each other, whereas before Mani was pitting himself against her resistance, grinding her down a little more every day.

Only where was Darius now? So much for his great poetic passion! So much for the cult of true love! Why had he stopped coming? Why had he quit so meekly? If one humiliation was enough to drive him off then he should never have come at all. Did he think she didn't know that Mani was reading a poem written by Darius himself? Did Darius credit her with so little wit? It seemed he did for he had abandoned her to face her fate alone, left her stranded in this hot furrow before stork and flame.

How she loathed what Mani Babachoi was doing across the street. How it sickened her. The burning ceremony Mani performed might be common to every *javanmahdi*, every youth of noble soul, it might be time honoured custom, but that did not make it any less shocking when she was the cause and it happened in front of her own house. Mani lowered the fiery rag towards his exposed forearm. To Gol's horror, he dabbed the flame up and down his arm, scorching several burns at once. She had rather burn her own arm than have him declare his love in this way. She threw a poultice over the screen and heard it land with a wet slap in the street. She turned her back to the screen, squatted on her haunches and closed her eyes. Glimpsed through the elm screen, flame had printed copper lines across the inside of her eyelids. Copper strings.

In those last peaceful moments before Mani Babachoi had invaded her life, Gol had been restringing her tanbur's copper strings. If only she could go back to that time now. Everything was so simple then.

There she'd been, sitting on a cushion on the worn rug, peacefully restringing her tanbur while her mother baked biscuits on the other side of the room. She threaded a copper string through a tuning peg. Holding the tanbur's headstock to her ear, she plucked the string as she turned the tuning peg, like drawing the note's true sound out of a well. As she did so, she cast her mind back to a conversation about Rumi that she'd had with Darius, whom she had bumped into at the pigeon-post. They had discussed Rumi's *'Alas, we are lost on a black sea...'* A poem of despair, said Darius, with its image of a ship steering by clouds. Against this, Gol argued that when set to music the true hopefulness of Rumi's quatrain emerged - all will be well so long as the sailors keep sailing - in the same way that lovers drew out each other's true nature, the melody drew out the lyric's true meaning.

'Who are you thinking about?' her mother, Roshanak, had asked.

'I'm not thinking about anyone. I was thinking about poetry.'

'Love poems!'

'No. If you must know, I was thinking about truth and meaning.'

'You won't get a husband talking like that,' said her mother. She slid the biscuits out on a long-handled steel tray to turn them over one by one.

'I was not thinking about how to get a husband.'

'Well, you should.'

'I was thinking about the ways in which the great poets make us see the world in new ways, how their insights increase our knowledge.'

'I don't want to know anything I don't already know.'

Gol was left openmouthed by this last remark.

'What, *madar?*' she asked.

'I am quite happy never to learn anything more.'

'But... how can you say that?'

'I have got all the thoughts in my head arranged just so,' said Roshanak. 'Like furniture in a room. If I were to let in a new idea, then I would have to rearrange all the tables and shelves. I'd have to shift all the furniture around my head.'

'Isn't that good?'

'No, it's not good! I don't want to have to move everything around. I've got it just how I like it. I've had it sorted this way for years.' She slid the long-handled tray back into the oven.

'But surely,' said Gol, 'you've had to change with each big event.'

'No, that's the blessing, you see,' said Roshanak, her voice echoing from the oven into which she was peering, 'of having your head set out just right: you only have to do the job once. Once it's done, then it's done for good. I thank God my house and my mind are well-ordered.'

'But every word we hear changes us, *madar*.'

'God help you, girl! Not me! What nonsense.'

Gol sat back on her heels to trim with a short knife where the strings were proud of the pegs. She listened to her father's footsteps as he pottered about up on the roof terrace, and to a thump of wing against wire in the pigeon coop. Silently her lips began to work. Take Ibn Hamza of Cordoba, she was telling Darius, now there's a poet whose words you could only reduce by setting to music... And that was when a strange, new voice was first heard outside the house, bellowing away as if for battle not for love:

'Gol Zarafshani, you are loved with a pure love by Mani Babachoi.'

'Who is he?' asked Roshanak.

'I don't know, *madar.*'

Her father hurried downstairs, escaping the newcomer. Gol took her father's place upstairs, where she crouched behind the elm screen and sneaked a look at the stranger. She knew she'd never met this Mani Babachoi with his horseshoe moustache, upright stance, and smart clothes. From the look of him she was sure that he'd made a mistake, and got her confused with someone else. His arms, then, had been a blank page - and now look at them: puckered and dotted with burn marks and thin scraps of bandage.

And now here she was, so many days later, still crouching behind the elm screen, still wondering how to stop him from disfiguring himself for her sake. She knew that she could never return his affection, and so he would bear these burn marks up his arms for years, and never look at them without cursing her. At least he had done his burning for today. Now she must only endure the poetry.

'Gol, Gol, I have failed to write a poem for you,' he called out, 'and so I will now burn my right hand to punish it.' She groaned, and shook her head in a mood of finality.

'That's it,' she whispered. 'That's enough.'

Trapped between the fire and stork, the field mouse must make a dash for it sooner or later. Her speed startled the caged doves into a flurry as she ran across the roof garden, through the skylight and down the seven stairs. She dragged open the stiff front door and stood in front of him before he even knew she had left the roof.

'Would you like to go for a walk, Mani Babachoi?'

He yelped in shock and jumped backwards, dropping the burning rag.

'This way,' she said, and set off waiting for him to catch up.

19

That first walk together was followed by another and another, and soon Gol and Mani Babachoi were walking out every evening. Upon their return, they would sit talking on the low clay wall of the abandoned corner plot across the way. One evening, unseen behind the screen, Gol's father, Atash Zarafshani called down some questions. Who was Mani's father? Where did his family live? He then invited Mani to call for Gol as often as he liked.

Roshanak Zarafshani also believed that Mani was an excellent suitor who would make a fine husband for her daughter. But so entirely was the musketeer carrying all before him, that Roshanak felt it necessary to intrude a few dissenting murmurs.

'Watch for his temper,' she told her daughter, 'a stiff-backed soldier like that!'

'He is kind and gentle.'

'*He* won't hold with your philosophising and your poetry, *I'm* sure! You think I am impatient with your ways, wait till you're tardy lighting the fire one cold morning with that young soldier your husband. He'll make you hop, my girl.'

'He is very correct with me always.'

'Out of doors he may be.'

'Is father a different man indoors from out?'

'I don't know,' said Roshanak, lowering her voice, 'he never goes out.' Together they listened to Atash sweeping leaves on the roof terrace, the slow scuff of his lame right foot following the quick scuff of broom bristles. 'Your young soldier,' Roshanak resumed, 'will nod and smile for now. For now he'll appear to like nothing better than hearing every foolish thought of yours, but he's not listening, he's biding his time.'

'No, Mani listens to me, not like you!'

'Oh, does he now? Let me tell you something, my girl, this listening is as painful to him as burning himself on the bare arm. Ceremony. That's what it is. Ceremony. What a man has to do to win a wife. But once you're married then it ends. Then you'll see how far you get talking about poetry and philosophy, and all your *Shab-e-Sher* nonsense. That's if you haven't already driven him off with such idle talk before the wedding,' she added, because she still believed he was a good match for Gol.

Gol resolved to give Mani a piece of just that part of her mind her mother warned her not to. 'I shall prove her wrong,' she thought. 'If I don't, if she's right, and I do end up driving Mani off by speaking to him of what is closest to my heart, then he was never the man for me anyway!'

As Gol and the unsuspecting Mani walked out the following evening, she bit her lip, impatiently waiting until they were in a narrow rutted lane between the sagging clay walls of orchards, before she asked Mani if he believed in poetry.

'I don't understand most poems,' he replied, not knowing he was being ambushed, 'and what I do understand I don't believe - unless it's Hafiz talking about the ruby cup: I believe that fellow liked a drink all right.'

'So why read out these poems to me all the time, then?'

'If I could sing, I'd sing you a song.'

'Songs lie too.'

'How the singer sings it makes it true.' They walked a few more paces up the lane before she said to him:

'Al Abbas bin Al Ahnef says, *There is no good in those who do not feel love's passion.* Do you agree?'

'I don't know,' replied Mani after a while.

'You must think something! What?' She was almost shouting. Mani looked startled.

'I don't agree,' he replied in a voice thick with confusion.

'But why, Mani? What don't you agree with?'

Mani took such a long before replying that Gol thought he must be angry with her, until he quietly said:

'It used to be, whenever we were on these walks, that your thoughts were not rocks thrown at my head, but odd lumps of minerals which you put in my hand. You'd invite me to cast my eye over them. I used to take pride in turning over in my hands these minerals. I turned them over, looked at them this way and that, and then, if I didn't understand, I would hand the clump of minerals back to you with the same care with which you had handed it to me, and no-one the sorrier for that.'

Now it was her turn to take a long time before replying.

'Isn't it the same now?' she asked.

'No, Gol, it's not the same.'

'Yes, it is: I'm telling you what matters to me and asking you to tell me if it matters to you.'

'No. You used to invite me to understand you, but now you defy me even to try.'

'No, that's exactly what I am asking you to do: to try. Try. Why don't you agree with the poet who says there is no good in those who do not love? It's a simple question.'

He sighed heavily as they walked along the rutted path between sagging walls deformed by tree roots.

'Lots of good people aren't in love,' he said at last, 'and there's plenty of bad ones who are.'

'No good person loves nothing.'

'What if they're just lonely?' said Mani. 'I was not a bad man before I met you, I simply didn't love. That's not a sin. That's a lack. I didn't know you existed. I was lonely.'

For the first time ever, she took his hand in hers. And they walked on hand in hand.

At home that evening, Gol was rubbing a block of beeswax on her kamanche, a small spiked fiddle. Sitting by her mother on the threadbare rug, and unaware that her lips were silently moving, she repeated to herself, over and over, her last conversation with Mani.

'Talking to yourself like an old spinster,' said her mother. 'What nonsense are you thinking about now?'

'About whether you need to understand a song before you dance to it.'

'You won't get a husband talking like that.'

Gol fixed her mother a look.

'I think I have,' she said. Her mother's face fell.

'What are you saying?'

'You're shifting all your furniture now,' Gol crowed, laughing a full, deep-throated laugh that brought Atash downstairs, asking,

'What is it? What has happened?'

Gol threw back her head and laughed even louder and more delightedly.

20

The following evening, Gol and her band of musicians were playing at a wedding party, after which she returned home and climbed the stairs to the roof terrace to talk to her father, who was gardening by moonlight.

'How did you do tonight?' he asked. She ignored the merry twinkle in his eyes that had been there ever since she and Mani had begun courting. She didn't want to talk about that now. She wanted to know that she could still talk to her father up on the rooftop late at night just like they used to, and about topics other than love and marriage. Plus, she needed to talk about work. It wasn't going well. Seemed the oil shortage was affecting even wedding singers.

'I tell you, father, gold teeth would have fallen from their heads sooner than coins. We had them all dancing and sweating, but the wedding guests fixed the coins to their forehead with gum arabic.'

'How do you know?'

'You could smell the acacia. It's unbudgeable that stuff. At the end of the night when we raked our metal harvest from the floor, there was just one shahidi and a few brass larins.'

'That was all the coins that dropped off all night? I'm amazed. Why don't you and the girls take your own gum next time? A big ball of elm gum. Offer it around free for the guests to stick coins to foreheads, and this way you'll be sure to shake down a fair wage.'

'I'll try it, but perhaps everyone's hoarding their coins for lamp oil,' she said. 'It's now twenty times last week's price.'

'Well, better a brass forehead than a dark house, I suppose,' said Atash. 'Why was Mani carrying his musket earlier? Is Darius coming back?'

'He's on duty tonight.'

'Where?'

'Guarding the oil reserves at the *majlis*. Mani hates this duty. These are meant to be emergency oil reserves for the city, but it seems every second merchant has a "special warrant."'

'From a friendly minister?'

'Yes, and so Mani has to watch these barrels of oil carried out under his nose. Oh, and I've news for you *pedar*, your old friend Hoseyn Ali Beg is made a Mirza. The Shah is sending him to Rome as ambassador.'

'Well, well, ambassador Hoseyn Mirza! Do you remember him, Gol?' She shook her head and smiled.

Hoseyn Ali Beg was a figure from Atash's past. Ten years earlier, not long after the start of the Shah's reign, they had been friends. They had both served in the same provincial governor's administration. Atash had served as assistant notary, Hoseyn Ali Beg as vice-governor. When the governor was executed for embezzlement, his entire staff - except Hoseyn Ali Beg who was needed to replace him - were sent to the front to fight invading Uzbegs. Atash found himself alongside soldiers half his age defending a walled town called Turbat-i-Haydari, south of Meshed. He was carrying a powder magazine when the Uzbegs shot burning oil-tipped arrows over the walls. The powder magazine exploded, and set alight his face, an arm, a hand and a leg.

Atash was invalided home, and home he had stayed, never setting foot outside the house. Seven steps led up to a roof garden fenced on all four sides by an elm screen. The screen was tall enough for him to potter about unseen by anyone passing by, even someone on horseback. Only twice in the last ten years, late on a starless night, supported on Roshanak's arm, had he limped to the end of the street, but that was as far as he went. Indoors was downstairs, outdoors was upstairs.

Within this limited precinct, however, he pottered about contentedly enough - just so long as Roshanak or Gol did not try to make him leave the house. When they did he flew into a rage. He saw their attempts to nag him back into the world as a withdrawal of loving kindness. They were trying to turn him out of doors. To evict him. They were setting him a punishing task when he had already been tasked - hadn't they noticed? - with carrying a heavy enough burden through the rest of his life as it was. Whenever Roshanak bought him a new ashplant walking stick, or whenever Gol asked him to accompany her somewhere, he snarled and stamped until both wife and daughter retreated.

It was not as if he were sitting on his hands, he reminded them. There were the messenger doves to be cared for, and they only had to look at the roof garden, from which the family earned a small but steady income, to see how hard he worked. Here he cultivated his own blue and green hybrid carnation, Sea and Sky, which he sold at the bazaar's little overflow market, the outdoor bazardeh. The carnation pergola's eight legs stood in six raised beds where he also grew squashes, mustard, tomatoes, onions and fruits - not to mention every single item stipulated on Roshanak's finicky lists of medicinal herbs. They had no idea what planning and hard work it took to grow so much in so small a space. None at all. Dark green mustard leaves spread under the compact heads of huddled red kalanchoe. Tomatoes rose from among pink dwarf mallow and onion clusters. Grapes climbed the back legs of the tall pergola entwined by striped carnations, and the soil was fertilised by the pigeons which warmed themselves by the chimney breast, against which stood their dovecot. But not only did Roshanak and Gol not appreciate how much planning and imagination it took to grow so many things on top of each other, they told him that the eight-legged pergola was a giant spider that held him in its maw.

Atash Zarafshani's great worry was that the catastrophe at Turbat had blighted his daughter's life as well. Too much family responsibility had devolved onto Gol's young shoulders. When not playing with her band - another vital source of household income, at least equal to the sale of Sea and Sky - she was running family errands, to places where he'd rather not show his face: toting pigeon crates to and from the maidan, delivering mustard seeds to the bazaar, finding the salvage-yard timber from which he'd constructed a wooden oil pipeline which - up until the present oil shortage - had piped a constant supply of oil to the numerous lanterns dotted around the roof garden, as well as to the lights and stove downstairs. Well, with such a life was it any wonder that she only ever played sad songs? But not anymore! Ever since she had gone for that first walk with Mani, things had changed. Now Atash and his doves heard happy tunes and dance music drifting up the stairs. Soon Mani Babachoi might ask his permission for Gol's hand. If she were married to such an excellent fellow as Mani - even Roshanak could hardly find a bad word to say about him - then no-one could say that Atash had failed her as a father.

It did his heart good to see her standing before him so confident and assured, and so colourfully dressed - she was still wearing her performance costume of funnel-shaped rainbow cuffs and a long-sleeved lemon tunic. If the catastrophe at Turbat had not blighted her life, however, the Shah's new plan of war might do it yet.

'Can Hoseyn Ali Beg stop the war?' she asked. He knew she was thinking about Mani. She was worried he'd be sent to the front. She wanted her father to tell her that there wouldn't be a war.

'If Hoseyn could stop the war,' he replied, 'Abbas wouldn't have made him ambassador.'

'He wants a war?'

'Yes.'

'But he's just had twelve years of war, why does he want another one? Is it for glory? Does he want to be slain in battle like all the past shahs?'

'Let me tell you how his grandfather Shah Tahmasp died, my child. It happened far from the field of battle. The palace servants who were waxing his legs left the depilatory on too long. Tahmasp fell asleep and died of his burns. Hot wax killed Shah Tahmasp! Sixty-six years old and he still wanted smooth legs like a girl.'

'So why does Shah Abbas want a war?'

'I don't know. He's got a big army and he wants to use it?'

'The Turkish embassy hasn't gone back yet, *pedar,*' she said. 'That must mean there's at least a chance that the Turkish ambassador might yet leave with a new peace treaty. The very fact that majlis and shah are still arguing between war and peace means nothing is settled.'

'*Inshallah!*' he said, and hoped it sounded more sanguine than he felt. It seemed to do the trick. She kissed his rooster cheek, and went downstairs into the house.

Alone on the roof terrace, under the moon and stars, Atash unrolled his prayer rug.

'Oh God, you are the One who sends forth and the One who delays. Bless Hoseyn Ali Beg's endeavours to bring peace. May Mani Babachoi not be sent to the front. Protect my wife and child from sorrow and from grief.'

On a more personal note, he thanked the All-Merciful for the three-quarters moon which, when Gol's wedding band came by for practice the next night, would allow him to escape to the roof garden, lamp oil or no. He climbed to his feet, and cast a last look at his garden. A cloud covered the moon. The wooden pergola became invisible, setting a constellation of pale carnation buds adrift in the night.

21

A faint sun struggled behind a hornpaper sky. Nat's eyeballs ached from the tears he was holding back. All this way for nothing. This was Masjid-i Suleiman. This was the fabled Fire Temple of Mithras to which Darius had led him. No oil gushers, no oil fountains, no oil ponds, no oil of any kind anywhere. Only dust, weeds and a derelict chimney on a sandy mound in a scrubby wasteland. The wind blew grit into his eyes.

He saw Darius knee-deep in a sand drift at the foot of the bricked-up chimney tower, and could hear his sobs, but, this being hell, every spring of fellow feeling had dried. Rather than going to his only friend in the world, he walked in the opposite direction towards a hillock covered in scrappy weeds.

Round the back of the hillock, he was out of the wind. He sat against a limestone bas-relief of Mithras and traced his finger over the pagan stonework. Bore-holed by dust-mites, the old impostor had lost his nose so that he looked like a syphilitic sailor. Nat ran his finger over raised glyphs which had crumbled away in patches. The Zoroastrians, or whatever they were, who knew how to read these glyphs, were long gone. It was a dead alphabet.

He flayed the glyphs with his steel-tipped knife sheath, hot tears running down his face. He hewed the glyphs harder and harder, faster and faster, for all that they withheld, and because ignorance and folly had been his only patrimony. Great chunks of Mithras broke off, and satisfyingly huge cracks opened up in the limestone.

Then the whole facade caved in. To his terror, Nat found himself perched over a black abyss. The earth wobbled as if he was on the top of a tall ladder. Running fissures opened in the ground beneath him. He rolled backwards. An ever-expanding crater chased him, the soil opening up beneath him. He got to his feet and ran. Behind him, the whole hillside caved in and collapsed into the black abyss with a noise like rolling thunder.

A cloud of dust rose where the hill once stood. The deafening landslip was followed by abrupt and total silence. The dust unveiled a green marble giant, a twelve-foot high statue of Mithras with his outstretched wings.

❖

Nat and Darius crept forward to peer over the edge of the crater at the winged Mithras. A cascade of rubble descended to a subterranean ledge on which the beautiful idol stood. Darius stepped gingerly onto this rocky stairway, fearing it would give way at every step. On all fours, he climbed backwards down the rocks to the subterranean ledge, Nat following after.

At the foot of the marble Mithras, Darius kicked a rock into the black chasm. They listened to its splash in flooded darkness far below. They lay on their bellies on the rocky ledge of Mithras's pedestal and lowered a lantern on the end of the rope. A deep cavern revealed its shape. Sandstone walls shot with zigzags of hard shale. At the bottom of the well bubbled a pool of boiling pitch. In this black pond hoops of hot oil rolled and tumbled over each other like eels at play.

'Oil,' cried Nat. 'Oil! Oil! Oil!'

'A furnace,' said Darius. 'It will incinerate our goatskins.'

'Even if we douse them first?'

'Yes. But look! Look! Halfway down. There!' He swung the lantern in the direction of a vug, a cave within the cave wall, a kind of alcove. On its floor, the swinging light discovered standing pools of shining black oil. 'There's our chance. That shelf there. The oil is shallow. It won't scald.'

'But how do we reach it? How do we get the oil out of the well?'

'I don't know.'

They reeled in the lamp, and clambered up the rubble cascade, past the green marble shoulders of the giant Mithras, and out into the open air.

The wind had dropped and the sun was shining. In the shade of a dead tree, Nat set a pot of Kulsum's *qaveh* to boil. Darius snapped a thick branch off the dead tree. The loud crack scared the mules to the end of their tethers.

'We can't make a jib crane out of this brittle timber,' he said, 'so all the ferryman's nails are useless.'

The coffee came to the boil. Nat offered him a cup but Darius asked him to pass him a drink of water instead. He then watched Nat wipe his hands on his seamy breeches, before thoroughly smearing the bottle's mouth with his dirty palm. Spotting a blade of grass in the lip, Nat sucked a forefinger and stuck it into the bottleneck to prise out the grass. Darius waved the water away:

'Perhaps I'll drink the *qaveh* after all.'

They sat with their tin cups steaming in the open. Darius took a swig, and pulled a face at its bitterness. As he sipped his *qaveh*, his gaze rested upon the marble idol. Only Mithras's head was above ground, like a gravedigger.

'Look at Mithras,' he said. 'Straight as a chess-piece even though half the hillside has caved in around his shoulders. We don't need a crane, we can hang the block and tackle around his neck. All we have to do is tie the saddlecloth to the other end of the rope. Then it's simple! I lower you down to that shelf of oil halfway down the oil well, and after you've filled up all seven goatskins with oil, I'll winch you up again!'

'Who made you the Shah of Persia? I'm not going down the well. You're the one who knows good oil from bad. You go down.'

'I'm the heaviest, you're the lightest - these are elementary engineering principles.'

'The same elementary engineering principles you used for your catamaran? You nearly drowned me in water and now you want to drown me in oil.'

'I didn't invent the key principles of physics, Nat, I merely apply them.'

'Key principles of cluck-cluck-cluck.'

❖

Naked but for suede breeches, Nat sits in the saddlecloth on the edge of the abyss. He leans back on the rope, the soles of his feet on the ledge. He is terrified as never before in his life. His eyes follow a trail of rope. The trail starts where the rope loops in and out of the saddlecloth's grommets to fashion the bosun's chair or sling he's sitting in. From there the trail rises to the maple block lassoed around Mithras's neck - how fragile that block looks now! From the block and tackle's pulley wheel the rope drops down to Darius, who has the rope looped over his shoulder and then wrapped around his waist like a village tug o' war team's anchorman. He looks at Darius's face. There is terror there too.

'I'm going to swing out and swing back,' says Nat, his voice trembling. 'To test. Brace yourself.'

He hops backwards off the ledge, swings out a few feet, and lands back where he left, on the lip of the ledge. He gasps and sags against the rope with relief. Darius hands Nat the lantern, then feeds more rope through the maple block around the marble neck.

'You will not swing back level this time, Nat.' Their eyes meet. Nat steps back off the ledge, and drops a few yards. Darius lowers him hand over hand into the dark depths. Nat listens to the pulley wheel chuntering, and to the block and tackle's maple box scraping against the icon's marble chest. Side to side it scrapes with every turn of the pulley wheel. As the bosun's chair descends, the lantern's light travels over shale zigzags in the sandstone walls. Halfway down the well he comes to the vug. Its pool of shallow oil glows bronze in the lantern's beam.

'Level,' he shouts. The rope halts its descent with a bump.

Nat kicks his legs backwards and forwards. He swings towards the ledge of the vug, and then back out again over the bottomless pit, his stomach turning over. Forward goes the swing, Nat's feet almost touch the ledge. Back goes the swing. Forwards goes the swing, and he leaps from the saddlecloth. He lands on the vug's oily ledge, slips and drops the lantern. He watches his only light somersault down into the pit.

'Whores in God's hell!' he shouts, his curse echoing around the pit.

Blackness. Then movement on the black pond far below. A smoothly expanding blue ring ignites the pit with a muffled whoompf. Abruptly, the black pond turns into a glaring disc of yellow fire. With a whoosh and a peeling sound, one whole wall of the cavern ignites, lighting up strips of shale and long zigzags of sandstone with racing flames. Nat screams in terror. A confetti of bituminous flames showers the cavern. Darkness returns for an instant before the black pit belches up more gobbets of burning pitch, which spatter the walls. Soon the whole cavern is seeded with spitting, sizzling, glowing yellow flakes of fire. Cowering against the back wall of the vug, Nat is better sheltered from the firestorm than Darius, who is spattered by scalding tar up on the ledge.

Petrol bats flit from wall to wall scorching Darius all over. He strips off his limpid rag of a shirt for fear it will catch fire. The black hair on his bare chest and belly, arms and shoulders, swoops and sweeps like iron filings drawn by a magnet. Having been too poor all his life to use the depilatory *dowa,* he has a full pelt. Molten pitch falls as slow as furry snow upon his naked, hairy torso. He can smell the singeing of his body hair. Each scalding gobbet that settles upon him fizzles another patch.

'Are you all right, Darius?'

'My poverty has made me flammable!' he calls down.

From his leather bottle, Darius douses his body hair as best he can, then pours water down the front of his shalwar to flameproof his loins. He sprinkles water onto the bundle of goatskins, then, with his own leather belt, straps the seven skins to the saddlecloth. Kneeling at the feet of the green marble giant, he lowers the bundle of goatskins down to Nat on the vug. The block and tackle clatters and rattles on Mithras's marble chest as he feeds rope through its trundling pulley wheel.

'Level!' comes Nat's voice.

Down on the vug, gritty fumes scrape the roof of Nat's mouth, and the noxious, metallic air makes his head woozy. He leans out and grabs the swinging saddlecloth in oily hands. He unstraps its bundle of goatskin sacks, hitching the rope to a natural sandstone pillar. Standing up to his shins in warm oil, he glides the mouth of a sack through the shallow pool. The sack bellies out. Stiff hide grows supple as it fills. He stands the full goatskin up, stoppers it, and ropes it onto the saddlecloth..

'Ready!' he shouts. 'Haul away!'

The goatskin sack swings out into the cavern, then ascends in jerky stages up towards the light. The block and tackle squeaks with every turn. He sees Darius reach out an arm and grapple the black sack, like a fisherman leaning from a boat to land a sea lion. The chamber darkens, for a second, its shaft of natural light eclipsed by Darius climbing the rocky stairway to attach rope to mule, which drags the sack up the rubble cascade to the light.

Nat is alone.

The only sound comes from the rumbling oil at the foot of the well, which sounds like an evening tide trapped in a rocky inlet. Nat skims the second sack's open mouth through the shallow pool of warm rock oil. As he does so, a starburst of pitch and embers illuminates the vug, which becomes suddenly beautiful. Quartz crystals, embedded in the vug's sandstone walls, wink and glint in the firelight. A molten squib lands on the oil pool and floats past him like a bronze sail at sunset. He wades through gold-rimmed ripples of oil. When he hears Darius climb back down the rubble cascade to the promontory at the foot of the marble Mithras, he shouts,

'We are going to succeed, Darius! We're on our way!'

A second time, the saddlecloth descends towards Nat. A second time he loads in a full sack of oil, a second time Darius winches it up towards Mithras's pedestal, a second time the harnessed mule drags the sack the last bit of the way up the rubble staircase and into the light. And so it goes, a third, and a fourth and a fifth time, with Nat shouting:

'We're on our way, Darius! We're on our way!'

On the sixth time, however, there's a hitch. A small stumble. A falling squib scalds the back of Nat's neck, he claps his hand to his neck, slips and falls. He lands on the very edge of the vug, and watches his hat drop down into the bottomless pit. His skin seems to bristle all the way up the back of his body from heel to head. For several seconds he stays absolutely rigid, not daring to blink. He looks over the vug's edge at the burning well where his life nearly ended, and sees his hat come floating back towards him, rising on an updraught from the furnace. His hat floats past him and carries on up towards Darius. A cruel practical joke occurs to Nat. With the sole of his boot he rolls a boulder off the ledge, lets out a scream, then hides at the back of the vug.

Darius hears the scream followed by a thud-splash far below in the oil well. The next second, right in front of his face, the lambskin hat disintegrates into flakes and burning embers. A message from hell. Nat has fallen into the bottomless pit.

'Nat! Nat!' cries Darius, but hears only his own deep voice straying lost around the chamber, echoing from wall to wall. 'Merciful God don't let him die! Oh, Nat, oh, Nat!'

There comes a small sound, barely audible above the great rumbling slurry of captured tides of oil:

A foldeh-roll a-fiddly-doe, a foldeh-ro-a-roo.

He listens. A cry of help? or death throes? or a belching of oil?

A foldeh-roll a-fiddly-doe, a foldeh-ro-a-roo.

The noise ceases. Darius lies down on the marble pedestal. He holds his breath and listens. It comes again. The same sound, clearer and more distinct:

A foldeh-roll a-fiddly-doe, a foldeh-ro-a-roo.

A squib shower lights the vug. Darius sees the hatless ghost of Nat Bramble leaning against a lumpy sandstone pillar, a fiery veil of golden nuggets falling before him, singing:

'*Love me little, love me long,*
Is the burden of my song.
Love that is too hot and strong,

Burneth soon to waste.

A foldeh-roll a-fiddly-doe, a foldeh-ro-a-roo.'

'Fool!' shouts Darius. *'Pedar soukteh!'* Your father was burnt.

'You can't live without me, Darius Nouredini!' bellows Nat exultantly. 'You were heartbroken!'

'I thought you had the money-belt!'

'Haul away!'

Darius hoists the sixth bag. Only one more goatskin to go, he tells himself. The lack of air in the vug, he fears, is playing with Nat's mind, making him giddy, bombastic, crazed. He hears him splashing about in the petroleum, and singing in the oil:

> *I loved a lass a fair one,*
> *As fair as e'er was seen,*
> *She was indeed a rare one,*
> *Another Sheba Queen.*
> *But fool as then I was*
> *I thought she loved me too,*
> *But now, alas, she's left me,*
> *Fo la ro la ro la roo!*

Out in the open air, Darius hitches the rope to the packsaddle. He slots his hands between the mule's suede jowls and the bridle's worn leather cheek straps and leads the buckskin away from the well. The rope from packsaddle to goatskin goes taut. The mule takes the strain, and struggles forward. From the hole in the ground, greasy and blackened, the sixth goatskin appears, and plops onto the earth. The mule tows the sack across the dusty scrub, along the greasy path made by the other sacks. Darius unties the sack and climbs back down to the ledge. He picks up the saddlecloth. It is caked in tar. He slices off as much tar-cake as he can with his knife, but it is no use. He cannot tell what is saddlecloth and what is pitch. He climbs down the rubble to Mithras's pedestal and calls down the well.

'Nat!'

'Ready!'

'No, forget about the last skin. Just come up now. The sling is more tar than saddlecloth.'

'I've got the last sack here, full and ready to go!'

'The sling won't hold. It's rotten.'

'It's not rotten, only filthy. It's still the same saddlecloth underneath.'

'It's too slippy. Come up now.'

'One more sack. The first four or five sacks clear our debts, six and seven earn us profit. We have come here for the seventh sack, or we've come here for nothing.'

'You're starved of air down there and don't know what you're saying.'

'Send down the sling. The longer you cluck like a hen the more I'm down among the fireworks. We'd have had the seventh sack done by now but for you!'

The block and tackle trundles. The rope descends.

'Level!' shouts Nat, and Darius begins swinging the sling.

When Nat grabs the saddlecloth his fingers sink into claggy tar, and he sees the truth of Darius's warning. This is a clump of tar on the end of rope. He should just climb on now, and be hoisted to safety before the saddlecloth gets any worse. But the seventh sack of oil is tied at the neck and ready to go.

'Climb on now,' calls Darius. 'Forget the last sack.'

Nat ties the neck of the sack to the sling and shouts:

'Ready!'

The sack swings out over the oil well, and he hears Darius's angry curse at finding that he is after all winching oil not man.

'Fool! You should come up now instead of this sack.'

'Just pull your rope.'

Nat watches the seventh and final sack rise up to the jagged circle of daylight far above him, with Darius grunting angrily on every pull. Silence. Nat is alone in the pit for the last time. He wipes the oil from his hands as best he can on the sandstone walls. At last comes the sweet melody of the block and tackle's trundle. In jerky stages the filthy beautiful saddlecloth sling appears before his eyes. Nat lifts his face in joy. He watches the tar-caked saddlecloth sling swing out over the abyss.

'Level!' he cheers. He reaches out to grab it but before he does, a squib of burning pitch lands on the saddlecloth. It gently blooms into flame. Nat keens a long, long howl. Darius looks down and finds a stricken helpless look in Nat's saucer eyes, wide as a lemur in the dark.

The fire is brief, but when the flare-up has died away it has taken the saddlecloth with it. Now there is just a frayed end of greasy rope jouncing around in the middle air of the cavern.

'Get me out, Darius! Darius! Get me out! Lay me out some more rope!'

'That's all there is!'

'It won't reach! Get me out!'

The rope dangles in the middle of the chamber, level with Nat's head, and beyond his reach. Without the plumb weight of the tarry saddlecloth on the end of it, Darius cannot swing the rope from up on the top ledge. Nat throws clods of petroleum sludge at the rope to try to set it swinging again. The third handful he throws actually strikes. The rope jounces a little, and then hangs dead still, exactly where it was before.

'Wait, I'll free some more rope,' Darius calls down. He scales the marble statue and plants his feet on Mithras's chest, either side of the block and tackle. In this way he is able to feed an arm's length more rope down to Nat, but at the cost of exposing his bare back to the slew of bituminous pebbles and scalding squibs that the well now spits from its depths. As the oily buckshot pelts Darius's hanging body, he roars and squirms, but hangs onto the rope. The block and tackle rattles with the weight of his writhing. A fat ember of pitch settles on top of his shoulder. Darius endures the ember burning itself out. He holds on, and must suffer the agony of the scorching skin on his shoulder because any second now Nat will leap from vug to rope, and so the rope has to stay where it is. He throws back his head and shouts,

Jump, Nat! Jump!'

'The rope's too far.'

'It's now or never!'

'I'll slip if I jump.'

'Do or die!'

'I'll fall!'

'Come on, jump! You won't fall!'

A sudden weight on the rope slams Darius's knuckles against the block and tackle's maple. Darius yanks back on the rope. Leaning backwards on the horizontal, his feet planted Mithras's chest, he hauls the rope hand over hand, lifting Nat out of the bottomless pit. He hears great gasping sobs of deliverance break from Nat's throat, followed by cries of exultation:

'Oh! I'm rising, Darius! I'm rising. Don't stop! Don't stop!'

Darius scales down the front of Mithras, using his bodyweight to hoist Nat faster out of the pit. At the foot of the idol, he once more hauls the rope hand over hand. He has saved Nat. He is reeling him in.

'We're on our way!' he laughs.

He hears a sound he cannot place. A creak in the earth. Mithras leans forward, churning earth and shunting rubble. The rope goes slack in his hand. The pulley wheel razzes in its maple box. A rockslide knocks him off his feet. Then he sees the most terrible sight of his life. The green marble giant topples headlong down the oil well. The winged Mithras stoops like a hawk for its prey, snatching Nat down into the fiery pit.

An ever-thickening dust cloud rolls over Darius. Coughing and spluttering and blinded by dust, he claws his way up to the light, climbing on rocks that seesaw under him, his feet dislodging rubble that follows Nat and Mithras down into the depths.

He escapes the pit and climbs out into the open air. He looks back at the stoved-in hillside shrouded in its pall of dust. Earth and rock lie where fire and oil shone. There is no oil anywhere save what is bagged in the sticky, filthy mound of goatskins. He throws handful after handful of earth over his head.

'I have killed you, Nat, I have killed you! You have drowned in oil! Oh God, surely Nat is under Your protection and in the rope of Your security, so save him from the trial of the grave and from the punishment of the Fire. You fulfil promises and grant rights, so forgive him and have mercy on him. Surely You are Most Forgiving, Most Merciful!'

22

Day after day, he rode back the way they came. Day after day, he tapped his heels against the mule's sides and listened to the four oil-filled goatskins glooping along. For this glooping sound, this small haul of petroleum, Nat had died. The painful burns on his back were earned while hanging upside-down, feet planted on the icon's chest, trying to feed Nat more rope. He had held on, despite scalding squibs, and when Nat leapt, Darius had been there to take his weight. These insistent burns should have assuaged his guilt, then, but they didn't - because the truth remained that Nat was dead because of him. A hill might fall into the earth, but a truth like that was indestructible.

He led the mule, he rode the mule, his boots were dusty, his boots were muddy, he waded through a cold stream, he was cable-ferried across the Karun River by the ferryman and his wife, until, on a snowy pass at dusk, he found himself back at the goatherd's hut on the mountainside where their expedition had first gone wrong. Thick snow hid the wreckage and donkey carcasses from sight. A small mercy. If they had not lost most of his father's oil-mining equipment Nat wouldn't have died. Inside the hut, where the only sounds were the mule breathing and the oil-stove burning, the Natlessness was like glue-ear.

How powerful were the destructive forces of the universe! And how the slightest attempt to improve things summoned them!

Just for seeking shelter in a bush, the donkeys were crow food on a cliff. Just for stealing a little lamp oil for his mother to sew by, that boy was ganched on a gatehouse hook by the Qizilbash. Just for selling the wrong poem to the wrong man, Darius suffered a face-full of pigeon dung in full view of his beloved. Just for begging the use of his own father's oil-mining equipment he was expected to marry his step-aunt. A simple ember landing on a tar-caked saddlecloth sent Nat plunging to his death in boiling pitch. Darius spoke out loud in the quiet hut.

'Why did I let you persuade me against what I knew was right? I should have refused to drop the rope until you agreed to leave the last bag and come out. It was in my power to save you, Nat.'

In his fitful sleep that night, whenever the wind scattered clods of earth or stones on the roof, Darius heard Nat singing his foolish ditty:

A foldeh-roll, a fiddle-dee do, a foley, rol-a roo!

The following day, Darius rode back through that green ribbon that ran between desolate stretches of rocky grey shale, the strange landscape where they'd talked about Mithras. He dismounted, unwound his leather bottle's long thin strap and lowered it into the bright sparkling stream that ran through the narrow seam of vegetation. He reeled in the bottle, and sipped the cold water. The stream, the blue irises, the purple vetches, the bees and butterflies, and the orange spikes of foxtail lilies that were as tall as a man - he hated them all for their vainglorious existence, because each and everything here had outlived Nat Bramble.

23

The oil shortage had plunged the parliament into near darkness. Two or three lanterns only lit the Shah and his ministers as Anthony stood before them. The Shah was dressed in red from head to toe, save for the black turban crest that rose like a plume of smoke. They said that when he dressed in red it meant someone would die at his hand that day. The Shah was looking daggers at him. So was Oliver de Cannes. Why? What had happened? Anthony lowered his eyes to the rug, a perfect twin of the Persian rug that hung in the Whitehall privy gallery between the Julius Caesar portrait and the bust of Attila the Hun - either of whom Anthony had rather face now than Shah Abbas in this temper.

The Grand Vizier handed him a silver salver upon which lay several dark brown sheets of vellum, covered in handwritten Latin.

Anthony's heart beat fast. Now he would know his doom. He picked the vellum sheets from the salver. The silence of the majlis deepened, the dark room seemed somehow to grow darker. Anthony's heart sank into his boots as he read the beginning of letter:

From Elizabeth, by the Grace of God, Queen of England,

- To the right mighty, and right victorious prince, the Great Shah, Emperor of the Persians, Medes, Parthians, of the people on this side and beyond the River Tigris, and of all men and nations between the Caspian Sea and the Gulf of Persia,

Greetings and most happy increase on all prosperity!

God a' mercy, how had this royal arrow come out of a clear blue sky to pierce his eye? Anthony was the garlanded buffalo on the sunny side of the square. His eyes filled with tears. He could not read the next line. He looked up and asked Abbas when the letter had arrived. Abbas didn't answer. He rose and approached Anthony. He unsheathed a brand new sabre, a replacement for the one he had left in the Tofangchi captain during the battle re-enactment.

Anthony could hear Abbas's heavy breathing. The sun and lion motif on the new sabre's single-edged steel blade was inches from his eyes. Was Abbas going to cut his head from shoulders where he stood? Or blind him? Instead, Abbas said,

'Thirty years ago,' and burst out laughing. A bewildered Anthony looked from face-to-face: Oliver de Cannes was laughing; the austere Grand Vizier was laughing; Mulla Abdulla Shustari was laughing; the Shah's blind brothers were both laughing, even that sour, old vinegar-faced Hoseyn Ali Beg was laughing.

'Queen Elizabeth wrote this letter to Shah Tahmasp my grandfather in the third year of her reign. Years later she wrote to my father, the old blind Shah Khudabandeh. My father and grandfather couldn't give them what they wanted, but I can. I can. She wanted what a rash of Popes, and Kings of Spain wanted. These Christian Princes always petition for a military alliance against the Turk. They have waited long, but now is the time. This morning I cut the Ottoman ambassador's beard off and told him to give it to Sultan Mehmed to eat. We are invading the Turk's lands from north, south, east, west, together with Christian princes! I will send Hoseyn Ali Beg and your brother bearing letters to all the Christian Princes setting out my plans for war!'

'My lord, the Christian Princes will ask why the Shah of Persia has not sent the elder brother, and will scarce believe it to be a true embassy if I am not there.'

'They will have my letter and carry gifts of great price.'

'Oh my lord, send anyone but me to the courts of Europe you insult the Princes and your great stratagem dies. Custom demands you send the elder brother.'

'Must it be you, Antonio?'

'Oh, great Shah, how I wish it were not so for I shall I hate this embassy that takes me from my lord and my love.'

Anthony covered his face with his hands, and then peeked to see how this had gone down. Shah Abbas wore a face of woe. The painted eyebrows and mournful expression gave him the look of a tragedian in old Athens. For a moment he appeared to be as blind as his two brothers, his green eyes unseeing as his raised face went slowly side to side, earrings tinkling in the hush. His chest heaved in his tight scarlet tunic and when he opened his mouth wide. Anthony expected a lion's roar but instead out crawled a boy chorister's squeak.

'I am what men, to mock me, call a Shah, when it seems I have no say in what most touches my heart. You, Antonio, must go to the courts of the Christian princes. But your brother stays here as hostage against your faithful duty and your swift return to the Shah who loves you.'

'As your majesty commands. I request only that I be the first to break this news to my brother.'

24

The following day, Anthony and Robert Sherley went to the top of the Shah Tahmasp tower, the tallest building in Isfahan. Its turret was tessellated with the skulls of deer and gazelle, leopard and lynx. Anthony had brought Robert up here to break the news that he was going to be staying behind as a hostage.

'Looks like a besieging army down there, all those tents and camp-fires,' said Robert. 'Except they're all leaving.'

'Last caravan before the war,' said Anthony.

Each day the tent city upon the western plain thickened like algal bloom, as more and more traders, pilgrims, migrants, merchants and servants camped out awaiting the departure of the caravan, to which they would hitch themselves for safe travel to every town and shrine from Isfahan to Istanbul.

While waiting for his moment to break the news, Anthony ran the quartz crystal perspective trunk, the Sultan's gift to the Shah from the Istanbul observatory, over the crowds and encampments outside the city wall, searching for Bramble, hoping to capture him within the ground glass disc's rainbow borders.

'I have been sending Elkin, Pincon and Parry daily into the cara-vanserai to seek out the villain,' said Anthony. 'The Ottoman caravan will leave in a day or two, taking Bramble and my silver coins with it if we don't bustle! He's down there somewhere among that filthy horde. But oh, it is shaming that even as the Embassy is about to depart my mind is not full of high statecraft but all taken up with finding that whoreson. Cock a bones, the agonies that slave has put me through! I need my three-hundred dollars for the Embassy! Am I to beg my stipend from Hoseyn Ali Beg, like the young housewife married to the old miser!' He lowered the quartz crystal from his eye, saying, 'Ugh! All is confusion! See if you can find my brand on one of these filthy sheep.'

'To escape detection so long,' said Robert, squinting into the perspective trunk, 'the renegade must have accomplices in Isfahan.'

'Bramble won't want to make a life here! He cannot leave except with a caravan and this is the first to go since he fled.'

Robert laid quartz crystal on bone sill, and looked his brother in the eye.

'When do we leave?'

The moment had come to tell him. Anthony would have to be very careful how he told him for nothing must jeopardise the Embassy. But tell him he must. This was the time and place. It was now or never.

'The Embassy,' Anthony began, 'will leave in two days. But there's something which you should -.'

'Two whole days! I don't know if I can last two more days in this place! Look what Abbas did to the governor of Ghilan yesterday. Hacked off his lips and nose for embezzlement. Then sends him wandering naked and blind, his head and arms in stocks, no man allowed to shelter him.'

'I'll thank the Shah to do the same to Bramble for his embezzling my silver, by God!'

Once upon a time, reflected Anthony, Bramble was supposed to have delivered the Sherley brother's escape fund. Those Dutch lion dollars were to have financed their plan to flee Persia together. The only sure way to do so was without telling Angelo and the other gentlemen of the party, whose continued presence would cover a pretend hunting expedition long enough for the brothers to get clean away with some Dutch merchants. But that was once upon a time. Now there was a new story with a new ending for Robert. No way out but by leaving Robert behind. Up here in this skull circle it would not matter how Robert shouted and stamped when the news was broken, nor what threats he made to tell the Shah how things really stood - no-one could hear.

'For embezzlement, Anthony! Why it could have been father!'

'You talk as if embezzlement were the family business! And besides, father would have had no cause to embezzle from so openhanded a sovereign. Unlike that ginger bitch, Abbas would have given our brother three ships no question. By the time we get back, Thomas will have put more gold back in the Queen's moneybox than she ever knew was gone.'

Chanting arose from a large angry crowd in the maidan. Robert trained the perspective trunk down on the crowd, and moved the lens a notch. Within the disc's rainbow blur of ground crystal he captured a redcapped Qizilbash parading a giant burnished steel battle standard. Two steel dragons stuck out from either side of the battle standard. Waving one arm, a mullah led the crowd in a chant. His mouth opened and closed as silently as a fish, but his words were amplified in the crowd's chants that reached the Sherley brothers' eyrie.

Hoping to dazzle his brother with his knowledge of these things, Anthony went into a long disquisition about the chant's political significance. The Shi'ih crowd were cursing the names of the first three Sunni Caliphs, he explained, whom they accused of robbing Ali of his rightful succession to the Caliphate. The Sultan was Sunni the Shah was Shi'ih.

'Shah Abbas is keeping his pulpits well-tuned,' said Anthony, alluding to the Queen's famous phrase about how, whenever war loomed, she used the clergy to incite a patriotic Protestant fervour. 'For Shi'ih Persia is surrounded by hostile Sunni states, just as our little Protestant island is surrounded by hostile Papist states.' Far from being dazzled, as he should have been, Robert said:

'Ah! That's the very point I've been wanting to tell you about. This is the great mistake you're making. I've read your whole stack of ambassadorial letters and they all contradict each other.'

'Wheels within wheels,' said Anthony, cryptically tapping his nose.

'No,' said Robert. 'Each letter contradicts the next. What helps Spain harms England, what's good for Venice is bad for Rome. Venice wants peace with the Turk, the Pope wants war. These letters are all at cross purposes!'

'Fear not, these letters will all carry well. I'm lucky, didn't you know?'

'They cannot all carry well. Either some will or others will, but not all at once, don't you see?'

'No,' said Anthony his voice rising, 'this is bigger than all that. Venice, Rome, Spain and England all set aside their differences to fight against the Turk once before at the Great Battle of Lepanto. They've done it before, they'll do it again, and these letters are the means to do it!'

'Anthony, Lepanto was before the Levant Company's trade with the Turk. England and Venice will never, ever give up this rich trade. These are new times, brother.'

'All times are new to the ignorant! You don't see the broad canvas.'

'No, *you* don't,' said Robert, 'your letter to King James cancels out what you write to the Queen.'

Anthony scowled, and a hot flush ran up the side of his neck. All his life his younger brother Robert had been a kind of wizard whose words had the power to alter substance, whose adenoidal, actuarial tone and manner somehow made it seem as if he were the elder brother. Anthony's best way of defending his achievements from such sorcery was to put some distance between himself and Robert.

'Perhaps there are things about the Embassy I haven't told you yet.'

'My heart bleeds,' said Robert 'that you have not consulted me more on this Embassy. I don't understand why you have cut me out. I have been an ambassador and you have not, and I tell you plain that the way you have enlarged the embassy ensures its failure.'

'Perhaps you don't know the true purpose of this mission.'

'I'm still waiting for you to tell me!'

Robert knew his brother wanted him to ignore the fine detail and applaud only the scale, but he was duty-bound to share his serious misgivings about this hopelessly compromised embassy of cross purposes. True brotherly love required Robert to point out to Anthony that his high horse was only painted white. The first shower of rain would reveal a poorly painted piebald nag.

'These letters will get you into a terrible tangle. They'll bog you down and sink you. I fear they will entrap and ensnare you in all kinds of ways that you don't yet see.'

'Trap, snap, ensnare, bog, mire, impede - these are your only joys, brother! Your very ecstasies! You want to piss on my achievement!'

'I do not, Anthony! I offer you good counsel as a loving brother.'

'You're cursing the embassy, this legendary enterprise before it's even begun, before it's even had a chance!'

'I simply urge you to form a single clear strategy from one or two commissions from one or two princes rather than drown in a welter -'

'Drown! Drown in the boggy mire, I suppose! Among all the tangles! Here I stand on top of the world, about to lead the richest Embassy the courts of Europe will have ever seen, on a mission to shift the balance of world power more than Drake, Hawkins and Raleigh combined, and all you can say to me is that if only I'd listened to your advice I wouldn't be in this awful mess, bogged down in a terrible tangle in the mire. You don't understand, Robert. Policy is indirect. Policy is a billiard table where a statesman must use the green to sink the red in off the cushion, only so he can come up and kiss the purple.'

'How you kiss the Shah's cock is your own business, but unless you select your alliances this Embassy is doomed before it's begun. Everyone understands this, everyone except you and your sweetheart the Shah.'

Up here in this bony turret among the deer skulls, Robert's wild words were harmless. Except what if he was to carry on raving unpredictably at ground level? Anthony couldn't risk the Shah changing his mind about sending him on the Great Persian Embassy.

'You are right,' said Anthony. 'Forgive me. I'm sorry not to have talked over the embassy more with you. But I promise that once we're on the road, I will disclose all I know to you, and I truly look forward to hearing your wise counsel.'

Robert burst into tears of gratitude to be admitted back in to his brother's trust. He embraced Anthony, and laid his cheek on his shoulder.

'Oh, the road, the road,' he said. 'Soon we'll be on the road, putting our heads together as we ride out of here, oh heaven! Do you know I've had my bags packed for days now? Saddle too. Watching the servants buckle those bags, I was able to breathe for the first time in months. I saw Wiston in every shirt fold, our father, our sister Cessalye, and Thomas, above all Thomas in every slammed lid and saddlebow. Oh, I can't wait. Soon, we'll be on the road together.'

A strange sound entered the bone ring. The sound was like a man breathing on his spectacles, only terrifically loud, as an ant might hear it.

Hur! Hur! Hur!

It came from the maidan. And now came the rumble and thump of the crowd jumping up and down, while still roaring their *Hur! Hur! Hur!*

'Look, a trick rider,' said Anthony, glad of a change of subject, pointing at a gymnast standing on the saddles of two horses.

'Then why the hosannahs?' asked Robert. 'Why the jumping?'

Anthony took the quartz crystal. In the glass disc, as clear as in a clasp locket, he saw the horizontal black moustache and fierce green eyes of Shah Abbas. In flowing green robes, Abbas galloped through the crowds. The horses he stood on were still galloping when he leapt down and, on the bounce, reappeared on a high wall near the mosque, leading the crowd and his soldiers in chanting against the Sunni caliphs.

Seeing the Shah's face so close in the lens he felt an overwhelming sense of suffocation, of being trapped. Abbas had a habit of falling asleep with his arms around one's chest, so that it was impossible to break his hold without waking him up. Whenever Anthony needed to get up in the night, he would spend perhaps half an hour lifting the royal arms by inches, so as to slide out of his embrace without waking him, but the moment Anthony finally placed his bare feet on the marble floor, he would hear a marble-hard voice behind him, demand to know where he was going. At such times Anthony's own reply always sounded like a request,

'I desire to use the chamber pot.'

Essex once told him he felt he was putting his head in a lion's jaw every time he kissed the Queen. Kissing Abbas felt the same. A panther in his prime, though, not a mangy old lioness. If his love was suffocating, his air of violence was a close, overcast day, its looming thunderheads throwing down spectacular bolts like the one that killed Angelo's manservant, or mutilated the embezzling governor of Ghilan, or which would - by Christ! - have chopped Anthony's own head off, had the ink had been a little fresher on the lioness's letter to the panther. He lowered the perspective trunk and was relieved to see Abbas reduced to a far-distant dot. Soon the Embassy would achieve the same feat!

Into the circle of bone bounded Shah Abbas dressed in scarlet with a posse of Tofangchi, his bodyguard of Georgian war orphans, the sons of slain Christians. The bodyguard spread out around the turret walls in silence until they had surrounded the Sherleys. Forgetting to drop to their knees, the brothers turned from the Shah before them to look back at the Shah down in the maidan. Their heads spinning they saw Shah Abbas both far-off and near to the eye, both down in the maidan and standing before them in the bone circle at one and the same time.

'A double!' cried the Shah delightedly. 'A double so that I may spend the last precious hours I have with my Antonio before he leaves with the Embassy.' The brothers dropped to their knees, and bowed their heads in silence. 'This tower, Antonio, was built by Tahmasp my grandfather, to commemorate the most successful hunting party ever to leave the royal stables. All these animals were killed on one hunt. Every one of them. Will you come hawking with me? Nothing shall rise before us that is not game! For flies I have sparrows, for larks and finches I have marlins and tercels to set upon them, for pigeons hawks, for buzzards peregrine falcons, and for deer and gazelles I have golden eagles. And five hundred dogs to fetch it all in. In this way we shall make a clean sweep of the country, and leave a silence behind! Come!'

The Sherley brothers walked towards Shah Abbas.

'Where do you think you're going?' the Shah asked Robert, who froze on the spot. He watched Abbas, Anthony and the Tofangchi disappear down the long, winding staircase, leaving him alone among the skulls, a ghost in the bright blue sky.

25

The darkness is absolute. 'Or am I blind?' Nat wonders. 'Did my eyes burn out when I fell through molten oil into the water below?' He is encased in sticky bitumen. 'What happened? I fell through oil into water, and would have drowned but for Mithras smashing through the underground water chamber.' He must have slid from the vadose down some kind of chute into these catacombs of hollow sandstone where he can breathe. Better to have drowned than lie here in this sticky, tarry grave.

'Oh God, hear me in the truth of thy salvation. Deliver me out of the mire, that I sink not. Let not the flood drown me, neither let the deep swallow me up; and let not the pit shut her mouth upon me.'

His arms are outstretched ahead of him as though he were diving into a lake. Rocks and earth pinion his wrists and ankles. He waggles the blind antennae of hands and feet, the only parts of him that can move.

'Dear God, let me die in the open air, out on the honest earth below Your sky. Let me be numbered among the creatures of the earth and air, and not the scuttling underground creatures.'

Oil trickles towards him along a slant chute. The approaching oil rumbles louder and louder behind him. The soles of his feet grow hot. No trickle now, but a glugging flood. Oil is scalding the channelled earth behind him. He flippers his feet in impotent frenzy. Hot oil clouts his heels, flows over his ankles, up his legs and over his body, then rises around his Adam's apple, then submerges his face. He holds his breath until his lungs are about to burst. The oil rolls away. He sucks air like pebbles on a beach when a heavy wave withdraws.

Slicked and greased, he finds he can move his shoulders a little, and wriggle his legs enough to shake off the sticky jagged clumps of tar shale shackling his ankles.

For several moments, he believes it possible that he is not going to die in this tunnel, that the last taste in his mouth won't be oil. Then, from far behind, he hears a sound which ends that small hope. A rolling heavy tide of oil. Like a condemned man manacled to Traitor's Gate for seven tides of the Thames, he can hear the dark tide that will drown him. Oil booms into the chute and thuds against the soles of his feet. He hurtles forward into a widening passage. The rip tide of oil passes over him. He breathes air again, gasping and spluttering on a chute. He crawls, he slips, he sprawls into shallow puddles of oil. He slithers blindly through a narrow opening that shelves steeply. He slides down a ramp of slick bitumen. A rock bangs his hip. Rocks clash. The clash echoes.

He wafts his hand ahead of him in the blackness. A wall. His fingertips trace one right-angled groove after another. Bricks. The product of hand and trowel. Man has been here before him. He crawls round patting a ring of bricks no wider than the span of his arms. And then he knows where he is. This must be the foot of the chimney tower, thirty underground yards from where the marble Mithras plunged towards him: a cathedral bell crashing down on the bell-ringer. He climbs to his feet at the base of the tower. He spreads his arms out and touches curving wall on either side. There is no breaking through these thick solid walls. He raises his arms as high as they will go, wiggling his fingers above him. He shouts 'Hoy!' and hears the echo climb the tower.

He crumbles loose powder from dry brickwork. The brick dust stings his wounds. His whimpering echoes up the chimney. He braces himself off the ground, feet pushing back against curving brickwork and inches up the inside of the tower. His whole body trembles and shakes. The pain in the muscles of his arms and thighs redoubles with every breath he takes. Up and up he climbs. The darkness is so immaculate that he has no sense of how high he has climbed. A large slab of dry mortar detaches from under his palm. He hears it bounce down the inner walls. A sickeningly long fall. His stinging palms press against the curved wall, but his whole body starts shaking and trembling so violently that hands and feet keep slipping.

A crunching blow to the ridge of his skull pile-drives his neck into his shoulders. Sharp dust prickles his eyes. He reaches up a hand and finds a rusty iron bar. He grabs hold of the bar with both hands. He lets his feet dangle over the sheer black drop of the inside of the chimney tower. He swings to and fro and finds he can hook the back of his knees over two more bars. He hangs from the three iron bars, right at the top of the tower, and sobs in the sweet relief at no longer having to brace his aching muscles against the fire-tower's walls.

He climbs up through the bars. His fingers touch a mortar ceiling. He runs his fingertips over the mortar, and finds a flint, which he excavates with his thumbnail. Perched on two bars, he uses the flint to dig out the mounting of the third. He scrapes and gouges at mortar until he can rotate the bar. He jerks the bar side to side, working it loose like a stiff door-bolt. Suddenly he is holding the full weight of the bar in his hand. He touches it to either cheek, and kisses the iron bar. He climbs through the gap he has created. He lies on his back on the two bars fixed under the cement ceiling. He thrusts the loose bar up at his coffin lid. He thrusts it upwards - once, twice, three times. *Tunk. Tunk. Tunk.* He cuffs dust from his face, and tastes it on his tongue. He adjusts his grip on the iron bar. *Tunk. Tunk. Tunk.* Ever larger chunks of mud, brick and mortar fall onto him. *Tunk. Tunk. Tunk.*

A slab clunks his cheek. Orange lights flicker on the insides of his eyelids. 'If I were blind, would I still see these orange spots?' He tunks the iron bar upwards with all his might, and strikes the very thing for which he has been mining: the first nugget of sky. He can feel cool air among the dust. There is a different quality to the blackness. He flails away with the iron bar, mining this rich seam in frenzy, digging out stars, a clipped moon, a galaxy, clouds - he can see them all!

Nat throws the iron bar, and hauls himself up onto the rim of the tower. He sits with one leg hanging outside the tower. He feels the wind on his eyes, on his eyelashes, on his lips, in his nostrils, in his mouth. He holds his breath to hear the dead tree's gentle clacking and creaking.

'Darius,' he calls out. 'Darius!'

All alone. But his prayer has been answered: he will die in the open air.

He coughs a long hacking cough. He stands up on the rim of the tower, legs apart with his arms raised aloft. He shouts to the elements:

'I am Nat Bramble! I am the sky miner! I gouged the stars and moon out of the earth! I knocked down the wall between death and life! Knocked it clean through!'

He squats on the round ledge, and leaps from the tower. He lands in sand. Curled on his side at the foot of the Fire Temple of Mithras, cowled in oil, more mineral than man, he sobs for the deliverance he has won for himself.

He lies immobile. The soft heavy sand flashes here and there with mica. The sands drift over him with the night winds. A delicious heaviness steals over him. 'If I don't stay awake the sands will bury me.' He blacks out, and the first ray of dawn discovers, scattered in the sand, a blackened barefoot heel, a protruding elbow, and a tussock of stiff, black hair.

26

Darius was approaching Isfahan as darkness fell. Campfires, hundreds of them, burned far and wide under the night sky. He led the mule through this plain of campfires, each of them thick with travellers waiting to entrain with the Ottoman caravan the following day. Drawing near the gatehouse - the same one where they'd seen the boy ganched - he found it was thick with merchants and their runners all shouting for oil at any price.

'Gold for oil! Gold paid for oil. New gold tomans for oil!'

'Oil, oil, who here has oil? Oil at any price!'

Darius lifted his face to the stars and whispered to the spirit of his dead friend,

'We have beaten the Baku convoy to the gates, Nat-jan!'

At that very moment, a gauntlet bit into his burnt shoulder and pulled him against a tall white horse. Leaning down from his jewelled saddle, Sir Anthony Sherley swept a lantern beam over his face.

'Would your excellency like to buy some oil?' asked Darius. The English knight pushed him away with his boot, and rode off, playing his lantern beam this way and that, hunting through the crowds.

'You search in vain, Sir Anthony. Your servant is free of you at last.'

Darius led his mule back out into the fields. He passed cooking smells, chatter, babies crying and laughter at one crowded campfire after another. Soon all these fell away to be replaced by only three sounds: tussock grass brushing his boots, oil slugging in its hides, and the footsteps of two men following him. Pretending to adjust the mule's harness, he turned round and walked backwards.

The two pursuers weren't Antonio's men. They were Persian. One wore a conical hat, turbaned with cambric, the other a pot-shaped hat with a tall, upturned brim and a feather. Neither Pot nor Cone bothered to disguise the fact that they had made him their quarry, but followed as fixedly as the ploughman his plough. They must have heard him ask Antonio Mirza if his Excellency wanted to buy some oil. He cursed himself for a fool.

Cone split from Pot, and went looping ahead of their prey. They were going to come at him from different directions. Darius spied a large campfire in a dell. His heart leapt up. He'd find safety in numbers. Saved! He hurried over the ridge of this sunken encampment. Empty. The campfire blazed unattended. He was alone.

The mule tossed its head. Darius pulled its jaw down, tightening the rein about his fist. Pot descended into the dell and stood before Darius. Up close, the pot-shaped hat was an expensive one, with plume fronds on its upturned brim. Pot stared into Darius's eyes but said nothing until Cone jumped into the bowl with a two-footed thud.

'You shouldn't have this oil,' said Pot.

'That oil belongs to a powerful merchant,' Darius replied. 'He will be very -'

Pot's fist struck his jaw. Darius rocked back on his heels. Then he seemed to turn to stone. He couldn't move a muscle. Not because the blow scrambled his brains, but because it affronted his soul, shocked him to the core, singled him out from the world, which carried on everywhere except inside the ringing cowl in which he now stood, as if a magic circle of immobility had been drawn around him. He stared numbly as Pot and Cone led away the mule. His gaze fell vaguely on the four bulbous goatskins waddling on the chestnut's back. It dimly crossed his mind that this would be the last time he saw those sacks, that packsaddle. And then he heard the oil go *gloop, gloop*. It was a soft, lulling sound, yet the glooping oil awoke him with more force than a pistol shot next to his ear. This was the oil that Nat had died for. He pulled a long oak branch from the campfire. He gripped it double-fisted. Its tip glowed. He strode towards the robbers.

'I cannot let you take that oil.'

The thieves turned and saw the club he was wielding. Pot drew a knife from his sash. Darius dropped the club instantly.

'Pardon, please. I beg your forgiveness! Please take the oil. Take it.'

'What were you going to do with that club?' asked Pot.

'You can have it,' said Darius. 'Take the oil. There's a curse on it anyway.'

'I asked you what you were going to do with that club when our backs were turned?'

Pot stepped towards him. Reflected firelight slid up and down the blade. Darius had seen the last of life beyond the little arena of this firepit. He would die here.

Just then, however, Pot did the very last thing Darius expected him to do: he turned a forward somersault! More astonishing still, from the wriggling ball of Pot's grey cloak there issued not one but two pairs of feet! Four legs wiggled in the air. Up flew the knife, its silver blade spinning high into the night to land in the firepit. Pot was wrestling a dirty, ragged dervish. Cone darted forwards and hopped about the wrestling pair, looking to stab the dervish. Darius picked up the oak club again, stepped forward and slogged Cone on the beige cambric headband. Cone slumped to the ground, his face sheeted with blood.

Pot scrambled to his feet and raised his fists against the filthy dervish. The two circled each other, looking to land the first blow. But then Pot caught sight of Cone on his back and dropped his fists. As if the fight had ended half-an-hour rather than half a second ago, Pot helped Cone to his feet, and together they staggered the few steps to the edge of the dell, where he lowered Cone onto the bank, unwound the cambric and used it to staunch the smooth weir of blood pouring from above his eye. Pot turned to Darius, and asked:

'What did you do that for? We weren't going to hurt you. We only wanted your oil. Look at all this blood. Are you mad? It's lucky he's still alive. If he wasn't wearing this you'd be a murderer you would, a murderer!'

'But you pulled a knife,' stammered Darius.

'Only to make you put the stick down.'

'You were going to rob me.'

'Who was stabbed? Nobody! Who's covered in blood? Him!'

'Will he be all right?' asked Darius.

'Go away!'

Darius walked off a few steps, then back turned to say:

'And you punched me in the face...'

'Go! Just go!'

Darius left them and went to thank the wrestling dervish, who was now on the other side of the blazing fire. Through the tall flames Darius watched him retrieve Pot's knife. A grimy face turned towards him and smiled. Darius screamed at the top of his lungs. He turned tail and ran, no longer caring about mule or oil or Pot or Cone. For he had seen a ghost. Behind him, he heard the ghost cry:

'Don't you know me, Darius? Don't you know me?'

Darius froze.

'Don't you know me?' called the ghost. 'Don't you know me?'

Darius slowly turned. The spectre stood behind the fire. A veil of burning embers rose before the apparition. Now illuminated by flame, now plunged into darkness, the ghost sang a strange incantation:

> *A foldeh-roll a-fiddly-doe, a foldeh-ro-a-roo,*
> *A foldeh-roll a-fiddly-doe, a foldeh-ro-a-roo.*

Darius feared he had gone mad. He sank to the ground, head in hands. A pair of arms encircled him and as they held him in their frowsy embrace, he smelt a sweet rank odour that could only be of this world.

27

The heat from the fire on their faces, Nat and Darius sat with their backs against seven goatskins of oil, while the chestnut and buckskin companionably rattled the sucker growth of the cherry to which they were tethered.

'But if you thought I was dead,' asked Nat, 'then why didn't you take the buckskin?'

'He bolted when the hill caved in.'

'When I lifted the packsaddle off him, I found the mutton fillet your grandmother put there to cure. I ate that mutton like a dog in the street. Then I loaded up the goatskins you left behind and rode after you. And this shirt I'm wearing belonged to the Karun ferryman. His wife fed me, even though I was a poor naked beggar who could not pay, and then man and wife together they winched me across the river on their new ferry. New wood, amber it was, our nails like shining copper pennies in the fresh timber. Did you see it?'

'I had eyes for nothing, Nat. I thought I had killed you.'

'Killed me?'

'With my idiot plan, my mad ideas.'

Nat took hold of both his hands and looked him in the eye.

'No, Darius, I have been more alive on our venture than I have ever been in my whole life.'

They embraced and Nat resumed telling his tale.

'After the Karun River, I was sure I'd catch you over the next hill or the next. I raced the setting sun on my shoulder. When it sank, I dismounted and led the mule. When it rose, I hopped into the saddle again. When I found you, the robbers were already following you. And here,' he said, raising the long knife, 'is the blade that might have killed you.'

'None of that at any time at all,' said Darius with a shudder. Nat grinned to hear his friend come out with his old saying again.

'Here's our treasure!' said Nat, throwing his back against the goatskins and smacking them with satisfaction. 'It is almost as sweet to be reunited with these sacks of oil as with you, my friend. Now we just have to walk the oil through the gate and set up on the maidan to make our fortune!'

'Alas, it's not so simple,' said Darius. 'Your old master Sir Anthony is out with his people hunting for you.'

'He can't stay at the gates forever, so shall we wait till he goes?'

'No,' replied Darius. 'Every second counts. What if the Baku convoy comes in while we're waiting out here? Our oil will be cheap as sticks. Everything we've done, everything we've been through, will have been for nothing. '

Nat got to his feet and walked to the steep riverbank and listened to the turbid river. Now and then a whitecap flashed in the dark. Well, if his fall through the bottomless pit had taught him anything it was that oil floats on water. He turned his head and said:

'The river. Let's bind these goatskins into a raft of oil.'

'And just leave our good mules here for thieves?'

'Or let them go.'

They untethered the mules, fed them kola nuts and slapped their rumps.

Then Nat and Darius roped all seven bulbous goatskins together, rolled them down a steep grassy bank into the fast-flowing Zayandeh River, and flung themselves aboard. The river whisked their oil raft to the city wall, where a heavy chain strung across the water stopped their raft dead. There was not enough slack in the chain to lift it more than a hand's breadth. They kneaded and dunked the raft under the chain, and through a narrow archway in the foot of the wall, and then flowed into Isfahan.

28

Sitting on their goatskins, Nat and Darius drifted across a wide ornamental lake. As loud and disordered as it was outside the city, all was silent and serene inside the city walls. They could hear the ripples made by the slowly twirling raft. A mandarin drake turned his eye of fire upon the two men who lowered themselves into the water, which came up to their chests. They waded through thick clusters of water lily and lotus, towing the bobbing goatskins behind them. They took hold of a willow's exposed roots to climb out of the water onto a garden rockery.

Dawn cracked overhead as they dragged the goatskins across mosaic-tiled paths, through flowerbeds, and over an empty lane. They came to a long pool with stone columns along its paved borders. Reflected in its sheen of greasy algae were the bearded barbarian Darius and Nat the asphalt dervish, his hair a tarry clump of tats. The goatskins landed with a smack in the pool, and they ran along the paved border, towing the oil raft to the end of the waterway, hauled it out of the water, crashed through some bushes, and were soon lost among thorns and briars. The muddy raft, coated in leaves and bark, became wedged stuck between the low branches of a pink oleander thicket. Together they tugged the rope with all their might, but it wouldn't budge. They were in a pink hell. Nat began to panic.

'It's getting light now, and here we are like poachers in a wood. Any second now a root is going to rip through these rotten sacks!'

They heaved on the rope one more time. The oil raft broke free and they tumbled backwards through the oleander to find themselves in a lane busy with market traders carrying their wares in bags and bundles, on mules and handcarts, to the maidan. Nat and Darius joined them.

In the breaking dawn, the mosque's dome glowed like a jellyfish. The goatskins made a high-pitched whine, as they dragged them across the maidan, and when they reached the foot of the bleachers, the base of each scoured sack was hot to the touch, and its hid singed bald. Darius sawed through the soggy rope netting. They separated the sacks. They humped each one up the bleachers, and stood beside their merchandise on the third stone step.

Hands on hips and fighting for breath, Darius said,

'We have brought our goods to market.'

Nat cast an anxious look at Ali Qapu Palace as a shutter opened on the second floor.

Leaving Nat to mind the oil, Darius found a ceramist in his workshop. Alas, the only ceramic tureens about the right size were snow leopards sitting proudly with the tops of their heads missing. Tall vases for reeds, they came up to Darius's waist but they would have to do.

On the third step of the white stone bleachers, Nat and Darius unstoppered a goatskin. Together they peered in at the oil, and saw their own wobbly heads before a cornflower blue sky. The black oil winked with golden bubbles. Unexposed since Masjid-i-Suleiman, this magical substance from the bowels of the earth had the power now to change their fortunes, and let them start again. Darius slowly poured oil from the goatskin into a snow leopard's head. All around them, the fir pole scaffoldings of market stalls were being erected. They looked at each other.

'Give me your hand,' said Darius.

Nat's eyes misted over. He was deeply moved that Darius should choose this very moment to solemnise their friendship.

'With all my heart,' he replied, and held out his hand.

To Nat's surprise, however, Darius seized his elbow, dunked his hand in a snow leopard's skull, then raised it high for everyone to see how it was gloved in fresh, black and shining oil. Then, Darius, the prolix poet and grand speechifier, spoke the most powerful and eloquent speech of his whole life - and it was only one word long. His strong, clear voice boomed across the maidan:

'Oil!'

29

Word spread. Tea rooms emptied. Venerable merchants, who hadn't run in years, nor slept since last night's crazed, hopeless hunt for oil outside the city gates, came running across the square. Nat tilted a snow leopard's brim to let these panting merchants glimpse the purity of their wares.

'Behold, the finest oil known to man!' declared Darius, as they swarmed round. 'No tarry sludge but pure oil from a secret reserve kept by ancient Zoroastrians for their pagan fire-worship rites!'

The first lot was sold for two gold tomans, about one hundred abbassi. But Darius would not sell the second lot until he had entered the first sale in his calfskin book. Only Nat could see that Darius wasn't writing anything at all but only pretending to enter the sale in his ledger, all the better to get the merchants slathering at the mouth. At last he closed his little book and announced:

'The bidding for the next jar begins at the closing price of the last.' The merchants shouted curses and insults. Darius promptly closed the book and stood there, eyebrows raised. The merchants fell silent. He nodded and opened his book again. Immediately, new bids were cried out, to which he theatrically cupped now one ear then the other.

'Two gold tomans and twenty-five abbassi!' shouted a merchant.

'Two gold tomans and fifty!' cried another.

'And fifty-five!'

'And sixty!'

'Sold!'

Once again Darius took an age pretending to enter the sale in his book, once again he announced that that starting price was the closing price of the last lot. Again the heckles, again the shut book, again the raised eyebrows, again the abashed silence, and once again the book was reopened and outcry bidding erupted.

Nat feasted his eyes on Darius at work. What a tragedy if Darius had never known this hour! He was born for this role. This was him: standing on a step, balding velvet coat buttoned over his podgy belly, lording it over the merchants, beating them at their own game, teaching them how much money they stood to lose if the game were not rigged, reminding them never to let the poor man pitch his talents equally against theirs or else they'd be poorer than he! No-one else but Darius could have rinsed more gold tomans from these merchants' purses. He was excellent at this. He was as unbudgeable as the solid tar of his hair. No matter how high the bids, he refused even to consider selling all his oil at once. Vast sums he waved away with a waggle of his fingers, flicking their offers back in their face. It drove the merchants livid, but they weren't going anywhere. In between taking the merchants' money, and pouring more oil into ceramic snow leopards, he feasted his eyes on Darius, and marvelled that the two of them created all this clamour and hubbub by their own labours, their own visions and dreams. They had defeated the odds.

The last lot of oil was sold, and the auction came to an end. Unsuccessful merchants, who had failed to purchase any of that morning's oil, went away darkly muttering that if Shah Abbas couldn't stop the Turk attacking the Baku oil convoys, upon which all commerce depended, then a quick war was needed.

The sky darkened. The Zagros Mountains slipped away behind a grey mist without anyone noticing. Charcoal clouds smudged the sky. It began to drizzle and then to rain.

Nat and Darius gathered their slough of empty, oily goatskins, and walked away, leaving a black stain on the steps of the stone bleachers.

30

Nat and Darius no sooner sold the last jug of oil and rolled up the empty goatskins, than they were seized by a ravenous hunger. Hunching their shoulders against the rain, they hurried to the narrow alleys behind the bazaar in search of breakfast. A giant basin of mast, for customers to fill a jar from, sat among the vegetables of the first food stall they came to.

'An advance,' Darius informed the stallholder, and dropped a silver abbassi in the scales. He lifted the basin of mast to his lips, tilted his head back and drank half. He handed the basin to Nat, who drained the rest. The curdled milk was delicious, but as Nat set down the empty bowl, his gaze became snagged on the single silver coin hanging in the balance, and a shadow passed over his joy when he thought of Anthony and the reckoning to come.

The drizzle turned to rain, but the stallholder would not let them stand inside. Instead he brought out a gong-sized plate of refried khoreshte fessenjun, the mutton chunks steaming in the cold and wet. The salad's clear green hazelnut oil glazed their oil-blackened hands. In no time at all, their oily fingers were leaving black prints on smooth white bones, from which every shred of mutton had been sucked.

Nat's heavy head drooped with tiredness but he could not stop laughing at the milk on Darius's beard and at his curly coriander moustache, or rather at the fact that he was unaware of them just as he was unaware of the curlicue of lettuce and humus decorating an eyebrow, and unaware of his ecstatic moaning and groaning each time his tongue discovered buried citruses, rogue sultanas and caramelised onions in the mutton stew or salad. The rain stopped. The nightingale, in a cage between a net of melons and a string of onions, chirruped and chatted.

'I've no room for the nightingale,' groaned Darius.

Nat keeled over, laughing uncontrollably. The stallholder brought out a pot of mint tea, took one look at the howling foreigner rolling around in a puddle, and hurried back inside. Darius clutched his belly against the pain of laughing on a full stomach. Tears streamed down his face. Each time they mastered themselves and stopped laughing, and were just getting their breath back, the nightingale started singing and that set them both off again. At last, they calmed down and dried their eyes, and finished their tea.

Darius reached a hand into the torn lining of his balding velvet coat, and brought out their earnings. They scrubbed tarry coins clean in a puddle, and split the money into two equal shares. Nat drew his knife, nicked an opening in his doublet's lining, and slotted his coins one by one into its satin panes.

'Stab me now,' he said, 'and I bleed coin.'

'You are armoured with loot!'

'I am honeycombed with gold and silver,' said Nat.

'But can you twist?' Not only could Nat twist, but when he did so the coins were as silent as a corset's whalebones.

'La!'

'Can you bend?' asked Darius.

Bending was another matter. He could no more bend at the waist than if he were wearing a suit of armour. The only way to touch his hand to the ground was by executing a ceremonial, courtly bow. Sweeping the back of his hand over the ground, he became aware of another presence.

A young nobleman was standing before them. The rain-soaked plume wilting on the stranger's hat obscured one half of a handsome face, the other half twinkled with the reflected light from the food stall's glass bead curtain. The nobleman introduced himself as Uruch Bey, First Secretary of the Persian Embassy, and congratulated them on the great success of the oil trading they had done on the maidan. The wind set the glass beads tinkling and sent light chasing up and down one side of Uruch Bey's face.

Nat was later to think back to this first encounter with Uruch Bey, a man who was to change his and Darius's lives forever. Right from the moment they met, Uruch Bey was a shimmerer. You could never tell Uruch's facial expression from a trick of the light. You never knew quite where you were with him. He was never one thing or the other. Even the way Uruch Bey spoke to them was ambiguous. On one level there was a comradely lack of hierarchy in his chatty amiability, and yet all the time he spoke, Nat and Darius shared a sense that they were being somehow pressed into service by an irresistible power. His manner was ambiguous too. He stood with a loose-limbed, easy grace and yet his sharp eyes were like diamond cutters when he asked Nat,

'Are you not one of Mirza Antonio's servants?'

'Yes, your honour,' Nat replied.

'Does he know you are here?'

'Indeed, your honour, Antonio Mirza commanded all his people to help any merchants bringing oil into the city.'

'He did?' asked Uruch. 'Did he also finance this venture?'

'Yes, your honour,' Darius replied.

'What's a lack of lamp oil to him, I wonder?' asked Uruch. 'How very strange. I shall congratulate him upon his servant's success when I see him. Now, where are you going, Darius Nouredini?'

'Only to my grandmother's humble barn.'

'Excellent. I shall accompany you.'

As he sauntered along beside them, he asked question after question about the oil venture, and about Darius himself. On the one hand there was something elusive, guarded in his character, and then on the other hand there was a startling ingenuousness in how he came right out and confessed that he was in a bind and needed Darius's help to put it right.

The bind was this: Uruch was depending on profits from a nascent oil market in Tabriz to provide for his family while he was away with the Embassy. His problem was that a few days earlier, the oil agent supposed to carry on the business in his absence had cried off, claiming the outbreak of war made the Tabriz-Isfahan road too dangerous to travel.

Uruch confessed that 'to his shame' he had been terribly lax in finding a replacement - except there was no hint of shame in his voice as he said this - having spent all his time instead in the much more pleasurable business of reading up on the fascinating places that he'd soon be visiting as First Secretary of the Persian Embassy: Rome, Prague, Venice, Madrid! His head had been so turned by the allure of these exotic courts and customs that he had neglected the duty of care he owed his family, for whose sake he must secure a replacement oil agent, and he wondered if Darius Nouredini might consider the post?

'But Tabriz is Ottoman, your honour,' said Darius.

'Not for long,' said Uruch. 'The Shah's army has its marching orders, and Tabriz lies too far from Istanbul for the Sultan to defend. I believe there's a rich market in selling oil to the camel-dung burners there. But as to details -.'

But as to details they were left hanging, and Uruch left open-mouthed, because Darius caught sight of his grandmother standing by the barnyard gate, and sprinted towards her.

Nat and Uruch stood and watched Darius run up the lane and

gather her in his arms. After each embrace, his grandmother's face was printed blacker and blacker by his tarry beard.

Down the lane, as they watched this reunion, a cold wind whistled around Nat and Uruch's hearts. Nat's own family were dead, and Uruch was about to leave his family with the Embassy and didn't know when he would return. He told Nat to tell Darius that he would call tomorrow, and then went his way.

❖

The following morning, Darius soaked in the public baths. The burns on his body grew less painful as he wallowed in the *hamman's* steamy water. After bathing, he had his hair cut and his beard shaved.

'You're lucky,' said the barber. 'Today's the first day the water has been hot for weeks. The Baku oil convoy came in yesterday noon. Please don't smile while I'm shaving your cheeks.'

They had beaten the convoy by a matter of hours.

Meanwhile back at the barn, Kulsum poured several cauldrons of hot water into a wooden trough for Nat to bathe in. Nonbelievers weren't allowed in the *hamman,* besides which everyone would have leapt out of the public baths as soon as he got in because he was as scabby as a leper.

He lowered himself into the trough of hot water and sat there not daring to touch the scabs, gashes and blistered burns all over his body. When his wounds began to seep, rusting the bath water, he stood up in the tub and let the air dry him, then stepped out of the water and gently lowered the ferryman's long shirt over his head.

He heard Kulsum crank the handle of a grinder in the yard, peeked through a crack in the barn's planking and saw her pour black powder from grinder to pot, and then hang the pot from a stick over the fire. *Qaveh!* He hurried out of the barn, and sat warming his bare legs by the little fire, waiting for the *qaveh* to boil.

A smooth-cheeked, well-groomed, apricot-scented Darius returned from the bazaar. He had a bolt of broadcloth over his shoulder for Kulsum's winter curtains, and two suits of clothes, one for him and one for Nat.

They got changed under the zigzag mulberry tree. Darius pulled on cream-striped grey calico churidars, a long grey damask shirt with a raised satin weave depicting silver firebirds, a black astrakhan coat, and a tall crown hat with a plume and a short floppy brim - just like Uruch's. Soon Nat was striding about the barnyard in narrow-leg midnight-blue churidar trousers, a sleeveless Bokharan jerkin, a fresh pair of brown buffalo-hide lace-up boots, and a brimless grey karakul hat. Nat loved the karakul's texture of convoluted grooves and ridges that looked like a tin-loaf brain.

Kulsum then handed him what he at first thought was a cushion before he recognised his doublet, which she had laundered and repaired.

'I have retrieved the heron from the oil,' she said. His fingers traced the couching's red outline. The red heron stood by his midnight pond once more. He shook the doublet and it made a sound like a muffled tambourine. She had even sewn the coins back into its lining.

She handed him a steaming tin cup of *qaveh*. He closed his eyes. He inhaled the aroma that told him the world was good and true. He drank. There it was. That earthy, nutty taste. A smile spread over his face. He didn't know why but drinking *qaveh* felt like a homecoming.

'Take time in your preparation of *qaveh*,' Kulsum told him, 'and God will be with you, and bless you and your table.'

31

G ol was on the roof garden sitting with her back to the elm screen while down in the street Mani prepared to burn his arms once again. Why, she wondered, even for the sake of the love growing between them, could he not stop burning his arms outside her house? Time after time she had asked him to stop. But he wouldn't listen. On this one matter he, who listened to her so well in all else, was deaf. Whenever she asked Mani to stop, something strange happened to him. A faraway look came into his eyes, as if he were speaking over her head to an invisible giant.

Who was this invisible giant who came to join them whenever she mentioned the ceremonial arm-burning? If Tradition, then why did Mani's replies take on a flippant, mocking gallantry? That smirking tone of voice flew in the face of the confidences they'd shared on their long walks. It made her wonder if all this elaborate ceremony was actually Mani's way of repudiating the intimacies they had shared.

The smell of smoking linen crept under Gol's nose. Orange sparks from Mani's taper drifted over the roses. The stubble burning had begun again. He was smoking her out. Was it crueller to watch or not to watch? Today it felt crueller not to watch.

Placing her hands in the soil, she squinted through the elm sticks as Mani dangled a burning rag. Yellow flame braided the linen. He lowered the flame onto the exposed flesh of his forearm, burnt himself and then hopped around in a little circle, flapping his injured arm up and down in the air. She lobbed the sealed poultice. He found her outline behind the elm screen and pressed the poultice to his lips with a dramatic flourish.

'As if,' thought Gol, 'he hardly knows me.'

She watched him apply the bright red and yellow binding, soaked in her mother's remedial salves to his arm, dabbing it between the motley strips she'd thrown down every day for weeks. He pulled a calfskin album from his bag. Now came the poetry. Let no neighbour's shutter, door or roof hatch be open, she prayed.

'*Sweet maid,*' he began, '*if you would charm my sight,*
And bid these arms your neck enfold –'

To Gol's intense relief he broke off. Perhaps he had finally sensed her discomfort. If it were so then she'd love him to the end of her days. She shot a hopeful look through the elm screen, fully expecting to find him wearing a look of contrition, the scales having fallen from his eyes. Mani wasn't, she discovered, looking in her direction at all, he was staring down the road. Whatever he saw there stunned him. His jaw fell open and his mouth gaped wide under his horseshoe moustache. Following his gaze, she scuttled on all fours to the corner of the roof garden. A sauntering Darius Nouredini in black astrakhan coat and plumed hat was approaching accompanied by a foreigner in fleece jerkin and karakul.

For a moment she experienced intense joy at seeing him in such fine fettle, but his reappearance complicated everything. Once upon a time, two suitors had been less trouble than one. Not anymore. Squatting on her heels, she clutched her hair in both fists. Why was everything so fraught and complex?

Down on the street, Mani taunted Darius,

'Have you acquired a taste for pigeon shit?'

'*Salaam,* Mani Babachoi. Allow me to introduce –'

'Hark! Gol's mother is readying another shovel load now. It will ruin your new coat!'

'Forgive me for interrupting the poem, Mani Babachoi. I pray you, continue.'

'Ha! Anyone can wear fancy clothes, or spout poetry, but have you any wounds of devotion?'

'Perhaps I am reluctant to show them,' mumbled Darius.

Mani pitched his voice so that Gol could hear his words.

'For days - or is it weeks now? - you haven't even been here. What sort of devotion was that? I have been here, Darius Nouredini, and have paid homage to my beloved every day. I have had the honour of meeting her respected father and mother. For I am an ardent suitor. But you? You debase this fine woman by your fitful hot and cold wooing. Have you wounds? No? Then be gone! Now!'

'We all have wounds,' replied Darius mildly.

'Like these?' demanded Mani, pushing up his loose white sleeves to reveal his forearms. Tapping the different coloured bandages that ran up and down his arm, he said: 'Look! It's quite a history I share with Gol now!'

'This showing of wounds, is it, I wonder, really *wajib*? Is it necessary?'

'Fine words like fancy clothes are only superficial.'

'So are wounds,' said Darius.

'No, they show the passion of the heart, not the skill of the tailor.'

'They are only skin-deep.'

'The coward has none!' said Mani.

Darius unbuttoned his shirt cuff. Mani laughed delightedly. So, Darius was going to roll up his sleeve and dab his triceps with flame, was he? This was going to be fun. Mani sat on the low wall opposite the Zarafshani house, and stretched his long legs out in front of him. Grinning from ear to ear, he threw a look up at the elm screen, where, with his keen musketeer's eye, he discerned three outlines: Gol had been joined by her father and mother. The whole Zarafshani family was gathering to witness the coward flinching and giving up the battle for Gol's hand here and now.

But why was Darius unbuttoning his whole shirt instead of just rolling up the sleeves? The shirt came off and Mani had his answer. Revealed to the open air were the hundred burns covering Darius's arms and torso. Up on the roof Gol screamed. Seconds later, Mani heard the shunting rasp of the stiff front door. Into the narrow street burst Gol, raven-black hair unbound and flowing. She tore open a week's worth of poultices with her teeth.

'Ah, dear Gol, that won't be necessary,' said Darius. 'Oh, one or two for decoration, I suppose.'

'What have you done? What have you done?' she asked, dabbing burns, scabs and blisters with the possets.

Roshanak followed her daughter outside, took one look at Darius's wounds and told her daughter,

'Bring him in the house.'

'Yes, *madar*,' said Gol. She cast a look at Mani, defying him to misconstrue, and the two women went into the house ahead of Darius.

Mani nodded, profoundly gratified by Gol's look. This was not the triumph poor Darius supposed. He slung his bag over his shoulder, bid a breezy farewell to both rival and rival's *shagird*, and walked away whistling the happy tune of he who trusts where he loves.

Alone together in the street, Nat watched Darius put his shirt back on and asked,

'Why are you bothering to get dressed first?'

'This will be my first ever crossing of the Zarafshani's threshold,' replied Darius, putting his new shirt back on. 'Am I to be half-naked when I meet Gol's father for the first time? You go in ahead, my friend. I shall follow.'

The door was open. A thin black curtain hung over the doorway. Nat entered. On the other side of the curtain, the room was dark. A single shaft of light fell down stone steps to the centre of a threadbare kilim. Around this slanting shaft all was dim. Nat heard muffled trilling from the rooftop pigeon lofts. Then a footstep.

'Father,' said Gol, 'here is a friend of Darius Nouredini.'

From a dark corner, Atash Zarafshani stepped into the light. The skin of his face was a patchwork. In patches, the melted face appeared like plaited brown leather, in others rough and pink as a pigeon's foot. In the joins between these patches grew seams of beard like ploughed-under sod. The father's hazel eyes followed Nat's. Doffing his karakul, Nat bowed and said:

'Thank you for receiving us in your home. My name is Nat Bramble.'

'Welcome, Nat Bramble,' said Atash. Nat felt a strange-shaped hand on his elbow guiding him to the corner cushions, where Nat no sooner sat down than he sprang up again. He must forewarn the squeamish Darius who went into paroxysms over the mildest deformity. If he didn't warn him, then his friend would completely disgrace himself when he saw how badly burned Gol's dad was. Nat must speak to Darius first, put him on his mettle.

Too late! Here he came ducking under the curtain, plumed hat on his head, astrakhan coat folded over one arm, peering into the darkness, grinning expectantly. Nat slid down against the wall, biting his knuckles at the disaster about to come, his heart sinking and a sickly feeling in the pit of his stomach. If only he'd been five seconds quicker. If only he could have warned him in time. Too late now. Too late for anything except to let Fate have his wicked way.

'Darius Nouredini,' said Gol, 'this is my father, Atash Zarafshani.'

'Where?' asked Darius, looking around, seeing nothing.

Atash stepped into the light and stood before him. Silence. Then Darius spoke.

'When I see your wife's great beauty, Atash Zarafshani, I know the wooing of her must have been a fierce hot business.'

Atash burst out laughing, and so did Roshanak and Gol, and then Darius too! Everyone was laughing except Nat, who whimpered the high-pitched note of someone who's just had a steel nail extracted from his foot. Then, Atash laid a three-fingered right hand gently upon his heart, and said,

'Welcome, Darius Nouredini. Please sit.'

'Not yet,' said Roshanak. 'Up on the roof, my beauty. Wait for me there.'

❖

Emerging onto the roof garden, Darius was confused. Why had Gol's mother sent him up here? That was one thing. Another was: Why didn't Gol ever tell him about her father's face? The bad leg, yes, the face, no. Yet while she'd never told him about her father's burns, she'd gone on often enough about the wonders of his roof garden. Now that he saw it with his own eyes, Darius didn't find it wonderful at all, just sad. The garden had the tragic overworked intricacy of replica palaces prisoners carved from soap. Every iota of soil fed some tap root or tuber. The soil was strained to breaking point. One more seed, one more stalk and this overworked soil might explode like an earthwork.

Or maybe that was just his own strained senses. He was about to explode with desire, quivering at the memory of the ends of Gol's long black hair sweeping against his naked shoulders and upper arms. It was so overwhelming a sensation that he had not felt her swabbing his burns with astringents. He had had no feeling for anything except the flicking of the ends of her hair against his body, the opium to the operation. Perhaps she would tend him again soon. Perhaps now.

He heard footsteps behind him. A woman's light, tripping step. Yes, perhaps now. The wooden hatch slammed shut behind her. They were alone together. Her footsteps drew near. Her hands spun him round and commanded:

'Take your clothes off!'

Darius walked backwards from Roshanak saying:

'... Sincere though I was in complimenting your beauty, I fear you have misunderstood exactly who is the object of my unceasing devotion, which is your daughter. I regret any confusion which may -'

'Off! Off!'

Darius turned his back to her and fumbled with the unfamiliar tab-braids of his new kurta, and then with the buttons of his shirt. He heard her tearing linen behind him. He froze. He dared not look round. When he did, would he see Gol's mother as topless as he? He heard her spit and rub her hands. He gasped in fright.

'Turn around, boy!'

The boy turned around to find her grinding herbs in a pestle and mortar. She sprinkled the mortar's paste onto a linen rag. These were the same healing salves, he reflected, that Gol used on Mani. She laid the poultice on his suppurating shoulder burn and pressed down with the heel of her hand.

'The other boy,' she said when she was done.

Darius slid his new damask shirt back over his stinging back, then walked to the roof hatch and called down for Nat.

Nat climbed out into the roof garden. At Roshanak's command, he took off his sleeveless fleece, unhooked the eyelets of his black and red English doublet with its half a heron, but he couldn't slide the Karun ferryman's long striped shirt over his head without help. Roshanak unstuck the little red blobs bonding shirt and skin together, like letter seals. Gently she detached Nat's shirt and raised it over his head.

Darius's eyes filled with tears as he saw how badly Nat had suffered in the underground chambers beneath the lake of pitch. So much pain was written in these welts, cuts and weeping sores all over his body, the worst of them on his back. A row of scabs buttoned his spine.

'Where have you been?' murmured Roshanak, stroking Nat's clumpy hair. 'Where have you been, my boy?'

Nat stood hunched, his knobbly shoulders sticking out of his skinny white body. Roshanak smoothed a poultice over an oozing wound on his back. He said nothing, but his whole body stiffened. She stopped. Then, after a little pause, he nodded his head, at which signal she laid another poultice on his back. Darius turned away, and left the garden.

❖

When Nat came downstairs again, Darius and Atash were in the middle of negotiations.

'Where will this dance be held?' asked Atash.

'In my grandmother Kulsum Nouredini's barn,' replied Darius, balancing a tiny ornate glass on his wide grey-striped calico thigh, and holding a Yazd biscuit in the other hand.

'Then you must invite Mani Babachoi.'

'Mani Babachoi!'

'Otherwise,' continued Atash, 'I am unable to grant permission for my daughter to attend your celebration, even in the capacity of hired musician and in the company of the other three girls in her band.'

'Why ever not?' asked Darius.

'Surely you see that if Mani Babachoi is not there, then it will appear to people to be a betrothal party between Gol and you.'

'How could I possibly invite him?'

'Gol will invite him. She sees him almost every evening. They have come to a happy understanding these last weeks while you were off prospecting.'

The colour drained from Darius's face. He replied in an ashen voice,

'Please bid your daughter be so kind as to invite Mani Babachoi.'

In the uncomfortable silence, the doves' burbling could be heard from the rooftop coop. To break the tension, Gol pointed towards the roof and made a weak joke:

'Our doves are smoking their hubbbabubbas again! They pick up many foreign habits on their travels.'

She flashed Darius a smile, but his eyes were so full of urgent questions about Mani that she quickly looked away.

'The Great Persian Embassy leaves in a few days,' said Atash. 'You will be glad to go home, Nat, but I suppose - '

Atash broke off, lifted his head up to the light and listened. Gol and her mother did the same. The way the pigeons were flapping and squawking, Gol explained to the guests, meant that a pigeon had had just returned. She ran upstairs and came down with a black and white dove wearing a purple satchel. Atash inspected the tired, hungry bird, and then prised open the satchel. A silk page, covered in writing front and back, fell open. He read the addressee's name, and told Gol where to deliver the page, and to take two fresh, well-rested doves with her.

'We will accompany her,' said Darius.

'No,' replied Roshanak. 'First you must finish your tea.'

And so the two adventurers sat and sipped their tea, while Gol left the house.

❖

Bird box on hip, Gol walked down a rutted lane between the muddy backs of houses. She regretted that she had not had a chance to tell Darius about Mani before her father had broken the news. Still, she hoped that for the new Darius, losing her to Mani would be a horseshoe dropped in a victory parade, a small loss, hardly noticed.

For what a victory Darius had won! Her heart rejoiced at how he had given his soul room to breathe. His special gift, it seemed to her, was for transmuting degradation into beauty. He did this in every area of his life. His poky stall in the bazaar he had made so studious a place that for whole minutes at a time she used to be able to forget she was between tinsmiths and metalworkers. Rather than let his dank and dismal family home seep into his soul, he had struck out for the mountain passes, and gone prospecting for oil in a ruined temple. And just now he had applied his special gift to the ugly scene of his last appearance as a suitor outside her house. Somehow he had effected a happy reconciliation, and was now sitting with her parents drinking tea and nibbling biscuits, as if her mother had never slung a shovel load of dung at his face to punish him for reciting Rumi's *Like This* without skipping the lewd parts.

But come to think of it, was the poem any more lustful than the one by Darius that Mani had recited, and for which his face had not been made a bird tray?

> *Gol, I yearn for your touch*
> *as silence before the final chord,*
> *aches for your fingers*
> *upon copper and silver tanbur strings.*

Gol stopped in mid-stride and froze where she stood. For the very first time, it crossed her mind that Darius might have actually felt the emotion his poem described, that what she had taken for conventional hyperbole, standard *gol o bobol* - rose and nightingale - bluster, might in fact be true, be real. She blushed to the roots of her hair to remember how her hands and fingers had touched and stroked his naked torso when dabbing him with the salves.

> *For until the touch of your hand*
> *the whole world hangs suspended,*
> *like a frozen waterfall.*

Suddenly she wished that her band had not agreed to play at his barn dance. She wished he would go away again, so that she wouldn't have to see him for a long while. Thank heaven she had already given her heart to Mani, otherwise she'd be in turmoil. But happily she was not in confusion. Her path was simple. All she had to do was go to the dance, play with her band, and dance once with Darius for politeness' sake. And the day after that, her love for Mani would proceed as before on its straightforward course.

32

A tangerine sheet hung in the centre of the barn to separate male from female dancers. It hung at chest-height, which was not nearly high enough for Darius, whose heart was full of dread at the prospect of seeing Gol dance with Mani. That sheet, the colour of tightly closed eyes, was all that stood between him and the sight of Mani's body pressed against Gol's. None of that at any time at all!

Division sheets sometimes became a mere formality, were reduced to a knee-high jump rope, or were done away with altogether in the small hours, by a carefree mood of high spirits, fun and frolics. Well, he wasn't going to stand for any of that at his party! He intended to be a stickler for protocol. Mani hadn't had even arrived yet, but the tangerine divider was all Darius could think about.

'Perhaps she won't dance,' said Nat, 'because the band need her for every song.'

'No,' replied Darius, miserably, 'she's already said she'll dance with me.'

'Her parents may prefer Mani Babachoi to you, but that doesn't mean she does.'

'No, Nat, I've lost her.'

He looked at Gol. Two dangling locks of hair swung in front of her ears as she swayed her head in time to the music that she and her band were playing. She was wearing a peach and plum striped dress with a row of domed brass buttons running down the front to a knotted sash of oyster silk. She had fabric flowers in her hair. Her eyes flashed in the oil lanterns' bright light. She had never looked so beautiful. The whole party was already a disaster and it was only just beginning! He shooed off the children who were playing chase around the division sheet and making it sag to waist-height, and then escaped into the barnyard, where he stood with his hand on his grandmother's bony shoulder welcoming the guests.

Some of the guests were the young men and women he knew from *Shab e Sher* poetry and song evenings, some were Kulsum's neighbours and their children. They were his neighbours, too, since Darius had moved in with his grandmother, having cleared all debts with his mother.

It may have cost him a quarter of his fortune to buy his way out of the *sigheh* and to compensate his mother for the lost oil-mining gear, but it was a small price to pay to redeem his soul. He had given her still more money to buy delicacies for the party: viands, fruits, sweetmeats and wine. Off she had gone to the bazaar, and gone so willingly that he wondered whether he might get along with her better now he had paid her off and moved out.

The pious Kulsum had invited the Sufi dervishes who now strode across the yard. Intense young men, they were nothing like the bearded wastrels of Safavid caricature. Only in their dress did they resemble the state's libel of them: their thick cotton skirts were frayed at the hem, their boots mud-spattered, and their shaggy coats crusty. One or two wore chimney-shaped *sikka* hats, the rest wore ragged headbands.

On the heels of the scruffy dervishes came the immaculately dressed Uruch Bey, bemused, as he strolled through the barnyard, to find a party going on. The First Secretary of the Persian Embassy crouched before Kulsum as if the sole reason for his visit had been to hear from her lips the full story of how Darius's father had gone into business with an

Azeri oil miner who dug a famous oil well as deep as the maidan was wide. Darius broke in, reminding his grandmother that he and Uruch Bey had a business affair to discuss, whereupon the First Secretary begged Kulsum to be excused, and was led by Darius to the twisted mulberry tree.

Uruch rested his foot on the bottom rail of the fence. Darius leaned back on the rail fence and hooked the heel of his new brown buffalo-hide lace-ups on the bottom rail in the same stance. He swung his raised knee from side to side, hoping that Uruch Beg would notice his new cream and grey-striped calico trousers. Let Uruch know he had found the right man. Uruch's mind seemed to be elsewhere, however.

'It will take a little time,' he told Darius, 'to persuade men in Tabriz to buy oil since that is not the custom there. Once they have experienced naphtha for themselves, they won't go back to dung.'

'Yes, but how can I sell them oil in the first place, when it costs so much more than the dung they're used to burning?'

'By selling at a loss,' answered Uruch, 'until they are used to oil, and then you raise the price to a level at which we can earn money.'

'What price is that?'

'You'll know. You have a gift. You are a natural merchant. That is why I wish you to accept this offer of employment. And there's not just oil to be sold. There are all the accoutrements that go with it, all the lamps and stoves. I propose that you take one-fifth of the profits. The rest you will give to my wife.'

'A fifth? Then how will I even cover my costs while I'm losing all this money every day?'

'I have deposited twenty gold tomans with a Tabriz *havaladar*, and I'll advance you five tomans now.'

Darius clasped his hands together on his belly and was silent for a long time.

'Let's say I keep fifty percent of oil revenues,' he said, 'and one hundred percent of the profits from selling oil lamps and stoves?'

'All of it? Outlandish! How do you possibly imagine that I would consider, even for a moment, agreeing to such terms?'

'Because you cannot bear to see so excellent a venture perish on the vine, and because you're about to leave with the embassy but still have no-one in place. In fact, you were being so attentive to my grandmother that I thought you were about to offer her the position.'

Uruch threw back his head and laughed.

'One hundred percent from sales of stoves and lamps and forty percent of the oil.'

'Fifty.'

'Fifty.'

The deal was done. Uruch handed him a red velvet purse containing an advance payment of five gold tomans. He pulled a ring off his finger, and told Darius the password he should use in Tabriz to effect the *havalar*, the word-of-mouth system of credit and exchange.

'Handing over my name ring,' said Uruch, 'makes me feel like I am going to my grave. Europe: Land of the Setting Sun. In the event of a Spanish knife in my ribs, the position you have just accepted comes with a lifelong moral duty to look after my family.'

Hand on heart, Darius declared,

'*Gorbanat.*' I die for you.

Hand on heart, Uruch replied,

'*Gorbanat*, Darius Nouredini.'

Darius watched Uruch Bey's satin-clad figure glide like a wraith across the paddock, and down the road. He closed his eyes and raised his face to the sky in elation. He must tell Nat the good news. The best thing of all about this position as Tabriz oil factor was that it gave Nat a future too.

As Darius hurried to find his friend, he spotted his rival, Mani Babachoi, accompanied by two friends, striding through the barnyard. The defiant thrust of Mani's chin, his puffed-out chest and nervous eyes told Darius that he expected the evening to be a trial of nerve. Seeing this, he was seized by an overwhelming imperative, perhaps it was some ancient hospitality instinct, to relieve Mani of any thought of grimly enduring this barn dance for the sake of Gol's honour. He bounded across the yard to embrace his startled rival.

'Welcome, Mani Babachoi! I am very glad to see you! Will you honour my Khanum Kulsum, whose barn this is, by introducing yourself and your friends to her?'

Mani consented to be led to Darius's grandmother. Riding boots creaking, he knelt on one knee to greet Kulsum, then he and his fellow soldiers passed into the crowded barn's music and dancing.

❖

Among the dancers, Nat was nodding his head to the beat of drum and dulcimer under the reed flute's wail and the sounds of Gol's tanbur and her singing. There was something too measured and too admirable in her phrasing. And in her playing too. She held the tanbur slightly to one side and away from her body as if she were demonstrating fingerpicking to a music class rather than singing a drinking song to a merry dance hall. In fact her singing made everyone a bit tense, with its odd mix of melancholy and precision - he could see why she was Darius's girl! The cheer that accompanied the chorus may have been the crowd's relief at the other girls joining in the singing and drowning out her voice's haunting beauty. They didn't want haunting beauty, they wanted to shake a leg.

The reed flautist, Sahar, set down her flute and passed among the dancers. When she got to Nat's side of the sheet, he saw she was carrying a ball of elm gum. Like fish feeding on ground bait, dancers crowded round to pinch a peck. To Nat's confusion, everyone then stuck a blob of gum onto their foreheads into which they pressed a coin. Soon coins on foreheads were bobbing about the barn like boat lanterns on the Thames.

Sahar stood before him, rubbed a peck of elm resin between her palms, and stuck a gobbet of gum to his forehead. He handed her a silver abbassi which she fixed to his forehead. As she pressed it to his skull, the band struck up a new tune. Her face fell.

'Oh, they've started the next one without me,' she said.

'That means you're free to dance,' said Nat, but she disappeared without a word. He supposed she was rushing to rejoin the band until her face bobbed up on the other side of the swaying sheet. He tossed the elm gum globe to a small boy, who caught it in both hands and ran off, a swarm of children running after him into the barnyard.

From what Nat could see of it, Sahar's dance looked very like Jenny Pluck Pears. Moments later, he and Sahar's top halves were dancing in perfect unison, plucking an imaginary orchard's invisible pears. When she disappeared to play the next song, Nat danced on alone for song after song. He had forgotten the bliss of dancing, the way it made you feel ten feet tall. Elation seemed to aerate his lungs with pure air, even in the humid crush of this musty barn.

Taking a breather and wiping the sweat from his face and neck, Nat was the only dancer who noticed the six dervishes take to the dance floor and spread out like dots on a dice. At first they hardly seemed to be dancing at all, yet the small movements they did make absorbed their whole concentration. Their eyes were closed as their bodies twisted and swayed. Then, by a spooky coincidence of will, each dervish began simultaneously to spin. The dance floor soon cleared of everyone except the six whirling dervishes, their heavy skirts fanning out higher the faster they span, dispersing the other dancers to the walls of the barn, as if by centrifugal force.

A thrill of subversion ran through the onlookers. The Sufi dervishes were all but outlawed by Shah and majlis. Their dance was the emergence of a powerful subterranean current in Persian life. It was a dance of defiance. Nat believed he understood what the subversive dance was saying better than anyone in the barn, and what it said to him was very plain:

There are other powers than those that rule.

The dervishes' revolving shoulders snatched their heads round in crisp clean strokes. The faster each dervish spun, the more composed he seemed to be. The whirling dervishes came together, horizontal skirt hems touching like adjacent cogs. The spectators stamped and cheered as the dervishes reached peak rotational speed. One by one, each dervish emerged from his blur, and came to a stop. With broad smiles on their faces, not a spiritual trance at all, the dervishes beckoned everyone back to dance, and joined in with the ordinary dancing.

Nat saw Gol and Mani dancing together, their hands joined over the sagging tangerine sheet. He went out into the cool night air, and found Darius.

'Don't go in the barn for a little while, my friend,' he told him.

'Are they dancing together?'

Nat didn't reply. Darius listened. He could hear reed flute, dombak and dulcimer - but no tanbur. Yes, she was dancing with him. He felt cold and sickly.

❖

Back in the barn, Darius's mother, Leila, standing behind the food table watched Gol and Mani dancing. If her son had eyes in his head than he must see what everyone else in this barn could see: the rapture on Gol's face when she was dancing with that handsome musketeer. They were really in love, those two. They looked right together - the girl with the fabric flowers in her hair, and the tall slim man whose loose sleeves revealed forearms studded with burns of honour and striped by frayed and bloodstained bandages, the only disorderly thing about him. Her son, on the other hand, still looked scruffy even in his new clothes.

Leila knew, with a mother's instinct, that Gol was not a spoon for Darius's mouth. Why couldn't he see it? He should stop pining, find a new woman, move on. Let his new fortune make him a new Darius. She'd help him. She'd cut that cord. He might not thank her now, but he'd thank her later when he had a wife and children. A plain wife more suited to him. A wife who'd be faithful to him, not a woman already smitten by a fine young soldier.

Her scattergood son had given her funds with which to buy all manner of cooked meats and fine wines, but Leila knew it was a waste of money to buy delicacies from the bazaar. Far better to bake your own fare. No-one would notice the difference. And rather than buy expensive fine wines, she'd used those stocks of Shiraz that a friend couldn't sell because they'd been left out in the sun too long.

Her son might have a fat purse for an afternoon but when that was gone - and with all this profligate feasting, dancing and chasing after unattainably beautiful women it soon would be - all he'd have left would be his family. He had to learn, one way or another, that he couldn't just buy his way out of family duty. She was sure Darius could still be prevailed upon to do that *sigheh*. Leila smiled as the handsome musketeer approached her food and drink stall.

❖

Nat and Darius sat on a low bough of the zigzag mulberry watching the moon disappear behind a black cloud.

'The silver coin,' said Darius, 'drops from the dancing night.'

'Is that a poem, *dostum?*'

'It's real life. We're on our way,' he said and clinked a gold toman against the coin glued to Nat's forehead, dropped it back into the red velvet purse, and handed the purse over. He told him the brilliant news about how they could go into business together as Uruch Bey's oil merchants.

'Say you will come in on this venture with me.'

'With all my heart, Darius.'

'I should warn you that war will make the road to Tabriz a dangerous one, my friend.'

'We'll have good luck. Tomorrow belongs to the misfit. Those who don't fit the present shape the future.'

'Like my grandmother's poor Sufis in their hillside hovels? No, alas, the powerful rulers shape the future. Look at Shah Abbas and your old master, look at their embassy to the Christian Princes: an exchange of gifts here, a letter sent there, and a wildfire of war burns from horizon to horizon.'

'An exchange of gifts, is it? Well, now, that reminds me! Here, I have a gift for you. I bought it in the bazaar.'

'You went to the bazaar? Are you mad? What if you were seen?'

'In these clothes?'

Nat reached into his doublet and pulled out the gift.

Brilliant white silk bloomed in the dark. A silk wedding blanket hemmed in ivory brocade. A series of tiny coral tubes were stitched to its corners with silver thread.

'A *sofre aghd,*' said Darius, in a hushed voice. 'Did you know this is what the couple sit upon during the wedding service? Did you know this is what the wedding gifts are spread out upon?'

'For you and Gol.'

Just then the tanbur's metal strings come clashing in on the song. Gol must have stopped dancing with Mani and was strumming again. The clouds lifted from Darius's face. He pocketed the silk blanket, and began cavorting around the barnyard, doing crazy dances with Nat. They were soon joined by a crowd of children who were spinning themselves dizzy, little, white-smocked blurs whirling round and round and toppling over. The children's foreheads now sported an odd miscellany of objects: sequin, pebble, peach stone, mother-of-pearl, button, mulberry, like the small shiny objects stitched to the wedding blanket. Nat and Darius picked up one child after another and span them round by an arm and a leg.

Then Nat and Darius, hand in hand, began dancing towards the barn. Darius was following the steps of Nat's *Dance Of Joy At New Employment* when Mani and his two comrades stormed out of the barn, and barged past him.

'Selling food to invited guests!' spat Mani. 'You are a cheap, despicable man, Darius Nouredini.'

Darius was confused. He watched the three soldiers disappear down the lane into the night. *'Selling food to invited guests...'* He ran into the barn and straight to where his mother stood behind the food table.

'What have you done?'

'They all love my lamb stew,' she replied.

Blank spots jigged in his eyes. As he blinked them away, he saw to his horror a brass dish full of shahidis and larins on the table.

'What have you done?' he cried, dizzy with fury.

'Yes,' said Masghoud. 'The lamb has been selling very well.'

'No!' shouted Darius. 'No! You do not sell the food!'

'As you wish,' said Leila primly. 'What about the wine?'

'No! No! No! Nothing is to be sold! Nothing! Everyone here in this barn is a guest!'

Leila leant forward over the bean curd.

'How can you be sure?' she asked conspiratorially.

Darius was struck dumb. It would take a year and a day to try to explain to his mother what was wrong with this question and she still wouldn't understand. When at last he spoke it was only to find out how much damage had been done to his name:

'How many people have you sold food to?' he asked.

'That was the first bowl we asked payment for,' replied Masghoud.

'Was it?' Darius asked his mother.

'Yes,' she said.

'No, it wasn't! You are shaming me! You are shaming *Khanum*! This food is to be given free to everyone! Everyone!'

'Bless you, Darius,' laughed his mother indulgently. 'Always loving an argument! Even tonight! Tonight of all nights! You go and enjoy yourself! We'll take care of all the food and drink.'

Darius whirled away and found Gol staring straight at him while she strummed her tanbur. He was mortified. She had seen him shouting at his own mother. He smiled weakly, rooted to the spot, until Nat hooked his arm and danced him round and round, before spinning off on his own, in giddy joy. Stripping The Willow up and down the barn, Nat crooked his arm with whosoever came his way, weaving in and out, until he stood before the musicians. He gestured for Gol to set down her instrument, and pulled her to her feet. Together they skipped along the tangerine sheet, all along the barn, where he presented her to Darius, and withdrew.

❖

Darius and Gol stood face-to-face either side of the division sheet. Over the sheet, came his hand, up to the sheet came hers.

As they swayed and zigzagged down the barn, the sheet spooled with them, a tangerine eel flowing along a riverbed, following their hips and shoulders as they danced their fluid, gentle measure.

Gol and Darius were wholly unaware that they had become the centre of attention, the only couple now dancing. Both were oblivious to everything except the alteration that was taking place in them on their first ever dance together.

Stepping backwards, Gol drew Darius towards her as far as the sheet allowed, and then Darius drew her towards him as far as the sheet allowed. She had the sensation that she was collecting Darius, piece by piece, and that he was collecting her, piece by piece. It was a careful, tender task, this collecting of one another. That was why they had to step so lightly.

The song ended. Gol looked up and saw they were alone on the dance floor. She dropped Darius's hand and hurried scowling back to the band. She sat in with the other musicians.

'Play fast!' she snapped.

Gol bowed her kamanche six-eight time, Maryam thwacked her goblet-shaped drum, Nargis blew a fidgety melody on the reed flute, Sahar hammered the santur's strings and together they launched into a skipping rhythm which soon filled the dance floor again. Everybody was dancing and leaping and the first coins dropped to the floor. Gol heard the dancers cheer each coin that dropped. The rest of the band ululated as one, swapping looks of awe at the power their music wielded over the polled unicorns, a stump of elm gum on their foreheads and all dancing madly. But all Gol was aware of was that she loved the dear dancing bear. Tonight she had danced with Mani and she had danced with Darius, and it was Darius who had discombobulated her. Poor Mani! It was Darius she loved.

❖

Darius was sitting in darkness under the zigzag mulberry staring at the wedding blanket. He ran his fingers over its brocade and touched the coral tubes, sequins and glass beads stitched into the white silk with silver thread.

'Why does Nat have more faith in my future than I?' he wondered. 'Why can he act as if Mani Babachoi did not exist, when I cannot?'

He looked up to find Gol walking through the white blurs of dizzy children. He hurriedly stuffed the wedding blanket into his pocket. Two warm, long-fingered hands took hold of his. He had never seen Gol's face so close. She kissed him on the lips. He leaned back against the tree trunk and she leant on him. Her head-tire of fabric flowers pressed uncomfortably into his cheek, snagged his top lip and hooked one nostril. Still, he didn't want to move. He told himself that life had become like an illustrated lyric - he and she on a bough embracing in the light of a silvery moon. Life had become *Like This*.

They heard guests bidding farewell to each other. A black horse whinnied somewhere in the field beyond the fence. The barn seemed far away, until they heard Maryam's voice calling Gol's name.

The spell was broken. Gol sprang from his arms and ran through the firefly blur of spinning children to the barn, where Maryam, Sahar and Nargis were talking to Darius's mother.

'If it's weddings you play, girls,' Leila was saying, 'we shall want to hire you for a wedding in a week or two.'

Gol was glad it was a business discussion - dry land after swamp. She tried to focus her mind on everyday matters. Yet how weird to think that she herself might soon be calling this woman 'mother'. Right then, Leila gave her a look as if she had read her mind, and Gol blushed hotly. Leila turned to her husband and said:

'What do you think, Masghoud, shall we engage these girls for the *sigheh*?' The band looked uneasily at each other. Gol spoke for them.

'You must excuse us,' she said. 'A *sigheh* is not quite a proper wedding. We cannot play for you.'

'What do you mean it's not quite a wedding?' returned Leila. 'For me, it is more than a wedding because it is my only son's only wedding. So, you must play. There. It's settled.'

'Your son?' asked Gol.

'My boy has set his heart on this so badly.'

'Which son?'

'God has granted me but one son,' Leila replied, 'Darius, my only son, is to be wed next week or the week after! It has been arranged for months!'

The ground reeled beneath Gol's feet. She could feel her friends' eyes upon her, but refused to meet their looks, to suffer their pity. Months! It had been arranged for months! This meant Darius's whole courtship of her had been a lie! That explained the wedding blanket she had just seen him stuffing into his coat. It was for the *sigheh*. No wonder he was so furtive and hasty in hiding it. Poor Mani, she had betrayed him for a lie. Staring at her feet, she heard Maryam speak to her. No words! thought Gol, and fled the barn, running down the lane into the night.

❖

After Gol had left him behind the twisted tree trunk, Darius got down on his hands and knees by the mulberry roots to thank Almighty God, the Most Gracious, the Ever Living, the One Who Sustains and Protects All That Exists, for the greatest blessing of his life: Gol. When he stood up again, clouds were disrobing the moon, just like in Rumi's *Like This*.

> *When someone quotes the old poetic fancy about*
> *clouds disrobing the moon,*
> *unknot the ties of your gown one by one,*
> *let your loose gown fall open, and say,*
> *'Like this?'*

Life had become a song. So much so that Darius began to worry if what happened just now behind the mulberry tree meant what he thought it meant and was not a mere enchanted moment. He needed to go back to the barn, and have Gol vouch for what had happened, for what it meant. Of course, he wasn't such a fool as to expect her to hold his hand in front of everybody, she had to break off with Mani Babachoi first. Yet he needed her to acknowledge - by a whisper, or look, or touch - that they were really going to live their lives together. He brushed the mud from his palms and knees, and walked into the barn.

He couldn't see Gol anywhere. She was not beside Kulsum, who had fallen asleep with a child on her lap. Nor was she by his mother who was loading food in cloth-covered jars. Nor was she with Maryam, Sahar and Nargis, either, but they were staring at him coldly.

'Why don't you leave her alone, you liar?' said Sahar.

'What lie?' he asked, but without a word the band members shouldered their instrument bags and walked out of the barn.

Darius was bewildered. What had happened? His mother came to him and said,

'Oh, my poor boy, she's gone to her Mani, you see.'

He looked at her in perplexity, sick with nerves. What was she saying? What did she mean? He ran out of the barn and onto the road, but there was no sign of Gol anywhere. He understood nothing except that he had somehow lost her forever. He sank to the ground in the road.

He recognised more of himself in the man who had lost Gol, than in that strange Darius whom she'd kissed, filling his body with golden light as he felt her mouth upon his. The kissing and the fabric flowers indenting his cheek - it had all been an engine devised by Fate only to produce this perfect occultation of the New Darius. Nothing less could have done it, nothing less could have shattered the new man. Nothing less on his triumphant homecoming party, the night of his great celebration, could have made him lie face down in the dirt, claw at the roadside weeds and writhe in the dirt. Nothing less than love being given after years of waiting and then snatched back again in a matter of minutes.

33

Watching Darius and Gol dance together, Nat knew he had been right to buy the wedding blanket. He grinned ecstatically to see his friend's dream come true, and then left barn and barnyard to walk the surrounding lanes.

His mind was a-whirr, his heart was full to bursting at the prospect of selling oil with Darius on behalf of Uruch Bey. Employment gave Nat a future. His life was no longer a thin ribbon of vegetation in a wilderness of shale. Each new passing day of life after Anthony revealed his own power, and made him stronger, more whole and alive. There were other powers than those that ruled. They may be submerged for a while, but, like underground rivers, paved over and forgotten, they had not gone very far.

Whatever he had been doing before he met Darius wasn't life. This was life. Life and a new job too! He hummed a melody the reed flute had played. He skipped and danced through the late-night lanes, past closed shutters and bolted doors. That reed flute was not wailing his exile, as in the Turk's poem, but rejoicing at his homecoming. Return to England would be exile. For here Nat had what he'd never have in England: the hope of a life beyond service. Not the life of an indentured servant, but the life of an oil merchant. He would make a life for himself here.

A breeze stirred a house front wind chime and set some hanging tin pots tinkling.

'WHERE'S MY MONEY, BRAMBLE?'

Nat jumped in terror at the sound of Anthony's voice.

Eli Elkin slammed him against a wall, and held him there while Anthony punched him in the eye. The raised stitching of his master's tapestry gloves gashed his eyebrow. Blood flowed down into Nat's eye. A second punch to the chin studded the back of his head to the wall. The pain as the back of his head banged the wall was worse than the punch.

Anthony gripped him by the throat Nat. Through his stinging eye, saw again the clove of garlic nose and the avid bug-eyes, and smelt again the ambergris in his master's beard.

'I led you, Bramble, across deserts, rivers and seas. At mine own expense, I had you schooled in the Persian tongue. Led you safe through half the world. Led you and all my people out of Baghdad, even at peril of my own life. When we first came here, Shah Abbas commanded me to give you to him as a slave. I refused an emperor to save you, Bramble.'

'On my life, Sir Anthony, I discovered that there existed in Qazvin a better exchange rate for silver! I tried to tell you, but Angelo turned me away from your chamber when you were sick with your stone. Hear me, Sir Anthony! It was precisely in honour of my obligation to you, and for no other reason, that I went to Qaz -.'

'Lying lawyer's bibble-babble!' bawled Elkin, cracking his billyclub against the renegade's knee. Nat skittered along the wall.

'Good news, Sir Anthony!' said Nat, hopping on one foot. 'Here, here, look, six gold tomans, here in this purse, good Sir Anthony.'

Anthony poured six gold tomans from red velvet purse to glove, and then poured them back in again, before attaching purse to belt.

'What's this, Bramble?'

'Six gold tomans equals three-hundred abbassi, Sir Anthony!'

'Numbers!' roared Anthony. 'Numbers! You dare bandy numbers

with me, boy! There's no arithmetic to wrong and sinful wickedness!'

'No, Sir Anthony, only restitution. Good my lord, here's restitution in full.'

Anthony pawed his straw and rye beard with tapestry fingers. Nat stared at the raised stitching of the gloves' autumnal forest-floor tapestry. What fresh lacerations were yet to come from those seams?

'Uruch Bey congratulated me,' he said, 'on the great fortune won me by my servant selling rock oil upon the maidan. A great fortune - those were his words. Not six gold tomans. A great fortune. So my question for you is this. Where's my money, Bramble?'

'I am rinsed, sir. Indeed I am. You have it all.'

'The only reason you are still alive is because Uruch Bey believes you were acting on my orders when you fetched the oil into the city. He says he saw you serve an oil merchant on the maidan. Is my fortune with this villain? You will take me to the den of thieves, Bramble. I am told it is a barn close by.'

'On the way back from Qazvin, it's true, yes, sir, that fearing to travel alone with your six gold tomans, and in return for security of passage, yes, I did help a merchant bring in oil, my lord.'

Nat hadn't seen or heard Anthony draw his rapier. A sharp hot needle pain pricked his throat. His eyes followed the steel sword all the way past the tapestry gloves to the cold blue eyes.

'Where is your accomplice?' asked Anthony.

'Accomplice, sir? I know no -.'

Anthony put an ounce more weight behind the sword. The cartilage of Nat's windpipe buckled. He dry-retched and his whole body grew very cold.

'To pop your windpipe now, I need press less than to seal a letter with my ring. A flinch will do it. A sneeze. A stumble by Master Elkin against my elbow. Any of these will dispatch you straight to hell. Now, is there anything in my past conduct, anything at all, that might lead you to doubt for even a moment that I will skewer your windpipe like calamari rings. Blink once for "No." Twice for, "Yes." So, tell me, where's your accomplice?'

Nat could not focus his terrified wits enough either to lie or betray. The air hummed. The rapier flashed and slashed. A ripping sound. Not flesh, but fabric. A clatter of metal. All the coins in his doublet scattered across the road.

'Where's your silver armour now, Bramble?'

'The cod's roe, Sir Anthony,' cried Elkin. 'Here's the cod's roe!'

The red and black doublet hung in tattered rags. Anthony kicked him in the belly. As Nat doubled over, Elkin's billyclub struck his shoulder, and sent him sprawling face down in the road.

A canvas hawking bag landed next to his head.

'Fill it,' said Anthony, sheathing his sword.

Nat crawled around the road filling the hawking bag with coins, like a potato-picker dragging a burlap sack along a muddy furrow. On hands and knees, he searched for any coins he may have missed. When he had picked up every last one, he lifted the heavy bag up to Anthony.

'This is all, sir.'

Anthony fastened the bag around his waist.

'No, Bramble,' he said, 'this is not yet restitution.' He drew his dagger and nodded to Elkin, who grabbed Nat by the neck and hair and walked him backwards to the wall. Anthony approached with the blade at eye-level. Nat writhed and thrashed his head every which way.

'Hold still,' said Anthony, and laid the flat of the dagger against his forehead. Anthony carved through flesh and elm gum.

Nat's last coin in the world clinked onto the road. The dancer's coin. He had forgotten it was there.

Anthony removed his left glove and pointed at his palm.

'Put the coin here, Bramble, at the meeting of the lifelines of good fortune and longevity.'

On his knees, Nat placed the gummy and bloody silver abbassi in Anthony's palm. He watched Anthony's fist close over the coin, and heard him step back a pace. Then he heard his own teeth clatter as Anthony kicked his chin. Pain burst an aurora behind his eyeballs, and exploded against both eardrums. He keeled over on his side.

'Ho! Ho! Ho! A day later, Elkin, and I would have missed him.'

'A very good omen, Sir Anthony. A sign.'

'Do you know, I think this *is* a good omen.'

Relief flooded Nat's body, for Anthony had dropped all talk of hunting Darius now that the hawking bag was five times heavier than when it had first left Anthony. Darius was safe. Nat would not be a burst goatskin laying a drag trail of oil all the way to Kulsum's barn!

A boot kicked him hard in the thigh. Elkin leant over him and barked,

'Up, Bramble! Up! Tomorrow we leave!'

34

The following morning outside the gates of Isfahan, Shah Abbas and his entire royal court were ranged on horseback to send off the Great Persian Embassy. The Embassy's caravan stretched far along the city walls. Proclamation of war against the Ottoman Empire ruled out travelling west through Iraq therefore the Embassy would travel northwest through Russia to Christendom, where Ambassador Hoseyn Ali Beg would present letters to all the courts of Europe.

Ambassador Hoseyn Ali Beg sat on his horse swaddled in shawls, as if already bitten by the cold northern winds of Europe. He scowled throughout the farewell ceremony. Just listening to the Shah recite the name of every last godforsaken place the Embassy would visit made Hoseyn feel exhausted. He cast a longing eye beyond the city walls at the tops of minarets, at the golden domed mosque. He was still in sight of Isfahan but already he was tired and homesick. If being made ambassador was such an honour, why did it feel like being exiled? He cast an envious look at his fellow majlis ministers who were staying. In a few minutes, they would simply turn their horses and ride back the short distance to their homes, wives, children, to their commercial interests and political intrigues - in short, their lives!

For all Hoseyn's gloom, however, there was at least one man among those staying in Isfahan with whom he would not wish to trade places. Hoseyn Ali Beg looked at Robert Sherley, the brother that Anthony was leaving behind as a hostage. From the Englishman's unconcerned air, it was clear that he didn't know what was about to happen to him, what part he was to play in this grotesque ceremony of leave-taking. Hoseyn winced and snapped at Uruch to stop humming.

The Shah waved his sword, at which signal hundreds upon hundreds of white doves emerged from a round dovecot, the size of a two-storey house. The doves flew to the front of the Embassy caravan, where they immediately turned round and flocked back to the giant dovecot, all squabbling and fighting to get back inside.

'A bad omen, Uruch,' he said.

'Scared by a hawk, Hoseyn Mirza. All shall be well.'

Hoseyn grunted.

❖

Robert Sherley's attention was wandering from the big sendoff. Hands on saddle-horn, he gazed longingly towards the orchards and barley fields on the horizon. Soon, let's say in one hour, he would be trotting past those trees and that waving barley, and he'd never see Shah Abbas again. A new chapter of his life was beginning: The Great Persian Embassy.

He glanced at Ambassador Hoseyn Ali Beg, and covered his mouth to hide his mocking laughter. Somewhere on the steppe a flock of goats was missing its shepherd. You could take him out of his yurt, tie a mink cape round his shoulders, and call him Ambassador, but his lowborn nature hung about him. He would be lost, utterly lost, in the courts of the Christian princes, which made it a small matter for Robert and Anthony to gain control of the Great Persian Embassy. Hoseyn's broad flat turban made him look like the supporting pedestal of a subsiding porch, and he was fated only to play a supporting role in this Embassy. Anthony would be the *de facto* or titular Ambassador once they got into Christendom, but Robert would be the real Ambassador, the effective policy-maker, doing his brother's thinking for him. After all, it was Robert and not Anthony who had ambassadorial experience, Robert who had concluded successful trade negotiations with the Moroccan court on behalf of the Grand Duke of Tuscany. He would be the real Ambassador behind the show Ambassador. He just had to keep a straight face until they were level with the barley and those orchards. That was all he had to do.

Suddenly, the Shah's voice cracked with emotion. So deep a silence followed that Robert thought he had been struck deaf until he heard a lone dove flap overhead. All eyes turned towards him.

'Have I have missed my place in the line,' Robert nervously asked himself. 'Is this my cue to trot forward and bid farewell to Shah Abbas? Yes, I believe it is.' But when he reached for his reins they were gone, and he found his horse being led to the side of the Shah's by a Tofangchi.

Shah Abbas kissed the reins then pressed them to his heart. Cheers erupted from Tofangchi, royal court, Great Persian Embassy and from the spectators.

'Am I a hostage, Anthony?' shouted Robert. 'What have you done?'

The mask of propriety that settled on Anthony's face made the blood drain from Robert's own. By the look on his face, Robert knew what the Shah and the cheering crowds did not: Anthony was never coming back! 'My brother has made good his escape by sacrificing me! Oh, I am betrayed where most I should trust!'

As his horse was led back towards the city walls, Robert concentrated on not fainting, on keeping dignity, on staying upright in the saddle, by taking deep breaths and breathing and blinking the black dots from his eyes. He was flanked by the Shah's two blind brothers, Prince Abu Talib and Prince Tahmasp, whose horses were being led along with his.

'So the three blind brothers are led away,' thought Robert. 'There's no shame in the princes' blindness, only mine. I knew Anthony would betray me, knew it from when I was on top of the tower with the crystal to my eye! I knew and yet I did not know. I didn't admit to myself what I already knew. Fool! The princes are past danger now, but not me, dear God, not me. One day Shah Abbas will find out that my brother has lied to his face and fled the coop. What will the Shah do to me then! I am at his mercy now. Oh, Anthony, oh my brother, you have abandoned me at the gates of hell.'

❖

The crowds watching the Great Persian Embassy depart were so deep that Darius could see nothing. He found a tree that looked as though it had been struck by lightning, and climbed the black stumps of charred branches, each about the size of a rolling-pin to the very top of the tree.

Too much was going wrong all at once. Nat had not come back to the barn last night. Earlier this morning, Atash Zarafshani had refused to admit Darius into his house, asking whether he'd ever been promised in a *sigheh*. When he hesitated before answering, Atash slowly closed the door in his face, leaving him looking down at the quarter circle the door had inscribed in the dirt like a compass-pencil.

On his way back from the Zarafshani house, Darius's way was blocked at the Sharestan Bridge by crowds of people in holiday mood. When he asked where they were going they told him they were off to see the departure of the Great Persian Embassy. Darius ran around the out-side of the crowd overtaking them all, plumed hat in hand and sweating in his astrakhan coat. When he came out at the gates, the crowds were so deep that he could see nothing of the Embassy. Now, from the top of the blackened lightning tree, he could see the whole train of the Great Persian Embassy. Nat was nowhere to be seen.

The two short men, Anthony and Abbas, faced each other on massive stallions. They looked like rich, overdressed children at play. Anthony, dressed in silver armour, sat very upright in the saddle, bracken beard thrust out. Was it possible to read Nat's fate in that bug-eyed countenance? Was this a man who had just murdered his servant?

Darius caught sight of Uruch Bey, his patron and benefactor, sitting on a tall smoke-grey horse. That wizened old fellow in the pancake hat beside him must be Hoseyn Ali Beg, the Ambassador and former friend of Gol's dad. Mounted behind Ambassador Hoseyn and First Secretary Uruch were a few secretaries and servants, but still no Nat. He glimpsed servants darting to and fro among the English party ranged behind Anthony, but could not see Nat among them.

Summoned by a nobleman, a footman limped forwards to tighten a saddlebow. Darius did not at first recognise this hobbling footman as Nat. When he did, he shook with anger to see the damage done his friend. There was a starburst of dried brown blood on the centre of his forehead. One eye was purple and almost closed, his mouth bruised and puffy. Those new clothes were covered in dust. He hobbled painfully. Not all the rigours of their oil venture had damaged Nat as much as a few hours with his old master. Yet now Nat must toil across the lands of Europe and northern Asia with that *shaytan*!

Nat limped down through a wreath of dust into a roadside ditch, where he disappeared from view. Moments later he popped up again wearing a pack fastened to his back by two crisscross leather straps, from which hung a blanket roll. Nat joined the line by the side of the road, behind the horses of the English party. Thank God for his new boots of brown buffalo hide, since he appeared to have no mule or pony to ride. Oh, how lonely and desolate a figure he looked.

'*Dostum! Dostum!*' Darius cried out, but the loud entraining of Great Persian Embassy drowned his cries out. All the way up the caravan's line, camels rose amid a cacophony of banging clanking baggage. Darius shouted fit to burst his lungs: '*Dostum! Dostum!*

❖

'Hark!' said Hoseyn, hunched in the saddle, 'the Turks are here already.'

'Let's go back into the city,' said Uruch, 'and see if we can negotiate terms.'

'An excellent suggestion, First Secretary of the Embassy. Wheel the horses! Yes, no point going now. The Turks are already here.'

'We can give the Sultan some of these expensive gifts intended for popes and doges!' said Uruch.

'We can offer Antonio's beard in return for Muhammad Aga's,' said Hoseyn, grinning. Again they heard the shouting Turk.

'*Dostum! Dostum! Nat-jan!*

The First Secretary of the Embassy turned in the saddle to find the shouting Turk. His blood ran cold. With unutterable sorrow he recognised Darius Nouredini, the oil factor in whom he had reposed the welfare of his family, perched up a tree and shouting like an Izmiri drunk.

But then Uruch realised that Darius Nouredini was calling to someone among the English party. He followed the direction of his oil factor's gaze and recognised the *shagird* - but only just, for the English servant had suffered a violent beating since Uruch last saw him. The *shagird* must have been a runaway, for why else would such punishment be meted out upon his return to Anthony Sherley? Uruch's guts rolled. This meant

Darius had lied to him when he had claimed that Antonio had financed the oil venture. This liar was the man in whom Uruch had placed his trust and the future of his family!

If the *shagird* heard what was shouted to him, he was too dejected, or too ashamed to lift his eyes to search for his friend's face. Just then, however, he slowed his walk, as if he could, after all, hear the words Darius shouted:

'You are the cork that bobs up from black subterranean seas, Natjan! You rise like smoke from pagan chimneys. You keep your footing on the sinking ferry. How can they ever drown you? How can they crush you? How can they quench your spark?'

Part Two

1

Cheering crowds lined the route from outside the city gates to Castel Sant' Angelo. Half Rome had turned out to witness the legendary Persians, fellow heirs of a great classical civilization, ancient Rome's most formidable foe. And the Great Persian Embassy did not disappoint. They wore bright silk turbans, rode magnificent white stallions, and altogether looked as if they had ridden straight out of the pages of a romance.

First Secretary of the Embassy, Uruch Bey, looked up at the children perched in trees who were shaking linden blossom down upon the parade. He cupped his hands and caught a falling blossom. One hundred cannons boomed an artillery salute from Castel Sant' Angelo. Uruch's giant white horse reared up. Using just his thighs and hips, he wheeled the horse to a standstill. This display of horsemanship set the crowd roaring,

'*Evviva! Bravo!*'

He blew the linden blossom from his hands towards some young women who screamed with delight. He touched his heart, lips and turban with his fingertips and they screamed some more.

Uruch trotted his horse forward towards Hoseyn Ali Beg, whom the Romans welcomed with chants of *Genghis! Genghis!* The grizzled old ambassador grinned from ear to ear, laying one hand on his heart and waving now up to the eaves and now down to the smallest child, as one and all cheered *Genghis! Genghis!* Uruch chuckled. It was true, it was true! Why had he never seen it before? Ha! That was *exactly* who old Hoseyn looked like. Genghis! Only Genghis with a headache and a bad back! Or Genghis's father!

Up ahead rode little, puffed up Antonio, dazzling in his steel doublet and blue puffball trunks, his silver ruff on his neck and shiny silver silk turban. He waved his arm like Julius Caesar home in triumph, as if he were an emperor who had taken all these Persians prisoner!

Behind him were his real captives: his overworked English servants dressed in carnation taffeta for the occasion. Uruch glimpsed Nat Bramble, his oil factor's friend and accomplice. Hard to believe this was Antonio's youngest servant. Travel had scored vertical grooves in his cheeks and there were black moons under his eyes.

Uruch wheeled his horse and rode the last stretch alongside the open carriage of Cardinal Aldobrandini, the Pope's right-hand man and military commander. As they reached Castel Sant' Angelo, he exchanged an excited look with the Cardinal. Together they watched the ambassadors dismount. This was it. It was really happening! It was glorious.

Trumpets blared a fanfare, choristers burst into song, and the Great Persian Embassy's two ambassadors proceeded up the steps. The Papal Guard locked halberds against the surging, cheering, crowd.

The ambassadors stopped halfway up the stairs. Uruch watched an argument in dumb show which seemed to be about who led and who followed.

Anthony shoved Hoseyn aside. The crowd fell silent. So silent that Uruch heard Hoseyn Ali Beg's fist land on Anthony's chin. Cardinal Aldobrandini placed red silk fingers over his eyes.

The two ambassadors wrestled on the steps of the Castel Sant'Angelo. There was some work inside - a bite, a knee to the groin - and then Anthony broke free. He trotted up the steps. Hoseyn grabbed the hem of his cloak and yanked. Anthony toppled backwards, his silk turban bouncing away into the crowd, and when he got to his feet, the back of his hair was soaked in blood. He swayed for a moment, and then ran up the steps.

Hoseyn had just reached the door when Anthony spun him round and caught him a loud cracking blow to the chin. Hoseyn's head rocked back, but the next instant he had one hand on Anthony's throat while punching his face with the other. Anthony hooked Hoseyn's legs out from under him and both ambassadors tumbled through the doors of Castel Sant'Angelo.

The ambassadors had arrived. The crowd let out a mocking cheer.

First Secretary Uruch Bey dismounted and climbed the blood-stained steps with as much dignity as he could muster, but he was scarcely through the doors when he found himself on the floor, trying to pull the ambassadors apart, and getting clipped with a couple of blows for his pains.

Uruch couldn't find purchase on Anthony's steel doublet, so he slid one hand in its waist and one in its neck and lifted Anthony bodily as if hefting an empty samovar. He bashed the samovar against the oak-paneled wall, and let the wretch drop to the floor.

'Lock the door!' ordered Hoseyn Ali Beg, pressing a wadded silk handkerchief to his bloody mouth. Uruch did as he was bid and pocketed the key.

As Anthony climbed to his feet, Hoseyn shouted:

'I am the Shah's ambassador! Not you!'

'No, I'm the ambassador! This whole Embassy was my idea. Everybody knows that. You heard the crowds cheer me!'

'Treason! They were cheering the Shah not you!'

Uruch broke in.

'When Shah Abbas,' he hissed at Anthony, 'hears that you attacked his Ambassador during the civic reception in Rome, I tell you he will deal with you like your Queen dealt with Essex.'

'Pardon?'

'She cut the traitor's head off last month after he tried to murder her in her bed.'

'Essex?'

'Essex!' barked Hoseyn. 'That's the fellow! I heard it too! Essex!'

Anthony opened and closed his mouth to speak but no words came. He looked from Uruch to Hoseyn. Tears flowed down his cheeks. He must get away from them. He must grieve alone. His heart was breaking. He fled past Uruch to the door. Locked. Tears stung his eyes. He could hardly see and stumbled as he ran to a pair of floor-to-ceiling double-doors. He rattled the knob, banged and kicked the doors, until they gave. Here at last would be a little room where he could try to comprehend the enormity of this loss. Stumbling through the double-doors, he found himself not in a little anteroom, but out on the balcony.

A huge cheer went up from the crowd down below. Anthony raised his hand in salutation. His tears could not be seen so he didn't need to dry them. Just wave. His face a rictus, he waved and waved, while sobbing so heavily that his steel doublet bashed and clashed against the stone parapet, drawing tiny sparks.

2

A fortnight later, Uruch crossed the courtyard of the Embassy's Palazzo della Rovere lodgings with a parcel under his arm intended for his oil agent's friend. Reintroducing himself to Nat Bramble, he was shocked by the venomous scowl that greeted him. Then, as if there were no such thing as hierarchy, the servant, his lip curling, accused the First Secretary of betraying him to Anthony on the night of the barn dance. How else, he wanted to know, were Anthony and Elkin able to waylay him on the road back to Kulsum's barn? Who else but Uruch could possibly have told Anthony where to find him? Uruch adjusted the cuffs of his dove-grey satin kurta, and raised his eyebrows.

'I did not know you were a runaway,' he replied. 'Did you not tell me the oil venture was Antonio's project? ...Talking of runaways, I thought these might fit you. They belonged to the defectors who left us for the Jesuits.'

Uruch handed Nat a bundled assortment of clothes balled in twine.

As they sat down together on the courtyard's stone bench, Uruch noticed how stiffly the servant moved. The careful way Nat propped the small of his back with the bundle of clothes was the precautionary act of an old farm labourer hoping to preserve his spine for one more season, not a young man of, what, nineteen? Antonio was a slave driver. Whatever hell came of Antonio's Papal audience, it was at least a chance for the haggard boy to sit in the courtyard an hour.

'The packet ship's just sailed,' lamented Uruch, 'or else I could have included a word to Darius Nouredini from you.'

'When's the next one?'

'I don't know. Perhaps not till we get to Lisbon.'

Nat's spirit sank.

'Whenever you next write, you must tell Darius that I defended his good name from Mani Babachoi's slanders.'

Nat told the First Secretary how Mani and Darius both loved Gol and how Mani had by chance bought the very poem that Darius had written for her and read it to her first, Nat then told Uruch about when he last saw Mani.

The Embassy had not been many days out of Isfahan, when it crossed paths, at the Kashan caravanserai, with soldiers on their way to the front, amongst who was Mani Babachoi, Darius's rival for the love of Gol. They soon fell into an argument when Mani said that Darius had no right to seek Gol's hand because he was already engaged.

'He earned the right,' Nat snapped back, 'when he went down into a well of fire! When have you ever done her so much honour, Mani Babachoi?'

'I have scars.'

'Yours were done for show, for empty ceremony. His scars are marks of love. He got them trying to free himself to marry Gol.'

'Well, he can forget about that,' said Mani triumphantly. 'Gol has done me the honour of consenting to be my wife.'

'Then yours will be a marriage built on a lie, since it rests on falsehoods about my friend.'

Nat had stormed off, heart beating and expecting Mani Babachoi's musket stock to crush the back of his skull. But when he dared turn his head, Mani Babachoi was still standing where he had left him.

❖

'Be sure and put it in your letter,' said Nat as the sky darkened above the Palazzo della Rovere courtyard, 'that I argued his worthiness for Gol Zarafshani's hand.' Uruch pretended to commit her name to memory:

'Gol Zarafshani.'

In truth, not only was the First Secretary only half-listening, he would never even have sat down with an errand boy in the first place, still less suffer his rudeness, did he not plan to employ Nat as a spy.

The black clouds began to rain on the courtyard. They were sheltered where they sat, but Nat shivered and picked at the bundle of apostates' clothes and pulled out a quilted black twill coat. The coat reached below his knees. It had a warm lining, thick in the nap. He could wear it all through a London winter, that is if he ever got back.

'I have seen you,' said Uruch, 'delivering your master's sealed letters and baton scrolls to the Spanish ambassador.'

'And I have seen you at the Spanish ambassadors, too,' said Nat, happy in his new black coat. 'Seen you there so often, indeed, that I thought you were to run off and join a monastery like those other three Persians!'

Uruch chuckled as if Nat had said something very witty, then said:

'The ambassador will pay in gold to read Antonio's letters to kings or queens.'

'Huh! Anthony will kill me first.'

Uruch pulled a silver signet ring off his finger.

'This is the Safavid seal ring, official letter stamp of Shah Abbas. Antonio has one, Hoseyn Mirza has one, and this one is for you. You open the letter, make a copy, seal it with this. How will your master ever know? He won't. He can't. Here, take the ring."

'No, Uruch, you must excuse me.'

Uruch nodded at Nat's seemly *Ta'rof*, the etiquette that demanded that one refuse a gift several times before accepting.

'Nothing threatens the Alliance more than Sir Anthony's intrigues,' he said. 'Disclose his secret proposals and you will save the embassy.'

'What's the embassy to me?' asked Nat.

'The safety of the Isfahan to Tabriz road, upon which my oil merchant, the esteemed Darius Nouredini, must travel, depends on the success of this embassy.'

Nat held out his hand for the ring.

'If Anthony ever finds it, I'll just say it was there when you gave me the coat.'

'Very clever,' said the First Secretary. 'Very clever. I knew I had picked the right man for the job. Now be sure to bring me copies of any letters that Antonio writes to any Prince or Pope, won't you?'

'At your service, First Secretary.'

Nat bowed and walked into the rain, with his little bundle under his arms. Halfway across the courtyard, however, he turned round and called back.

'Oh, one more thing, Uruch. This is a dangerous undertaking and I ask you to give me a solemn pledge.'

'Name it.'

'Leave me that grey satin kurta when you defect to the Spanish.'

3

Hoseyn Ali Beg looked down onto the rain-lashed Piazza Scossa Cavalli. The rainstorm had turned day into night. Italian servants lit candles and withdrew. At least these candles were wax and not tallow, the animal fat they were burning in the English quarters. How he missed the steady cheerful light of a string of proper oil lanterns! Flickering candle-light made him feel he was hunkering in some cave. The door opened and Uruch walked in with that picking step of his.

'What were you talking about with Antonio's boy all this time?'

'I gave him the signet ring just as you told me to do.'

'And the rest of the time?'

Hoseyn was jumpy. Three of his staff had defected from the Embassy. If the First Secretary turned apostate, as well, the Shah would summon Hoseyn home for execution. Since the Jesuits gave Uruch that Bible they had so helpfully translated into Farsi, Uruch's nose was hardly out of it. Uruch was as happy in Rome as Hoseyn himself was miserable. A little too happy. Something was afoot. 'What else did you talk about with him? What else?'

Intending to shame Hoseyn, the First Secretary began to relate every last petty detail he could remember of his oil factor's love triangle involving a soldier and some woman called Gol Zarafshani. To Uruch's dismay, Hoseyn, far from being ashamed, asked question after question about the love triangle, as keenly if they were going over the Papal order of ceremony or something important or seemly. Uruch couldn't believe his ears. He was appalled. Perhaps Antonio had cracked the old fellow's skull during their fight on the Castel Sant' Angelo steps. One would think that after such a humiliating spectacle as that appalling brawl, Hoseyn's every word and deed would now be bent towards regaining at least a modicum of ambassadorial dignity. But no, he was hungry for servant tittle-tattle about who kissed whom in the barnyard!

'You are meeting the Pope tomorrow, Hoseyn Mirza! What does any of this matter?'

The Ambassador sat down cross-legged on the rug before the fire, and gestured for Uruch to join him. Uruch sat opposite and waited. Hoseyn seemed lost in memory. He stroked his drooping white moustache, which was like a pair of twin compasses.

'Many years ago,' he said, 'Atash Zarafshani and I both served a governor who was executed for embezzlement. I replaced the governor, whom I'd served as deputy, but Shah Abbas sent the rest of the governor's staff, every last man, to the Uzbeg front, and not as administrators or quartermasters, either, but as foot-soldiers. All except me. I don't know why.'

'He knew your character, Hoseyn Mirza.'

'The same crimes for which the governor was executed were not unknown to his deputy. At that time in my life. In that place. Never since, I want you to know, never since. I was the governor's deputy, Atash Zarafshani was just an assistant notary and completely innocent. But Atash suffered, and I was made governor. He was terribly injured in the war, disfigured, and I was given a seat in the majlis.'

Hoseyn told Uruch how it was this new chasm in rank, and not the disfigurement, that made things difficult between them. There was an awkward New Year visit - Gol was a little girl then. Down there in the poor, clay-built part of Isfahan, a fur-trimmed majlis minister was visiting a humble pigeon breeder and crippled soldier. Impossible to compliment him on his roof garden or his birds without the air of condescension. So when Atash Zarafshani thanked Hoseyn Ali Beg for the great honour of the visit, they both knew that a little less honour would have meant a great deal more friendship. He hadn't seen him since.

Hoseyn stuck out his bottom lip.

'Guilt weighs down your soul,' said Uruch.

'My guilt's no help to Atash Zarafshani - or his family. What would have helped my old friend was if I had been able to send him the truth about Darius Nouredini's innocence on this packet ship. That would have helped.'

'His daughter has another suitor.'

'A soldier in a war that is worse than any we have ever known thanks to this Embassy having failed to deliver the alliance upon which hung any hope of victory. That's why we lost those three defectors: the prospect of a Turkish war is a stronger argument for apostasy than any number of Farsi Bibles. A letter! I will send a letter to Atash Zarafshani, and you must find a mail ship soon. The one great merit of Darius Nouredini's suit is that he is not a soldier. If this whole Embassy achieves nothing more than clearing his name and persuading Atash that your oil merchant is a fit husband for Gol, then at least the years will not have been wasted.'

'Indeed, Hoseyn Mirza. For is it not written in the book that he who saves one man saves the whole world?'

'Which book is that, Uruch? Which book is that?'

4

Sir Thomas Sherley's ship the *Golden Dragon* was anchored off Kea, nearest of the Cyclades to Athens. A full moon lit four boats rowing from ship to shore as Sir Thomas led eighty men in a raid on the almond-shaped island. They crossed a broad plain and began the steep two-mile climb to the hilltop town of Ioulida.

As they slogged uphill, the raiding party muttered behind his back. If you are going to attack by the light of a full moon, they complained, why not just attack by day and be done? One hour later, Sir Thomas stood in a deserted plaza in the centre of Ioulida, splashing his lantern's light up and down up the white walls of empty white houses and locked white churches.

Tallest and eldest of the three Sherley brothers, Sir Thomas pushed his long brown hair off his wide forehead. Broad shouldered, broad-nosed, his open mouth and knitted brow gave him a baffled yet determined look, dogged and uncomprehending. He looked like a gentleman farmer on his way back from market, stopping in his tracks upon realising that he has been shortchanged.

Ioulida was a ghost town. Except he knew it wasn't. Candles were still glowing in the wayside cupboard shrines. He led a search through the streets of the hilltop town. He ran down a narrow alley and at the end of it there was the full moon playing Peep Bo with him. When the rest of the search party gave up, he ran on alone the length and breadth of all Ioulida's mazy walkways. At the end of every alley and every flight of steps, he saw nobody, only the fat round moon, framed in the square of the passageway like its reflection in a well, saying, Peep-Bo! Peep-Bo! Peep-Bo!

Sir Thomas returned to the central plaza by the large church where he found his men sitting about and giving him sour looks. Grumbling and cursing, the *Dragon's* crew began the long walk back to the sea. They straggled downhill in darkness, which became darker still as they entered a deep gully hidden from the moonlight.

Stones and rocks pelted them from the high cliffs either side of the gully. Hundreds of roaring Greeks charged at them from both sides, all swinging staves, rakes and hoes.

'Stand! Stand!' bellowed Sir Thomas, as his crew fled all around him screaming 'The Turk! The Turk!' The next second he was fleeing himself. He emerged from the gully into a running battle on the plain. 'Stand! Stand! To me! To me!' he cried, waving his rapier. But the crew could see their ship in the moonlight and ran pell-mell for the small boats.

A rock caught Sir Thomas on the forehead as he watched them go. Blood poured into his eye. He did not see the stick that cracked his kneecap. The pain was intense. He kept his footing, but was hobbled and limping now. He slashed his rapier around like a cornered crab with only one claw left. In hand to hand combat, Sir Thomas's sliced, slashed and stabbed at his Greeks attackers in the moonlight. A hoe struck the side of his head. He fell to the ground. The heel of a boot crunched the bones of his sword hand.

The villagers stripped him stark naked, using his own garters to tie his arms behind his back. Two Ioulidans had been killed in the skirmish, and so there was not a man, woman or child who did not kick, punch or scratch Thomas, or tug his beard or pull his long hair before they slung him into a tiny stone shed, where he was shackled to the wall.

On the third day of his captivity a few Greeks came into the cell and removed his leg-irons. They stood him on his feet, and tied his hands behind his back with his gaiters again. The Greeks led him to the edge of a rocky promontory. He squinted against the bright glittering azure sea far below. His captors began talking in their barbarous tongue. They were trying to tell him something, and were pointing at the long drop to the rocks. He knew this game. He wasn't playing. Let them throw him off the cliff and have done. He would not humour them. He would not be their sport.

'Yes, yes,' he said in English, 'a long drop. Jagged rocks. A painful death. Quick about it. You will not make a Sherley wail or beg base life from primitives! I am Sir Thomas Sherley, you dogs!'

Then it began to dawn on him that they were not going to shove him off the cliff. It was something else that they were trying to tell him. They pointed at the marks on his ankles and bare feet where the leg-irons used to be, then pointed down at the sandy crescent of the bay. They seemed to be saying that the reason his irons had come off that morning had something to do with the azure bay down below. He looked back down at the shore.

And then he understood what they were trying to tell him. A great cry escaped him. His knees gave way. He lay on his face in sharp thistles and sheep droppings. They had kept him in irons only so long as they had feared a rescue attempt. No chance of rescue now. He was forsaken, utterly forsaken. The *Golden Dragon* had gone.

5

Their instruments at rest, Gol, Maryam, Nargis and Sahar sit with self-effacing stillness, against the wall of a courtyard crowded with wedding guests. The hired musicians are waiting for the speeches to end before they resume playing, none more impatiently than Gol for whom life has become one long wait. Waiting for Mani to return from the war. Waiting for any word of Mani. Waiting to hear if he's dead or alive.

What a lot of speeches there have been since the band's last song! And what a long speech this last one is! She strokes the drumskin of the dombak she has primed and ready to go. She'll play drum on the next song, which will begin – if these speeches ever end - with a double-time drumbeat: *doum-tek ka! doum-tek ka! doum-tek ka! DOUM!* She can't wait to puncture the heavy, slow silence with that *doum-tek ka! doum-tek ka! doum-tek ka! DOUM!* But wait she must. Wait she must.

She stares up at the neat rectangle of sky above the courtyard. The edge of a cloud tears with tedious slowness.

She looks at the newly weds, gifts piled before them on the bright silk wedding blanket, the *sofre aghd* sewn with little mirrors and embroidered with silver brocade. They are both younger than Gol. Here's yet another couple moving on to the next stage of life, while she is stuck fast. Betrothal to Mani should have brought Gol change: escape from a father who never left the house, and from a mother who never changed an opinion. She is not living, only waiting.

Once, when she was a little girl, she asked her father what made the mosque's blue walls shimmer. He showed her how each blue wall tile was glazed with a solution of tiny metal specks in suspension. She stroked the glaze under which flakes and flecks of copper and nickel were suspended like stones in ice. Suspended in a glaze.

She starts jigging her heel on the ball of her foot. Heel clacks against slipper with the blurry speed of a kingfisher's wings. Will this mullah never end? Must he pause between every last phrase so as to let its full triteness sink in, leaving ever longer gaps between one choice word and the next? At least he is the final speaker. When he has done the band will at last be able to strike up again. For now she must endure this interminable waiting.

Even Darius has grown up and moved on. A few weeks ago, she caught sight of him in the maidan's middle distance haggling with a couple of merchants. There he was, the New Darius, a self-possessed man of affairs, his hands full of practical gestures, the flat of his hand chopping a fraction off the top of a commission, a forefinger rolling revenue into next month. All his old dreaminess was gone, leaving only these cold, sharp gestures. Well, they say good fortune hardens the heart. Except his heart had always been harder than she'd ever suspected, hadn't it? He'd never really been the wide-eyed poet of her imagination. His betrayal of her was cold. She never really knew him.

She closes her eyes and breathes in through her nose and out through her mouth. When she has done this seven times, she opens her eyes to find that the shadows in the courtyard have somehow thickened. More than that, the courtyard is completely silent. The mullah's speech has ended! It ended long ago! Her heart skips a beat. Everyone is waiting for her. Late! She is late! She has missed her cue. Maryam and Sahar are frowning at her.

Gol seizes the dombak and beats the drumhead in double-time:

doum-tek ka! doum-tek ka! doum-tek ka! DOUM!

Maryam grabs her arm. All the wedding guests in the courtyard hiss: *suss! suss! suss!* All eyes are upon her. She lays the dombak down, ashamed from head to toe.

The mullah turns his head towards her, and makes a joke about the intemperance of young women, then resumes his unending blessing.

6

Musket and bird basket slung across his back, Mani Babachoi scaled a steep mountain path through prickly bushes. Only an hour after daybreak and already it was hot. He was leading a three-man scouting party. From the top of the ridge, he'd be able to see to the far horizon and to search for any distant puff of smoke that might be a clue as to the whereabouts of the Ottoman army. The two other scouts – Abadani boors - were dawdling far behind in the foothills.

This suited Mani well, because on this pristine and beautiful morning he was, contrary to military regulations, going to release the homing dove carrying his love letter to Gol. Weeks and weeks he had spent composing the letter in his head. It was all very *gol o bobol*. Just her sort of thing, he was sure. Pale green lizards turned tail, rattling purple thistles as they flicked away into the bushes. Perhaps they heard the two birds in his basket, the army bird and the stout black and white dove that was a gift from Atash Zarafshani.

'This is for your letter to my daughter,' Gol's father had told him, his scaly hands closing Mani's upon the bird, its heart beating hard and fast against his fingers. 'A token of my blessing upon your engagement. Not my fastest, but my strongest dove. He will fly fifteen hundred parasangs at a go.'

Later that same day, when they were alone together on the roof garden, Gol said,

'Darius is a hypocrite. He's the type of man who preserves the purity of the bride in his left hand by dint of the whore in his right. For men like Darius, marriage does not mean the entwining of two souls at all, but the perpetuation of the eternal purdah between men and women. He fooled me. I don't know why it should hurt so much, since we were never lovers, but it does hurt. He has destroyed my trust. Who can be sure of anything in this world anymore?'

Mani's eyes had rolled back in his head, 'She is mine!' he thought. 'She is mine!' Victory over Darius was so total and complete that he even forgot his jealousy about the close friendship Gol had enjoyed with him for all those years before.

When his platoon had crossed tracks with the embassy's caravan, however, Mani ran into Nat, who argued that Darius was not the hypocrite Gol thought he was. The young foreigner's passion convinced Mani he was speaking the truth.

Should Mani write and tell Gol the truth about Darius? No. What she didn't know couldn't hurt her, but it could destroy Mani's hopes. No, now was not the time to write, not now when he was so far from home, and when Darius was in Isfahan. In her contrition Gol would be too receptive to the honeyed words the new rich Darius poured in her ear. He would convince her she was too fine and precious a rose for a soldier's wife. Well, a pox on that! Besides, hadn't she told him herself that she was over Darius? So there an end. Why tell her at all?

But then he heard her again plaintively saying: 'He has destroyed my trust. Who can be sure of anything in this world anymore?'

Mani hauled himself up between two jagged rocks. He cuffed sweat from his forehead and from his horseshoe moustache. He heard a noise above him. Footsteps? He listened again. The mountain was quiet. Probably just falling scree. He looked down at the other two scouts toiling far below him. He rubbed the bumps and dull discs on his arms where the self-inflicted scorch marks had healed. He listened to the two doves burbling in the basket. Their trilling carried him back to how he and Gol first met. And he heard his laughter echo off the rocky hillside.

The first time he saw her she was playing at a wedding with her band. They didn't meet. He never spoke to her, she didn't notice him. Strange how these things work, but for some reason what stuck in his mind, the thing that made him fall in love, was the delight in her eyes as she looked across to her fellow musicians whenever the music changed pace, swerving from one mood to another. He found out her name but no more than that.

Then a week later, he chanced to see her selling those stripy blue and green carnations – the Sea and Sky hybrid - in the bazardeh, or little bazaar. Gol's mother was doing the actual selling, while Gol herself was cutting stalks from a bunch of blue and green. He bought flowers for his mother, but failed to catch Gol's eye. When he returned the next day, Gol and her mother were gone, and there was a man selling meatballs in their place. He never hated a stranger so much as that oaf selling meatballs.

He went for long walks through the city streets. Truth be told, he was in no way searching for her, but rather the opposite. He was hoping to see another woman of equal charisma to bring him to his senses, to extirpate this wedding singer from his blood, and let him go back to how he used to be. He wasn't used to going round like half a person. He didn't like it. One other woman, of equal beauty would do it. Even if glimpsed for only a few seconds, her existence alone would be enough to calm his blood, be enough to let him drop this lunatic obsession with the fiddle-player with the raven black hair. He would be able to say to his madness, 'Look! There are other woman of uncanny charisma and blood-troubling beauty out there.' Yet even when they swapped a passing look with him, pretty women now stirred him as little as they did the Shah.

Walking, walking, walking through Isfahan's back streets in rain and wind and sun did at least take the edge off the gnawing hollowness that he had suffered ever since he first saw Gol. It had gone on for months this lonely walking, which he did whenever he was off-duty. One day, he was ill with a coughing fever, but still felt compelled to walk and walk, with a blanket around his shoulders. Woozy with sickness and fatigue he became utterly lost among tiny back streets, and passed a roof terrace crowned with sky-blue sea-green striped carnations. The Sea and Sky carnations! He stopped and listened to the trilling of doves. Boxes of them were stacked on top of each other on the roof terrace. He sat on the low wall of a vacant lot opposite the house, and wrapped the blanket tightly around his shoulders. A few hours later, he heard a stiff front door being dragged open and – boom! - there was Gol.

The very next day, Mani - fully recovered - marched straight to her house to declare his love, equipped with poem and burning taper. After a week he was running out of poetry and bought from the bazaar a perfect poem about a female musician, little suspecting that the chubby poet who sold it to him was his rival.

❖

At last Mani reached the abandoned hill fort, a squat stone box high on a ridge and dragged open the door. A cool breeze fluted through an espial set deep into the rough-hewn wall. He crossed the dirt floor to look through this rocky window, and then jumped back and flattened his back against the wall.

The entire Ottoman Army was within shouting distance. Tens of thousands of Turks! How had he not heard them? Had the hillside acted as an acoustic shadow? However it was, from this little stone hut on the ridge he could hear and see tens of thousands of enemy soldiers. He could hear dogs barking, and even the odd canteen clank. Mani ran back to the door and made warning gestures at the Abadanis, trying to tell them to keep their heads low and their mouths shut. He crept to the edge of the window again and looked down. Ottoman cavalry, artillery and transport were camped on the plain, and the horses corralled. With his marksman's eye he could make out details such as the silver chasing on a musket stock, and the folds in the paper hats of the men digging latrines. In the middle of the plain, the cannons were limbered, the cavalry mounted, the men formed lines that marched or ran. His heart beat fast as it hit him that he'd caught the Ottoman army rehearsing its battle plan. Here before him were revealed the battlefield tactics which they were going to deploy against Allahvirdi Khan's troops.

Hands trembling, he spread the army-issue silk on the broad slab of rock which formed a window ledge and drew what he saw, cross-hatching blocks of artillery and sketching arrows swooping this way and that to describe the swing of cavalry. When the manoeuvres finished, Mani folded the silk into a satchel which he strapped to the sky-blue army-issue dove.

As he watched the Turkish soldiers, he was struck by the fact that these men were different from all others he had ever seen before in his whole life, they wanted to kill him.

If they did then Gol would spend her whole life thinking Darius betrayed her.

He smoothed pale pink silk on the rocky ledge and weighted down the four corners with pebbles. As soon as his reed pen inked the first black words on the pink silk, he saw the poverty of the flowery love letter he'd been meaning to send, with all its *gol o bobol* bluster. This was truer. Mani wrote and told Gol that her first love, Darius Nouredini, had been faithful to her all along.

Outside, the Abadanis arrived, groaning and wheezing after slogging up the mountain track, and flung themselves down on the bank beside the door. A few moments later, he heard the knock of bottleneck on bowl.

Mani flapped the pink page around to dry the ink, folded it into a satchel and took Atash Zarafshani's black and white dove from the bird basket. Its keel – or breast muscle – was hard as a wrestler's biceps. As he hurriedly harnessed the dove, he muttered to him:

'Fly like a musket ball, my champion. Rip through headwinds right across *iran zamin.* Find Gol on the roof among the Sea and Sky carnations. That's how I found her, after all! That's how I found out where she lived! You know your way back to the Sea and Sky, my beauty. Go and find her.'

He heard scuffling outside. A scream. The Abadanis' bodies thudded one by one against the door. Turkish voices. He watched the door rock on its hinges. The echo in the little stone lodge punched his eardrums. The door wouldn't open because of the weight of the two dead Abadanis upon it. He heard their bodies being dragged away.

When the three janissaries burst through the door, and levelled their muskets at his head, he was holding a bird in each hand.

❖

The janissary captain, a Magyar from the Elayat of Budin, takes a pace forwards. Both the birds the Persian spy holds are already harnessed with silk satchels containing vital intelligence about the army's precise location and strength – perhaps even its battle plan. The success of the Ottoman strategy depended on surprising the Persians. Therefore this whole war could hinge on the secrets carried by two birds – one black and white, one blue – in this little stone lodge.

The Magyar takes another step forward, but as he does so, the Persian lifts both arms, threatening to launch the birds if the Magyar comes any close. The Magyar stops. The Persian's floppy sleeves have fallen to his elbows, revealing track marks on his forearms. An opium addict. A poppy demon. Therefore unpredictable. Yet there is calculation in his eyes. He can be reasoned with. The Magyar lowers his musket, and signals for the Egyptian janissaries behind him to lower theirs too.

Mani hears the musket stocks rest on the ground.

'Will you sacrifice your life for a couple of doves?' the Magyar asks him. 'It's very early in the morning to die. So why not hand them over and then you can go. We're just scouts, like you. We're no firing squad. Our orders simply say to gather intelligence. So why not give us the doves and then we can all sit outside and finish the last of that wine, eh?'

The Magyar holds out his hand.

The blue dove hits him in the face. Mani spins on his heel and lobs the black and white dove out of the deep-set window.

The Magyar shoots him where he stands. The shot's reverberations give way to the sound of flapping wings. All three janissaries slash at the blue dove flapping around the stone lodge. One blade connects. Abruptly, a plum-coloured spray sprinkles them, but the sky-blue bird keeps flying round and round the stone lodge, misting the dusty air with its blood. It drops and rolls into a clump of bloody feathers in the corner.

The Magyar cuts satchel from dove, and spreads it out on the broad slab of a window ledge. He turns to his comrades,

'This nest of spies has got our battle plan!'

A groan from the floor. The Magyar scoops up the limp sky-blue bird, and crouches beside him.

'You see, you dumb poppy demon! We got the bird anyway. Here's the bird, fool! Look!'

Trackmarks cannot turn his head, so the Magyar holds the dead blue bird over him, its blood dripping onto his face.

Mani's eyes locate the blue dove. To the Magyar's shock, a broad smile lifts the ends of the Persian spy's horseshoe moustache. Mani looks the Magyar in the eye. He works his mouth to be able to speak, then rasps his last words:

'You got the wrong bird.'

The Magyar shakes him, shouting,

'What secret is greater than a battle plan? Do you have a spy in high command? A general? Tell me! We have doctors. We can save you. What's the secret? Tell me your great secret!'

He stands up and tells the Egyptians to go though his pockets. Empty. All empty. He kicks the dead body.

7

A golden hawk, Shah Abbas's finest, hovers high in the air. His wings span the whole plain west of Isfahan, south of the Zagros Mountains. The Shah's hunting party are specks now. Dots. The barking dogs cannot be heard so high. Hunting dogs don't leave a hawk long with his prey.

The golden hawk tilts his wings. The bells on his legs tinkle in the current as he changes direction and soars away from the hunting party. Let the beaters with their petty lures and gyres beckon the falcons, the tercels and the clumsy young eagles. The royal hawk is above and beyond them all. Any prey now caught belongs to him alone. Dogs will not be able to snatch his kill away to give to men.

He hangs in a clear sky. Halfway between himself and the ground, the golden hawk sees a black and white dove. Black and white and directly below like mouse tracks in snow. The black and white dove is hindered in his flight. Some impediment in the flap of the wings. A patch of pink or purple on its back. A wound!

The golden hawk folds his wings and stoops. Dropping like a stone, he snatches the dove on his way down. On the ground, his talons hold the fallen dove as his beak shreds the black and white feathers. The pink patch the colour of a raw wound is not a raw wound. It cannot be eaten. The hawk rips silk to shreds, then tears at feathers with his beak. Plum-coloured blood oozes out onto the black and white. Now he is getting somewhere. Now here is flesh. The dark meat is the same colour as always. The taste is the same taste as always. All is as it should be.

By the time the yapping, barking, howling dogs arrive, the men on horses following after, the hawk has eaten his fill, and is content to flap to Shah Abbas's royal gauntlet. The hunting dogs may have his leavings.

Torn feathers and tattered fragments of shredded pink silk covered in black writing blow this way and that, scattered on the breeze, lost forever.

8

After the Vatican awarded him fourteen hundred gold escudi, Anthony set out from Rome a well-contented traveller. But travel broadens the mind, the road lends perspective. He had not been very many miles upon the Appian Way before he began to consider whether he had not been rash and over-hasty in accepting this award of fourteen hundred escudi. Sure, it *sounded* a fine sum, but when weighed in the scale against all the hardships of a journey between Rome and Isfahan, he found it wanting. So he had gone to Venice instead and taken out a year's lease on a sumptuous palazzo on the Grand Canal. He was so flush that he paid the lease in advance, but soon had cause to regret acting out of character in this way.

He'd only been in the palazzo a fortnight when he was found guilty of extortion against a Persian merchant, and sentenced to three months in the New Prison with immediate banishment to follow his release. A whole year's rent he'd paid! It was all Queen Elizabeth's fault. The long arm of the Queen had robbed him of funds. Spooked by the damage he could do to England's relations with Venice and the Mediterranean trade, she'd forbidden all English bankers to extend him credit. What else could he do, what other course was left him but to try and lay hold of the Persian merchant's silk bales?

On being sent to New Prison, Anthony dismissed all his followers save two, Elkin and Bramble. He kept Elkin next to him in jail for protection. Elkin wasn't complaining. Stranded and penniless the rest of the lower servants were pulling an oar in the stinking galley ships. Jail was far better, especially an apartment cell like Anthony's with fruit, good meat and a fire. Bramble, meanwhile, came and went, running errands and delivering mail. Anthony lodged Bramble at the palazzo as a sort of nightwatchman, chiefly to make sure that the owner, on hearing of Anthony's incarceration, didn't try to let the Grand Canal property to anyone else - it was the principle of the thing. He had paid a year's rent in advance, and so it stuck in his craw to think of anyone else having the run of what was his.

One morning in the cell, Nat stood beside the oak desk he had just shifted from palazzo to prison listening to Anthony's rings clack through hot wax, sealing the letter he'd just written to the King of Spain.

Anthony wore two rings side by side. One for Essex who sent him east and one for the Shah who sent him west. The mourning ring for Essex, a white skull with eyes of jet on a band of gold, was of a piece with Anthony's whirligig sword hilt that went up and down and all around, like the trail of a bee set in steel. His master disdained to own anything unless the artisan went blind in the manufacture and so couldn't make a copy! The signet ring, however, was identical to his own, and one day Nat would make a copy of one of Anthony's letters and sell it to his enemies. So far the opportunity to do so had not presented itself. He would know the moment when it came.

'Deliver this to the King of Spain's ambassador, Bramble.'

'At once, Sir Anthony.'

Instead of going to Spanish ambassador's residence, Nat went straight back to Anthony's abandoned palazzo on the Grand Canal by Rio San Maurizio. What joy to have the whole pile to himself! Even though there was no-one but himself to fetch the food, it was still fun to bang the gong and shout a loud summons down to the empty scullery. More wine, I say! More cheese! He couldn't help but feel like a conquering general bathing in the bath of the conquered king!

Except not conquered yet...

Nat sat at an ornate writing desk. With his pocket knife he carefully slit the sealing wax and read the letter that Anthony had just written to King Philip of Spain's Ambassador.

If His Majesty King Philip assembles a Spanish invasion fleet of but twenty-five to thirty ships at the mouth of the River Scheldt in his Dutch Dominion of the Low Countries, he shall find England can in no way defend herself. The best places for an invasion force to land are Sandwich, Harwich, Ipswich, Hull, Hartlepool. Twelve hundred to fifteen hundred men will do it, but you must take London.

England relies upon the Turkish navy as a counterweight to Your Majesty's ships out of the Mediterranean, but, acting under my orders, the Persian will soon overrun Ottoman ports, and Your Majesty will be lord of half the world.

The treason was eye watering. This was the strongest meat yet, more treacherous even than last week's letter to the King of Scotland telling James how the best way to get the English crown was to ferment the Irish war because this would so impoverish the English that they would cry out for deliverance from the Queen, and the City of London merchants would welcome him as liberator.

Only where was the market for the traitor's letters to the King of Spain? Who could he sell this letter to? Or the one to the King of Scots? He knew no-one in Venice he could sell these to. If only Uruch was in Venice. Uruch would pay Nat gold for this letter, gold enough perhaps to buy a passage on a ship back to England, but he doubted he'd ever see Uruch again. The Great Persian Embassy was last heard of in Lisbon, as Nat knew from Anthony's letters. All of which left Nat like the card player who, for want of a stake, folds his winning hand, folds his two kings.

He thumbed the Shah Abbas signet ring that Uruch had given him from the honeycomb lining of his patched black and red doublet. Out slid the cod's roe. He cracked a shard off a scarlet block of wax and held it on his knife over a candle flame. He drizzled the sealing wax over the cracked boss, and stamped the ring down hard to reseal the letter. As if he knew the liberties Nat was taking with his image, Shah Abbas's livid and scarlet face stared up at him from the fresh wax.

Nat turned to the invisible guests crowding the salon, and bid them adieu. He kissed his fingertips at the ladies, then bowed to the lords, and set out to deliver Anthony's letter to the Spanish ambassador.

9

In the New Prison annex under the Doge's Palace, Anthony was reading a letter from his sister Cessalye about their brother Thomas's sufferings in his Turkish gaol. Anthony pored over this last letter from his sister, hoping runes could be read in it, the runes of Tom's fate, be it life or death. Let it be life. Dear God, please let poor Tom live.

My most honourable dear brother,

Lord, lord, by what strange fate are all my three brothers now prisoners! Thomas in the Seven Towers, you in Venice, and Robert a hostage in Isfahan, where he is much alarmed because Shah Abbas now throws cold looks upon him for want of any word from you.

Sultan Mehmed reprieved Thomas from execution and was about to set him free but died the night before he was to sign his pardon into law! I do not know how Thomas survives this setback, for I confess that I scarce survived the news! All hopes now lie in the gift of the new Sultan, Ahmed, who is I hear a boy of fourteen or fifteen. God help us!

It goes hard with Thomas in the Seven Towers ever since the Turk discovered he was brother to the famous Sir Anthony Sherley, sole instigator of the Persian invasion of the Sultan's country.

Thomas has neither clothes, bed, fire nor blanket. His new dungeon is quite the worst he has yet endured. He is shackled to a damp wall, and there's frost on the stone floor. But on his first night in the new cell, when his eyes grew accustomed to the dark, he found he was not alone. There was another prisoner there, an English convict who told him:

'Do not worry about the damp, sir. Be of good cheer. The cool air of this dungeon is rich in healthy minerals and can preserve a man's health and life for many a year.' Alas, the poor, good fellow died in the night.

Thomas fears he himself can't hold out much longer, being so much weakened by many strange sicknesses, and having endured many grievous tortures right up to the mock executions he now suffers when the guards are drunk or bored.

One bright star glows in all this black night! James, King of Scots, sends Thomas money and still pleads with the Queen to intercede on our brother's behalf, though she obstinately refuses to petition the Sultan to let Thomas go, it being an article of faith with her that the Great Turk is England's counterweight against Spanish might - so forget about justice and right!

Let us pray that Sultan Ahmed frees poor Thomas,

God bless and keep King James, our deliverer!

Your loving sis, Cess.

Anthony stared into the fire. A cell is not a place where a man can endure bad news. Away down the corridor another prisoner was howling and wailing. He feared that he would soon be howling himself. He had a gut-twisting presentiment that today was the day when he would receive the letter saying sweet Tom was dead. He had sent Bramble to collect mail from the packet ship just put in at the Levant Company's dock on the Riva degli Schiavone.

Poor Tom, ill luck had followed him all over the world, right to the hell of Kea Island. Ah, he should have listened to Anthony and never gone to sea. Hadn't Anthony warned him against it? On their very last conversation together, he'd warned his big brother of the pitfalls of storming an island.

'I took Jamaica once, Tom, and precious good it did me! The Jamaicans fled, taking all their worldly goods with them. I got nothing out of the invasion but a ton and a half of meat. Cock a' bones if that wasn't all I got for taking Jamaica! By Christ's blood, I'd have been richer taking Smithfield meat market!'

Thomas had always been outshone by his younger brothers' achievements. That was the problem. There was Anthony, a Colonel with Essex in France where he had been knighted by Henri IV, and now the favourite of the Shah of Persia. Aye, and there was Robert, four years in the court of the Grand Duke of Tuscany, whence he was sent as emissary to North Africa, now instructing Persian generals in artillery. At thirty-six years old Thomas had yet to do some great thing. It looked like he'd found his path to glory when he got into the court of James, King of Scotland.

One misty day, Thomas and Old Sir Thomas Sherley, his father, who was then England's Treasurer for War, rode out to meet two Scottish ambassadors at a remote spot in the Sussex Weald, near the Sherleys' Wiston seat. These clandestine meetings were never in the same place twice, but the topic for discussion was always the same: how to obtain the funds that James, King of Scotland, needed to raise an army. On this particular day, the Earl of Mar turned in the saddle and addressed a question to Young Sir Thomas:

'So, if not the West Indies, then where is the honey pot, eh? Where's the world's great gold mine, do you think?'

'The Mediterranean Sea is where, my Lord. A lake of prizes. The only problem is rules and regulations. The only problem is the Queen. She has slapped a moratorium on hunting for prizes in the Mediterranean. She's not just a signatory, but she herself actually framed and drafted the treaty banning piracy and privateering in the Mediterranean, so dear does she and all her faction hold the Levant trade, and so high does she rate her rank alliance with the infidel Turk.'

'King James has signed no such treaty,' said the Earl of Mar. 'Nor will he ever.'

'I offer to hazard my life and estate,' said Thomas, 'to attempt to take from the Turk his treasure and lay it at King James's feet!'

Old Sir Thomas Sherley diverted from the Queen's war chest all the funds needed to equip his eldest son with five-hundred men and three ships, each one bearing a fine English name: *Saint George, Virgin* and *Golden Dragon*, and which all flew the Grand Duke of Tuscany's red fleur-de-lys banner (the Duke himself a shareholder in the venture) as they sailed across the Mediterranean.

The three ships had stalked the Straits of Gibraltar without joy for so long that the victuals ran out. They had attacked the next ship they saw, a hulking great Venetian merchantman. For eight hours straight the combined crews of Sir Thomas's three ships battled against the Venetian galley soldiers. One hundred of his men were killed, with many more wounded, maimed and mutilated, before they at last took the Venetian ship, and found its hold full of gravel for building roads.

That night on board the *Saint George,* disaffected officers, crew and walking wounded came together for a meeting.

'Tom Sherley never even parlayed beforehand,' said the outraged pilot. 'Had he done so, then he'd have *known* there'd be no prize worth the life of so many men.'

One and all, they voted to leave Sir Thomas Sherley's fleet, and that night the *Saint George* sailed away.

With his two remaining ships, *Dragon* and *Virgin*, Thomas Sherley put in for resupply at Livorno, the Tuscan port which the English called Leghorn. The *Virgin's* crew absconded when they went ashore, and so Sir Thomas had to hire survivors of a recent shipwreck, making the captain of the shipwreck, one Peacock, pilot of the *Virgin.* On behalf of the *Virgin's* new crew, Mr Peacock thanked Sir Thomas for giving some forty-five Greek, Italian, Irish and English harbour bums a rare and unexpected opportunity, and then set sail in the *Virgin,* never to be seen again. That left Sir Thomas with only the *Dragon,* and one hundred men.

It so happened that two Levant Company Vice-Consuls, Sir Nicholas Roe and Sir Nicholas Colthurst, had just arrived in Leghorn from the Republic of Venice, and got wind that Sir Thomas was planning to attack the Ottoman island of Kea. Any such attack on a Turkish possession by an English ship could result in the Sultan revoking the Levant Company's harbour rights and licence to trade in the Mediterranean. Roe and Colthurst therefore instructed the *Dragon's* crew in their legal and moral duty to jump ship or mutiny, or else run the risk of being hung for wrecking the Turkish and Levantine trades in which English merchants and the Crown had invested so many years of hard work. But Sir Thomas, accompanied by the Duke of Florence's envoys, had returned with meat, beer and pay. A fresh wind filled out the topgallant and the crew stayed aboard in hope that Sir Thomas's luck might change.

It did not. Thomas achieved fame as The Least Successful Pirate In The World. Captured by the very islanders he was supposed to have been pillaging and marauding, and now being tortured by the Turk for a ransom he was too poor to pay.

Or worse. Soon the letter might come telling Anthony that Tom was dead. Tortured to death. Executed. Where was that jackanapes Bramble? Damn his eyes! Damn his dawdling and shillyshallying. What was keeping him? A man's life hung in the balance.

He chucks more logs on the fire blazing in the cell. He picks up the poker. He'll brain Bramble with this when he gets in. In fury, he whacks the poker against the grate so hard and it makes such a loud noise when he does so, that it takes him a moment to register the sound of iron key in door. His stomach goes hollow. Here comes the news.

The guards admit his servant. Bramble bends a face of tragedy upon Anthony. He knows the news already. He must have heard the news off the passengers on the boat. Thomas is dead.

'Sir... I... have sad... terrible... I -'

'I'll know the worst right now rather than hear you stutter me down to hell!'

'Indeed, I bring bleak news, sir.'

'What did I just say?' shouts Anthony. 'Spit it out!'

Tears tumble down Bramble's face.

'The Queen...' he gasps.

'What's the bitch done now?'

'Her Majesty has left us, sir.'

'What?'

'Queen Elizabeth is dead, Sir Anthony. James of Scots is the new King of England.'

Anthony lets out a long whoop of joy and begins dancing around his cell, crying out with an exultation that sounds like rage,

'The Queen is dead! The Queen is dead! A curse upon her bones!'

Nat's astonishment gives way fear. Anthony becomes ever more maniacal. Nat senses that he is capable of doing any abomination, and in that instant, Anthony's wild gaze falls upon him, seizes his wrist and swings him towards the fireplace. Nat struggles, but this crazed Anthony is as strong as a runaway bull and Nat clatters to his knees before the fire. Then Anthony drops to his knees beside him. For want of an altar he is kneeling on the Persian rug before the New Prison cell fireplace, hands clasped together in prayer. And there they are, master and servant, side by side, praying into the rising flames.

Palms pressed together, Nat looks out of the corner of his eyes at Anthony, red and sweating. He breathes heavily, his eyes are malevolent little wicks of reflected firelight, his stench – unleashed by that little jig around the cell – is peppery. His red beard goes up and down as he prays into the fire like a pagan in the Temple of Mithras summoning Ahriman God of Darkness and his forces of death and destruction. The flames wobble with the panting fervour of his master's prayers.

'God bless and keep King James! Our deliverer and hope of the age. Hear me now, Lord. Let no mischief overtake him all the long way down from Scotland. Let no assassin's shot come near him at Jedburgh, nor no suspicious pottage be set before him at York; let no plaguy-breathed petitioner sneeze on him at Hitchin, but let him come safe to the throne to do Thy Blessed Work on Earth!'

10

King James had been on the throne for less than a month before he successfully petitioned the Venetian Doge and Senate to pardon Sir Anthony, who returned to his palazzo on the Grand Canal in triumph.

It was bruited that Anthony would soon be recalled to Whitehall and made either Lord Chancellor or Secretary of State. A bindweed of gondolas tangled among the palazzo's mooring posts as English office-seekers and petitioners vied for influence from the new king's anointed, and merchant bankers fell over themselves to extend him lines of credit. The mooring posts themselves Nat had newly painted in the Sherley livery, blue with coiling gold bands.

One evening, an impressive and forbidding looking *felze* – a gondola with a roof on it - was moored to the blue and gold posts. The *felze* carried the crest of the Levant Company, England's richest and most powerful corporation, alongside the City of London's red dagger crest.

The booming sound of Levant Company Governor Sir Henry 'Customer' Hythe's laughter, came from an upstairs window of the palazzo, where he and a couple of Levant Company Vice-Consuls were being royally entertained.

All night long Nat had been running up and down the stairs with Anthony banging the gong every five minutes for more tobacco, more wine, more meat, more fruit, more logs, or to fetch that map or those papers.

Around midnight the supper party was still going strong, with the Customer feeding Anthony top secret English espionage on Turkish naval strength in return for a promise to persuade King James to restore the Levant Company's monopoly, recently suspended to punish the corporations' nonpayment of tax.

Halfway down the stairs, Nat sat slumped against the wall, dog-tired. He was dressed for the evening in the new Sherley livery: stripy blue and gold sleeves and stockings with blue and gold garters on his knees. What looked like black knee breeches were actually shalwar rolled to the knees. A gift from Uruch in Rome, the shalwar had been among the bundle of defectors' castoffs. Now Nat feared being cast off himself.

Ever since Anthony's release, Nat had feared being stranded with no money in Venice. Once King James repatriated Anthony, Nat would have no way of getting home. How would he eat? Where would he sleep? Every third thought filled him with a sickly, nervous dread, a heaviness in the limbs and spine that made Nat feel as though he was carrying a heavy box or crate on even those rare occasions when he wasn't weighed down with Anthony's burdens. This fear of being cast adrift without a penny tied a knot in his stomach that wound itself tighter and tighter every day.

He was under no illusions that Anthony might take him back to London with him. Not after Anthony dismissed twenty or so of his followers with a flick of the wrist when he was sent to prison. That was brutal. No back pay, no retainer, no sense of *noblesse oblige* towards men who had been halfway round the world with him. He had simply discharged his whole party, everyone except Nat himself and Elkin. Gone! Just gone!

Sitting on the servant staircase, Nat listened to the convivial hubbub up above and felt the knot in his stomach grow tighter. What if, this very night, Customer Hythe were to invite Anthony to sail back to the Pool of London with him on board one of the Levant Company's ships, the *Consent,* the *Great Suzanne* or the *Mayflower*? Anthony would shake Nat from his boot heels like dust. Then where would he be? He'd be where the rest of the Sherley party's lower servants had ended up, every man jack of them. He'd be in the galleys, sweet Jesus. And that was how his life would end. Sickness and disease felled oarsmen quicker than they could be resupplied. You smelt a galley ship before you saw it. Even from far out beyond the harbour bar the stench reached the quayside, so strong was the smell of human excrement. It was the Aldgate ditch put out to sea with colours and a mast. The galley men shat where they sat on the rowing bench. They stood up and sat down on every stroke, and with each day of the voyage – as the grim joke went - had less far to travel. Nat pulled a face like Darius passing a three-legged dog.

How had such an abomination as a galley ship appeared in the world, he wondered. What could have spawned this man-devouring Sea-Monster? He heard Darius, when he was leaning against his mule in the Zagros foothills, say,

'It takes a lot of work by a few dedicated men to make an unjust world.'

That was the truth of it. A few sharers' profit had spawned the ocean-going Sea-Monsters. The sickness and disease of the rowing bench was the health of the moneyed incorporation.

The gong dinged the dented sound it made when Anthony booted it instead of striking it with the hammer.

'Bramble! Up here now, jackanapes! Bring up that Muscadelle, Bramble! To speak truth, Customer, the New Prison was a most excellent wine-cellar!'

Nat hauled himself to his feet.

'The Prophet Muhammed,' Darius once told him, 'would rather a man did one hour of deep reflection, than sixty years of worship.' But, oh Darius, where was a serving man to find a whole hour?

Nat carried the bottles upstairs and was ordered to bank the fire. As he knelt with the fire tongs, Nat bent an ear to the conversation. He soon heard news that thrilled him to the marrow, set his blood on fire, and gave him hope that his fate might not be death in the galley ships after all.

Customer Hythe was telling Anthony about the recent arrival of a Persian envoy.

'… Of course Venice doesn't want to upset the Turk,' the Customer was saying, 'and so he's not at the Palazzo Ducale, but they've lodged him out of sight at the Palazzo del Camello - the Camel Palace! Ha! - way over in Canareggio.'

'What's this Persian's name?' asked Anthony.

'I've got it here somewhere,' said Vice-Consul Roe ruffling through some papers. 'Yes. Here it is. Uruch Bey.'

'Ah, he was First Secretary to my Embassy, and - one moment. Hie! Why so many logs on the fire, Bramble? Pull some out or you'll burn my palazzo down! Now, where were we, gentlemen? Uruch Bey. That's right. Yes, I may pay this Persian envoy a little visit tomorrow.'

'Well, I'm afraid,' joshed the Customer, 'that this envoy only comes with a diplomatic portmanteau, and not three-hundredweight of silk!'

Silence. In a voice that chilled the room, Anthony enquired,

'What do you mean by that?'

'Nothing. A jest. A poor jape. Forgive me, only I'm just so anxious about the suspension of our monopoly and these back-taxes the king has slapped on us. We all are.'

'Leave it to me,' said Anthony, an expansive wave of his arm knocking a map of the world from the table to the floor. Upon landing, the map curled itself up tight, as if fearing further assaults by Anthony or the Levant Company. Nat retrieved the map from the floor and gave it back to Anthony.

❖

It was nearly dawn when Nat handed the Levant Company delegation their hats and cloaks. He lit their way down the steps with a flaming brand, leading them out onto the jetty, where they stepped into their waiting *felze*.

All's Nat tiredness fell away. He ran upstairs, taking the steps two at a time. Perhaps he would find Anthony already at work, writing some treasonous stuff. Any kind of treason would do just so long as he wrote a letter for Nat to sell to Uruch. When he reached the landing, however, he was dismayed to find him on his way to his bedchamber.

'Sir Anthony!'

'Goodnight, Bramble,' he slurred.

'Forgive my boldness, Sir Anthony, but the Spanish ambassador sails on the noontide tomorrow and I fear, begging your pardon, that you may sleep past noon. Therefore, now's your one chance to write a letter to the King of Spain, should you wish so to do, for any reason, and have your servant deliver the letter at first light without disturbing your much deserved rest, so please you.'

This was the longest he had ever spoken to Anthony in one go. When he was done, Anthony just stared and stared. Nat looked down at the floorboards. When he looked up, the stone-blue pop eyes were still boring into him.

'Ink,' said Anthony, at last. 'And the veal.'

Nat opened a drawer and took a few sheets from the ream of pure white vellum which Anthony liked to call 'the veal.' Nat stirred the ink, dipped his master's pen and began heating wax in a candle flame.

Anthony took up the pen and scratched away, now and then pausing to refer to the spy's report on the Turkish navy, and all the time humming to himself. He signed the letter with a flourish which spattered black ink spots over the vellum and his white sleeve.

'Wax, Bramble.'

Nat dripped hot sealing wax on the letter fold. Anthony stamped the face of Shah Abbas in the scarlet wax, propped the sealed letter against the back of the desk, and rose from his chair.

'God give you good night, Sir Anthony.'

Anthony padded out of the room and up the stairs.

Nat forced himself to count to seven. Then he stepped to the desk and sliced open the freshly sealed letter.

Your Illustrious Highness and Christian Majesty, Philip, King of Spain and all the Portugals,

Upon English State Secretary Lord Sir Robert Cecil's request to the Levant Company for intelligence about Ottoman military strength, serious matter has been discovered which urgently touches your territories.

The Sultan's navy is massing sixty warships at Constantinople. On the second day of this month, ten thousand men, of whom five thousand are combatants, went aboard....

He stops reading. This is it. The right thing at the right time. Here's something that Uruch Bey will pay for in gold. He will take him Anthony's signed original. To escape detection, all he has to do first is substitute a copy of the letter to take to the Spanish ambassador. This needs no forger's art. Servants do the actual penning of most gentlemen's letters. Half the time Nat scrivens Anthony's letters anyway. The Spanish ambassador will think nothing of reading a letter in his handwriting, instead of his master's.

He opens the drawer, and takes out a fresh fillet of veal, which seems to glow in the breaking dawn. He squares the sheet of vellum on the desk. Using Anthony's letter knife, he slits a few stitches in his doublet's lining, from which he thumbs out the seal ring of Shah Abbas that Uruch gave him. He stirs the ink. Pen nib squeaks on vellum as he copies.

Your Illustrious Highness and Christian Majesty, Philip, King of Spain and all the Portugals.

A creak on the landing. Footsteps. Nat holds his breath. He listens. Anthony fills his piss pot. Footsteps. He hears Anthony shuffling about his chamber. Go to bed. Go to bed.

No time to copy out the whole long letter. Besides Uruch may give him enough to get home, which means covering his tracks is academic. Instead of the whole long intelligence report about the naval dockyards, therefore, he draws a stick man with a crown on his head, and dashes off the following dedication:

I, Anthony Sherley dedicate this portrait what I have just done to Your Catholic Majesty in hopes that you will make me an admiral. I like boats and have my own sailor suit, I know several nautical terms such as, 'Lay her a-hold' and 'Take down the topsail.' I promise not to lose every single ship in my command like my idiot brother Thomas, the least successful pirate in the world.

The wax is still warm. Nat folds the vellum, and presses his Shah Abbas seal ring into the wax. Boot heels approach the door. Nat's heart bumps against his ribs. He props the forgery at the back of the desk, and pockets the original. The door opens. Nat jumps up from the desk.

'Tired as I was,' says Anthony, belting his sword over his nightshift, 'I lay awake. Couldn't sleep, you see, for the question going round my skull. Why does my servant want me to write a letter to the King of Spain? Why?'

Answer being: he's going to steal my letter to the King Philip and sell it to Uruch Bey at the Camel Palace.'

'But here's the letter, sir, seal unbroken.'

Anthony inspects the seal. The wax seal – applied when only luke-warm - breaks. The letter springs open. Nat backs towards the window. Anthony looks from stick man to Nat's hand.

'What's that ring on your finger?'

Nat climbs out of the second-floor window onto the steeply sloping zinc porch in the breaking dawn. He springs from the porch and, with his eerie sense of balance, lands on a mooring post. He hears Anthony roar for Elkin. He leaps from one post to another, aiming for the jetty. Anthony and Elkin get there first. Now he is stuck at the top of a post. They jab their swords towards him. He hops from one mooring post to another until he is out in the middle of the river.

'Swim for it and the letter's destroyed,' mocks Anthony.

Elkin pulls his dagger from his belt, takes aim and throws. Nat hears the blade thud into the wooden mooring post only inches below his foot. Then he hears the dip of an oar. He looks up. A *felze* comes swoosh-ing by. Nat hops onto its roof, leaps from the roof of the boat onto the far bank of the Rio San Maurizio, with the gondolier cursing him in Veneto, and Anthony, across the water, jumping into his blue and gold gondola and shouting,

'The Camel Palace, Elkin!'

11

Nat ran through Canareggio's cold dawn alleys under lines of dripping laundry. Rust flaked from the studs in the door of the dowdy Camel Palace as he banged with his fist. There was no sound from the house. From the look of its peeling paintwork and the purple loosestrife sprouting from cracks in the wall, the whole palazzo might have been abandoned. He bent double to get his breath back from the running. He was wheezing so hard that he didn't hear the door open. He looked up to find a man with a poignard beard in the Spanish style staring at him. It took him a moment to recognise Uruch Bey.

Nat held up the letter with its broken seal. He warned the First Secretary that Anthony had caught him in the theft and was on his way here. Uruch fetched his cloak and turban and they plunged into the byways of Canareggio, where they would be safe from Anthony and Elkin, who didn't know this part of the city.

Hands behind his back, Uruch led Nat through a dank alley, where roosting pigeons gurgled in the broken eaves.

The sight of Antonio's servant made him sad. Nat – wasn't that the name? - looked as haggard as a youth could be. His hair stuck up in neglected clumps and spikes. Saddest detail of all somehow was the contrast between the blue and yellow satin garters and the rest of his clothes, which were the by-now seamy castoffs that Uruch had given him in Rome. The shiny blue and yellow satin resembled the gaudy ribbon on a mangy monkey dancing beside a poor busker. And just as the monkey has no sense of the indignity of its gold-braided jacket with the jingling bells, so Nat seemed oblivious to the humiliating blue and yellow livery.

They emerged onto the Rio Della Sensa, its waters a frothy rind of cabbage heads, pig trotters and flotsam, and turned onto the New Pavement Canal, where Uruch stopped before a statue of a merchant wearing a broad, flat turban. This was Alfani, he explained, the merchant who did for Venice what Darius was doing for Tabriz: he brought them their first oil.

Nat's heart soared to hear Darius's name mentioned again, but how to describe the bitter, crushing dismay he felt moments later on learning that Uruch had not one shred of news about him, nothing beyond the fact that sales were up. That was it. That was all Uruch knew, or cared to know about Darius Nouredini. Nat cursed the First Secretary under his breath.

They arrived at a hole in the wall café with a few barrel kegs outside for seats. Uruch sat down and gave Nat a zecchino and sent him in to fetch tea.

Once inside the dark cafe, Nat sniffed the air.

Qaveh!

At this early hour there were only two others there, one Arab, one Ethiopian, both of whom an ecstatic Nat startled with a greeting which was much too hearty for that time of the morning. In Nat's mind he was among brothers of a secret caffeine sect. He returned with Uruch's tea and a steaming cup of black *qaveh* for himself.

Garrulous from the first swig, he told Uruch – who, like Darius, couldn't stomach 'the Turk's bitter beans' - about how coffee was unknown in England, how Darius's grandmother had introduced him to it, and how Darius had claimed that it was discovered by Ethiopian herders who noticed their goats cavorting about after they'd been eating the coffee bush.

Uruch interrupted this babble to say,

'The Ambassador instructed me to find out the whole story about Darius and Gol when next I saw you.'

'Why?' asked Nat. 'What's it to him?'

'He knows Gol's father.'

'Atash Zarafshani?'

'You would not believe the Ambassador's interest when I told him the story you told me about how Gol Zarafshani got engaged to Darius but then found out that he was already betrothed to another woman.'

'No, no, no,' cried Nat. 'That's not what I said at all! That's not the truth of it! You have a head full of bees!'

Uruch stared him out of countenance. Nat lowered his head and mumbled,

'Forgive me, First Secretary.'

Nat put Anthony's letter to King Philip of Spain on the table.

'Read it out, please,' said Uruch.

When Nat had read out the whole letter, Uruch said nothing. The First Secretary picked it up and walked to the edge of the canal. He stood there completely immobile for so long that a heron landed on a mooring post not six feet away. Nat watched Uruch's fingers revolve the letter, while his wrist twitched. It looked as if he were itching to send the missive spinning into the canal.

The long silence unnerved Nat. The knot in his stomach wound itself still tighter. He remembered the rumours in Rome that Uruch would defect to Spain. He already looked half-Spanish, truth be told, with that chin beard and wearing his sleeveless doublet over his satin kurta. Nat feared that he had brought the letter to the very last man he should have done. Uruch's desire for Spanish preferment was greater than his detestation of Anthony. Of course, Uruch would give the letter to King Philip's ambassador as a way of proving his value to the Spaniards. He would say to the

Spanish,

'Look how I stopped this falling into Venetian hands. Tell Antonio to be more careful in future – oh, and by the way there's his English servant to be wrapped in a carpet and chains and be dropped in the lagoon off Pellestrina.'

With a sickly feeling in his bones, Nat grasped the enormity of his blunder: he had brought intelligence proving a member of the Persian Embassy to be a traitor in the pay of Spain to a member of the Persian Embassy who was himself a traitor in the pay of Spain. Upon such blunders servants are executed. Why hadn't he seen this before?

A grey heron flapping off the mooring post was the first Nat was aware that Uruch was dancing. He looked up to find the First Secretary twirling round and round in a little dervish dance and cackling to himself.

'Nat-jan,' said Uruch, dancing round and round, 'you have ended Antonio's career. This letter shows him passing naval secrets of Venice's vital strategic ally to her chief enemy. Should Spain even wrest control of the Mediterranean from the Turk, Venice would become a fishing village. It would be the end of the Republic! Quick! We must bring this letter to the Collegio.'

'You go. What do you need me for?'

'You must accompany me to the Doge's Palace to vouch for how this letter came into my possession.'

'God's hooks! You're going tell them I stole it! They'll arrest me. They'll throw me into the New Prison!'

Uruch walked slowly towards Nat and stopped right in front of him.

'You stand as a marriage witness vouchsafing the honour for Darius Nouredini at his wedding, should that day ever come, to the only daughter of Atash Zarafshani, who is Hoseyn Mirza's dear friend. The witness must be a man whose word is proven. There is only one place where you can vouch for Darius: the Doge's Palace. That is where you prove your word.'

Nat heard boot heels clattering about on an *altana,* one of those precarious-looking wooden platforms on Venetian roofs, and wished for one fixed and certain thing in his wobbly ledge of a life. Then again, his one great talent was balance, the ability to keep his footing on sinking cable ferries, or the greased pole in the Datchworth fete, or when hopping between mooring posts this morning. But why did his life always pitch him up on these precipices? Why did the ground always open up beneath him?

Into his mind flashed the time when he was hewing the stone glyphs at the Temple of Mithras and half the hillside fell away to leave him perched upon a precipice. It was exactly the same here in this hole on the wall café in Venice. One minute he was sitting drinking qaveh with Uruch, and the next he was supposed to present himself as a letter-thief before the highest court in the land! He didn't trust Don Uruch at all – but only Don Uruch had the power to get the ambassador to write a letter that would mend Darius's broken heart.

12

In the white marble Anticollegio, the small anteroom to the senatorial Collegio, Nat could hear the indistinct Veneto hum of the Senate arraigning his old master. The longer Nat waited the more scared he became. One then two then three hours he had waited in this sepulchre. If the Senate were going to find Anthony guilty, wouldn't they have done so by now?

This delay could only mean one thing. They were going to let him go! The Senate couldn't touch King James' favourite. Pardoned for spying, Anthony would know he could stab a false servant through the heart with impunity. What if Anthony came out this way? He would kill him on the spot. Nat would find that fussy sword hilt, the one he'd always hated cleaning, sticking out of his guts. He had walked into his last room. He couldn't leave because the Doge's private guards, the scudieri, stood at the doors. He was trapped in this white mausoleum. This was his tomb. He was the graveyard caretaker accidentally entombed while sweeping a family vault.

The Senate was rising. It had come to a decision. Nat was so frightened he couldn't focus his eyes. The door opened. A bustle of footsteps were coming his way. They were going to file right past him!

In walked the two most powerful men in Venice. Doge Marino Grimani, the *corno ducale* on his head like a great white whelk, followed by Senator Giacomo Foscarini, a bear of a man with cropped brown hair and a full brown beard. Nat looked right past them. He craned his neck this way and that, trying to see Anthony before Anthony saw him. He might

only have a split second. Out came Customer Hythe and sundry Levant
Company officials. Where was Anthony?

There he was flanked by scudieri, but they weren't restraining
him. They'd taken his sword away, but he often had petty knives concealed
about his person. Nat drew back against the white marble wall, hoping his
master wouldn't see him in the few seconds it would take him to cross so
small a room. Then Uruch came bounding in, eyes shining, and rapturously
announced,

'Banished! Nat-jan! He's banished!'

Anthony swung round. His bug eyes started from his skull to see
his betrayers side by side. He took a pace toward the two confederates.

'As for your part in this, First Secretary,' he said. 'I'll tell Shah Abbas
to slay your whole family and your village!'

'Do you honestly imagine your word carries any weight whatsoever
in Isfahan?' replied Uruch.

'You gave the Shah's ring to my servant.'

Nat lifted his hand,

'Here's the ring, Sherley.'

'Ha ha, bravely done, lad,' laughed Anthony. 'You're a spunky lad.'
He seized Nat's wrist, and, from a sheath in the small of his back, whipped
out a blade shaped like the ace of spades.

Nat rabbit-punched Anthony's face with the Shah's ring. The knife
clattered on the marble floor. Anthony staggered back, blood flowing from
the wound below his eye.

The scudieri separated the two Englishmen. Nat shook from
head to toe, but no longer from fear. He was a shaking mill-house. An oil
gusher. Whatever cap rock had been damming up all his power all his life
- Anthony, famine, England, fear - was blown sky high by this rebellion.
This anteroom was no sepulchre but the threshold to a world in which all

was possible. The rules had changed.

Three scudieri lifted his old master bodily into the air, and carried him feet-first out of the room. Eyes bulging, face bloody, Anthony clung to the doorway's marble architrave, like a man hanging by his fingertips against the cyclone that was hurling him out the door.

'There's nowhere you can go in the whole wide world, Bramble, where I cannot stretch out my arm and smite you! My brother Thomas will be waiting for you in London!'

'I'll end the pirate's career just like I have ended yours, Don Antonio!'

Taking a running jump, Nat stamped Anthony's fingers off the marble doorway, and the scudieri whisked him away.

'Thomas will kill you, by Christ!' shouted Anthony along the corridor and down the stairs. 'He'll kill you! He'll eat out your heart!'

Nat heard angry words behind his back, and turned to see Foscarini jabbing the Customer's chest with his forefinger,

'And as for *you*,' growled Foscarini, 'if the Turk discovers you are giving intelligence to his enemy-in-arms he will close down the sea! *Capice?* The Sultan has only to contract his fist to shut down the entire Mediterranean! Then there will be no bread in Venice, and not a ship on the Thames either.'

An outraged Customer swelled his chest, and said,

'Senator Foscarini, I demand an apology.'

'Last warning!' growled the crop-headed brown bear, and cuffed the Customer round the head a couple of good loud blows, then commanded the scudieri in Veneto dialect: '*Portelo fora prima che lo copa mi, cole mie mano! Portelo fora prima che lo copa mi!* Get him out of here before I kill him with my own hands.

After the scudieri escorted the Levant Company's three representatives off the premises, Foscarini thanked the First Secretary Uruch Bey and his accomplice.

'My thanks to you both. You have saved the Republic.'

Uruch and Nat bowed low.

'Will Cavaliere Antonio,' asked Uruch, 'return to the new king who loves him?'

'We'll warn King James not to incur our grave displeasure by allowing his repatriation. No, Antonio will be sailing with you, Uruch Bey, upon the *Santiago Matamoros,* the St John, Killer of the Moors. He will not be returning to England unlike this brave *ragazzo*.'

'Nat Bramble at your service. Your honour, I fear I will be an old man before I see London again. For Sir Anthony has stranded me penniless and far from home.'

'This purse shall pay your passage home.' Foscarini chucked him a frog-shaped green velvet purse.

To Uruch's horror, Nat's paw no sooner snatched the velvet frog from the air than - with an appalling lack of *Ta'rof* - he stuck his snout in the purse. Worse, he then began counting the gold coins there and then. When Nat went so far as actually to bite one of these gold zecchinos, Uruch blushed to the rim of his taj. Mercifully, Foscarini only laughed and said,

'Do not distress yourself, Uruch Bey,' said Foscarini. 'Can you blame him? He was in Sherley's service a long time, after all!"

13

The following day, in the Piazza San Marco, Uruch asked Nat to tell him the true story of Darius and Gol. They were sitting on the pedestal steps of a winged lion and looking out over the lagoon. Uruch was sailing for Lisbon in a few hours and wanted to get the story straight for Hoseyn Ali Beg. Accuracy was paramount since Hoseyn would put it all in a letter to Gol's father, and so Uruch took out his commonplace book and pen to take notes as Nat told the tale.

And that's how it came about that the First Secretary of the Great Persian Embassy sat on the stone steps taking dictation from the former skink, runner and dogsbody of the disgraced Sir Anthony Sherley.

When they were done, they both walked down to the water's edge and looked at the ships anchored in the lagoon. A few ships flew City of London flags.

'I'll sail home on one of those,' said Nat.

'In the Collegio they were saying that Sir Thomas Sherley's been pardoned by King James and is sailing from Naples to London. Beware of Sir Thomas when you get to London.'

'I'm sure he is just another swingbreeches like his brothers.'

'Bravely said, Nat, but he is vicious. You heard what Antonio said: his brother Thomas will be his sword arm and vengeance in London. The only thing you can ever believe from Antonio's mouth are his threats. I fear for you, Nat. I fear this half-crazed pirate Thomas Sherley will hunt you through the streets of London.'

Just then, Eli Elkin came marching towards them through the square's market stalls, his shoulders twitching, head snapping this way and that and as uncomfortable as ever in his own skin. On top of which, he must have fallen asleep drunk in the sun, because his face was red, his mouth was dry and he reeked of stale wine and worse.

'You're going to help me,' he said, and unfolded a single sheet of paper in a deliberate, pedantic way as if Nat had been trying and failing to unfold it all morning. Thrusting the paper under Nat's nose, Elkin asked: 'What's it say?'

'It's a testimonial,' said Nat. Elkin exhaled the long breath of exasperated patience. He counted to five and then said,

'I didn't axe you what it be. I axe you what it says. Now read it to me.'

' "*To whom it may concern,*' read Nat out loud. "'*I hereby recommend for good and honest service in any task, Eli Elkin, a right faithful Christian, who, here in Venice, as well as in Rome and Persia, has ever been a most loyal factor unto His Excellency Sir Anthony Sherley, Knight and Ambassador.*'"

'That's it?' asked Elkin. 'No credit? No name of no Jew who must give a fixed sum in dollars?'

'No.'

'Nothing saying pay such and such a sum to the said party, which is me, which is the bearer?'

'Just what I read.'

Elkin snatched back the letter and folded it into four, giving Nat a contemptuous look. He twisted his neck, rubbed his eyes, and asked,

'Do you know if they need rat catchers here, Bramble? Only I was thinking that, what with all the rivers and cellars here, they must do.'

'Rat-catchers?' asked Nat.

'That was my trade. That's how I first met Sir Anthony and his brothers. I was the Sherleys' rat-catcher in their Blackfriars townhouse.'

'I'll pay you one gold zecchino for your letter.'

'So this is a credit note, after all,' shouted Elkin. 'You cozen me, villain!'

'You ask anyone who can read,' said Nat.

'This letter is the fruit of two years' hard service. All I ever got from him beyond *per diems.* And you have it from me for one coin? You play me false.'

'Here you are, have it back, then.'

With a curling lip, Elkin sold his testimonial for one single zecchino. He grabbed hold of Nat's jaw, growling,

'Give me that frog purse or I'll snap you like a twig.'

Uruch stepped in and broke Elkin's hold with a swift sharp blow to his arm.

'Hide behind your infidel,' sneered Elkin. 'You'll never brave me man to man.'

'Man? What man?' cried Nat. 'You've snaffled your snout in Sherley's palm like a bitch her master, and now you're for galleys, Eli Elkin! But not me. Not me.'

'No, not you. No matter what fate God sends me, I had rather give honest service as a true Englishmen, than be you, Nat Bramble. Because for sinners such as you, Hell spews out a special Man Of Fire, clothed head to toe in the Fire Everlasting. Hell's Fiery Man comes to summon the wicked betrayer down into the very worst pit of Hell. Mark my words! Hell's Fiery Man comes for you, Bramble, he comes for you!'

And with that, Elkin turned on his heel, strutted off and disappeared into the crowded Piazza San Marco.

14

Three days later, the Levant Company's ship the *Mayflower,* one hundred and eighty tons burden, thirty-eight crew and one paying passenger, Nat Bramble, set sail from Venice for London.

Nat hooked his hammock by a stack of barrels marked 'Oil of Petrolio'. What a luxury to have nothing to do all day! To be a masterless man! It was still illegal to be a masterless man in England but he wasn't in England. He was in the hold of the *Mayflower* in the Mediterranean and he was free. To celebrate his freedom he took out his knife and scored N-A-T B-R-A-M-B-L-E into one of the dark resined stanchions, carving a winged Mithras underneath.

For the first week of the voyage he did nothing but sleep, eat and sleep. The slugging of oil in weathered barrels lulled him in and out of dreams seasoned by the hold's odour of cumin and pepper. His daydreams were further spiced by a bold new ambition: Why not do in London exactly what Darius was doing in Tabriz and create a market for oil as combined heat and light?

Londoners used oil for everything *but* heat and light. The petroleum in these barrels would be used as liniment for killing lice and fleas. Oil lacquered canvas to make the waterman's tarpaulin, and caulked the severed heads on pikestaffs on London Bridge Gate. Oil soothed coughs and toothache, cured gout and fixed new stones in the street. Oil sealed the seams on hulls, and sealed wounds as surgeon's caustic. But why not approach Customer Hythe with the idea of importing Persian oil lamps, stoves and heaters? The Levant Company would make him Clerk of Works, and sit him behind a broad oak desk in Levant House, from where he would control the whole operation, buying Ottoman barrels and selling them from Galley Quay into the Cornhill Exchange.

He was so excited by the idea of going into trade that he began to study the hold's freight. He unscrewed barrels, popped trunk lids and unstitched the tops of sacks to investigate the contents with a merchant's eye. He learnt to distinguish between the odours of nutmeg and cinnamon, turmeric and pepper. His palm scooped out something excitingly labelled Dragon's Blood Powder. He dabbed scarlet grains on his tongue, and the red-hot spice sent him coughing and spluttering to the water butt.

Scrawled on casks and barrels were names of many more things he'd never heard of before. What was the use of soda ash, borax, scamony, storax or sal ammoniac? Who wanted this cargo? Why would you bother to travel halfway round the world at vast expense only to bring back this stuff?

Up on deck, he asked a group of chess-playing mariners to explain. Borax was used for putty, they told him. Soda ash was used for making glass. So there were your modern windows. Scamony and storax were glues, and sal ammoniac was your metalsmith's soldering flux. Matter-of-fact though these answers were, they opened a world of wonder in Nat's mind.

Back in the hold, he wandered among this citadel of merchandise and saw it in a completely new way. What the *Mayflower* was carrying were all the ingredients for a nation. The elements of a city. A commonwealth in storage crates. Stacks of state. A raw nation.

Here were the building blocks for any type of country you could think of. Nothing was set in stone. The glass and the putty could be used for any kind of window you could possibly imagine. There was nothing to say where to put the window, how wide to make it, whose it would be, or how many you could own. There was absolutely nothing in the ingredients of putty and glass, nothing in the nature of the raw materials borax and soda ash, to say that most windows should be mean and small, and only a few rich men's windows vast and full of light. Multiply that fact throughout the hold, apply it to everything here, and this ship might be used to build a city with justice for its covenant.

If nothing was set in stone, if there was nothing inevitable about who got the big windows, who got the small, or about whose rules ruled, then nor was there any natural reason why he should return to London on the same terms as he left it: a serving or labouring man. This cargo itself seemed to confirm his dream of becoming a merchant upon his return. Just the thought of it sent his head reeling, as if he were dizzy or suffering sunstroke. What an idea!

The following night, when the ship entered the bay of Biscay, a storm blew up. The *Mayflower* pitched and tossed. Nat was kneeling in the hold, investigating cargo with his lantern, when the floor tipped like a two-wheeled cart. He slid thirty feet along an aisle, only coming to a halt when he wrapped himself around the base of a wooden post.

Fixed to the foot of the post was a pair of iron shackles. On all four sides of the beam were identical shackles. Another pair was set level with his neck. He brought the lantern close to the wood. Strange glyphs were crudely carved into the post. The beam had been coated with pitch since these marks were scored into it. He took out his pocketknife. The black pitch had been applied so thickly that he didn't so much scrape as slice it from the timber, just as Darius had once sliced tar from the saddlecloth sling. This done, he slowly raised the lantern up the length of the beam.

Like wood lice scuttling out of a burning log, names appeared. Names etched in Greek, Cyrillic, Arabic, Hebrew and Latin letters. Names carved into the timber with, it seemed, whatever was to hand: iron nail, belt buckle, coin, bodkin or perhaps the manacle's hinge itself. By a manacle's bolt his lamplight found a Greek legend: 'Kidnapped To Be Sold.'

As the ship shuddered and rolled, Nat tottered from one timber to another, scraping at the pitch with his knife. God a' mercy, he found names etched into every single post of the *Mayflower*. He walked up steep aisles, his legs shaking with the presence of a great evil. He found a post where the same hand had etched four or five sets of initials together. What was the meaning of this grouping together? A whole family? A father entering the names of his wife and children? A priest indenting his flock? As Nat raised the lantern up the beam he came upon a winged Mithras and N-A-T B-R-A-M-B-L-E and was ashamed to have wantonly carved his own name among these grief-stricken testimonials.

That night he was afraid of the dark. He only had an hour's candle left. He feared that if the light perished, then all the ghosts of the slaves who had been carried in the Levant Company's *Mayflower* would crowd upon him. So he concocted an oil lamp by pond-dipping his lantern in the Oil of Petrolio barrel and burning a tarry length of baling twine.

Even with the oil lamp burning a bright, steady flame, the moaning waves that thudded against the hull, and the timbers' groans and squeaks were voices lurking in the dark corners of the hold, the voices of those who had been kidnapped and sold, who had been manacled in hoops and chains at the foot of the timbers, hidden behind the soda ash which was used for making glass, and the borax for putty.

In the morning he asked the chess school about the slaves. They told him that the Levant Company did not itself trade in slaves, but that if it wanted to retain its harbour rights, the Company must suffer its ships being used to transport Christians, who were snatched from their beds all round the Mediterranean to be sold upon the block in public marts at every Levantine port.

It was late afternoon before Nat dared go back down in the hold. Lit by shafts of daylight from the hatches, it was not as frightening as it had been the previous night. He ran his fingertips over the names. Then he looked around at the citadel of merchandise.

Here was no embryonic city of righteousness. The *Mayflower* was a Sea-Monster who gorged herself on human flesh, just like the galleys. Multiply *that* fact throughout the hold, apply it to all the rich commodities piled here, to the tuns of borax mined for a pittance and loaded for less, and what did you end up with? The reason why it took a lot of hard work by a few dedicated men to make the world so unjust was precisely because nothing was set in stone.

In ways that Nat couldn't fully explain, his dream of becoming a merchant was dispelled by the discovery that the *Mayflower* was a slave ship. The trade secret no longer seemed to be an understanding of how all these commodities might be used, of why they were bought and sold. The trade secret now seemed to be that the poverty of the poor made the riches of the rich. Scratch the trade and discover the sin. He no longer felt full of capacity and ambition. He felt like krill in the belly of a Sea-Monster, and he didn't know where he'd be thrown up.

❖

'It's a shame you're a university man,' the *Mayflower's* master told him when they reached Rotherhithe, 'for half this crew are sick and we'll be shorthanded in the Pool.'

'Oh no, sir, I'm no university man. I have been nothing but a general dogsbody time out of mind. I'll fill the breach for you, master.'

'No, I'll have no readers, for readers is too proud and curious to hump a sack of macadamia nuts. On your way.'

'Sir, I'll hump any sack or any barrel you care to name, and what's more, I can tell you what's in them, no matter what language is scrawled upon the barrel head. That'll save you from opening 'em up only to have the wind take your dragon's blood or scamony!'

When the *Mayflower* was mooring at Galley Quay, and the Levant Company's quay master, Mr Levitt, came aboard to inventorise the hold, her master pointed out Nat Bramble as one who was able to read what was written on chests, boxes and barrels.

Quaymaster Levitt looked Nat up and down.

'Can you lift a hundredweight in each arm?'

'And whistling like a carman all the while.'

'You shan't be paid for whistling,' said Quaymaster Levitt. 'Only lifting. Work well today, do what I say in every particular and, if you do, I'll employ you as a warehouseman on Galley Quay.'

'I'll not fail you, Mr Levitt.'

The quay master sent Nat back down the hold where he hooked a lowered rope net to bales of currants. The jib-crane was the block and tackle's squeak and trundle. He heard his voice echo around the oil well as he sent up another bale of currants in the rope net:

'We're on our way, Darius, we're on our way!'

And so Nat's first job back in London was the evacuation of the hold that had been his home for six weeks. When he climbed out of the hold onto the deck, a pigeon landed beside him on the *Mayflower's* rail. He listened to the bright cries, and shouts and laughter, he looked down at all the dockers and merchants on Galley Quay, and over and over he repeated to himself in delight:

'London! I am in London again! This is London! London! I am home!'

15

King James entered Richmond Palace Chapel for the very first time. An involuntary moan escaped him and echoed around the chapel. It looked more like a bawdy house. The checkered parti-coloured ceiling was festooned with plaster roses of every gaudy hue that English artifice could devise. The peach and rhubarb rood screen looked like the headboard of a whore's bed. The chapel was above a wine cellar, its hatch propped open to reveal wine bottles - *wine* bottles! - stacked below. Scottish kirks were flint chisels cracking open the heavens. But above this checkered ceiling, a suite of offices was interposed between prayer and God. He heard administrators' high heels knocking on the plaster roses. He heard women giggling, too. Good God Almighty, his wife's bedchamber window opened into the chapel! He shouted at one of the Danish ladies to close the window and the shutters.

Bawdy house or not, it would have to do, for James never needed Divine Guidance more than now. A few hours earlier, Venetian ambassador Scaramelli had very formally, very serenely plunged him into the greatest spiritual crisis of his whole life. Sultan Ahmed had sentenced Sir Thomas Sherley to death, staying his Imperial hand only to allow the King of England to enter a plea of clemency.

'Plea?' asked James. 'Am I to *beg* Sultan Ahmed?'

'If Your Majesty seeks Sir Thomas Sherley's release, you must petition the Sultan with a personal letter. Nothing less will do.'

'Will Venice, our go-between with the Turk, do nothing to save this Christian soldier?'

'The Serene Republic of Venice would rather see the pirate hung, Your Majesty.'

How simple a thing would it be to write a letter to the Sultan, had he not sworn very publicly never to have any dealings whatsoever with him or any other Mohammedan. No letters, no treaties, no trade.

'For merchant causes I will not do things unfitting a Christian prince,' he vowed before untold merchants in the Guildhall, and promptly suspended the Levant Company's corporate charter to show the City he was serious about ending trade with the heathen.

'That fine speech,' Crookback Cecil told him, his long, spindly fingers fiddling with his pendant like the evil hobgoblin of the folk tale, 'has cost Your Majesty four-thousand a year.'

'I am laying up treasures in heaven, instead,' James had replied, and felt like a true king for the first time since the coronation, pure and righteous and sure he was doing God's will.

But now, to save one Christian was to pollute Christianity. To help one, harmed all! Either he must break an old, private vow to Thomas, or a new public vow to the merchants. Whatever he did was wrong. King James knelt before the rhubarb and peach rood screen.

'Help me, Lord, for I am frozen by the altitude of my position and know not what to do. If I write to the Sultan for the sake of Sir Thomas, I will change forever the destiny of these united kingdoms. Hear me, oh Lord, for we are at the pinpoint of the protractor, and decisions taken now will spread far and wide. Am I, your servant James, to reign, or is the City of London to reign instead? To write to the Grand Turk robs me of my last argument against dealing with Mohammedans, and my kingdom's future course will be charted by the Levant Company. Cecil and the City will suffer this *teuchter* to wear a silk cape and sit upon a throne only so long as I serve merchant causes. Shall I lose my crown, dear Lord? Shall I lose my power all for the sake of one sinner, your servant Thomas, who may not even live so long as it takes my letter to reach the Sultan Ahmed! Tell me, oh Lord, what to do.'

Between his praying palms, James held a scrap of paper as worn as a dusty old moth wing. He unfolded the letter and reread words he already knew by heart:

'*Without Your Majesty's express letters to the Grand Turk for my liberty I am likely to end my miserable life in most wretched servitude. Twice in the last month, galley-masters have come through the jail picking out slaves for the galleys. A bout of sickness saved me the first go. The second time they could not find the key to my cell, and so they rattled the lock only. A third time and I shall not be so lucky.*

May God command King James, his anointed, to reach out his royal hand for the deliverance of his most loving subject,

Sir Thomas Sherley

And the King wept when God told him what to do.

❖

Three months later, at the crack of dawn, a King's Messenger alighted from a royal barge before the onion-shaped towers of Richmond Palace. Following the sound of guitars, he walked to the tennis courts, where he found King James drunkenly entangled with the bodies of Philip Herbert, Susan Vere and Gentleman of the Bedchamber Jim Hay, all of them still dressed in costumes from the masque they had performed the night before:

Zeus Mounting the Goddess Europa In The Form of A Bull.

King James told the King's Messenger to hook the message on his buffalo horns and retire, whereupon he forgot the letter until an hour later when Susan, wearing a stag's antlers, locked horns with him. As they rutted on all fours back and forth across the service line, the message ripped and fell onto the dewy grass.

King James rescued the pierced document, and, having focused his eyes, read the words the *Khatt-i-humayun,* the Imperial Ottoman Writ. He broke the carmine seal and discovered three sheets of very fine, coral-white paper, one written in Turkish, one in Latin, one in Greek. Choosing the Latin, he rubbed some dew in his face, and extemporised a translation.

To King James of England,

May Allah, the Most Merciful and Most Forgiving, be glorified by the clemency of kings, and may the mercy of kings be a beacon to their subjects.

I have heard a brother sovereign's plea for clemency on behalf of his justly condemned subject Sir Thomas Sherley. Notwithstanding this man's fault, I give him to the King of England, King James who has begged his release.

James, my brother, we are both new sovereigns, but I have learnt that there is no might nor power, except by Allah's leave, the Exalted, the Wise, the Lord of the Worlds.

Tumbling lists of titles and territories followed Sultan Ahmed's elaborate calligraphic signature.

First light strained through the tennis net in long rays, which fanned out over the wet grass like a protractor's degree markings. The pinpoint of the protractor. For a moment, James remembered what he'd lost, and frowned, but then forgot why he frowned. In fact, why be disquieted and downcast? After all, was this not Sir Thomas Sherley's pardon from

Sultan Ahmed? Aye, it was! And did it not prove King James to be a right royal fellow who never forgot a friend? Yes it did! A splendid good fellow! Why, if ever a man was entitled to be entwined in the arms and legs of so many pretty pieces all at once, was it not he?

'Susan,' he said. 'King James is a splendid good fellow. Pull off ma canions, Susan, Jim and Philip. The bull will mount. All three sweet bums are my Europa, my demesnes and territories - for if Great Zeus is to be denied a godhead's rule, then, by God, he mun hae his prerogatives and perquisites!'

16

Darius Nouredini pokes his toe in the ash and cinders at the base of the burnt-out tree, the same blackened trunk from which he caught his last glimpse of Nat Bramble when the Great Persian Embassy was departing. Even this monument to what's gone is going. The trunk has snapped in two while he was in Tabriz, and now forms a triangle with the earth. Migrating cranes pass overhead, flying north.

He reflects upon the ways in which his life is better or worse than it used to be. To be an oil merchant is better by far than selling blank albums in the bazaar. The road between Isfahan and Tabriz is safe following Persian victories over the Ottomans. What's also better is that he's left home. In Isfahan, he's building two handsome rooms abutting his grandmother's house. In Tabriz, he loves to close the door upon his rented single room. So quiet, so peaceful, so entirely his. A room of his own. A brass key in a brass lock.

So much to the good.

'But I have lost Gol. The hope of her. I might meet a woman prettier, wittier, wiser, kinder or sweeter - but never all at once. From now on, life will be a poor shadow of what it might have been had it been lived with Gol. And I have lost Nat to the far frozen wastes, with its trembling candlelight made of rendered hog fat. I will never see him again in this life, and nor, due to his heretical beliefs, the next. Each morning I pray the day will bring me a fresh memory of Nat, for even my memories of him are fading.'

He is suddenly thirsty, but his leather bottle is empty. He climbs down the steep, sheer grassy bank, unwinds the bottle's long strap, and casts it into the water. When the leather bottle is full it tugs like a heavy fish on the line, and he reels it in. He takes a folded cloth from his pocket and dries the outside of the leather bottle, but just before drinking he stops with the bottle poised at his lips. A brightly sparkling memory of Nat has come back to him. Darius stands stock still, halfway up the bank, not wanting to lose this fleeting memory, like a fisherman not wanting his slightest motion to scare away a rare fish.

Yes, he sees him doing it now. Ha! Ha! That's right! Nat could never pass the bottle without first smearing it with his filthy paw. But it was his way of doing this that was rare. Not only was befouling the bottle's mouth the right and proper thing to do, it had to be done thoroughly. Nat would first wipe his hands on his seamy breeches, or on the mule's sweat-flecked flanks, or even once on a tuft of grass littered with sheep droppings. Then, with a show of great scruple, he would besmirch the bottle's mouth, wanting his friend to appreciate the pains he was taking. Darius hears his own chuckle echo in the leather bottle's neck. As his chuckle dies away he hears quite another sound. A buzzing. He looks upriver. A dead goat, buzzing with a flotilla of flies, drifts placidly out from behind the reed bed.

Darius shrieks and upends the bottle, pouring the contaminated water out onto the bank.

'None of that at any time at all!'

It strikes him how, but for that memory of Nat coming to him when it did, he'd have drunk the water poisoned by that raft of death. Memory saved his life.

Directly below him, a clump of rushes snags the goat's stiff legs. The dead goat nudges the bank. Darius throws an arm across his mouth and nose against the rankest stench he has ever known. To inhale might prove fatal. He scrambles up to the top of the bank and turns round. The rushes snap and crack one by one, releasing the carrion downstream.

If this carcass follows the same route that he and Nat's goatskin raft once took and slides into the city, it will poison Isfahan's water. People will sicken and die. He casts a look round at the empty plain, but there is no sign of anyone who can take his place. He must go down into the pit of death himself. His eyes sting and smart with the injustice of it all.

'Oh, how easy it would have been for me never to have seen this dead goat at all! It must be ten days dead by the high stench of it. Dead of the goat plague too.'

He unwinds his turban from his head and winds its beige linen around his nose and mouth. He takes his shirt and sandals off, then climbs down the steep grassy bank, and backs into the cold river.

The riverbed shelves steeply, and he is immediately chest-deep in water. He swims to the fetid carcass which the fast-flowing, deep middle of the river bears along. Up close to the evil stench, he barely has time to lift the mask from his mouth before he vomits into the water. He paddles his hand around to disperse the spooling strands of sick. Wrapping the facemask over nose and mouth again, he swims upwind and upstream of the goat's carcass, grabs its horns, and clamps its soggy flanks between his thighs. Once he has the goat's body in this leg-lock, he lets go of the horns, and strikes out for the bank. With every stroke, his heavy breathing sucks in the facemask, and ghostly goat horns butt his behind.

He swims from sunlight into the steep bank's cold shade, where he stands in the slimy toe-sucking silt. He presses goat to bank with both hands. It takes all his strength just to pinion her weight against the bank, let alone lift her. He looks up. The riverbank looms as high and sheer as a cliff face. His facemask slips and falls. As he jerks out a hand to catch it, disaster strikes.

What happens next is so horrific that for several seconds he simply cannot comprehend the event. Somehow the heavy goat slithers into his arms, her bony forelegs clamp him in an embrace, and her mouth dabs his lips. Her lips part to reveal reeking yellow teeth. Her wispy white beard wipes his chin. He screams in the goat's face. Her weight buckles his knees. The only way out of her clutches is down. He sinks underwater, where he grabs her hind legs in one hand and her forelegs in the other, and surfaces with the heavy carcass across his shoulders.

Like a shepherd carrying a stranded goat out of a snowdrift, he digs his toes into the bank and, little by little, scales the bank, falling to his knees every few steps, until he cannot get off his knees. He does not have the strength to carry the dead goat on his shoulders all the way to the top of the bank. He's nearly there, but spent.

He dumps her down, and a tide of filthy water surges from her mouth. He lies panting, sprawled on the incline just below the carcass. With his last reserves of strength, he begins to wrestle and shunt the dead goat uphill, hoping nothing falls off. Between heaving gasps, he bellows in fury. Slowly, slowly, the goat begins to rise up over the brow of the riverbank. He has done it! Almost there! The dead goat rolls back and a hoof clouts him on the temple. He punches her on the beard, and slips onto his side. He lies on his back, wearing sashes of algae and goat fur, his hair braided with bindweed, and laughs a helpless, defeated laugh.

17

The Sea and Sky had just come in. The rooftop pergola was a single dome of blue and green striped carnations. Bathed in the dome's blue-green light, Atash Zarafshani was cutting and bundling bunches of carnations, while Roshanak and Gol were away in the bazardeh selling an early batch. Harvesting the Sea and Sky, the unique hybrid he'd bred himself, was usually a happy event, but the sad tune Gol hummed this morning was on his brain, and worked its way into the rhythm of the cutting, the bundling, the stacking.

Since Mani's death, she'd only ever sing or strum sad songs. From up on the roof, he couldn't actually make out the words of this morning's dirge, but guilt filled in the gaps. In the same way that Darius once convinced himself that Nat was performing a *Dance of Welcome For A New Boat*, so Atash persuaded himself the song Gol sang was *Lament For The Lack Of A Proper Father*. That's what he heard in the song, and it was ruining his day, and ruining the happy harvest of his only success, the one thing he'd been able to make a go of since that powder magazine exploded in his face: the Sea and Sky carnations.

A dove came in. Atash left off bundling a batch of Sea and Sky to reach into the dovecot and remove its message. The patch of yellow silk fluttered between his scaly thumbs. When he saw to whom the message was sent he was astounded. It was addressed to the very last person he expected ever to receive a message by carrier pigeon. It was addressed to himself.

Esteemed Atash Zarafshani,

Let it be enough for wagging tongues that Shah Abbas's own royal ambassador hereby vouchsafes the good name of your daughter's suitor. A sigheh alleged against Darius Nouredini is a certain falsehood perpetrated by malicious matchmakers. He was not foresworn. His name is worthy even of that most rare and precious of daughters, Gol Zarafshani.

May I, old friend, who have grievously failed in my embassy, yet succeed in this humble suit. Inshalla,

> *Hoseyn Ali Beg.*
> *Lisbon.*

Here was a message that had sailed from Lisbon around the tip of Africa to Ormuz, and flown by dove relay to his hand. Yet it had still to reach Gol. Atash realised at once how this yellow silk could mend her broken heart, and change her life. She thought that love was only death (Mani) or betrayal (Darius). Atash's heart burst with excitement to think of the good news he could bring her. Love wasn't just death and betrayal at all! It was only death! He couldn't wait to tell her. A letter that had travelled over vast distances of sea and sky must not get stuck under the imitation Sea and Sky before reaching Gol. Atash had not left the house in daylight hours for years, but now he must.

He went downstairs and squared his shoulders before the front door, a blackthorn walking stick in his hand. And there he remained. His courage failed him as he listened to the voices in the street, and thought of all the streets he would have to walk to reach Gol. The bazardeh was way over on the other side of the city. The unpaved streets were not so smooth and flat as the roof tiles – and he fell over enough at home as it was. If it was raining or cold he could have worn a floppy hood to stop people staring, but the day was hot. Why not wait until night when his daughter would return? he asked himself. She'd waited long enough. He leant his bumpy forehead against the door.

If Gol had only grieved a day or two he could have waited a few hours before giving her this message, but because she had grieved for month after month after month, he couldn't bear that she should suffer one minute more than she had to. Here at last was something he could do for her. He took a deep breath, put his good hand to the door-handle, and pushed. The stiff front door described a quarter-circle in the dirt as its lowest corner dragged over the ground.

Atash walked further from the house in the next hour than he had in the past ten years, banging his blackthorn stick on the ground. He had not thought it was so hot a day when he set out. Or had he simply forgotten that it was hotter at ground level than up on a roof? Sweat seeped from his hairline and coursed over his numb face. He could only feel the sweat when warm drops, fat as summer rain, tapped his unburnt chin, collar bone or trickled down his one ear lobe.

He came to a bridge he did not recognise. Perhaps it was new. At the far end of the bridge was a tavern, its windows and shutters all open. A dozen pairs of eyes in the gloom seemed to be staring at him. Idle drunkards. Opium eaters.

The faded stripy rag over the tavern door disgorged a few drunks onto the bridge right in his path. Three men shouted at him. Mockery had found its meat. But God would protect a father venturing to lift his daughter from sorrow.

He quickened his pace, buckled and fell. His stick clattered to the ground. He lay on his back, squinting against the sunlight, groping for his stick. Three heads appeared above him, crowding out the sun, three petals around the sun's yellow stamen. Three exceedingly odd petals. Atash blinked the sweat from his eyes and focused on the three faces. One petal lacked a jaw, one had bullet-flecked cheeks of subcutaneous buckshot, and the third was disfigured by a star-shaped powder burn.

The three odd petals helped Atash to his feet, handed him his stick, and led him into the tavern, where almost every man turned out to be a wounded, disfigured or damaged war veteran. When Atash told them his pressing hurry to pass an important message to his daughter, the stocky one with the bullet-flecked cheeks, who turned out to be the tavern-owner, whistled for his son, and sent him to deliver the message to Gol in the bazardeh.

A glass of mint tea on a brass tray was handed to Atash. Golden light, reflected from the river, percolated through the coloured glass of dormant lanterns and empty bottles suspended from the tavern's ceiling. A few musicians were rehearsing in a corner, but sweeter than music came the sound of something he had sorely missed: political gossip.

The whole tavern was alive with the rumour that the Turkish commander-in-chief Cigala had been spooked by reports that Persian spies, a mountain scouting party, had sent Allahvirdi Khan his battle-plans by way of messenger pigeon, and so the Turks had camped on the plain at Ezurum for months, too scared to move, paralysed with indecision, until the Persians swept onto the plain and crushed them.

Atash leaned back against the wall. From the corner a one-legged flautist played a sweet, bright trill. His daughter's songs were so uniformly sad that he had almost forgotten that music could be happy at all. But perhaps that little strip of pale yellow silk he had sent her with the tavern-keeper's boy would change all that.

18

Why do you need a note from some ambassador before you decide to trust him?' demanded Kulsum Nouredini, Darius's grandmother. 'You spend eighteen months thinking him a liar, then, on a stranger's say-so, you don't! Why wasn't Darius's word good enough for you all along? Have you so little idea of him? No eyes or ears in your head to know what little store to set by any words that come from the lying mouth of that mother of his?'

'How is he?' Gol asked.

'You are not his only sorrow, Gol Zarafshani,' Kulsum replied, shaking hay out into the cribs. 'He suffers for his friend. He grieves over what happened to Nat-jan.'

Gol stared at a hoof print in the dirt, while Kulsum described how Darius had stood by a burnt-black tree and watched the Embassy depart, and had seen Nat-jan battered and bruised, his doublet slashed to ribbons, which meant that Nat's money from the oil venture had fallen into Antonio Mirza's hands.

'Darius grieves as much from this injustice as from your bad faith. In fact, the one compounds the other, since you were not there to comfort and console him. And I'll tell you one last thing, Gol Zarafshani. If by your lack of faith you've lost your chance to marry such a man as Darius Nouredini then you have your punishment already, and there an end!'

And with that Kulsum blew her white fringe from her eyes, shooed her away like a cloud of midges, and went to fetch more hay.

❖

A few hours later, Gol found the blackened tree trunk Kulsum had described - or at least what was left of it. For the wind, despising all dead things, had snapped the trunk in two. The top half hung down to the ground, forming a triangle with the earth.

Gol sat with her back against the charred tree plucking her tanbur. Here she was at another of Darius's haunts, just like yesterday when she went in search of his old bookstall. Not only was it not there anymore, there was not the slightest trace of its ever having existed. The narrow booth had been subsumed either by the tinsmiths on one side or the coppersmiths on the other, it was impossible to tell which, so completely had it been obliterated - as if her memory of Darius in the stall was the memory of a dream.

She would stop haunting the old places of Mani and Darius. She would begin living again. She listened to the river puttering invisibly beneath the steep bank, and it suggested a key and a tune. A song landed in the palm of her hand like a ripe apple. She called the song *The Haunt*. As she sang it for the first time, the chord changes and the melody were so inevitable that she felt she was singing a famous old song, as if it had always existed, and not just been born this second.

I will not be a ghost when I die,
I haunted too much when alive
all the old places we used to go.
no ghost life for me
when I am dead

if you see a ghost,

in the shape of your clothes

at the foot of your bed,

or your misty shaving mirror,

if you hear one moaning by our old tree,

it won't be me,

when I die I'm done with haunting

when I die.

She hears an animal grunt nearby and peers round the snapped triangular trunk of the blackened tree. A goat lifts its head above the grassy riverbank's ridge. The goat must have fallen into the water and is now struggling to clamber up the steep bank. A hoof digs into the grass, slips and the goat slides back down the bank. As it does so, its howl of frustration sounds strangely like a man's. Then the goat makes an even more astonishing noise: it laughs!

She creeps towards the riverbank. What she sees next fills her with horror. A savage barbarian slams the goat's head on the bank over and over again. He wears a tribal headdress of reeds and bindweed. His hairy chest and stomach are streaked with algae, mud and goat fur. Welts and whorls scar his back. A rampaging madman murdering all in his path? An escaped prisoner killing his supper with his bare hands?

She runs back behind the snapped black trunk, and squats behind its widest part. Her heart thumps in her chest. She peeks out. Goat and barbarian are wrestling. The wounded goat is fighting off the barbarian. Together they roll out of sight and down the riverbank.

Silence follows. Has a kick from the goat knocked the barbarian out? Or has barbarian vanquished goat? She holds her breath. The barbarian emerges above the top of the bank, dragging the dead goat in a headlock.

Gol pulls in her head and presses herself up against the trunk. She draws in her elbows tight beneath her ribs, willing herself to become one with the dead tree. But then to her horror she notices her tanbur lying in plain view. She reaches out a hand and snatches the bag behind the black tree. She listens. It is the silence, the immaculate silence, which tells her she has been detected. The barbarian has seen her.

She looks to the horizon measuring the distance she has to sprint. She sets down her bag. She will leave everything behind. She must sacrifice belongings for speed. She balances on her toes, coiled and ready to spring. She takes a deep breath, and flinches at the sound of the barbarian's voice.

'Gol, Gol,' he calls. 'Help me! I can't move this goat by myself. She's slipping!'

She runs to the lip of the muddy bank and looks down.

Darius and the flyblown rotten carcass are slithering through the long grasses back down towards the river's reeds. She drops to her belly, crawls headlong down the bank and grabs a goat leg, halting the slide just before it hits the water.

'Thank you,' croaks Darius, a bullfrog among the reeds.

They hang, one above, one below the carcass. Then, Gol pulling and Darius pushing, they heave the dead goat up the bank onto the flat, where each grabs a hind leg, and together they haul the carcass away from the riverbank.

Dumping the bloated beast, they stagger a few steps, fall to their knees and vomit in chorus. They wipe their hands and faces with tussocks of grass. They run, holding their filthy, sticky arms away from their bodies, towards a bend in the river, upstream from contamination.

The bank is shallower here. They wade in and submerge themselves in the crystal-clear, sunlit water.

Gol swims upstream on her back, looking up at the white clouds and the azure sky. She feels the touch of his palm under her shoulders and then, like the nudge of a fish, under the backs of her thighs. Very slowly he glides her round in the sunlit water. Her ears are underwater, and so when he speaks she can hear the deep watery echo of his voice but not what he is saying. His lips are cold and soft when they touch hers. His warm mouth tastes of pondweed. His touch leaves her.

She opens her eyes, and swims on her back, steering by clouds. When she rolls over, he is nowhere to be seen. She swims round and round in a circle. No Darius. She swims to the bend in the river and finds a hairy starfish floating on his back. She wades towards him and places one hand between his shoulder blades and the other under his knees to buoy him up in the sunlit water. She spins him slowly round and round, the crown of his head bowing the current, the river peeling reeds and slime and goat-fur from his hairy chest and smooth shoulders, revealing the scars earned in the oil well under the Fire Temple of Mithras. She kisses his cold lips. His arms enfold her and they tumble over each other like otters at play.

Hand in hand they climb out of the river, and hobble barefoot through grass and thistles to the burnt-out tree that forms a triangle with the earth. He drapes his astrakhan coat over the cracked trunk's apex. Behind this modesty screen she changes into his calico shirt, and spreads her wet clothes on the grass.

She sits shivering beside the astrakhan screen. Darius's hand appears over the top. She closes her long fingers upon his as if resuming their dance either side of the tangerine screen in Kulsum's barn. Only instead of dancing, she lifts the astrakhan coat and wraps it around them both. They sit shoulder to shoulder, dripping water into cinders, teeth chattering in the sunshine.

Part Three

1

Nat walked onto London Bridge, a sack of his landlord's barleycorn over his shoulder. He passed from sunlight to shade as the bridge's tall houses met above his head to form a covered arcade echoing with cries:

Strawberries ripe and cherries on the rise!

Buy my dish of great smelts!

Salt, salt, white Worcestershire salt!

What d'ye lack?

The woman shouting, *Fine Seville oranges!* took one look at Nat's dirty clothes flecked with birdlime and rested her throat while the ragamuffin passed.

'The day will come,' he vowed, 'when I will buy up all her fine Seville oranges and bowl them one by one down the street through the filth. Yes, that's what I'll do. Or else I'll buy every last strawberry ripe and cherry on the rise and eat them right in front of her.'

Pretty pins, pretty women?

Quick, quick, periwinkles, quick, quick, quick!

Brass Pot Or An Iron Pot To Mend!

Fine Writing Ink!

The covered arcade opened out to the sky again, and below him roared the Long Entry waterfall. Long Entry was the steepest, narrowest, loudest arch of London Bridge. Before they chained its mouth, Long Entry was known as the sawmill, since any boat that fell into its torrential waters was chopped into tiny pieces. He could still hear its roar as far as the gaudy pile of Nonsuch House.

At the southern end of London Bridge, he turned into the narrow passageway that led to the corn mills. He joined the knot of people standing on the sack floor, sacks between their feet. Quitrenters, immigrants, the poor and the thrifty brought their grain here to be ground.

When Nat's turn came, he emptied the Beijderwellens' barleycorn into a battered wooden hopper. The corn slid through a funnel in the floorboards to the revolving runner stones below. He took the stairs and followed the barleycorn down to the stone floor's thundering grindstones. A miller, white from head to toe, doused a scorching runner stone. Steam hissed as loud as a cymbal crash. Nat coughed in a speckled cloud of chaff. A man could choke to death on the superflux of grain, the want of which had orphaned him. He crossed to the stairs, each flight being set against a different wall to save the mill house from being shaken to bits. One hand on the newel post, he looked back the way he came and saw falling flour obliterate his footprints. Down he went to the low sheds of the meal floor, the lowest floor, where a little boy was hunting through a fog of wheat to whack rats and mice with a stick. The cast-iron waterwheels sounded like a limping ogre, his walking stick coming down hard and angry on the third beat, clank, clank, CLANK! clank, clank, CLANK!

Nat emerged from the gloomy depths of the meal floor onto a sunlit jetty, where the whole wide, magnificent sweep of the Pool opened to him. All those people waiting up at street-level on the dusty sack floor didn't know what they were missing. Here lay a grand vista where you would least expect one: not up high but down low. The Pool of London was bright and sunny, except for the mist and spray over Long Entry, which was spanned by a small rainbow, as if it had concluded a separate covenant with God. A dozen Levant Company ships rode at anchor, flying the City of London's red dagger flag. A sail-foist full of eels glistened, and a barge loaded with sea-coals winked. All manner of skiffs, ferries and lighters were plying their trades across the glittering Pool, and all the bankside cranes were nodding and swinging.

Nat loved standing on the jetty for its contrast to the lack of perspective in his own life. Across the Pool, a giant merchantman moved out of St Katherine's Dock. The ship's hull planks were the same dark brown as the warehouses, and it looked to Nat as if a warehouse were detaching itself from the City of London to sail free. What appeared to be fixed and stuck in place might yet go some place. For the past three years he'd been stuck in the rut of Galley Quay, working in the Levant Company's warehouse. The old dream of being a London oil merchant had died. What was the use of knowing about oil in London?

'I learn something in one place only for life to fling me where it's useless.'

But perhaps not all he learned in Isfahan was useless, he considered, catching sight of his two best doves, Petrolio and Mithras, looping the Tower of London. If not pioneering the sale of oil, then perhaps he might yet introduce his countrymen to another Persian innovation: messenger pigeons. Unlike a barrel of oil, pigeons could be bought for sixpence. Here was a venture needing no rich patron and no capital.

Messenger pigeons were unknown in England. As far as the English were concerned no-one since Noah had ever received a message by pigeon. The idea that a pigeon could bring a merchant in Cornhill the price of silk in Bruges was as fantastical as Mercury the winged messenger flying about the Greek Islands. Sunlight caught the underside of Petrolio and Mithras's wings as they raced back towards the coop that Nat had built them on the Galley Quay warehouse roof.

Into Nat's thoughts intruded a sound more striking than noise on silence: silence on noise. The corn mill seemed to hold its breath. The master miller had disengaged the grindstones. For a few seconds, Nat could hear the river softly lapping at the jetty by his feet. He waited for the sound he knew was coming next. The chink of the master miller's switch lever striking the pit wheel gearing, the chink that announced that the Thames was about to power the enormous wall-mounted drum wheel that hoisted the flour sacks up three flours to the street. He loved how that single sharp note set off a great cacophony. Tap one peg in one cog and the whole mill house began to tremble.

Chink went the miller's lever, followed by the ringing of the drum wheel chains, taking the strain against the river. Next, the black oak drum wheel on the wall began its trundling turn, powered by the immemorial force of the Thames, and then the chains rattled as they whisked the flour sacks up three floors to the street.

Chink! Ring! Trundle! Rattle! Whoosh!

As the empty sling was lowered back through clouds of flour dust, Nat saw the saddlecloth lowered down to him in the vug, ready for another goatskin full of oil.

The miller switched the gears from drum wheel back to grindstone, and the mill house resumed its regular throbbing, clanking, skirring din. Nat climbed three flights of stairs to the sack floor, where he heaved the landlord's flour onto his shoulder, and walked back through the shops, taverns and houses of London Bridge. In one window a spherical waterglass multiplied candlelight. An oil lamp would do the job much better. Ah, it was agony to have the solution to the whole city's heat and light problem when you could not put it into practice! But perhaps, were Nat to succeed with the messenger pigeons then the Levant Company might finance his plan to import oil.

He passed the Three Neats' Tavern, which marked the end of the

Bridge, and walked up New Fish Street. On Crooked Lane, he stood to one side to make way for merchant families in velvet and furs, who were crowding into St Michael's Church of the Murdering Mayor, its bells ringing for evensong. Nat looked through the churchyard railings at Walworth's tomb and monument, upon which was inscribed in antique script, all the 'u's in the shape of 'v's:

> *Here vnder lyeth a Man of Fame,*
> *William Walworth callyed by Name;*
> *Who with Covrage stovt, and manly Might,*
> *Slew Wat Tyler, in King Richard's sight.*

The red knife on the City of London's crest was in honour of the dagger with which the Mayor of London, Sir William Walworth, murdered peasants' leader Wat Tyler during a parlay under a flag of truce. After Walworth stabbed Tyler, King Richard galloped up and down screaming at the peasant petitioners, 'Villeins ye were and villeins ye shall remain! In bondage ye shall abide!'

'A warehouseman ye are,' the red dagger told Nat, 'and a warehouseman ye shall remain. On Galley Quay ye shall abide!' And to make sure he never forgot it, the red dagger was everywhere he looked as he walked home: on street corner signs, on tabards hanging outside shops and warehouses, on ceramic tiles in guild halls, on flags flown by half the ships in the Pool, and on shields held by dragons roosting in the middle of Cheapside. The red knife gave the City of London's short answer to the equalising instinct in the hearts of common people. For equality was a tropical cyclone that levelled whole cities.

'Tempests in state,' said Sir Francis Bacon, 'are commonly greatest when things grow to equality, just as natural tempests are greatest about the equator.' Nat stroked the scar on his forehead where Anthony's red knife had sliced off his last coin from the oil venture.

At Old Swan stairs, he dropped the flour sack into the boat, and began the long row home. The river gave off that whiff of the green sea that it somehow retained even above the Bridge. He pulled past the wooden warehouses lining the river, behind which rose banks of red, pink and orange roofs, and behind them the towering megalith of unsteepled St Paul's, that primeval slab in the sky that could be seen from seven counties.

At Hay Wharf, he had to go round a moored ship. He detested being in the middle of the broad river, where the wind blew across the wide reach, for fear of his atoms being scattered to the four winds.

Not once, but twice in his short life his whole world had scattered on the wind. The first scattering had been when he was nine: the Datchworth famine which killed his father, mother, sister and brother, along with half the village, and every girl he had impressed at the summer fete by being the boy who won the cheese hat for walking the greasy log. The second scattering had been his loss of Darius. This double scattering left him an arbitrary figure in a landscape, Godforsaken, a third-growth forest, all scrappy dogwood and bramble, a scattering of chaff upon the muddy Thames.

He scarfed his nose against the noxious outflow from Water Lane, and then rowed through the harum-scarum junction where Thames met Fleet at Bridewell dock, with its swinging jib-cranes, barges and lighters, the flat-bottomed boats used for rowing goods from ship to quay. He ran along the gunwale with the boathook to squeeze the skiff through the river traffic. He had that skill which lightermen called 'the walk', the ability to step to all parts of the boat without losing your footing come rain or shine or choppy tide. If you didn't have 'the walk' it could take you an hour to get your boat through Bridewell dock's log-jam. Bobbing and weaving, and running nimbly on the gunwales with his eerie balance, Nat was through in a matter of minutes.

After Fleet Bridge it was easy rowing. The river was far quieter on this last stretch. A starling's *chink* sounded like the master miller's switch lever. Soon Fortune's solid oak drum wheel was going to turn for Nat. The chains would rattle and he'd rise, rise, rise, driven by the mighty waters of justice. *Chink*, called the starling, *chink, chink, chink.*

Nat moored the skiff to the Turnagain Lane landing. Flour sack on one shoulder, oars on the other, he walked to the Beijderwellens' house on Seacole Lane.

2

'Three years!' exploded Customer Hythe. 'Bramble has worked three years on Galley Quay, and in all that time no-one thought to inform me! And now come goods and a letter from Spain addressed to Mr Nat Bramble - Mister indeed! - care of the Levant Company, if you please!'

... And in Venice, he thought darkly, this same Bramble had witnessed Foscarini duff him up like a drayman his boy.

Customer Hythe, Governor of the Levant Company, was sitting in the walnut-paneled chambers of the Levant House on Fylpot Street with his Vice Consuls Roe and Colthurst. He picked up the English translation of the Spanish letter and read it out loud to them.

Esteemed friend Nat Bramble,

Since last we spoke in Venice, I have been lodged with Jesuits in Valladolid.

His Majesty King Philip and Queen Margaret stood as godparents at my baptism in the Royal Chapel of the Palace at Valladolid, where I was dressed in a suit of white satin. On that day Uruch Bey became Don John of Persia, and King Philip gave command of his royal and Christian generosity that I should receive 1200 crowns a year.

I was resolved that after my baptism I would return to Isfahan to fetch my wife and children, and carry them out of the country by way of Ormuz which the Portuguese now hold in the name of his Catholic Majesty, my godfather. But he forbad it. I protested that the plan was already far advanced, a ship's cabin paid for, an hour set to sail. His Majesty told me that my plan was no secret to the Shah, who would imprison me the moment I set foot upon Persian soil.

And so here in Spain I stay, striving daily to believe those doctrines, which I as yet do not fully understand but which are, it seems, necessary to belief, and are called the Mysteries of the Faith. Jesus told my new namesake John: 'Marvel not that I say ye must be born again, for except a man be born again he cannot see the kingdom of heaven.' I confess I am not yet born again for I miss my family, and my homeland, and marvel too much at what I have lost.

Mr Nat Bramble, a sum of money has been conveyed to me by means of havala, *our Persian system of remittance. The funds come from Isfahan by way of Ormuz and Cadiz. Darius Nouredini has arranged for you to be paid monies still owing to you from the oil venture, the expedition to the Temple of Mithras in Masjid-i-Suleiman. Darius has prospered selling oil in Tabriz, but cannot enjoy his prosperity while you are poor, Antonio Mirza having robbed you. This sum of money is half of his half of the Temple of Mithras money, and arrived with me almost two years ago. To my great distress I have not, up until now, been able to fulfil the role of* havaladar *because of the wars between Spain and England. While war raged, your money stayed in a locked drawer, during all of which time I felt like a low thief, little better than Antonio Mirza himself.*

How relieved I am at last, therefore, to be able to send you this bill of credit to be drawn upon Don Zuniga the Spanish Ambassador in Fenchurch Street. Upon production of this bill the Ambassador is to pay you the sum equivalent to one hundred Spanish dollars in English coin, to the value of no less than twenty-five pounds sterling, nor to exceed thirty pounds sterling.

I send you also a gift of my own. When we sat near the Camel Palace in Venice, you told me of your love for the Arab drink qaveh. Well, since peace with the English, King Philip has begun to expel those Spanish Arabs who turn their face away from our Redeemer, as well as those so-called moriscos, *who only pretend to love Christ Jesus but are really infidels too. The King is expelling all of them. Every day of the Grand Expulsion, Sunni Arabs, exiled from Grenada and Cordoba, leave tons of excellent qaveh behind them, piled high in the cellars of their deserted houses. Spanish Catholics have no more taste than Shia Persians for qaveh, and so sacks of beans are free for the taking. All this great circumstance of war and peace means that I send you a chest of beans!*

If you find a market for this commodity in London, inform Don Zuniga and I shall send you more chests of qaveh beans. Then we can establish the trade on a proper footing with commercial articles drawn up between us, and - God willing! - I may help you prosper in London as Darius prospers in Tabriz, by finding a market for qaveh as he has found for oil.

By the way, as well as these bags of qaveh beans, I discovered a bag of cocoa beans from the Indies. The chief use of these cocoa beans with them is in the manufacture of a drink that they call chocolate. Shall I send them also?

If through sale of qaveh and chocolate you become a rich merchant with servants of your own, I trust you will dress them better than that awful blue and yellow livery that Antonio forced you to wear!

To speak of the Devil, he is at large here in Spain where he has become, would you believe, Admiral Don Antonio Xerley, all of whose schemes and shallow plans for wars infect feeble-minded ministers in Madrid and Cadiz - and may yet lead to war.

But let me end on good news. Indeed, I save the best for last. Darius Nouredini wishes you to know of his marriage to the daughter of Atash Zarafshani. I enclose a strip of the hem of the actual wedding blanket upon which husband and wife sat on their wedding day. I pray that they are blessed with children, from whom they may never find themselves - as I, for my sins, find myself - half the world away.

Inshalla!

(or, as they say here, Oxala!)

I remain, as ever,

your altered never altering,

Don John of Persia,

the erstwhile Uruch Bey

'Well, what are we to make of this?' Customer Hythe asked his Vice-Consuls Roe and Colthurst. 'What does it mean? Is it in code? So fantastic a farrago simply has to be code! But what sort of code?'

'By commodity?' suggested Roe. 'Cecil's merchant-code?'

'His what?' asked the Customer.

'Cecil tells his spies to make up their codes merchant-wise, so that "chocolate" might mean frigates, say, and "qaveh," the assassination of King James.'

'Inshalla!' barked the Customer, and all three men burst out laughing. It was an assassination the City much wished.

'And perhaps pulling the strings behind it all,' speculated Colthurst, 'is your double-triple-gaming Don Antonio Xerley!'

'If so,' said Roe, 'could this be part of the Thomas Sherley plot? Could Bramble be waving his flag on Galley Quay to signal Sir Thomas's confederates?'

'Flag?'

'Bramble's been seen waving a flag on the end of a pole up on the roof at Galley Quay.'

'What? What?' exploded the Customer. 'You saw Bramble - the letter thief who sunk us in Venice - you saw Bramble up on my warehouse roof waving a flag at foreign ships and still you never told me!'

'Calm yourself, Customer. Upon this letter's arrival, I enquired after Bramble of the quay master who told me that he is training pigeons to fly further every day and so he waves this flag at the birds to send them on another circuit around the Pool, and to stop them coming home to roost too soon.'

'Show me these goods sent to Mister Bramble of Galley Quay.'

'Here's a sample from the chest,' said Colthurst.

'Lentils?' asked the Customer, who scooped a handful of hard green pulses and then let them clack back into the sack.

'Qaveh beans, Customer,' replied Colthurst. 'In Constantinople they sip of this black qaveh drink in little china dishes as hot as they can suffer it. An aid to digestion, they say and it also lends alacrity.'

'Black?' asked the Customer. 'The drink comes black from these green beans?'

'They first roast the beans until they are as black as soot,' said Roe. 'And tasting not much unlike it!

'Besides these beans,' said Colthurst, 'there's a grinder and a couple of pots in the chest.'

'Valuable?'

'Gewgaws.'

'So the only thing of value here,' said the Customer, 'is the bill of credit, then. Now, as to this, there is an issue of probity here. This money is not ours to receive, but nor can we be party to a Spanish paymaster paying a Spanish agent. I propose, therefore, that we endow the Merchant Taylor School with a sum exactly equal to the bill of credit, viz a twenty-five pound bursary to help poor boys gain an education.'

'It speaks well of you, Customer,' said Roe.

'Inform the clerk of works and tell him to dismiss Bramble, too.'

So saying, the Customer scrunched Don John of Persia's letter and bill of credit into a ball and threw them both in the fire. 'Now gentlemen, if you are ready, we must meet the King.'

3

Stepping out of the kitchen door into the back garden, Nat was vexed to find Miep, his landlord's daughter, already up and about. If that wasn't bad enough, she was feeding sugared almonds to his scrawny, speckled brown pigeon called Parboyl.

'Don't feed him,' snapped Nat, snatching the tatty dove out of her hands, 'or he'll never fly to Galley Quay.'

'It's only a bite,' she said, putting the rest of the almonds back into the pocket of her grey, square-cut, bibbed apron of a dress.

'No, not even a bite. Give him food and he won't know whether he is coming or going. He'll start thinking this is his home, and then fly back here with the messages which the Levant Company want me to train him to carry. '

It was her fault he had begun the day with a lie. Nobody at the Levant Company even knew he kept birds on the warehouse roof, let alone wanted his birds for carrying news. He was ashamed of himself. What was he thinking? Why bother to puff himself up in front of her of all people?

'Nothing but food draws him home?' she asked. 'That's his only loyalty? Don't the other doves draw him to Galley Quay more than food?'

He knew that this was her roundabout way of asking him if he had any other reasons apart from bed and board for lodging at Seacole Lane. Any reason that might have to do with her perhaps.

For two years now, Nat had lodged in a back garret of the Beijderwellens' house on Seacole Lane in Snow Hill, opposite the Saracen's Head inn. He had first seen the Beijderwellens when apprentices had stoned the Dutch Church on Broad Street.

The Dutch Church windows possessed the largest panes in the parish. Enough of smashing petty Papist stained-glass leads that made no more noise than cracking an ice puddle with your heel, the Dutch Church panes smashed with a sound like the noonday chimes! The apprentice boys had tried to get the crowd going, tried to get them to join in. Those Dutch didn't want to be English, they were shouting, so why were they here? They kept to their own language, their own churches, and even wanted to bring over their own king. Come on! Clubs! Clubs!

Nat did not dare help the Dutch who were trying to drive off the mob, but he had a barrow with him that he trundled to the city ditch to find some timber to board the broken windows. At the stinking ditch, an open sewer, he pulled on his work gloves, took up a few duckboards, washed them in a puddle, and put them on his barrow. He carried the duckboards back to the Broad Street, where the Dutch were shovelling up a crunchy slush of broken glass. Watching them board up the church windows, he hoped they wouldn't ask him where he got the timber.

One cold, rainy day a month or so later, the quay master at Galley Quay sent Nat on an errand into the Steelyard, the Hanseatic, Dutch and Flemish dock, where he'd run into Mr Beijderwellen. When Nat compared the tiny sentry box of a hut where the Dutchman clerked to his own cramped lodgings on St Lawrence Lane by Cheapside, Mr Beijderwellen had said he had a garret room to let on Snow Hill for a shilling a week plus chores.

The air was clean and clear on Snow Hill. On holidays and summer evenings, Nat had only to cross Holborn Bridge to be among Saffron Hill's cattle-grids and open fields, and from his dormer window he was greeted each morning by the lurid pub sign of the Saracen's Head Inn. What with his thick black moustache and his scarlet clothes, the Saracen reminded him of Shah Abbas in one of his killing moods.

❖

Nat tried tossing Parboyl, but bird clung to glove. He pumped his hand up and down but couldn't shake him off. Miep tried. The bird took off. Her eyes, which were very dark for so pale a pudding face, flashed with delight.

'*Vloeg, dvif!* she cried. '*Vloeg weg, lief dvifje!* Fly dove, fly away, sweet little dove!'

Up Parboyl flew, circling the Turn Again Lane rooftops. Nat was exalted to see his bird find its direction and fly straight for Galley Quay. As he watched Parboyl disappear over Newgate Market, he heard Miep ask the same novice's question he had once asked Darius:

'How do the doves know where to take each message?'

'The doves only know how to fly home,' he explained, with a far-away voice as if he were reciting an old poem. 'That's all they know, but they know this one thing very well. No matter where they are, they can always get back to their dovecot. And when they are released that's the one direction they fly, with a message strapped under their wings. I'm trying to train him to fly to Galley Quay so don't be feeding him here.'

He heard a flutter and a thump behind him. He wheeled round. There on the lid of the rabbit hutch was Parboyl. Snatching him up in his fist, Nat rounded on Miep:

'You and your sugared almonds have done this! It's pointless. A peacock will fly more than him! Every day I carry him to Galley Quay and home again.'

'*Dvifje! Lief dvif!* Clever Potboil, you have made Nat your carriage.'

'Parboyl. His name's Parboyl. Not Potboil. Have you risen so early just to bate me?'

Miep watched a shadow fall on him. Old Man Bramble was back. She never knew which Nat she was going to get. One minute he was all boyish zest, and the next he'd be Old Man Bramble with his mubblefubbles. One minute he'd be bursting with plans and schemes and dreams, his brown irises shining like conkers, and the next minute he'd be all sour comments and twisted grimace and what was the point of anything he'd like to know.

She had need of Nat's keen spirit, and wished it were not such a guttering flame. She needed his bright spark against the drizzling sea-fog of her elder brothers' and her father's snippy, narrow, discouraging platitudes, a sea-fog that she feared would infect her soul with the rheumatic fever that had claimed her folks. She sought him out to nourish what was different in her from the men in her family. They had an amused contempt for anyone who did not do as they did. The world was as it was with good reason, and depended upon the simple application of well-worn principles which had been revealed to the lucky Beijderwellens as to few others and which allowed them all to earn a steady wage at the Steelyards. No wonder her mother retreated into the mysteries of faith, a netherworld of spirits and apocrypha. When the English lodger arrived, she felt that his very existence gave the lie to the Beijderwellen philosophy, gave the lie to the way they always told her that once she'd seen a bit of the world she would think like they did and know that the world was as it was and couldn't change. Because unlike them, Nat had seen a little of the world and he was still full of zesty projects and impossible schemes just like her! Well, half the time, he was. When he wasn't being that knock-kneed twenty-one year old codger. Though closer in age to her than her brothers, he had already done more than they would in a lifetime. The problem was he rated himself too low.

She thought she could do something about that. She made him her project.

'Never mind the Levant Company,' she told him. 'Why don't you set up your own pigeon post? Why not be an independent trader? Why not build your dovecot here?'

'I won't be here for very long.'

'You've been saying that for the last couple of years. I wonder what keeps you here?'

'Well, I should tell you that I've come to an arrangement with your father. An arrangement concerning you, Miep.'

'Me?' Despite herself she blushed to the roots of her hair. He took her hand in hers and looked deep into her eyes.

'Well, I have been living here for two years now, and during that time we've spent a lot of time together, you and I, and so I have spoken to your father, and told him how I felt about you, Miep, and he has, I'm happy to tell you, agreed to my request to knock a penny off the rent every time you talk to me.' She snatched her hand away. It was no use. He was just like her brothers. What happened to people past the age of twenty to make the spark go out of their eyes?

❖

Nat couldn't understand how it was that she had no inkling of the vast difference in experience in status between her and him who had once served secretary to a knight of the realm. What possible interest did she think she might hold for him? There was a chasm of degree and of experience between them. Truth be told, he sometimes forgot to remember this chasm, and would be chatting equably and enthusiastically as if they were indeed friends - before he'd suddenly scold himself, his cheeks and ears burning with shame. These piecemeal collusions were how the prisoner becomes habituated to his cell, and the pigeon to its hole. But not this woodcock. He had travelled too far and lived too widely to fall for a moon faced Dutch girl with freckles and red hair that stuck out unevenly as if she had been lying in straw. The hair came out of her linen cap in two bunches. The first rays crossing the kitchen garden's dewy grass shone upon her bare calves, where her yarn stockings were rolled down to the ankles. The ginger hair on her shins turned blond as it caught the early sunlight. She caught him looking and so he said,

'You look like the four of hearts.'

'*You'll* never see the five,' she shot back.

He laughed. She was herself to herself. She had an independent spirit. He recalled how big that word independence had been with him when he was her age - and the recollection made him feel done in, spent. She reminded him of all the vim he'd lost. He wasn't sure he wanted to be around her and feel so loose-toothed and over and done with. He didn't resent her verve. He liked the independent way she'd hacked a short fringe that exposed her forehead all the way to the hairline, and the way she went barelegged in clumpy leather mules that wanted to be clogs, he liked her quick tongue and ready wit, but her vivacity made him feel hollow and tapped out. He knew he was hollow and tapped out. He just didn't want to be reminded of it all the time. And so he called her old scold, old crone:

'One year under the Spanish is like ten anywhere else,' she replied. 'I'm wise because of my one hundred and fifty years.'

'Tell me something wise, old woman.'

'You think that courage or heart or spirit is something you have like a flame in a temple and when it goes out that's that, but it's not. It's something you get by doing.'

4

The Levant Company had convened a meeting at the Guildhall with King James, who was trying yet again to abolish their monopoly on importing Mediterranean and Asian goods.

The high-ceilinged Guildhall was dominated by the two towering wooden effigies of Gog and Magog, carved and painted grotesques of London's ancient demons, the evil giants who had to be vanquished before the city could be built. With goggle eyes and gaping gobs, Gog and Magog glared down in amazement on the assembly.

Customer Hythe slid an opened ledger across the table.

'These accounts show the great revenues that the Levant Company renders Your Majesty's Exchequer each year in import duties.'

King James slammed the ledger shut with a great boom that reverberated off the high ceiling as if Gog and Magog had drawn a sharp intake of breath.

'By trading in yon Mohammedan lake, the Mediterranean,' said the King, 'you put oor Royal Dockyards to an expense of boat-building far in excess of the tallies totted in yon ledger. That's the truth of the matter, and all the sultanas in the world will nae make it false. My brave Sir Thomas Sherley puts it right well: instead of spending all oor treasure building fleets to protect yon currants, I might hae the sewers and drains, the fountains, pleasure gardens and public walks which every other Christian kingdom save mine alone, it seems, is adorned withal. He tells me the more profitable course is to switch trade away from Venice and Constantinople, altogether, and into the free port of Livorno, which some call Leghorn, where there are no imposts to be paid such as we must pay the heathen. He tells me yours is a naughty trade. I hear ye've contracted a kind of moral gonorrhoea from the Sultan. So, I'll not renew your monopoly. The past was yours, right enough, but I shall award the coming years' prosperity to my champion, Sir Thomas. For we are at the pinpoint of the protractor, Customer Hythe. D'ye know what that means? It means the deeds we do now will radiate far and wide for centuries to come!'

So saying, he swept out of the hall with all his retinue - all bar Secretary of State Cecil.

Everyone else shrank back as those two great powers in the land, the Governor of the Levant Company and the Secretary of State, glowered each other. The Customer raged at Cecil:

'You were supposed to have told this bumpkin King what was good for him! You were supposed to lance this Leghorn boil on his brain, bring him here to sign the charter, and arrest Tom Sherley, who is a great a threat to trade, and yet is somehow he's still at large. Your spies are sleeping!'

Who'd have thought so small a man as Crookback Cecil could produce a voice as loud as he did in response to this?

'My spies are dying!'

His shout filled the hall. Gog and Magog went ooh.

'This very morning,' Cecil resumed, 'my best agent was blown up by a tripwire grenade Tom Sherley placed in a lantern.'

'Then hang the pirate for murder!' stormed Customer Hythe.

Gog and Magog went aah.

'How can we when we stole the lamp from his chambers? You're not in the Sultan's seraglio now - there's law here, Customer, law! I need evidence before a king's favourite can be imprisoned and tortured.'

'Give the Scotsman the note you got from the Doge!'

'Hearsay,' replied Cecil, long elfin fingers fiddling with his ame-thyst pendant. 'A note from the Venetian ambassador warning that Tom Sherley is plotting with one Basadonna to destroy the Levant Company is not evidence. Documentary proof is what I need. A scribble. A jotting. A confidential list of goods. Trade secrets. Anything that shows him to be a traitor plotting against England's most vital corporation.'

Customer Hythe bowed.

'Do you follow him?'

'Not even God can follow a man through London,' replied Cecil. 'Once we have him on a charge of treason, we can extract the whole truth in the usual way, King James or no.'

'How do you propose to get this evidence, my lord?'

'I don't know. Do you?'

Gog and Magog awaited his answer with bated breath.

❖

The merchants returned from the Guildhall to the Levant House on Fylpot Street.

'Lord, Lord,' said the Customer, as the clerk of works helped him out of his goose-turd-green velvet cloak. 'From above and below, by secret plot and public law, the company is under attack! Woe to the man who tries to enrich the realm! Woe to him! Have you dismissed Bramble yet?'

'Forgive me, Sir Henry,' said the clerk of works, 'only with the move from Billingsgate I've been so busy that I've not had a chance to.'

'Don't. I have a job for that serviceable villain after all. The rascal knave has already ended the career of one Sherley, perhaps he'll destroy Sir Thomas too. I do believe Providence put that Spanish letter into our hands to remind me of Bramble's existence. I'll visit him tomorrow on the roof at Galley Quay.'

5

Nat climbed out onto the roof of the Levant Company's Galley Quay warehouse. This roof was his domain, and his alone. No-one else ever came up here except him and his pigeons. A crossing wind rippled the bright silver puddles.

Here on the roof, Nat's round, salvage timber dovecot was a kind of Temple of Mithras where he kept alive the flame of his days with Darius. He couldn't say exactly what it was about those days that he was trying to keep alive, though. The sense of when life was larger? The memory of what it felt to love? Of when life seemed something he could shape and not be bent by? Maybe all of those things. He didn't know.

He was proud of the dovecot's ingenious design. He'd built it from a back axle and two old cartwheels. He'd stood the back axle on end, weighted the bottom wheel with broken bricks and on the top wheel set an empty forty gallon barrel for a pigeon house. He'd carved eye-level pop-holes into the dovecot, and topped it with a pitched roof made from two sides of a wooden box.

He unplugged a dowel peg, and the front half of the barrel swung open on its hinges like a doll's house to reveal two pigeons sitting in their pigeonholes.

'What cheer, Petrolio? What cheer Mithras?' He lifted them out, one in each hand.

He'd named Petrolio for his colouring, a neck of iridescent green and purple exactly like spilt petroleum in sunlight. Mithras's crop was still a little swollen, and so he fed her a few crushed oyster shells, before scattering millet, peas, barleycorn and firethorn berries in the dovecot.

He sat on the riverside parapet and from his doublet took Parboyl, who was named after how Nat was going to cook him. With his tatty, speckled brown feathers and a beak barnacled by a fat white cere, he was as ugly as the other birds were beautiful.

On London Bridge, the windows of its tall houses were glinting in relay as the morning light touched each one. When sunlight reached the middle of the Bridge, igniting the gold-leaf paint of Nonsuch House, it was time to pull on his hide gloves and go down to the wharf to work.

Trade had so diminished that the Company was abandoning its Billingsgate warehouse. Nat and the other hands spent a long day stacking evacuated Billingsgate stock into Galley Quay, the Company's last redoubt. All day Nat stacked bales of raisins, coils of wire, and hundredweight pepper bags. It was exhausting work and no-one could stop for a break. Not until late afternoon did the warehousemen have a moment to share a jug of small beer on the Thames shore.

'All this ache and blisters for what?' asked one, after he had taken his swig. 'Used to be that the more work in hand, the more you were sure of long usance at least. But once this lot is stacked, there's not one man in two will be working here by next week.'

Nat wondered who among them would be dismissed. Would it be last in, first out? Or would the quay master's say-so decide who stayed or went? Or perhaps Nat would rescue the fortunes of the Levant Company with the aid of his messenger pigeons, and the competitive advantage they'd bring! Perhaps he'd be the rescue of every last man here!

At the end of the day, when the others went home to their suppers or the alehouse, Nat went back to the roof and his pigeons. He was training them to fly further and further by waving a flagpole (a rag tied on the end of a broomstick) to stop them coming home to roost too soon. This evening, however, he was going to try something new. He was going to attach a satchel to one of his birds. He wasn't sure if it would slip and tangle the wings and cause the bird to drop from the sky, and so he tied it to the worthless Parboyl.

He sat astride the parapet and fastened the blue silk satchel to the brown and white speckled feathers. He kissed the rolled-up cotton script for luck and tamped it into the blue satchel.

'Get in there, it's your birthday, Parboyl, I shall be more sorry to lose this satchel than you for I was up half the night making it.'

He tossed the bird into the sky. Parboyl spread his wings and glided the five yards across Galley Quay Alley to alight on a dormer window's gable, where his beak ripped the blue satchel to shreds. Bird looked past scarlet-faced human to scarlet firethorn berries in the dovecot. Guessing his intention, Nat gripped the flagpole in both hands and prepared to clout Parboyl like a shinty ball far into the Pool.

There was insolence in the direct route the bird took to the berries. Parboyl flew straight for the dovecot as if the man with the stick wasn't even there. Nat swung his pole with perfect timing. Right before the sweet strike, Parboyl did something astounding. He tumbled forward in mid-flight and rolled under the swinging stick. Nat raked the air, lost his footing and fell on his arse in a puddle.

It was in this position, rainwater soaking through the seat of his galligaskins, that he looked up to find Customer Hythe looking down on him from the white wooden cupola, blue-plumed hat upon his untidy fair hair, and goose-turd-green cloak flapping in the breeze.

Nat jumped up from the puddle, and wiped the seat of his baggy black galligaskins, as Customer Hythe said:

'You're the item that was old Anthony Sherley's page, are you not?'

'Master Bramble, sir. Except I was more in the way of his secretary, Sir Henry.'

The Customer frowned at the dovecot that Bramble had had the temerity to build on Levant Company property. An upended axle with a barrel stuck on top, it looked as though a beer wagon had overturned in a slurry of pigeon shit. The Customer swallowed his disgust, climbed over the cupola's low wall onto the roof terrace, and addressed the skink directly.

'So now why is the Customer talking to you when there are currants to be counted, eh? Well, I'll tell you the reason. The reason is this -'

'Because there are no currants, sir?'

'What?'

'No ships, no currants,' said Nat, waving his arm at the Thames.

The Customer narrowed his eyes. There was something unsavoury about Bramble. He seemed somehow not to have come by his knowledge fairly and squarely as Sir Henry himself had done. His literacy smacked of the looted silver candlestick in the soldier's knapsack. What would have been clever in a gentleman was low cunning in him. Yet perhaps these unnatural wiles might yet make him the very dog for the Sherley foxhole.

'But do you know the reason why there are no ships and no currants, Bramble, eh? D'ye know that?'

'No, sir.'

'The dearth is caused by a plot against our Levant Company, which is to say a plot against England. A plot led by Sir Thomas Sherley in conspiracy with an Italian named Basadonna.'

'By piracy, Sir Henry?'

'No, Sir Thomas lives in London now. His seafaring days are over. It is a subtle and Machiavellian plot. It is an Italian plot. Sir Thomas passes confidential lists to Basadonna.'

'What's on these lists, sir?'

'They're lists of goods. Order forms. Who buys how much at what price. Then with their fleet of swift ships and a warehouse in Livorno, they undersell us, scoop the buyers out from under us.'

'Go slower, sir. I have not followed.'

'I am glad you have said that. Good. I would not have a man nod five times and then carry my Southwark parcel to St Albans. It shows wit to admit incomprehension. I shall explain. Sir Thomas and this Italian Basadonna conspire to sell goods for less than we do, even if they make a loss. Because Sir Thomas and Basadonna don't care about the trade. Basadonna's business is the ruin of old England and the raising up of Livorno. And Sir Thomas's fixed intent is to destroy the Levant Company. To this end as well as his trade conspiracy, he slanders and libels us to King James himself.'

'What does he say in these libels, sir?'

'Sermons from a pirate! It is no simple thing to win harbour rights in Constantinople, I tell you. The Sultan requires our ships for certain tasks, tasks which we perform to safeguard trade, which means safeguard England, for the two things are the same.'

'What sort of tasks, Sir Henry?'

'The full picture to him who has a wall big enough to hang it on. Now, Bramble, you've bust the seal on a fair few Sherley letters in your time, I happens to know, don't I? So tell me, lad, got a way of secret writing, have they? A secret conduit for exchanging treasonous letters? Family codes? Ciphers?'

'Secret anything was against Sir Anthony's nature, sir. Display and show were a religion with him.'

'And guile and subterfuge with Sir Thomas. I have a commission for you, Bramble. You will find out and steal Sir Thomas Sherley's treasonous correspondence and bring it to me.'

Nat feared his next question would earn him a cuff round the head as the Customer exploded with righteous indignation.

'Do you wish me to steal Sir Thomas's letters, Sir Henry?' Far from erupting with insulted honour, however, the Customer impatiently waved the suggestion away. 'Sir Thomas Sherley's letters are opened daily. Orders of the Privy Council. We don't want his letters, Bramble, we want his lists of goods, his lists of our trade secrets before he uses them to eviscerate England. What I need from you, Master Bramble, is to find out how Tom Sherley passes these mercantile espials to Basadonna, the Italian. With any one of these lists in hand we have proof of the existence of a plot. Proof enough for Cecil to show the King. Letter me no letters, I want his treasonous lists.'

'Do Lord Cecil's spies visit his lodgings when he is out, Sir Henry?'

'Ransacked monthly. No bloodstone found.'

'Bloodstone, Sir Henry?'

'Ah, the art of subterfuge has come on apace since your day, Bramble. Nowadays spies hide messages in a bloodstone worked like paste and made hard again, so that it cannot be broken but one way or else the message is destroyed. No bloodstone found. No cipher codes found. His gewgaws and lanterns broken open.'

'Lanterns?'

'He is in a small way a merchant of eastern lanterns. He imports them a box at a time.'

'Then it's clear this must be how he gets the messages. The lanterns.'

'All searched,' said the Customer. 'Broken open, emptied out, top and tail. The sole purpose of his importing these gewgaws is to provide him with a pretext to meet with Italian merchants up and down the river. One of Cecil's spies, investigating a lamp at Whitehall, lit one and was blown up as if by a grenade. Bang! Seems they have to be lit just so, but we can hardly ask Tom Sherley how.'

'I have less idea than any man about Sir Thomas Sherley. I couldn't even tell you where he lives, Sir Henry, so I respectfully decline the offer, sir. But if the Customer will allow me two minutes of his time, which I know to be ten of any other man's, then I shall expound my scheme for the use of messenger pigeons in commerce.'

'Have you forgot your wet bum so soon? The piebald pigeon that pitched you in the puddle should be proof enough that foreign new-fangledness withers on the vine. Let me tell you a story. Once upon a time, Bramble, I tried to grow a medicinal poison called the tomato plant, but contrary to what certain suggestible sharers had me believe, I proved that the to-ma-to can no more be grown in England than the greengage. And it's inedible to boot! I learnt my lesson about novelty, then. Cost me five-hundred that little lesson did. Why, only yesterday I had a Spanish fellow try to interest me in a scheme to import Arabian beans from Cadiz.'

'Qaveh?'

'What? Aye, that's the boy: qaveh! And a drink called chocolate too! Chocolate! Tusk, tusk, tusk, if I went with every skyey scheme put in my way, the Levant Company would not last out the season. Forget these intelligencing doves and sentient starlings. You have ended the career of one Sherley, but he was not the worst of them. Sir Thomas is the worst. He is the eldest brother and the most dangerous.'

'For as long as I've worked for the Levant Company,' said Nat, 'I've hoped that the Customer might one day remember me as a former secretary who speaks Greek and Persian and who might be asked to translate documents from Cyprus Island or Patras better than any here can, and that you would recognise me as one who might be given a clerk's position or decide what goods we buy from where, and not as a doer of knavish deeds.'

'Not until yesterday did I know that you were working on Galley Quay. Soon as I learn you are here, up to the roof I come to seek you out. And that's the truth of it.'

'I fear, Sir Henry, that if I steal papers from Sir Thomas, you will never trust me with clerking confidential mercantile documents, and I will forever be humping silk bales about the quay.'

'Ability, not birth, is what counts on Galley Quay,' said the Customer. 'Apprentices can become members of the Company for twenty shillings when they are twenty-six. If you do not do this, there may be no Levant Company to employ you or anyone.' He flapped a goose-turd-green sleeve at the river. 'Look out upon the Pool. All's barren. If Sir Thomas's plot holds sway, we will be back in Boudica times with nothing on the river but a detritus of half-foist skifflers, penny-ferry piddlers and shrimpers - a flotsam and jetsam which counts for nothing in the great scheme of merchant venture! All because Sir Thomas Sherley's Machiavellian stratagem has unbalanced the world's trade.'

'But what can a poor warehouseman do?'

'When England is off-balance, the smallest actions of the merest Bramble have mighty sway. To borrow a phrase of His Majesty's: we are at the pinpoint of the protractor. The actions we take here have wide effects. In this present hour, with England off balance, a twitch of the hand on the protractor now decides the fate of the land for good or evil for all time. Let the pin slip or wiggle in its point and a Sherley's world shall radiate far and wide.'

'But, sir, I never met Sir Thomas. How will I present myself to him?'

From his right sleeve, the Customer produced a sealed and beribboned letter.

'Anthony Sherley has become - there is no nice way of putting this

- a Spaniard. The Sherley brothers compete as to who can be the biggest traitor. Anthony is a Spanish admiral, Thomas... something worse.' Then the Customer hardened his voice.

'Do you know anyone else who lives in Spain?'

'No, sir.'

Nat's heart beat faster as the Customer handed him a letter that had touched Anthony's hand. He sniffed the cream white paper folded decimo quarto. There was no whiff of ambergris. Nat examined the blobs of blood-coloured wax. The way Cecil's spies had cracked and resealed each wax boss was excellently done. Hairline fissures were visible in the wax, but you could get that from a courier riding over rough ground on a cold day. It was almost perfectly resealed, and they didn't have copies of the seal rings.

'You will deliver to Thomas this letter from his brother in Spain, and pretend to be a messenger from the docks.'

'No, Sir Henry, if I deliver this, it is too clear you sent me. But this letter from Anthony reminds me that I've another way into Sir Thomas's service.'

'Very good.'

'Is Sir Thomas at Blackfriars in the Sherley townhouse?' asked Nat.

'Sold to pay the father's debts. He lodges at the Brown Bull in Aldgate now.'

'Sure, I cannot succeed where the best intelligencers have failed.'

'They did not hate all Sherleys as you do.'

'I hope I hate no man, sir.'

'You haven't met Thomas yet.'

'If I am going to be absent from Galley Quay for a fortnight,' said Nat, 'then please may I have my wages in advance, Sir Henry.'

The Customer produced from his sleeve a brown velvet purse with golden strings.

'Here's rather more than that.'

'Who will explain my absence to the quay master, sir?'

'Myself. I will await your report at Fylpot Street a fortnight Friday at three o'clock.'

The Customer stepped over the wall into the cupola, then turned back to Nat and rested his gloved hands on the cupola's wall, like a Paul's' Cross preacher in the covered pulpit looking out over his open air congregation.

'Beware of Sir Thomas,' he said. 'He is a man disfigured by hate and bitter vengeance. Those three years in the Turk's jail soaked his soul in vinegar like your prizefighters' knuckles. Traitor though he be, yet I pity him his rough usage in Turkish dungeons, fed bread and water on the floor like a wolf. For three years he endured cruel tortures, and expected execution with every dawn. Well now, that kind of suffering does not make you a merry dancing fellow like his cousin Wil Kemp! They say suffering burns off a man's sins. Don't believe it. It burns off the last of his virtues. It breeds monsters. He blames the Levant Company for all the tortures and privations he suffered. He believes our Vice-Consuls argued for him to be kept clapped in irons. My God, I am glad it is you going into his chambers and not I. Believe me, your bravery shall not be forgot. Only beware of him, Bramble. He's not gentle like Sir Anthony.'

6

In Aldgate, in his seventh-floor garret at the Brown Bull, Thomas Sherley was reading a letter from his brother Anthony. The letter explained why Thomas's imprisonment in the Turk's dungeons had gone on so long. It appeared that a former servant of his brother - one Bramble - had intercepted his letters.

As Thomas read Anthony's words, he had a sensation that the very bones of his forehead were constricting. One night, during his imprisonment in the Seven Towers, the guards had bolted an iron hoop around his head and told him they would be back at first light to tighten the bolts and crush his skull like a walnut. Orders of the Sultan, they said. He had spent the night wearing the iron hoop, awaiting his execution, preparing for a terrible death. The next morning, some other guards entered his cell. Without a word, they unbolted the iron hoop and took it away. Thomas never knew whether this meant he was to live another day or another year. From that day on he had worn an invisible iron hoop around his head, which now tightened with this news. He fell to the floor clutching his skull in both hands.

All those letters Thomas had written with broken or frozen fingers, every page his scurvy lips had kissed in blessing as he sent it on its way, all those days he had gone without food so as to be able to bribe a friar to carry a letter - every single one of those letters, along with most of Anthony's letters to him, had been sleeved by Bramble, who had sold them to the Sherleys' enemies, singlehandedly tripling Thomas's jail time.

He jumped to his feet and paced the garret's threadbare Persian rug with his side-on way of walking which was another product of his captivity. It came from when he was transported in chains from Kea to Constantinople. For five-hundred miles, a great, heavy galley chain shackled his ankles under a donkey's belly. At Izmir something between his hip and groin had cracked and given him this slightly side-on, loping stride, as if he was turning his body into the wind, as he prowled the seventh floor garret, trying to control himself. The more he thought about this thieving Bramble the more enraged he grew.

Were it not for this incubus, this Bramble, his letters from jail would have reached his family and he would have been set free. At the very least, his father or Anthony, or Cessalye his sister, would have sent him the money to afford a prison servant and meat and a fire in his cell. Instead he had lain buried alive in an unmarked grave - and now he knew why. The name of the beast was Bramble.

Thomas stroked the bald patches in his hair. They were curious gaps. They came from where he had rubbed the back of his head against the dungeon wall for hours on end trying not to lose his mind.

The poisonous Bramble had made Anthony suffer too. He had stolen hundreds of Anthony's silver dollars, as well as a letter about Turkish naval strength, which he had sold to the Venetians who had expelled Anthony. An exile in Spain, Anthony had not been able to raise funds in time to save their father, Old Sir Thomas Sherley, from being arrested for debt on the public highway while riding alongside King James himself. There you had the upside-down sickness of the time: a base villain - named after the bush he'd been whelped under - could unseat the King's right-hand man.

Thomas grabbed his long hair in both fists. All the pain and grief and torture and fear and lice that he would have been spared but for this

one demon, this incubus, this foul forging evil villain Bramble! He kicked
the wall, denting the plaster with the toe of his boot. He picked up a chair
and dashed it on the floorboards, screaming. He heard the muezzin outside
his cell calling the faithful to prayer. He heard the spanner knocking against
the bolt in the iron hoop around his head as it tightened. Bellowing in fear
and fury, he snatched up a chair leg to defend himself, but then stopped.
That knocking wasn't a spanner on an iron ring around his head. It was
someone at the door. It wasn't the muezzin singing but his landlady telling
him he had a visitor.

❖

'Someone here to see you, Mr Sherley.'

Nat heard Mrs Da Silva walk downstairs. He stood alone before
the oak door. On the other side of which was the eldest Sherley brother,
who was not gentle like Sir Anthony. He knocked. No reply. He knocked
again. Silence. He lifted the latch, opened the door and entered Sir Thomas
Sherley's chambers.

Thomas stood on a Persian rug in the middle of the room, holding
a broken chair leg in each hand.

'May I, Sir Thomas, present my letter of commendation, my testimonial from your brother?'

'My brother?'

'Sir Anthony.'

'You were my brother Anthony's servant?'

'Yes, sir.'

Thomas laid the chair leg on the table beside his rapier. Nat
watched him approach. He was much taller than Anthony, with immensely
powerful shoulders, and led with his right leg when he walked. The rolling

of his big shoulders and the slinging of his right leg forwards reminded Nat strongly of a lion's slouching gait. And the bald patches in his hair and beard were gaps in the pelt of a mangy lion.

'But I have just had a letter from my brother.'

Thomas took the letter from Nat and walked over to his desk. He tilted the letter towards the lantern that burned before the dirty diamond-latticed windows.

To whom it may concern,

Hereby do I recommend for good and honest service in any task, Eli Elkin, a right faithful Christian, who, here in Venice as well as in Rome and Persia, has ever been a most loyal factor unto -

His Excellency Sir Anthony Sherley, Knight.

As Thomas read the letter he seemed unaware of the guttural noise, part growl, part hum, that he was making.

'Alas,' said Thomas, 'I am too poor to offer you employment, Master Elkin, but here is my hand in fellowship.'

Nat hesitated. Was it lawful for a commoner to shake a knight's hand? But Thomas clasped his hand in both of his, and smiled a smile that showed he had lost a fang.

'How did you know to find me here, Master Elkin?

'I asked at the Sherley townhouse in Blackfriars, or what once was the Sherley townhouse, begging your pardon, Sir Thomas.'

'Sit down. Sit, man, sit. I said fellowship, didn't I? Well now, Master Elkin, if you were in Persia with my brother, then I have a treat for you. A little something from the east. We shall have jasmine tea!'

He dropped two pink and silver pods into a can hanging from a pole over the grate. Soon a bright jasmine smell infiltrated the garret.

'The testimonial was written in Italy,' said Thomas, stirring the pods.

'Aye, sir.'

'My brother has not been in Italy these last five years.'

'No, sir.'

'How have you lived in the meantime?'

'Piecemeal to speak true. Here and there, on the quays mostly.'

Thomas froze. His humming growl ceased.

'Which quays?'

'Broken Wharf, Trigg Stairs, Galley Quay.'

'The Levant Company has warehouses on Galley Quay, has it not?'

Nat's stomach turned over.

'Yes, sir, I've been working there this week, hauling goods from Billingsgate, and hope to do so again.'

'Hope not so!' cried Sir Thomas, and then more quietly: 'Hope not so. Have a better hope, I mean. Think of your soul, good Master Elkin.'

'I seek better employment with you, Sir Thomas.'

'Well in that case,' said Thomas, 'what information can you bring me from Galley Quay?'

'Since losing their monopoly, the Levant Company dismisses men every day. They've had to give up their Billingsgate warehouse, sir.'

'Have they now?' His frame was shaken by a rapid succession of rasping hup, hup, hup's. 'That is good news!'

'Good news, Sir Thomas? Many labourers will lose their livelihoods. These men all have families to feed, sir.'

'The argument of footpads,' replied Thomas.

Sermons from a pirate, thought Nat. The ruined pirate set the steaming can of jasmine tea before them, a Sherley serving a Bramble. The precise way in which Thomas set out two tin goblets, and the way he poured the jasmine tea seemed to Nat to be the movements of a prisoner used to parcelling out his meagre ration of activity over the course of a whole day. One action at a time. There was anger, too, in the exactitude of his pouring. Where Anthony was choleric, irascible, busy, Thomas had a deep, still anger, which was much more ominous. They sat almost knee to knee on two wooden chairs in front of the broad oak desk. The furrows between his heavy eyebrows sharpened as Thomas frowned.

'What is that noise?' he snapped.

For a moment, Nat thought that Thomas had somehow suddenly become aware of his own growling hum. The next moment he realised what noise he meant, and replied:

'Oh, I have a pigeon in my breast. He won't fly, so I carry him into Snow Hill where I live and release him. It is a lazy one, sir.'

'A pigeon?'

'In Isfahan and in Damascus they use them instead of riding post. A safe way to send letters, Sir Thomas.'

'You send letters, do you?'

A blunder. A grievous blunder. Nat tried to distract Thomas from what he had said by producing Parboyl's brown and white domed head.

'Here he is, sir.'

Thomas ignored the bird and stared deep into Nat's eyes.

'Letters?' he asked.

'Would you like to hold him, Sir Thomas?'

'What kind of letters?'

'None as yet,' replied Nat, putting Parboyl back inside his jerkin as he spoke, 'but I hope that I can sell these intelligencing doves to merchants and sheriffs and those who need a discreet way to communicate.'

'Merchants...? You mean the Levant Company?'

'A man must live, Sir Thomas.'

'By conniving in the capture and death of other men?'

Nat's heart turned over. Did Thomas know why he had been sent here? The throaty rasp grew louder, the head twitched, and then the pirate said:

'Slaves. Slavery is how your Levant Company profits in Turkey. Christians kidnapped from their beds in maritime villages all round the Mediterranean. Children, mothers, fathers. Christians, Arabs, Jews and Moors. Snatched from their beds and sold in every Turkish town. Man, woman or child, they stand on the block like animals at auction. Sold from Turk to Turk. Shipped from harbour-market to harbour-market in Levant Company ships and only in Levant Company ships. None but our fine English merchants stoop to handle this trade. None but Levant Company ships bounce down the coast with Christian slaves. Are you proud of your work for them?'

Nat sat bolt upright as he recalled the timbers in the *Mayflower*'s hold. His eyes grew wide, as he said:

'I do believe I saw the names of those poor captives scored above their manacles in the hold of one of the Levant Company ships.'

'One? One? Ha!' A hollow, parched bark. 'Inspect the hold of every ship in their whole godforsaken fleet! The *Royal Merchant*, the *Trinity Bear*, the *Samaritan*, the *Mayflower*, the *Gift Of God*, the *Jesus*, the *Christ*! Not one, but all, man, all! That's the Levant Company's stock in trade!'

'If our English merchants don't do it,' said Nat, 'someone else will.'

With extraordinary speed, Thomas's arm slammed the table.

'No-one else will! No-one!' he shouted. 'Venice refuses even to sell arms to the Turk. Do you know what happens if a Venetian sells even so much as one ball shot to the Turk? The Doge confiscates his ship, all the goods in its hold are forfeit, and the merchant himself is condemned to the galleys for a fixed time.'

Again the muffled growl, the strangulated throaty hum, resumed in the back of Thomas's throat, only now that he got into the story he tossed his head jerkily, and smoothed the bald spots in his hair and beard with the tips of his long fingers, one after another, as he went on:

'The Levant Company sells the Sultan hundreds of barrels of gunpowder and munitions, fuses, lead, muskets, swords. The Levant Company of Fylpot Street and Galley Quay. Customer Hythe brings much slander to our nation.'

'The French trade with the Turk, Sir Thomas. The Poles too.'

'Truffles - that's what the French sell. The Poles sell mink and buy horses. That's your French and Polonian trade into Turkey! But the English, by Christ's blood and tears, keep three shops of arms and munitions in Constantinople, and transport Christian slaves around the Ottoman Empire. Only the Levant Company, only the English do this. All the others - Poles, French, Venetians - refuse to abet the kidnapping of Christians. This is the Levant Company you hope to serve, Elkin.'

Nat noticed how the more excited Thomas grew, the more he fiddled with a curious iron pendant that hung from a leather strap around his neck. In shape it was a crooked dogleg, an elongated letter Z with the lower limb bent outwards to point straight at Nat. Its screw-threaded tip showed it to be the missing part of an unknown mechanism, a clock winder, chuck key or crank handle perhaps. Just as Nat was wondering whether this might be a clue as to where the secret lists were hid, Thomas asked a question that made his heart skip a beat:

'Do you know Nat Bramble?'

'Sir?'

'Do you know Nat Bramble?'

'Why, yes. He was of Sir Anthony's and your brother Robert's party, sir.'

'As were you.'

'Yes, sir.'

'So you must know Bramble too.'

'Yes, indeed, sir.'

'What was he like?'

'We had different duties.'

'But you journeyed together through all those countries. So why won't you tell me about him?'

'Well, I hope to speak no ill of any a Christian man, sir.'

'Ha! Then you would speak ill if you did speak of him. That's plain. I see through your diplomacy!'

'Then I have failed in my Christian duty, Sir Thomas.'

'Speak on and you serve a better one. Where did you see him last?'

'That would be Venice. By which time he was Sir Anthony's secretary, I believe.'

'Have you seen Bramble on Galley Quay?'

'I, sir? No.'

'But you said you have been working there?'

'I have, sir, not him.'

'If you see Bramble, be sure to tell me, won't you?'

'I will, Sir Thomas.'

Nat turned his head away and tried to focus on something that would calm him, but instead his gaze fell upon an object that made his head spin: a Baku lantern. Three brass flames embossed its reservoir bowl. A perfect replica of the lantern that Nat dropped down the oil well at Masjid-i Suleiman was now burning away on the top floor of the Brown Bull east of Aldgate! On the floor beside the desk, lay a straw-lined box holding a dozen more Baku lanterns. So these were the trinkets the Customer meant, these were the gewgaws Thomas sold as a pretext for meeting with Italian conspirators.

'Bramble betrayed my brother, and sold his confidential letters to the Levant Company, who rewarded the villain with a sinecure. He is therefore daily complicit in the transporting of Christian slaves.'

Sermons from a pirate again - and yet the slander stung enough to provoke Nat to want to sting him back.

'What a cruel twist of fate that the Levant Company should have been saved by you of all people, Sir Thomas.'

'By me?'

'Is it not strange, sir? I myself was skinking at the supper when Sir Anthony reminded the Customer that it was you who saved the Levant Company.'

'Destroyed, I rather think he said. Ha-ha! You misheard, Master Elkin, you misheard. The Customer's spies have broken into these chambers and searched my papers often enough for fear of my intent to raze Galley Quay to the ground.'

'Saved, he said, sir. I remember Customer Hythe agreed with him, and said that when King James petitioned the Great Turk to release you he lost the right to refuse to sign Muslim contracts into law.'

'What are you saying, boy?'

'His Majesty licensed the Levant Company and all its works only to save your neck.'

Thomas stared deep into his eyes.

'You are a clever one.'

'I'm just telling you what I heard, sir.'

'Can you read and write?'

'Yes, sir.' Nat felt Thomas's fingers close around the back of his neck.

'Were you my brother's secretary in Venice?'

'No, sir, that was Nat Bramble.'

'Nat Bramble.' He could see the blood vessels in Thomas's stone-blue eyes as they searched his own.

'Yes, Sir Thomas.'

'Not Eli Elkin?'

'Nat Bramble.'

'How did you get home?'

'On the Levant Company's *Mayflower,* Sir Thomas.' The fingers of Thomas's other hand closed upon his throat.

'Then you lie. For how could you afford the passage home, when my brother cut all his people loose, far from home, without a penny?'

'Oh no, sir. Sir Anthony deposited money for our pay and passage home with an English merchant in Venice.'

Thomas pulled Nat forwards by the neck. Nat's chair tipped onto its two front legs. He braced an arm on the desk to keep the chair from tipping over entirely. What mistake had he made? What slip had let Thomas see through his imposture?

'God forgive me!' For the murder he was about to commit? 'God forgive me, but I half-believed the city merchants' slanders about my brother.'

He let go of Nat, and jumped to his feet.

Suddenly Thomas clutched his skull with both hands. He gave a sharp yell of pain as if he was suffering a brain aneurysm. He jackknifed so suddenly that it might have been Anthony with his stone. The next second he was rolling around on the threadbare Persian carpet, with Nat hopping clear of his long legs.

'Can I help you, Sir Thomas? What's the matter?'

'Out! Get out! Out!'

7

In the Pool of London a herring ship was approaching Galley Quay on its way to Fresh Wharf. Eli Elkin sat astride the ship's crosstree stirruping his boot heels in the top-rigging. He was trying to catch a glimpse of his mother's parish church, Saint Katherine Coleman's, but since he had been away so many new tall houses had been built along Seething Lane that he couldn't even see its steeple.

He was coming home penniless, after long years of service over-seas. If it turned out his mother had died in his absence then he did not know how he would feed himself, or where he would lay his head. He should have been home years ago. Three long hard years it had taken him to get home, and all because that whoreson Bramble had ruined Sir Anthony Sherley, and then swindled Elkin out of his testimonial letter.

One look at the Pool was enough to rob Elkin of any last hope of gaining a foothold in the city. Every barge had its bargemen, every crane its crew, every warehouse its hands. With bitter envy, he watched the lightermen unloading Portuguese, Spanish and Levant Company ships, the wherrymen ferrying their passengers to Horsleydown Stairs, and the shouting crane crews on Tower Wharf unloading grain for the Tower of London, the bargemen shooting the rapids under London Bridge at Gut Lock and Pedlar's Lock. Three years earlier Elkin might have been able to find a foothold in London. Too late now.

London Bridge was the very image of a city full to bursting. The only bridge across the Thames, its every square inch was put to use. All manner of extensions hung off the back of the bridge's tall buildings, like so many travellers clinging to the sides of an overloaded coach. Too late for Elkin to hop on that coach. In the middle of the bridge, Nonsuch House was full of rich Dutchmen, Italians and Spaniards, he had heard. There was no habitation for an honest Englishman anywhere in this city. Perhaps there might have been three years ago, but not now.

Sitting up on the crosstree, as the herring ship creaked on the flood tide through the Pool, Elkin found himself eye-level with the sail-lofts and taking-in doors of all the new warehouses that now lined the river. The topmast's City of London flag flapped in his face, and he pushed it aside as the ship drew level with the flat roof of a warehouse on Galley Quay, where a young warehouseman was scattering red berries for some pigeons. The breeze rippled the flat roof's standing puddles turning them into silver discs, and, in that moment, Elkin recognised the young warehouseman: Bramble.

Let wrongdoers beware! The Lord God would always find out wickedness even when it hid upon rooftops. Sure, it was Providence that the first man Elkin should see upon his return was the very cur who made it so hard for him to get back home for all these years. There would be no escape from justice now for the renegade who denied Christ and worshipped Ali in the mosques, for the villain who had forced Elkin to work his passage home on more ships than he could remember, for the traitor who betrayed Sir Anthony to England's enemies.

As close now as if he were leaning out of a first floor window and Bramble were on the pavement opposite, Elkin would hardly need to raise his voice to make the cur jump out of his skin! He put his hand to his belt. His knife and his billhook were both with his blanket roll at the foot of the mast. God's hooks! He cast about for some weapon near at hand with which to murder Bramble. His eye fell upon the wood and metal gantline block.

Elkin was shaking so violently that he was hardly able to unfasten the gantline block from the rigging. He freed it and stroked the spur of iron that jutted from the block's end. This deadly missile would kill him surer than a pistol ball. Elkin stood up on the crosstree. He wound his fist and forearm around the broad City of London flag to lash himself to the topmast. He leaned out from the topmast, swinging the wood and metal block in his free hand. He watched Bramble sit down on the roof's low parapet with one of the pigeons on his lap. Yes, let him spend his last breath mumbling to a pigeon instead of shriving himself for Divine Mercy!

'Jesus Christ, Our Lord God King on Highest, make my aim true!' Elkin shut one eye, took aim at Bramble's skull, and hurled the block with all his might.

Pigeons scattered. A black tile cracked. Bramble cried out. Jumped up. Untouched.

The herring ship pitched. Elkin clung with both arms to the mast. The flag wrapped itself around him. When Elkin fought free of his red and white cocoon, he was anguished to see Bramble still alive. The only consolation was his enemy's confusion. Bramble was bewildered, and was looking up, down and all around.

That the gantline block had missed his skull meant only one thing. The Lord God did not wish to grant Bramble a quick death. Instead, He wanted Elkin to tell the Sherley brothers where to find him. Elkin lifted his eyes to the heavens.

'Hosannah to King Jesus, who has brought Thy servant Eli home, after so many years away, to make of him an instrument of Thine and the Sherleys' Vengeance upon the traitor Nat Bramble!'

8

Come the Friday when he was supposed to present his findings about Sir Thomas Sherley's conspiracy to Customer Hythe, Nat was down in the Beijderwellen's cellar with Miep, beheading carrots at the shoulder and sliding them into damp sand to stop them sprouting.

'Three o'clock I'm expected at Fylpot Street, but what's the point of even going I'd like to know. I've nothing to tell, no intelligence to pass on. I might as well not go. In fact, I'll stay here.'

They knelt side by side on an old jute sack, working by beams of light cast by drill holes in the brickwork.

'Tell him you visited Thomas Sherley in his chambers,' replied Miep, slotting a headless carrot into wet sand, 'but that when you went there you found him too suspicious, too cagey, to let slip any intelligence.'

'You mean tell him I've failed at the only task he ever set me.'

'Except this time when you see the Customer,' she said, 'he doesn't catch you sitting in a puddle on the roof in dirty clothes. This time you dress like a secretary and take him a written report.'

'No, no, if I just present him with a written report about nothing then he'll think I've no more judgement than a Dutch girl.'

She stuck her knife into the damp sand and blew on her fingers for warmth. Well, that's shut her up at least, thought Nat. She who presumed to advise a man who'd been halfway round the world. Perhaps at last the sense was dawning on her that affairs in the world of men were a sight more complex than Miss Puppyfat could ever understand.

'Ah,' she said, 'but you're not going to give him a report about nothing. You're going to use your report as a clever way of reminding the Customer that you have more knowledge of the Mediterranean trade than a whole Turkish bath full of his Levant Company men. Your report will go, when Thomas says such and such I believe he is referring to the price of broadcloth in Aleppo, which as we all know tum te tum, tum te ta...'

Nat shook his head at her. He gouged a manky bruise from the side of a carrot, and then wiped his hands on his rough suede breeches.

'When I go to see the Customer, I'll wear my Persian attire. *That's* what'll remind him of who I am, and of the position I once held as secretary to a knight. Aye, and my lucky heron doublet, plus a few, choice Italian garments too!'

Miep was flabbergasted. He had done it again: flipped straight from being the hard-bitten, broken-spirited codger to this naive, headlong boy who believed the solution to all his problems lay in the dressing-up box. Gone straight from one foolish role to the other, ignoring every word of wise counsel along the way.

'I'd love to see you in your finery, Nat,' she said gently. 'But for today, why not dress like a sober clerk of works.'

'No, you don't understand,' he said. 'If I dress like what I have been, not what I am, then the Customer will be ashamed at having let me languish without advancement, and will therefore -.'

'Make you company jester.'

He laughed. He was suddenly happy to be down in this cellar with Miep, burying carrots in sand, and in this happiness he was ready to bury the Sherley hatchet too.

'Miep, I believe I should leave Thomas Sherley be.'

She sat back on her heels, wiped her knife upon her knee, and turned towards him.

'Then do,' she said.

'I will. Thomas, you see, he's not like Anthony. He's not subtle or cunning. Not really. He's just a little cracked in the head from all those years of licking rain off the cell wall. Oh, he slanders the Levant Company, all right, but not half as much as the men on Galley Quay.'

'Or in the Steelyard.'

'A blunt knife is what Thomas Sherley is.'

'A blunt knife is more dangerous than a sharp one. You are wise to let him alone.'

'Oh, am I now?'

'Succeed as a spy,' she went on, unable or unwilling to hear the condescension, 'and the Customer will never trust you as a confidential clerk or secretary. That would be an end of you with him.'

'Well, I'll meddle with Tom Sherley no more, even if it does put me out of favour with the Customer.'

'Bravo, Nat. Bravo.'

He looked at her black, sparkling eyes in her pale face. Light from the holes drilled in the brick made her white skin glow and the ends of her orange hair translucent.

'Miep...'

'Do your carrots,' she said.

They worked in silence aware of each other's breathing and tiniest movements. When the work was done, the sand was packed with hidden carrots, and there was a new awkwardness between them.

On his knees in the cellar, he watched her carry the bucket up the stairs, the frayed hem of her dress swaying against her bare calves.

Was this love? It couldn't be. It wasn't grand enough. It was nothing like those soaring sonnets Darius had recited for Gol. It was nothing like Rumi's *Like This.*

❖

That afternoon, Miep was halfway through building a cucumber frame, when Nat appeared in the garden dressed for his Fylpot Street interview. She was aghast to see him dressed like a storybook fool and to hear him talk in a stilted, stagey way too, like a Blackfriars chorister playing a foreign prince.

'Miep, the story of my life is in these threads. My friend Darius gave me this sleeveless fleece jerkin. In Rome, the First Secretary of the Great Persian Embassy gave me these pink and purple shalwar kameez. Sir Anthony made me wear these blue and gold stockings to match the blue and gold mooring posts of his Venetian palazzo. He wanted his retinue to look the part. Well, do I?'

She was so ashamed for him that she felt herself blush to the roots of her hair. The tips of her ears tingled with shame. She wanted to shout,

'You look like a fool in your Persian motley! As though the Saracen has climbed down from the pub sign to mince along the street!'

Even his English doublet looked crazy because no-one had worn that bumfreezer style since the old Queen's reign. Of course, he decided not to wear his one non-ridiculous garment, that handsome black coat, and laid it on top of the rabbit hutch.

'Perhaps wear that black coat on top,' she said.

'Why hide my light under a bushel?'

'Just for sobriety's sake, a little black.'

'And turn up stewed and reeking? Fie on it!' There was no talking to him in this mood, and so she gave up.

For his part, Nat felt he was squaring the circle. His life was a scattering no more. Everything was coming together! When he tossed Parboyl, he flew like an arrow for Galley Quay. There were good omens everywhere! He looked off heroically in the direction of Newgate and the City of London, and was crushed to see Parboyl flying back to him.

'*Dvifje! Lief dvif!*' exclaimed Miep, irritatingly, clapping her hands together.

'That stringy speckled runt,' said Nat, 'hasn't the first idea about being a homing pigeon. He's supposed to fly *home*. Home to the dovecot I built him on Galley Quay. Not round the corner and back to where he started from.' He snatched Parboyl from the rabbit hutch roof and stuffed him into his doublet. He'd launch him in the City.

Nat set off for Fylpot Street, rehearsing what to say to the Customer, but soon the stares directed at his outlandish clothes made it impossible for him think of anything at all. Miep was right! He should have dressed as the sober secretary. Should have worn that big black coat he got from Uruch. One look at this getup and the Customer would never offer him a position anyway. He was a public fool in his renegade motley. Perhaps there was still time to go back and change? No, he was more than halfway there now, just coming into the City at Bishopsgate, its turret a spray of severed heads. Each City gate displayed severed heads on pikestaffs to supplement the red dagger on the wall. Walking through Bishopsgate's echoey gatehouse, Nat heard a Qizilbash captain say, 'A warning to thieves!' As he emerged onto Chamomile Street, he saw a sight which scared him every bit as much as those red-cloaked Qizilbash once did: an apprentice gang a dozen strong.

The apprentices were playing a grisly game of hobbyhorse with a severed head, which had toppled, complete with pikestaff, from the Bishopsgate. One apprentice - big for a jockey - rode the hobbyhorse up and down, galloping towards passers by to make them scream and run away.

Nat hurried past, hugging the walls. Even before he turned round he knew the shouts at his back were directed at him.

'What thing is that? Hoy! Stranger! Stranger, hoy!'

'How dare you come by here?'

'Make him kiss the skull! Make him kiss the skull!'

'Ride him down!'

The jockey ran ahead of the mob. Holding the hobbyhorse in one hand, he spun Nat round with the other and grabbed his lapel.

'Kiss the skull! Tongues!'

It was a squashed leather face with long black eyelashes on the eyelids and the jaw swinging free. The dead head butted Nat hard in the mouth. A cheer went up from the mob that came running. Nat struggled but couldn't get free of the hand grasping his jerkin.

Jockey smashed the skull against his ear. The world went white. Blood trickled down the side of his neck. The hand on his lapel now seemed to him the most malevolent object in the world. He couldn't shift it. This hand would be the death of him. The other apprentices were only a few strides away.

'Kiss the skull!'

With both hands Nat took hold of the dead man's ears, plucked the severed head from the pikestaff, and piledrived the skull onto the jockey's own head. As they cracked together, one of two skulls made a sound like a smashed marrow. The jockey collapsed into the filth of Chamomile Street.

An apprentice club swung at his head. Nat ducked and felt the air raked above him. He turned and sprinted down Bishopsgate. Behind his back he heard the apprentices roaring,

'Clubs! Clubs!'

He stumbled round the corner into St Ellen's path, skidded and scrambled down an alley and vaulted into a kitchen garden. He stamped through leek rows, past garlic heads and runner bean poles. He tried to hurdle the kitchen garden's far wall, but his muddy shoe, heavy with soil, slipped on broken glass cemented into the brick, and he landed on his ribcage on the other side of the wall. He heard the apprentices come crashing through the beanpoles.

He stood up, wheezing and winded. He ran down Bury Street, snuck into a doorway and flattened his back against the door, pressing his throbbing forearms against its wood. Parboyl fidgeted at his breast, making the hooks of his doublet minutely squeak and creak. The next moment, there came a deafening, skittle alley clatter of wooden clubs in Bury Street. For sheer terror his legs seemed to give way like ninepins as the boys drew near.

He sucked down a deep draught of lung-scorching air and burst from the doorway into Bury Street. A great halloo rose up from the apprentice boys. Nat heard their feet pounding the street behind him, drawing ever nearer to his heels. He ran into the Aldgate crowds. Dodging and weaving through carts and barrows, jinking between carmen, carters and housewives, he escaped the mob, but was so scared that he didn't stop running until Threadneedle Street, where he heard the bells strike the quarter hour. A quarter past three. He was late! He'd missed his Fylpot Street appointment with the Customer. God damn those boys to hell.

Halfway down Threadneedle Street, Nat stopped to get his breath back. Next to him on the narrow cobbled pavement was a signwriter's ladder. At the top of the ladder, the signwriter was applying the finishing touches to a glossy wooden tabard showing three yellow needles on a black background. Three brass flames on a lantern bowl. As the signwriter's maulstick rocked the sign to and fro, this fresh black and yellow gloss paint winked and the yellow needles flickered like flames that gave no heat.

Suddenly Nat knew how Thomas Sherley smuggled stolen trade

secrets out of the country. His resolution to leave the ruined pirate alone perished like paper in flame.

Before the clocks struck the next quarter he was outside the Brown Bull.

9

Mrs Da Silva, mistress of the Brown Bull, remembered Nat's face. 'Sir Thomas is most desirous of seeing you,' she said. 'Come, let us see our garret knight.'

Nat followed her up several flights of scuffed wooden stairs. Sir Thomas was it now? He must be paying his rent on time. Perhaps his ship had come in. Perhaps all the wealth that once flowed to the Levant Company now flowed to him instead.

'Sir Thomas and his man are more out than in these days.'

A manservant too. Mrs Da Silva knocked at the door to Sir Thomas Sherley's garret chambers. No reply. She opened the oak door and called in to the outer room:

'Sir Thomas...?' She closed the door. 'Well, he shan't be long,' she said, 'his lamp's still burning.'

'May I wait for him here, ma'am?' She looked him up and down. 'My clothes are muddy, ma'am, only because I was chased by ruffians.'

'I'm not surprised you were chased,' she retorted. 'You must learn to do as my husband did when he first came over. A Portugal man, but you'd never have known it to look at the clothes on him. Mr Da Silva valued his marriage more than mass and went to proper protestant church. You should worship right too.'

'I do, ma'am.'

'You should dress more like the English and all. You should go to their churches and leave your mosques behind. You may wait there for Sir

Thomas.' She pointed to a small hard chair and went back downstairs.

Nat crept along the landing. He lifted the latch, pushed open the door and entered the empty chambers. He crossed the creaking black oak floorboards and the threadbare Persian rug to the desk, where a lantern was lit despite the daylight coming through the grimy windows.

The lantern cast a wan amber over Sir Thomas's correspondence, his reckonings, chits and bills. Nat had eyes only for the lantern itself with its embossed Baku symbol: three brass flames that looked like moneybags.

The lantern held a slender reed of flame on a thin white wick clamped, top and bottom, by a steel caliper. He lifted a little catch and its half-compass pane swung open. The naked flame flickered blue and gold.

This was the mysterious Baku fire that Darius had told him about when they were in the goatherd's shack on the Zagros Mountains. A fire that lit a room but did not burn paper.

He tried to blow it out, but the flame only wobbled. He placed the snuff cap on top to extinguish the flame, but when he took it off again the flame still burned. He turned the lantern round. There was a socket on the back of the lantern to raise or quench the flame, but it was missing its crank handle. What went into the socket must be that crooked dogleg of a screw-bit which Thomas wore around his neck.

'One of Cecil's spies,' the Customer told him, 'lit one and was blown up as if by a grenade.' An explosive charge was hidden inside the lantern. Fiddle with the socket without that crank handle and the lantern would explode in his face and leave him looking like Gol's father.

His next thought was simply to snatch the lantern, peg downstairs and run to Fylpot Street. There was a danger to this course, however. Mrs Da Silva would know he stole the lantern. If his hunch was wrong, if the lantern held no lists, Thomas would call for his arrest, the Customer would disown him for a thief, and Nat's head would be stuck on a pole on

Bishopsgate. One more dead lantern-thief on the gate. Another hobbyhorse for the apprentices to ride.

He put his fingers to the edge of the flame. Cold fire it was not. Curse you, Darius, it's hot! Only not scorching heat. No. He rubbed his thumbs over the three brass flames embossed on the lantern's belly, building his courage for what he knew he now must do. It was one thing to hear a tale on a windy night, quite another to trust his fingers to the flames. The flame trembled as Nat slowly let out a breath, and then righted itself, burning heavenwards again. One moment he was staring at the flame, not daring to touch it, and the next moment his hand was in.

Blue and gold fire gloved his hand. Tepid flames danced over his hands, tingling the little hairs on the back of his hand like a hot, desert wind. He forgot all danger, forgot the need to make haste before Thomas's return and even forgot the need to be quiet, but laughed in pure delight at the madness of being able to paddle his fingers in flickering flame. When he withdrew his hand, it was as if he were taking it out of an oven rather than fire.

He blew on his fingertips to cool them, then put them back into the lantern's flame. He squeezed the tall thin wick. Paper! This was, then, no wick at all, but a paper cylinder, conducting, not feeding, the cold fire of Baku. A stem of white paper clamped in a caliper of steel by means of two tiny thumbscrews, top and bottom. He tried to turn the top one but it was stuck fast, the same with the bottom screw. The longer his hands were ablaze, the hotter they became. 'Leave your hand there long enough,' Darius said, 'and you will think it fire then. Cold fire will slowly cook your flesh.'

Nat put both hands into the fire and tried to pick the paper from the caliper, but there was no prising it loose. The blood in his hands seemed to simmer. He began to panic. He tried turning both screws at the same time. It worked. The two screws turned in concert, triggering a sequence of submissive clicks. The caliper opened with a hiss, and Nat plucked the white paper cylinder from the fire.

Instantly, the room dimmed as the yellow flame collapsed to a blue squall in the lantern's greasy base. Blue flames flopped and writhed like landed fish, ever weaker. If they died he was done for because there was no way to relight the lantern without it blowing up. The whole Brown Bull might go up. The lantern sputtered.

Nat ripped an old invoice in two. He rolled it into a cylinder, which he slotted into the caliper. The paper burst into flames! Nat saw his own terrified face light up the sooty windowpanes like a firework in the sky. He ripped and rolled another strip of paper from the litter on Thomas's desk. This time he first wet the paper tube's ends in his mouth. He then slotted it into the caliper and let go. The paper didn't catch fire. The Baku flames only coiled around it like runner beans around a beanpole. Saved.

Nat reached in, tightened the thumbscrews top and bottom, and closed the lantern. His hands stank of Baku oil, a weird admixture of saltpeter, marsh vapour, and rock oil, a stench that took him right back to the vug in the Temple of Mithras.

He unrolled the secret scroll he had plucked from the fire, and read the cramped handwriting:

Sgr. Giovanni Basadonna,

Following buyers confirmed:

Messrs Salter, Sadler, Antrich, Ward buy:

currants at 5 shill bale,

pepper per bag 3 shill;

indigo per chest 100 shill,

Also, Steadman, Luck and Littler sell tin at £4 per cwt.,

Sr. Thos. Shrl, esq.

Nat danced an ecstatic little jig. Just what the Customer ordered! A list of who bought how much gross of what commodity.

Boots on the staircase. His flesh went cold. He stepped onto the landing and pulled the door to behind him, but there was no time to drop the latch before Sir Thomas Sherley appeared in a tall silver hat with a jewelled plume.

'Ah, Master Eli Elkin, is it not?'

Nat bowed low.

'At your service, Sir Thomas.'

'I really am very glad to see you again. Come in, come in. Oh, what's happened here?'

'Sir Thomas?'

'Who opened the door?'

'Mrs Da Silva, sir. Yes sir, she looked in and said I was to wait here for your return.'

'And so you waited there, and then I returned, and now we go in together, I and Master Eli Elkin in person.'

Nat sneaked a look at the lantern. Its flame was still burning steadily. The new paper cylinder held. But what if it were now to wilt? He sleeved the secret scroll. Suddenly he smelt the oil that had got all over his hands and fingers when he was trying to stop the blue flames from dying. His greasy hands reeked of it. They were church censers, filling the room with the Baku concoction. He wiped his hands on his doublet.

Sir Thomas took off his tall silver hat with its pearl-encrusted plume, and swung off his long black cloak. Nat gawped at the brilliance, the sheer expense of Thomas's new clothes. A silver shot-satin doublet with bronze slash-pane sleeve-heads. Silver knee-length canions with chunky black brocade. White leather gloves with silver knuckle studs. Silver garters on dazzling silver hose.

But as Nat was staring at Thomas's clothes, Thomas was staring at his:

'Why aren't you dressed like a Christian, Elkin?'

'Clothes earned, Sir Thomas, in the service of your noble brother.'

'I hoped I would see you again, Master Elkin.'

'Have you now a position for me, sir?'

'You were born for it.'

'Sir Thomas?'

'Master Elkin, here's work for you!' cried Thomas, and then still louder: 'Here's work for you, I say, Master Elkin! Come quick Eli Elkin, Elkin! Here I say, here! Elkin! Elkin!'

From the landing came the tread of boots.

'Your pardon, master, only I was fetching -.'

A bag of sea-coal dropped to the floor with a heavy chunk. A small cloud of black dust rose around Eli Elkin.

Nat's knees sagged as he saw again the vindictive leer of that uncomfortable, small-featured face with its exposed gums, upturned nose and bunched eyes. Elkin hopped up and down.

'Ha! ha! The fish is on the hook! This is that same whoreson Bramble, Sir Thomas. Look! Look at his clothes! I told you he worshipped Ali in the mosques! See how what I told your honour about him is true!'

'Lock the door, Master Elkin' said Thomas.

Nat heard the key turn in the iron lock. Thomas punched him in the head and he crumpled to the floor. He heard the sound of steel rapier being drawn from steel sheath.

Nat came up with his knife in his hand and squared off against Sir Thomas. For a moment it was a fight: two men facing each other, weapons drawn. Then Thomas slashed with his rapier, Nat parried with his knife, and that was that: one blow from the sword was all it took to snap the knife in two. Nat heard the end of his knife's blade fall onto the rug, leaving him holding a half-inch stump of steel by the handle. Then he felt the point of Sir Thomas's rapier pricking the hollow of his throat - exactly as his brother had done back in Isfahan - his windpipe squid for the Sherley skewer.

Thomas steered Nat backwards round the room with his sword point, grunting, humming and growling. Elkin tripped Nat's heels, sending him crashing to the black oak floorboards by the fireplace. Thomas's knee pinned down Nat's shoulder as he punched his head against the floorboards. He raised his sword's silver pommel for the deathblow to Bramble's temple. Elkin grabbed his wrist.

'Not here, sir, not yet,' he said. 'Beg pardon, sir, but seven flights of stairs is a long way to haul a carcass. Better not do the deed at home, Sir Thomas.'

'Unhand me.'

'Sir Thomas.' Elkin swept his wool cap off his head and bowed his head. 'I humbly beseech your forgiveness, Sir Thomas.'

'Bind your foul copy to the chair, Elkin! Bind him fast, arms, legs, and feet.'

'What cheer, Bramble?' Elkin's fetid spittle sprayed Nat's face as he roped him to the chair, talking all the while. 'Stealing from his lordship, that's hanging, Bramble! You and your cleverness!'

Thomas took the crooked dogleg from around his neck, slotted it into the back of the lantern, and turned down the flame until it disappeared. Nat knew he was going to die by the fact that Thomas did all this in plain sight. He watched him put a pistol in his belt and clip the lantern to his hip. Elkin followed his master out onto the landing. Thomas leant both hands on the balustrade and Elkin closed the door. Through the thick door Nat heard Thomas say:

'Bring Bramble to Old Swan stairs at five, Elkin. That's where I'm meeting Basadonna, who'll slit his throat on the *Buontalenti* and dump him in the sea.'

'Saving your honour, but from here to Old Swan's a long way to wrestle a live one.'

'Make your mind up, man! First you say don't kill him here, now you say don't kill him on the ship! Where can I kill him, I'd like to know?'

'Not where but when, Sir Thomas. After dark, we can do him in any alley you please.'

'No, we'll miss the tide.' A sigh. 'Nothing's ever simple is it?'

While his fate was being decided, Nat rocked the chair and put his weight on his feet. He waddled, half-man-half-chair, across the room, and sat the chair back against the door. His fingertips found the long iron key in the lock. He turned the lock, and listened to its tumbler turn. He heard Thomas say,

'Since it must be done in daylight hours, bandage his face so there's none can recognise him.'

Nat withdrew the key and waddled back to the centre of the room.

'Give out that a sawbones has trepanned him with the crown-saw,' Thomas was saying, 'to remove a nail that lodged in his skull following an alehouse fight. Blood may help.'

'Oh, he'll look like the part, Sir Thomas.'

'See that he does, Elkin. This is more important than my vengeance and yours. The slaves, Elkin. Think of those poor captives. Think of the slaves.'

'I was half a one myself, Sir Thomas, in the Venice galley where Bramble put me.'

'From Old Swan,' said Thomas, 'Basadonna's people will row him to the *Buontalenti*, and there an end of him. We shake the dust from our feet, and return to our work, Elkin.'

'God's work it is, Sir Thomas.'

'Old Swan at five, Elkin.'

Nat heard Thomas's footsteps go downstairs. Elkin rattled the handle, and then flung himself at the door. A shower of ceiling plaster sprinkled the threshold.

'You shouldn't have done that, Bramble. Now you put me to use of my bill hook here, and you shall rue that soon enough. I say, you shall wish you never gave me cause to use this bill hook soon enough.'

Nat heard the bill hook scrape the door a long single stroke, and then rap it sharply. He jumped.

'D'ye hear that Bramble? That's your destiny. This iron shall soon mar ye. Top hinge first, methinks. Fall to your prayers, Bramble - if Ali will hear you - for I shall soon have this door off its hinges.'

Nat tipped the chair onto its side. Face down on the Persian rug, he scrabbled behind his back for his broken knife. With its snaggle-edged stump of blade, he sawed at the fetters binding his wrists.

The door squeaked under the pressure of the bill hook's levering. Elkin sang while he worked.

'Rats or mice,
Have ye rats or mice?
Polecats, weasels?
Or have ye any old sows sick o' the measles?

Nat heard iron against iron, hook on hinge.

'I can kill vermin,

And I can kill moles,

that creepeth up and down,

and peepeth into holes!'

He snapped his fetters. Both hands free, he rolled on his back with the chair legs pointing straight up at the ceiling. He sawed at the rope binding his ankles. Kicking the last fetter from his legs, he rolled free of the chair and onto his feet.

'When I get in,' came Elkin's voice, 'I shall split your nose so your face looks like the sign of the Spread Eagle. Ohh-hoo, I can hear it now!' A loud crack sent a fissure running up the door.

Nat saw the billhook through the crack. He backed away in terror. His heart thumped so hard he thought it might burst. And then came the strangest sensation of his life, far stranger than putting his hands in fire, a sensation so astounding that he froze in the middle of the room, not daring even to breathe.

His heart came loose. It squirmed out of his chest and escaped his doublet. His heart spread its wings and flew across the room to perch on a shelf. Parboyl stared from Nat to the door, cocking his head from side to side. In his pocket, Nat found a fistful of firethorn berries, and held them out.

'Parboyl, come here!'

Parboyl walked along the shelf, fixing an amber eye on the berries, and flapped to his hand, hawk to glove. Nat grabbed the bird and chucked the berries on the desk. With his free hand, he plucked the paper cylinder from his sleeve. He clacked pen nib in inkpot, and on the secret scroll he scrawled:

5 o'clock on Old Swan Stairs. Sir Thomas Sherley will be there.

In flagrante delicto.

He folded the secret scroll into the miniature blue silk satchel, looped the satchel over Parboyl's head, knotted its straps under the bird's keel, opened the lattice window above the desk, and tossed him into the London sky.

Nat heard the door whine as the bill hook strained at the bottom hinge. In terror, he saw the foot of the door sway from side to side.

Elkin kicked the door. The bottom hinge flew off. Nat saw a muddy toecap through the gap. Elkin heaved and strained against the middle hinge, grunting his threats all the while.

'Gouge... you... up... I shall! Score grooves... in your... cheeks... with this bill hook of mine.'

Parboyl flew back in through the open window to alight on the desk. His ragged pink claws paced towards the rest of the berries. He had only gobbled a few when Elkin kicked the door a ferocious bang which sent Parboyl flapping out of the window for good.

Growling in rage, Elkin hurled his body against the door. The whole room reverberated. The fire tongs hanging in the andiron hummed.

The fireplace! Nat went to the grate. It would be a short climb up the chimney to the roof. He reached his hand over the grate's glowing embers to the flue. The chimney was too narrow to get an arm up, let alone a man. He groaned in dismay. The next second his hand and sleeve burst into flames. He leapt into the centre of the room flapping his arm. But then he stopped trying to extinguish the flames and touched them with his fingers instead. Cold fire. His hands and sleeve were still greasy with Baku oil.

A plan of escape seized Nat. He dragged the box of Baku lanterns from under the desk, lifted lantern after lantern from the straw, unscrewed every one, and poured the admixture of marsh vapour, saltpeter and rock oil all over himself, and in a circle on the Persian carpet. He put his foot in the glowing embers of the fireplace. Within seconds, cold fire danced all over his body, racing up and down like light.

With flaming fingers, he removed the chair from in front of the door, then returned to his circle of fire in the centre of the rug, where he slit his doublet and hung the knife handle in the slit. The black embers of his bonnet's plume, fine enough even for cold fire to incinerate, floated towards the heaving door.

The door flew off its hinge. Elkin burst into the room and stared in horror at the ghostly apparition before his eyes.

The ghost of Nat Bramble stood in the middle of the room cloaked in the Fire Everlasting. The handle of the dagger with which the coward had murdered himself stuck out from his body. Flames rose all around the ghost like a protestant martyr. But martyrs went to heaven and here was Hell's Envoy! A red heron peeled off the ghost's black doublet and flew upwards in flaming red strings, becoming invisible as it rose.

Elkin staggered backwards, tripped over a chair, fell down on his knees and clasped his hands together.

'Jesus defend me!' he cried. 'Hell's Own Fiery Man has come to summon me down into his furnace.'

Bramble's ghost extended an arm of fire to point straight at him. When the thing spoke, its voice was an unearthly growl.

'You! I come for you! Lucifer sends me hither to fetch ye, Eli Elkin, down to the Lake of Fire. Canaanites, Hittites, Satan summons all sinners and shall annihilate all the cities of these nations. Hell's Own Fiery Man lays hands of fire upon thee, Elkin, abominable sinner, for thou art damned!'

A finger of flame anointed Elkin's forehead and chest. Elkin rolled himself on the carpet to extinguish this unholy blessing. Legs of fire stepped over him, walked out the door and down the stairs.

'Follow me down, sinner. Do not delay.'

'Not I!' screamed Elkin. 'I defy the devil!'

Elkin jumped up, ran into Sir Thomas's bedchamber and locked himself in. He sank to the floor, where he rocked to and fro, howling, gibbering, insane.

10

A burning man strolled out of the door of the Brown Bull. Screaming citizens leapt out of his way. The burning man crossed the street to the horse and cattle trough, but he didn't jump straight in, as everyone expected him to. Instead, he sat on the edge, dipped his neckerchief, and began to rub the flames off his breeches as if they were chalk marks.

As the fire subsided, the full horror of the assault Nat had endured at Sherley and Elkin's hands struck him. His body began to shake. He splashed his face and neck and became aware of the onlookers crowding round. He must get away from this gaggle of hard-faced gawkers. He stood up, slipped on the wet cobbles and fell to the street. With that stumble, the spell was broken that had suspended the onlookers' ordinary sympathy. This was no bizarre prodigy, the crowd now understood, but a man like them all. Old and young, male and female, were suddenly helping him to his feet, all asking questions at once:

'Can you stand up?'

'Is the pain bad?'

'Have you any people at the Brown Bull?'

Nat turned back to the trough to scoop some water into his mouth. A cobb grabbed his wrist.

'That water's dirty,' he said.

The cobb carried the tall wooden scuttle on his back so easily that he looked like a giant insect that had learned to walk on its hind legs. The row of well-worn leather straps across his torso might have been an insect's thoracic segmentation grooves.

'I've got clean water here,' he said.

'I have no coins,' said Nat.

'You offend me, master,' said the cobb, unslinging the wooden water scuttle and standing it upright on the ground.

He dipped his willow ladle. Nat trembled as fresh, delicious, conduit water coursed down his throat, and over his chin and down his neck onto his chest.

'Hold still,' said the cobb. 'Don't wear it, drink it.'

He poured another draught down Nat's gullet. A young woman placed her shawl around his shoulders. The faces and words of all the men and women around him changed the tidal flow of his heart. He no longer resented the crowd's curiosity, but felt ashamed of his own unworthiness of their kind concern. He gave a stunted little wave, forgot to say thank-you to the cobb for his water, and the woman for her shawl as he handed it back, and hurried away, hot tears running down his face.

Stumbling through the Aldgate streets, many emotions crowded in on him. He sobbed with relief at having escaped the Brown Bull with his life. And he wept with grief that the crowd's goodness had been there all along, but as invisible as the River Walbrook underground. The crowd had been harbouring kindness like a fugitive. Why did this kindness, so natural to citizens, only appear as a break with daily life? What made people foreign to their proper natures? What force channelled a city down such closed and narrow culverts? The bells of St Michael's Church of the Murdering Mayor struck four. Nat ran towards Old Swan to do what he could to wreck Thomas Sherley's plan and be revenged upon him. Once this latest Sherley was destroyed, then Nat would help build God's city of justice.

11

Customer Hythe paced his walnut-paneled Fylpot Street office. He grew cold at the thought that he had been double-crossed by Bramble, who had not kept his appointment. The Spanish spy had flown the coop. If not in the pay of Spain, could Bramble be playing a double game? Was he a double agent secretly working for Thomas Sherley all along? Thomas Sherley's spy inside the Levant Company? And exactly what intelligence had Bramble been stealing? The Customer's heart sank. Downstairs from the Galley Quay warehouse roof, right below Bramble's dovecot, clerks registered how much of what went where for whom. The order book was there.

No-one carried more tonnage than the Levant Company. That was its great advantage. But steal its order book, and advantage became disadvantage. Light boats sail swift while greater hulks draw deep. A rival corporation's smaller, swifter ships could beat the Levant Company's three-hundred tonners to market. A hostile nation or corporation, a Basadonna or a Thomas Sherley needed only a spy on the inside to supply order books and shipping manifests stolen from Galley Quay.

The Customer might not know whether Bramble served Spain or Thomas Sherley or rival English corporations, but he knew for certain how Bramble sent the stolen trade secrets: by way of his intelligencing doves!

The Customer had been in the east. He was well aware how such tricks were done. He had heard tell what pigeons could do. Once, during a Chinese famine, for example, pigeons had been used to steal rice from the

Emperor's granary. They flew over the walls of the Forbidden City, gobbled the rice, flew home, and were given quicksilver to make them puke the rice. Back and forth went whole flocks, until they had coughed up a ton of rice, in return for which they were at last given a meal they were allowed to digest, while the stolen rice was washed.

Instead of rice, Bramble's doves were flying to the Spanish ambassador in Fenchurch Street, or to Basadonna on the *Buontalenti*, carrying a ton of intelligence about the Levant Company's order book. Either way, the company's sharers would not let the Customer remain long as Governor once they learnt how he'd lost so many orders to the competition.

The Customer had one last hope to save his position as Governor. There was still a chance he could catch Bramble on the warehouse roof at Galley Quay. From its hook on the wall, he lifted down his ceremonial yatagan, the wavy steel sword presented to him personally by Sultan Murad III. He belted its ivory scabbard around his waist, threw on his goose-turd-green cloak and slammed the door behind him.

Twenty minutes later, the Customer stood before Bramble's pigeon house on the Galley Quay warehouse roof. The birds were trilling inside their forty-gallon barrel. He unplugged a dowel peg and the coop swung open.

He looked in the pigeonholes. Nothing there. He was about to close the dovecot door again when he noticed that the turd tray was a stack of paper with writing on it. He angled his head to read. From the first few words he realised that this was a stack of Levant Company shipping manifests.

The brace of pigeons fluttering pell-mell inside the barrel were in the way. He unsheathed his yatagan and slashed. A scarlet spray striped the inside of the barrel and a pigeon with a chevron-striped tail dropped down dead in a corner of the coop. He sliced at a blur of wings. The second dove, green and purple, flumped down. He lifted the stack of shipping manifests and carried it to the edge of the roof, where he tipped the still squirming brace of pigeons off the end.

'A short last flight for you, my pretties,' he said, watching the birds crash onto the wharf down below.

He set the stack on the cupola wall, where he peeled away one damp rippled sheet after another. Quarterly reports from the old Queen's reign. Bills of anchorage in Crete or Patras. Sailing times of ships long since sunk or sold. These were not trade secrets. This was old, old, stuff. This wasn't spying, it was the petty pilfering of sheets that would have been used for privy paper or kindling.

Yet there must be something to it, or else why the twitching of the Customer's infallible antennae? Was this collection of musty old bills Bramble's canny way of giving himself an innocent pretext for taking valuable topical documents up onto the roof, so that, if caught in possession of the new lists, he could always say, 'Are these bills trade secrets? My, my, they all look the same to me. I've been using these old sheets of paper as the doves' turd trays for years. Begging your pardon, I thought they were all worthless.'

The Customer heard a light scraping, scuffling sound. He looked around. At first he saw nothing, but then on the copper roof of his cupola, he saw a tatterdemalion brown and white-feathered pigeon, its claws struggling to find purchase on the smooth surface. Strapped to its back was a neat blue satchel. So this was how Bramble received his instructions! Now the Customer would find out from whom: whether Spain or Tom Sherley. He unsheathed his yatagan.

The brown and white pigeon cocked its head, its amber eye went from coop to Customer, who stood between pigeon and coop, with his sword raised. The bird flew straight for its coop as if the Customer were not even there. The Customer let the pigeon come on. When it was an arm's length away, the Customer slashed. The pigeon closed its wings and tumbled forwards under the sword. The Customer scythed the air, hacking his black satin kneecap. He sheathed his sword. When he looked round, the brown and white bird was settled in the dovecot, feasting upon seeds and berries. The Customer shut the dovecot's door.

'Now to bring the mountain to Mohammed,' he said.

He rocked the pigeon house and toppled it over. Barrel slats smashed apart on landing. The structure had been made from an axle with a cartwheel at one end and a barrel at the other. He put his foot on the axle and rolled the dovecot around the roof. As the coop trundled its arc, the Customer saw through smashed slats the dazed brown and white dove, flailing and flopping around, struggling to stand then falling on its head. The Customer reached in and grabbed the pigeon. He ripped off the blue silk satchel, chucking the bird over his shoulder. Then he removed his gloves for the dainty work of winkling a tiny folded wad of paper from the satchel.

The cramped brown handwriting was so tiny that the Customer had to hold the thin slip of paper at arms' length and rear back his head to read it.

Sgr. Giovanni Basadonna,
Following buyers confirmed:
Messrs Salter, Sadler, Antrich, Ward buy:
currants at 5 shill bale,
pepper per bag 3 shill;
indigo per chest 100 shill,
Also, Steadman, Luck and Littler sell tin at £4 per cwt.,
Sr. Thos. Shrl, esq.

'So ends the career of Sir Thomas Sherley,' he cried. Here was enough to hang the pirate. Oh, the workings of nemesis were beautiful indeed! For Sherley's secret agent Bramble must have sent this message from Galley Quay, but instead of flying to Basadonna, his pigeon had come home to roost!

There was a postscript - or so it seemed since it had been written in another hand:

5 o'clock on Old Swan Stairs. Sir Thomas Sherley will be there. In flagrante delicto.

The Customer hurried down the cupola stairs, barking commands at one and all.

Within an hour, the King's Messengers had a Privy Warrant to apprehend Sir Thomas Sherley at Old Swan stairs, and to deliver him into the custody of the Lieutenant of the Tower, Sir William Wade, who by Privy Order was to wait on Tower Wharf steps until sunset.

The Customer would deal with Bramble himself.

12

Giovanni Basadonna was standing up in the cathedral turret of Saint Mary Overy. The bell beneath his feet tolled the half-hour. Half-past four. Thomas was late. He should be in the top corner window of Nonsuch House by now, there to await Basadonna's signal that all was clear for him to proceed to Old Swan for five o'clock.

Basadonna looked across the river to Old Swan stairs to see if any traps had been laid. Old Swan seemed clear. He checked the approaches, running his eye along the north bank landings above London Bridge: Anchor Lane, Emperor's Head Alley, Old Swan again - still clear - then Catherine Wheel Alley, Black Raven Alley and Fleur de Lys Alley, all the way to the Bridge.

White water hurtled from a couple of London Bridge's arches. The river hissed through Long Entry's narrow vaulted arch with the ferocity of venom spat from a cobra's mouth. Rivers were not so wild in nature as they were in the heart of this city. The gaily-painted Nonsuch House was out of all proportion with the rest of this pontoon bridge. It resembled a noblewoman lifting her skirts from the puddles of the flooded alley down which she had got lost. He felt like that dainty noblewoman himself when standing in Black Swan Alley, Bull Wharf, or whichever riverside alley or squalid stockyard or corn mill Thomas might choose to meet him in next. Except Basadonna was muddying his boots for a noble cause. He and Thomas were organising the evacuation from the City of London of that enterprising class of merchants who were being crushed under the yoke of the Levant Company's monopoly. From now on, London's merchant venturers could fetch their Eastern imports straight out of Livorno's *Riviera di Levanti*. Everything was ready - ships, crews, warehouses. All that was wanting were regular lists of these merchants' import orders before the *Buontalenti*, now anchored in the Pool, outraced the Levant Company to the Mediterranean and back again with the goods.

Beneath Basadonna's feet, the cathedral bell tolled five o'clock. As it did so, two official twelve-oared barges converged on Old Swan stairs. A sheriff's Posse Comitatus. Basadonna's heart sank through the soles of his feet to the tolling bell. Oh, what had Thomas done? How had he given the plot away?

Basadonna crossed the turret, took off his brown velvet cloak and turned it inside out. He swung his cloak over the eastern parapet. Its bronze shaft-satin lining caught the late afternoon sunlight. He flashed the lining in the direction of the *Buontalenti*. Moments later, a boat rowed out from under the shadow of the *Buontalenti*'s bows into the late afternoon sunlight, the six oars dropping from vertical to horizontal like a water-beetle, as it cut a course for Horsleydown Stairs on the Southwark shore.

Basadonna crossed the turret and swept his cloak over the north-facing parapet. A flash of bronze lining was the signal to warn Thomas, who should be in the top corner window of Nonsuch House by now, not to go to Old Swan, but to meet at the first stage of their rat run: deep in the meal floor of the London Bridge corn mills.

A casement window opened in the top corner of Nonsuch House. Sunlight glinted on a pearl-encrusted feather in a tall silver hat. Thomas leaned out, looked towards the turret where Basadonna stood and waved.

In the jauntiness of the wave, Basadonna saw the difference between them. This was not the dismay of a merchant venturer whose plans have come to naught, but the huzzah of a Christian soldier when battle is joined. Basadonna swept his cloak off the turret wall and onto his shoulders, fastened its ties at the chest and made for the spiral steps, cursing Thomas, cursing himself, and hoping only that he could get away.

13

As the church clocks struck five, Nat ran down the long passageway of Catherine Wheel Alley. He emerged onto rotting, neglected steps and looked upriver. Two twelve-oared barges were bobbing off Old Swan stairs. The barges were crewed by the Sheriff's posse, his levy of a dozen able-bodied citizens and constables. Nat lifted his arms in exultation. His face shone with triumph. This posse was all his doing. He had levied them, him and his trained dove. Parboyl had carried the message to Customer Hythe! Nat was about to see justice roll down like mighty waters!

Except where was the posse's urgency? Why had they shipped oars? Why were they sitting about so? They should be ramping up and down the bankside, ripping tarpaulins from every barge that could hide Sir Thomas and his Italian. They should be trying to roust them out of every shed between Lion Quay and the Customs House. Yet here they were, getting sunburnt faces on the petty swells of smooth water above the Bridge. A couple of constables had even removed pipes from the tops of their boots. White threads of pipe smoke knitted the two barges together. He saw the Customer emerge from Old Swan Alley, flanked by Sheriff and Alderman. Aha! This would make those alehouse constables hop! But to his dismay the Customer stood on Old Swan stairs passing the time of day with the boat crews.

Nat was aghast. What could be further from Isaiah's vision of justice rolling down like a mighty torrent than Old Swan's contented, late afternoon hum? Here above the Bridge the river was as still as a millpond. Tufts of down floated like flob on the brown water. A bullfinch sang its snorer's whistle of a song. Stirred by the breeze, a few downy tufts of rosebay willow herb rose into the air. Nat's gaze followed their ascent, and caught sight of a bright flash at the top of St Mary Overy's turret on the Southwark shore. A man draped a cloth of bronze satin across the turret wall and then whipped it away again. A signal flash! Who was he signalling? Nat looked across to the upper windows of Nonsuch House. A corner window opened. A glittering plumed hat leaned out of the window. A silver-knuckled glove waved at the Southwark church tower.

Nat jumped to his feet and shouted upriver to the Old Swan posse:

'View halloo! There's Sir Thomas Sherley there! View halloo! He's in Nonsuch! View halloo. Sir Thomas is on the bridge!'

'And how do you know for whom we wait, sirrah?' the Sheriff shouted at Nat, 'and you be not in league with Sir Thomas Sherley and sent by him to cully us, eh? Row down there, lads, and take up the traitor's boy.'

Seeing the barges making for him, Nat sprinted through Catherine Wheel Alley and along Thames Street. Blackraven Alley and Red Cross Alley flashed by as quick as fence posts.

On London Bridge, he slowed, gasping for air, hemmed in by crowds. The roadway was loud with hooves, carts, barrows, pedlars' cries and carmen's shouts. A glinting plume on a tall silver hat ran out of Nonsuch House and headed south. Nat bobbed and weaved through the crowds after him, but the Bridge was such a confusion of shop-signs and oversailing gables that there was no clear view one way or another. Nat lost sight of the silver hat, but kept running and searching through the crowds.

Thomas must still be on the Bridge, which meant he still had to cross the Pool. There were bound to be more Sheriff's barges in the Pool.

Nat would raise the hue and cry when the villain made his dash for the *Buontalenti*. He knew the perfect espial, not up high but down low, from which he could survey the whole Pool. He ran into the corn mills and down one flight of stairs after another, all the way down, through grist and chaff, to the cloudy meal floor, where the Thames throbbed through the cast-iron edge-wheels, clank, clank, CLANK, clank, clank, CLANK.

14

Basadonna found Thomas lurking behind a timber prop in the depths of the corn mills. He put his mouth to the Englishman's ear to be heard over the clanking chains.

'How are we betrayed?' he asked.

'They set an intelligencer upon me.'

'Who?'

'That same Bramble who betrayed my brother in Italy.'

'No, I mean who set him on? Who knows about us? Is it Cecil? The Customer? Were you careless, or are we cursed?'

'We'll find out presently,' said Thomas, 'I've captured the spy. My man Elkin will deliver him to us.'

'We can't stay for him, Thomas. You must come aboard at once.'

'Yes, only first let my man Elkin bring Bramble aboard.'

'No, no, you don't understand. There's two boats of sheriff's men at Old Swan and Customer Hythe himself! *Andiamo!* The launch is coming.'

Three Livornese scullers came rowing against the tide towards the corn mills, but something close by caught Thomas's eye.

'Giovanni!' he said. 'Look!' He pointed through the meal floor's dust cloud at a figure whose violent haste said he had as little corn to grind as they. 'Bramble!' They watched their betrayer clatter against a bolting-hutch, then rush to the water's edge to look out over the Pool.

'*Alora,* we'll take him with us for a tongue,' said Basadonna. 'He'll tell us what he knows in the hold.'

❖

Nat emerged from a cloud of dust and flour onto the sunlit jetty. He looked out over the Pool. There were no Alderman's or Sheriff's barges in the Pool, nor any search parties scouring the riverside. On Tower Wharf, way over on the other side of the river, the Lord Lieutenant of the Tower stood with a few Yeoman Warders. Too far to halloo. Sir Thomas Sherley had got away! The *Buontalenti* let down her topsails like a great white sigh of relief. Nat's eyes welled with bitter tears. He was never to have justice. He worked his jaw and mouth trying not to cry.

A knuckle-studded punch in the gut doubled him over. A gloved hand lifted his head by the hair.

'What cheer, Master Bramble?'

Thomas and Basadonna stood before him covered in chaff. Two white angels of death. Basadonna picked up a length of baling twine from the jetty, leaving an eel of black oak in the flour dust. He lashed Nat's wrists together in front of him. The bound captive looked down at the whitewater whirlpool under the mill wheels.

'Swim for it, Bramble,' mocked Thomas. 'It's your only chance.'

The scullers threw out the sternfast and let the current turn the boat about face. Basadonna hitched the boat to the jetty, and hopped aboard.

Thomas shoved Nat into the launch. Standing in the well of the boat, Nat braced his legs against its rocking. The six oars in the sky made a floating stockade of the launch. He heard Basadonna mutter some Livornese to the scullers, after which they all scowled venomously at the prisoner standing in the boat.

'They're hard-faced,' thought Nat, 'not because they believe I deserve my captivity, but because they know I don't. At Horsleydown stairs they were three innocent rowers, and now at London Bridge they are accomplices in a heinous crime. That's why they look daggers at me.'

Thomas jumped onto the sternboard. Nat listened to the last flick-flacks of rope being unhitched from the mooring post and readied himself for the sudden lurch the launch was about to make. He wriggled his wrists but the knots were tight. There was no way to pull his hands out of the baling twine that lashed them together.

The water under the corn mills churned so violently, that the scullers in the *Buontalenti*'s launch kept all six oars on the vertical, not daring to dip a blade.

'*Attenzione!* shouted the front sculler as Thomas cast off.

The launch did not swoop downriver, but swung to one side and crashed against the slimy wall of Borough Shore Lock. Nat wobbled as the launch swung back into the midstream, and began to surge downriver.

Then came one of those moments when the body is way ahead of the mind, when action is quicker than thought. Before he even knew what he was doing, Nat stepped onto the gunwale, and stamped a vertical oar flat. The oar slammed on the corn mill jetty with a bang. He ran along the oar to the jetty and was free. Without his weight upon the oar, the current dragged its blade from the jetty, and swept the rocking launch downstream to the Pool.

Nat sprinted across the landing stage to the waterwheel. He lay on his belly and held his fetters out to the waterwheel's edge blades. Ten times, twelve times the edge of a paddle nicked but did not sever the twine binding his wrists. He looked behind him. The launch was back! Standing on the sternpost, Sir Thomas grabbed hold of the mooring post and vaulted onto the jetty.

Nat thrust his wrists further into the waterwheel than he had dared before. A paddle's edge blade caught his fetters dead centre and dragged him forwards on his belly. The waterwheel had him in its cast-iron jaws and was diving down into the deep. Nat sawed twine against paddle as he sped across the jetty on his front. Snap. His hands came free. He watched a strand of snapped twine, still stuck to the cast-iron edge wheel, disappear through the soggy wooden casement and down into the whirlpool. That might have been him!

He looked over his shoulder. Thomas Sherley was running over the wooden boards towards him. Nat jumped up, ran into the meal floor and just had time to crawl under a bolting hutch before Thomas flew into the mill and up the stairs.

Thomas hunted Nat through the revolving runner stones. He manhandled one dusty miller after another, each time sure that the next man he spun round by the shoulder would be Bramble. He tripped over a grindstone and a shelf of grain fell from the brim of his leather hat. He ran back downstairs and hurled flour sacks this way and that.

Hiding under the bolting-hutch, the smell of singed grist in his nostrils, Nat saw Thomas's boots approach. The mill house clanked so loudly that it was impossible to hear footsteps or even shouts. No way for Nat to know when it was safe to make a dash for the river. That's what he would do, he decided. He'd swim for it after all. He slithered out from under the meal bin and ran for the jetty, and ran right into Basadonna, sword in hand. Nat turned tail. From the dust cloud came Thomas, rapier drawn, covered in flour from head to toe.

Basadonna and Thomas closed in on him. Another step and they'd both be a sword's length away. They would kill him here. A savage glint shone in Thomas's eyes. He would strike first.

There came that sound more shocking than noise on silence: silence on noise. Thomas and Basadonna stopped dead in their tracks. The corn mill seemed to hold its breath, until a single sharp note chimed:

Chink!

Chains began ringing, and then, as the drum wheel on the wall trundled, the clicking of the chain links became a rattle.

Of the three men, only Nat knew what was coming next. He ran for the tarpaulin sling full of flour sacks. Before he could reach it, the tarpaulin began to shoot up with a whoosh. It was at eye-level and rising when he leapt and turned a high somersault. The sling snatched him in midair like a hawk its meat, hoisted him upside down among flour sacks up through the ceiling. Chains ran all around him. The immemorial force of the River Thames shot Nat three floors to street level. Covered in white flour, he clambered from the tarpaulin sling and ran out of the corn mills onto Bridge Street.

'Hoy! You there!' yelled the Bridge Estates warden, raising his staff to block the sprinting spectre's path.

Nat dodged him, ran into the Chapel grocers, down the stairs and out the old crypt's undercroft onto Chapel Pier. He slipped and slid through the reeking seaweed slime of Chapel Lock, and out onto the stone bulwarks of the upriver mooring.

The breeze hulled the flour from his clothes as he hunted for a boat to steal. What he needed was a fast skiff or sail foist to whisk him to Tower Wharf where he could alert the Yeoman Warders before the traitor went aboard the *Buontalenti*. Instead, the only boat was a turnip barge. A pair of twenty-five foot paddles lay on the turnips.

He cursed his luck and untied the mooring rope. Though full to the gunwales with turnips, the boat rocked unsteadily as he stepped onboard. This was no flat-bottomed barge but a long skiff, heavy, but faster than she looked. As he rowed parallel to the Bridge he began to hope that he might be able to head off Thomas Sherley after all. Through Little Lock arch, he saw him on the launch, already halfway to the *Buontalenti*. Too late now to head him off or even to alert the Yeomen.

Nat turned the boat around. Standing up, he slung his whole body into every push and pull of the oars, like a man trying to uproot church railings. He grunted and howled with every stroke. Above Long Entry, a voice whispered in his head that he was charging in the way a wounded beast charges the hunters, hurling himself at death. He ignored the voice, shipped the long oars and let the boat's nose swing downstream.

Tunk! The heavy chain suspended across the approach to Long Entry cut into the turnip mound and stopped the boat dead. Chain against turnip blocked his way. There was not enough slack in the chain to lift it more than an inch.

The ton load made the boat sit lower in the water than the chain. Low enough to slide under if he threw the turnips overboard. Except if he did that then the boat would rise, and he'd still be stuck behind the chain! He couldn't throw the turnips overboard, but he could redistribute them within the boat. He started lobbing turnips, two at a time, from the middle to the front.

Leaning out of windows on the Bridge, people shouted urgent warnings:

'That's Long Entry! Pull away. Pull away, save yourself!'

'He's mad. He's sawing the log he sits upon!'

Nat heard a wet slap on the water right beside his boat. Rope. He looked upriver. Two watermen in a double-sculled wherry had thrown him a line. The waterman had rowed as close as they dared, but even twenty yards away they had to strain at the oars to keep their wherry from being sucked down into Long Entry.

'Grab the rope!' they were shouting. 'Forget the load! Save yourself! Take hold of the line, we daren't come nearer. You can't survive. It's self-slaughter! Grab the rope!'

The towrope floated on the surface beside his boat for a few seconds, and then slowly sank. Nat knew their words were true enough, yet somehow they didn't ring as true as the iron chain squeaking as it swung - a little more with each armful of turnips he lobbed - nor as true as the whitewater roaring in Long Entry below. A few more turnips would do it.

A woman up in a third floor casement window screamed. She could see what he could not. The turnip boat was slipping under the chain and into the cataract. The first Nat knew about it was when the chain tripped his ankles. He tumbled sideways as the boat slid completely under the chain. The boat then tipped down at a forty-five degree angle into the steep rapids. White water boomed and hissed under Long Entry's fan vaulting. It was a waterfall trapped in a crypt. Turnips rolled and bounced and smashed against the wall, while he clung to the tiller. The tiller jerked him around like a glove puppet. The boat was foundering. The sawmill was chopping it up. Only woodchip, turnip mash and a pulped corpse would be spat out into the Pool. A blizzard of white water filled his ears, eyes, nose and mouth.

And then the boat accelerated. Only when he plummeted into the oil well had he known such terrible velocity. The sudden acceleration left his stomach behind. No pebble ever skidded over an icy lake faster than the turnip boat ripped out of Long Entry, and sped across the Pool.

Nat's arms and thighs scorched with the effort of keeping the tiller pressed to his side. The boat carved a crescent through the Pool, casting up a white wall of water. By fluke he missed a merchantman, a sail-foist and a wherry, and then, clear before him in the open Pool was Thomas. The turnip barge's course would bring him close enough to swing the twenty-five foot oar. He'd poleaxe Thomas, knock him off the raised dais of the sternboard, and into the river.

❖

Thomas turned to see a giant swan's wing of water speeding across the Pool. His first thought was that one of those cantilevered extensions had fallen off the back of a tall house on the bridge and made a great splash. Except the risen spray stayed risen, the white water rose sheer from the river as it sped ever nearer. From out the swan's wing emerged a runaway boat.

Hanging on to its tiller was Bramble! The swan's wing vanished back into the water as the turnip boat came out of its curve, and headed straight for the *Buontalenti*'s launch.

Thomas pulled the pistol from his belt. He untied the twists of his dusty cloak and let the heavy black broadcloth fall into the well of the launch. He felt limber. Every faculty was alert. He pitied the uselessness of the long oar Bramble brandished, like an ancient Briton waving a cudgel at a Roman general. Was this the best that London could throw at him? After all Lord Cecil's spies? After all Customer Hythe's bribes and plots? Was this hectic, on his doomed last charge, really the best that London could do?

He watched Bramble push the tiller in panic, trying - too late - to steer the barge out of pistol range. The torque was too strong. The skink could no more change the boat's curve than avert the destiny written in the lines of his palm. He was set upon a course. The boat would come within six feet of the pistol point. Thomas didn't miss from that range. He cocked the pistol and took aim at the scar on Bramble's forehead.

❖

The river flashed beneath Nat. He saw Thomas take aim with the pistol. In frenzy he pushed against the tiller with all his might, but it wouldn't budge. If he couldn't veer from the pistol range then he'd ram the launch and throw Thomas off balance so that his shot missed. A collision would encumber the launch, and stop Thomas escaping so easily. An angry metal mosquito buzzed his ear.

Nat yanked the tiller with all his might and unleashed a thunderstorm.

The speeding barge swerved with twenty times its speed. He knew by its violent lurch that he was the sorcerer whose spell accidentally summons a hurricane.

With a thunderclap the two boats clashed. A cannonball would not have exploded the launch into smaller pieces. The barge's prow ploughed a brown surf of wood chip, splintered planks and snapped oar.

As Nat was catapulted through this wooden blizzard, a sharp object pierced his gut. The pistol's ball had found him in all this wooden fog! He spun in the air and fell into the dark cold river.

The cork bobbed up from the black river. He broke surface, among the floating wreckage of the *Buontalenti's* launch. The pain in his side from the bullet wound grew by the second. He struck out for the barge which was still intact as a battering ram. He swam through the bobbing noggins of a turnip shoal and hauled himself aboard. Blood oozed from his waist. If the pistol ball had entered his gut then his life was over.

He ripped at his clothes to see where he was hit. Tearing open his blood-drenched shalwar kameez, he found not a bullet wound but a shard of wood - simple wood – protruding from his belly. He plucked it out, and then lay on his back among the turnips laughing the helpless sobs of reprieve.

❖

Back when Nat's turnip barge was still stuck behind Long Entry's chain, Lord Lieutenant of the Tower of London Sir William Wade was anxiously pacing Tower Wharf. Six o'clock and no sign of Sir Thomas Sherley. Secretary of State Cecil's note clearly stated that Sir Thomas would be arrested at Old Swan at five o'clock, and be rowed in a King's Messenger barge to Tower Wharf, where Wade was ordered to keep him close prisoner.

'He is to be met at Tower Stairs by you, Sir William, you will then escort him to the White Tower.

The jabbing forefinger of that *'you, Sir William, you'* betrayed Cecil's nerves. Never a light thing to arrest a King's favourite, one whom Wade had seen at court cutting such a fine figure in the latest fashions. Worse still would be the bungled arrest of a King's favourite. But no blame could be laid at Wade's door, he was sure about that. He was where he was supposed to be at the time he was supposed to be there.

Suddenly his Yeoman Warders ran to the edge of the wharf, all jostling for a better look at the Pool. A runaway barge - full of turnips by the looks of it - had fallen through Long Entry. A man was trapped on board. The turnip bargeman climbed to his feet in the stern holding a single oar in both hands like a club. He was dressed in Tamburlaine's iridescent baggy breeches and a Biblical shepherd's fur-lined jerkin.

Something in the way this Turnip Tamburlaine stared so fixedly ahead made Wade and Warders follow his stare to a foreign launch with six oars flashing and dipping in and out of the water. Standing on the little stage of the launch's sternboard, a tall figure with a silver plumed hat sloughed off a dusty cloak to reveal shimmering satins and silks.

'Sir Thomas Sherley!' cried Wade. 'There's Sir Thomas! Arrest him! To the barges, men! To the barges!'

Not a single Yeoman Warder moved. They were no more able than Wade to tear their eyes from what was happening on the river. Light flashed off the chased silver metalwork of the pistol that Sir Thomas Sherley had levelled at the Turnipman. A puff of smoke appeared. Then the shot was heard.

And then with a jerk of the tiller and a swerve like a shark, and a sound like a house falling down, the turnip barge drilled through the launch. Sir Thomas Sherley and his Italians were thrown into the air as if by a mine or mortar, and the Yeoman and Wade were all running to the river steps.

❖

Thomas swam to Tower Stairs, where a Yeoman Warder pulled him out of the water, took his arm and helped him up the steps.

'My heartfelt thanks for your aid,' said Thomas, his ears ringing and a little dazed. On Tower Wharf, excited Yeoman Warders crowded round. 'Now, lads,' he asked them, 'who's seen my pistol and sword?'

'In the river, sir,' answered a Yeoman.

'A purse of gold to the man among you who fishes 'em out! Ah, my Lord Wade! The Pool's become a tiltyard this day, has it not, my lord?' No reply. That Yeoman Warder, meanwhile, still had hold of his arm. 'I shall need no handing from here, thank-you.'

'Yes, sir,' replied the Yeoman, but did not relax his grip.

'Why does he still attend me?' Thomas wondered. 'Am I cut and bleeding worse than I know?'

As he inspected himself for blood, a second Yeoman Warder clamped his other arm between elbow and shoulder. Thomas looked at the hands upon him, and stopped in his tracks.

'No, good fellows,' he said. 'Oh no, not one step further, no. Here's a Tower too many. I'm just out of the Turks' Seven Towers, you see, and cannot enter here. Wade! Let me send a note to King James. A note from me might save your house and title, Wade. Unhand me, lads.'

'Yes, Sir Thomas,' said a Yeoman, 'once we have you safe within.'

The iron vice tightened on Thomas's skull. His eyes bulged out of his head. He bucked and writhed and fought free of both Yeoman Warders. More came running, until nine or ten Warders surrounded him. Thomas kicked and punched in all directions. Once again, as on the island of Kea, he found himself surrounded and fighting for his life. They would have to kill him first. He found himself possessed by an overplus of strength, speed and guile. As he threw punches left and right, one Yeoman Warder after another fell to the ground. His knuckle-studded gloves sweetly dropped two more Yeomen, but then he tripped over a fallen Yeoman and was down. Hands grabbed all his limbs at once and lifted him off the ground. As they carried him up the wharf towards the Tower, he shouted:

'They're going to rack me! It's your Christian duty to let me go!'

Upside down and looking behind him, he craned his neck this way and that, seeking rescue. Where was Basadonna? Couldn't he see what was happening? Why no rescue? Where was sweet Giovanni? And then he saw him. There he was. There he went, scaling the *Buontalenti*'s white rope net with all the agility and conscience of a Gibraltar monkey.

'God, oh God! Why hast thou cast down thy servant and raised up the wicked!'

The *Buontalenti*'s rope net shone brilliantly white against its dull hull. At the foot of the rope net a debris trail straggled along the inky river. Thomas followed the trail of shattered planks that led to the turnip barge. The last thing he saw before the Yeomen Warders carried him around the corner, was the malevolent incubus who had destroyed his and his brother's life, and left the slaves upon the Mediterranean a helpless prey for the *Mayflower, Royal Merchant, Grace of God* and *Samaritan.* And what was Bramble doing? He was throwing back his head and laughing.

15

Body trembling, teeth chattering, Nat rolled onto his side on the turnip barge, and passed out. A few minutes later, an eeler bumped the barge.

'Eee! He's alive! The tilting turnipman's alive,' the younger of the two men in the boat exclaimed. 'Pass him some canaries there, dad. Warm up the boy.'

They helped him into a sitting position and he took the flask and sipped warm rum. They handed him into their boat, where long black eels flowed around his shins and ankles.

'And where's your people?'

'The Strangers' Quay of the Steelyard, but I've got to return this turnip barge to Chapel Pier.'

With both sweeps and a tablecloth sail, the eelers towed the barge away from the Tower of London They passed the Customs House, Galley Quay and Billingsgate. Lamps were being lit on London Bridge as they rowed up through Little Lock, and scudded south along the Bridge to Chapel Lock, where they moored the barge.

Then the eelers lifted some hessian from a writhing mound of pink crabs, and wrapped it round Nat's shoulders. Father and son pulled towards the Steelyard.

Nat closed his eyes. Flows of glistening eel-black oil coiled around his ankles at Hell's Door, pulling him down into a petroleum quagmire. He heard hooves clip-clop. Flames sprouted as harmless as flecks of foam from the flanks of two mules, a chestnut and a sooty buckskin as he and

Darius crossed the Pul-i-Shah, the King's Bridge. He opened his eyes to find himself inches away from innumerable softly clacking pink claws. Clippety-clop, clippety clop. He closed his eyes, and sank beneath the black sludge of a vug halfway down a deep cavern wall. He opened his eyes to find Miep rowing him upriver from the Steelyard.

'Where are we?' he asked.

'Between Baynard's Castle and Blackfriars,' she replied. 'Soon be home and dry, Nat.'

He closed his eyes and sank back into the vug's black sludge. He opened his eyes and found Miep basting his forehead with elm gum before pressing a coin there. He closed his eyes. Miep was as naked and sweating as he, and covered in a light dusting of almond ginger crumbs.

'Oh, don't give me that sweetmeat, Miep, or I'll think this my home.'

He opened his eyes and found Roshanak whispering Dutch prayers over him as she laid a purple mallow and woundwort poultice on his neck. From outside, he heard the creaking of the Saracen's Head pub sign across the street. The lurid red face was no Saracen but Shah Abbas, who was directing a gang of apprentices to attack Darius. Nat feared for Darius's safety as he walked past the apprentice boys down Seacole Lane. He tried to warn him, but the garret window was stuck fast and couldn't be opened without a crooked dogleg key. Darius had no sense of the danger he was in, being too preoccupied with calling up to Nat at his garret window,

'None of that vomiting and befouling of thyself at any time! None at any time at all.'

But as Darius drew level with the apprentices, far from attacking him, they doffed their caps and bowed, because he was now a merchant in a long velvet cloak.

Darius walked with Nat through the Beijderwellens' back garden down to the Turnagain Landing of the Fleet. They turned back and, Darius pointed at Miep's window and asked,

'Why have you not used poetry?'

Then they were standing at Paul's Yard bookstall, conning by heart poems they couldn't afford to buy, while the shopkeeper accused them with his eyes of stealing with theirs. As they walked to Newgate, Darius asked,

'What's the first line, Nat, what's the first line?'

Nat cudgelled his brains.

Twenty somethings would I go... tum-te-tum-te-ta?
Something, something and Earth's trees
And seaweed in the air...
Twenty ways...?

'No, it's gone.'

He stopped and his friend walked on ahead. Darius passed into the City at Newgate. No red dagger emblazoned the city shield, just the red scrawling of slaves in unfamiliar Greek and Arab script. The *Mayflower* softly bumped into Tower Stairs and a voice said,

'Eee, he's alive. Have some bullfinch.'

❖

When Nat opened his eyes, Miep was leaning over him. He held her hand and looked at her with clear eyes. His fever had broken. She sat on the bed. He heard her clumpy shoes land one by one on the floor. She lifted the sheet and rolled into the bed beside him.

It took the next hour for his hand, crawling slower than a worm, to cross the inch to her ribcage. She turned into his arms, kissed him, and they lay there, listening to the street outside.

Seacole Lane and Snow Hill were stirring at first light, but it might have been the First Day, so novel and distinct did every sound seem. The creak of a cart wheel, the metallic scrape of a night-lamp being taken off a sill, the ring of shod hooves, a baby crying, a man coughing - they all sounded new-minted, fresh and vivid.

Not so the sound of coals being put into the kitchen grate downstairs. The Beijderwellens were stirring. Miep leapt out of bed, and was gone.

Nat suspended a long ginger hair between the thumb and forefingers of both hands. Light inched across the room as slow as his hand had inched towards her ribcage and he was still holding the hair when the sunlight set it shining.

Time to get dressed. Only where were his clothes? He looked beneath a folded pile of hemp towels on the wooden chair next to his bed. No clothes there, nor in his drawer, nor under his bed, nor in the blanket box. He looked back at the chair. He noticed a wooden button. Not like a towel to have a wooden button, was it? Was this a pile of eiderdown covers?

With a sinking heart, he realised that the oatmeal-coloured pile of hemp on the chair were his clothes. The river must have ruined his treasured old clothes. The Beijderwellens had bought him this whole new suit. He knew he should feel grateful, but he was too cast down by this porridgy concoction.

He pulled on woolly oatmeal breeches, a hempen doublet with wooden buttons, and a worsted shirt with a fall collar like a Northamptonshire bumpkin. All that remained of his old attire were his grey shoes of untrimmed suede, their red stitching the one splash of English colour in all this Dutch porridge. 'This is the end of me.' He stuffed an oatmeal slop cap in his oatmeal pockets and went downstairs.

At the head of the breakfast table Mr Beijderwellen said,

'Ah, Lazarus has arisen! How do you like your elegant new suit, Mr Gentleman Secretary!'

Nat bowed and thanked him for his kindness and then thanked Mrs Beijderwellen for her care of him in his sickness.

'And Miep, too,' she replied. 'And the Lord.'

He looked about for Miep but she wasn't there. He excused himself from the table.

❖

Miep was down in the cellar waiting for Nat to leave before she came upstairs. She knew his way of blowing hot and cold. She couldn't stand him cold now. The way he saw it, no doubt, she'd caught him between sleep and wake. Tricked him. Got under his defenses when he was half delirious.

She shivered as she sat on the damp sand bank that they'd sewn with headless carrots. She wished she'd thought to bring a blanket or shawl or that big black coat of his which he never wore down here. Too late now.

The door opened and a block of hard light shone in. He was coming downstairs. Or would he now just see her as his slut? Would he now be of the opinion that she came with rent? A perk of the lodging. Bed and board. She sprang to her feet.

He walked through the thin rods of light cast by drill holes in the brick wall. They stood face-to-face in this cat's cradle of light. He offered her the black coat. She put it on. He put his hands inside the coat and held her round the waist, and looked into her eyes. She saw that his eyes were shining. He said,

Twenty journeys would I make,

And twenty ways would hie me,

To make adventure for thy sake.

To set some matter by thee.

Fire heat shall lose,

And frosts of flame be born,

Earth's trees shall seed the sky

Seaweed the air adorn,

Fire, earth, air and water, yea the globe itself shall move,

Ere I prove false to faith, or strange to you.

16

At midday, Nat set out for Fylpot Street to claim his reward. It was a cool day but by the time he came into the City at Ludgate, he was sweating in his thick Dutch clothes. The prickly kersey stockings itched and chafed through Pissing Alley, Canon Street, and all the way to Fylpot Street. The tall, top-heavy Levant House, each storey oversailing the one below, cast jagged shadows onto the whole street. The Company imposed its forms and patterns on the land. A Levant Company clerk led the man in the brand new Dutch suit to the Arcade of Curios, and told him to wait while he enquired after the Customer's will.

Alone in the Arcade of Curios, Nat listened to an indistinct hum of chatter and clinking glasses from a farther room. He examined the Arcade's wares, a miscellany of trade samples displayed on shelves and in cabinets. Indian cogwheels, Chinese printed silk, Turkish swords, Cypriot marble, Russian hides, and, from Persia, an old friend, a cork-stoppered clear glass jar of rock oil labelled 'Oil of Petrolio'. The oil and water had separated. Most of the jar was water. A rind of rock oil floated on top like the head on a pint of beer.

Nat shook the jar and the water turned grey. He shook the jar again, and there it was, black and viscous.

He recognised Customer Hythe's brash, puffed-up tone as it rose above the other voices behind the door of the adjoining suite:

'The nicer points are being discovered in the Tower as we speak.'

'But how was the trick done?' someone asked. 'How did he evade our best for spying, surveillance and house searches? What was his secret way of communicating with this Italian after all?'

'Magic,' cried the Customer. 'Fire that burneth not! Since no such thing exists in nature, the Yeoman have put his feet to the fire to find out his trick. Still claims it was cold fire no matter how his corns melt in the hot one!'

'He confesses all else?'

'Confesses? Why, man, he proclaims! Boasts how he fought to abolish what he calls our naughty trade.'

'If we don't transport the Sultan's slaves someone else will,' said Roe.

'Aye, and if we don't, we'll ship no other commodity besides,' said the Customer. 'The Sultan will snatch back our harbour rights and there an end of all honest trade. Let well alone, say I. For trade is a delicate tapestry. Pull one thread in the name of reform and you find yourself knee-deep in unsold silk bales. Let well alone.'

'Tom Sherley,' said Colthurst, 'is no righteous Moses leading the captives out of Babylon. He's a sharer with Basadonna in the profits sure enough. And hasn't he bought more fancy Neapolitan clothes than are found in even my wife's wardrobe? I tell you, gentlemen, his noble quest was for rich profits in hopes both of saving Wiston, the Sherley's Sussex seat, and of redeeming old Sir Thomas his father from the Marshalsea, where he lies half the year like Wiston plate in the pawnbroker's window.'

'True enough,' said the Customer. 'But you only have to look at the seditious libels he printed to see that Thomas fancies himself a holy warrior against the Levant Company. In which role, by the way, no man ever pissed in the wind as hard as he. For I have brought you here, gentlemen, to make an announcement. King James has made recompense after I told him that his royal meddling with our charter was to blame for this foreign plot against us. He was most contrite and by way of recompense grants that a private consortium, headed by myself, will collect customs duty on all foreign imports. I will be Customer in person and in deed: Collector of His Majesty's Customs and Excise.'

'Just like your father in the old Customs House,' said Colthurst. 'You have come full circle, and inherited your father's position.'

'Earned it, Nick, earned it. This office comes with powers my father never had. Collector and Controller. I am to set the level of that customs duty as I think fit for the benefit of the company. By the powers invested in me, we shall in future endure no division between company and England. Gentlemen, here's to the public weal and private commerce indivisible!'

'Here's to the Customer! Here's to Customer Hythe!'

Cheers rang out, boots stamped the floor and hands drummed tables.

❖

Nat felt ashamed of his role in Thomas's capture. He had been on the wrong side. Thomas's 'plot' had been a campaign to end the Levant Company's stake in shipping slaves from one Ottoman port to another. Knowing that posters and sermons alone were not enough to end the slave trade, Thomas and Basadonna had gone into competition with the Levant Company hoping to ruin them by shipping Eastern imports from the free port of Livorno. No Levant Company, no slave trade. That was the plot for which they had locked Thomas in the Tower.

'Oh, what have I done?' he whispered to the oil.

Blinking back tears, he watched the petroleum resolve itself into its two constituencies. Oil detached itself and formed discrete black strands in the water. How honest of rock oil to divulge its true properties in this way, to show its true separateness, to reveal that what looked compounded was always two constituents, Customers and Brambles. Customer Hythe had made him his gull, had used him to an evil end. In the reflection of a spindle of drifting oil, he saw him standing behind his back. Nat whipped round to face him.

'So you have escaped the hempen loop,' said Customer Hythe, 'as some call the hangman's noose. Now why is *your* neck not upon the block?'

'But, sir, you must know that it was I who sent you that messenger dove.'

'I know no such thing! I know the dove was sent to you! I know it was I who intercepted it on Galley Quay just when you thought me safely kicking my heels in Fylpot Street, waiting for your report which never came.'

'Consider, Sir Henry, that I got these wounds from Sir Thomas.'

'When thieves fall out fists will fly. Are you still in touch with Sir Anthony?'

'No, Sir Henry!'

'And yet there are these letters sent you from Spain, aren't there?'

'Letters from Spain, Sir Henry? On my life I never -.'

'On your life it will be if I catch you on Galley Quay again. You cheat your doom today, but you shall not be so lucky again. Believe it! Avaunt, cur! Shoo! Shoo!'

17

Come for your box?' asked Galley Quay's master as he slung a smashed barrel into a tall brazier's flames.

'Box? What box? I never owned any box!'

'It's in the warehouse. If it's still here in half an hour it goes in the brazier, shot and lot. Put it on your barrow or leave it for the flames.'

Feathers rose on an updraught from the pyre. With horror Nat suddenly recognised what was being chucked into the flames. He snatched his dovecot's door from the quay master's arm.

'That's mine!' he cried. The quay master shoved Nat down onto the muddy wharf, and shouted,

'Nothing's yours!'

Nat snatched his woollen hat from the mud, ran into the warehouse, up the stairs, and out onto the roof terrace.

A compass circle of white droppings marked the spot where his dovecot once stood upon its cartwheel base. All his pretty pigeons were cremated. Smoke wafted up to the roof from the wharfside brazier. Smoke, cinders and a speckled downy feather that settled on his hemp doublet. He picked it off. Brown and white. The only scrap of Parboyl to survive the flames. One of his keel feathers, by the looks of it. Hot tears stung his eyes. He didn't know why he should be distraught at the incineration of this unbiddable runt, why it grieved him more than the loss of his two best birds, Petrolio and Mithras, but the tears rolled down his muddy face and would not stop. The tatty brown and white pigeon had faithfully carried

Nat's message to the Customer on Galley Quay - hence the Sheriff's men at Old Swan stairs - only to be cremated for his good service.

A flutter of wings, a scrape of claws, and Parboyl landed clumsily on the cupola's copper roof, where he fussed and struggled to keep his footing.

'Parboyl!' cried Nat in elation.

A breeze swung the cupola's brass galleon. Parboyl took fright, and flapped awkwardly to the warehouse's parapet, and nervously tore out his own feathers. Could he smell Mithras and Petrolio's cremation?

Nat held out a handful of firethorn berries for so long that his arm ached. Despite the pain, he kept his arm still as a scarecrow's, knowing the merest flinch would scare Parboyl up into the skies. Lose him now and he'd lose him forever, because this was his last time on Galley Quay. Not daring even to turn his head, the scarecrow's gaze fell on the Tower of London's White Tower where Sir Thomas Sherley was jailed.

'And what punishment have I deserved,' he thought, 'I that put him there? To fancy myself the scourge of the Sherleys was to play a role I could be proud of, but that pride was bought at the cost of distorting Thomas beyond recognition, turning him in my mind into what I knew he was not, a bigger, badder Anthony. That was the Customer's false picture, and I made it mine. The Customer told me Thomas was my enemy, and I made him so because I wanted to feel important. And the Customer called the Levant Company my ally, when it is my enemy and the world's.'

Nat felt a small weight land with a little bounce upon his palm. Scaly feet curled round his fingers. A beak pecked. Very slowly, he brought his free hand across his body. Hardly daring to breathe, he stroked Parboyl's domed head with his thumb.

'Clever boy, right there where the lines of short life and bad luck cross.'

After a while, he gently introduced Parboyl to the inside pocket of his new hempen doublet. The skinny pigeon nestled next to Nat's heart and settled down inside his doublet. Together they left the warehouse roof for the last time.

❖

In a corner at the back of the warehouse, Nat found a hardwood trunk, its brass hasp decorated with Arab scrollwork. He turned the key and lifted the lid. The trunk was packed tight with jute bags. One bag was torn at the corner, spilling a few grey-green beans.

Nat scooped up the hard pellets and let them rattle back into the bag. Perhaps this was ballast and the real treasure lay hidden beneath. But when he squeezed his arm between the tightly packed bean bags, all he found were a few loose beans. What a joke! He closed the lid and examined the back of the box. Thickly painted green lettering read:

Kaveh/ Cafe/ Coffy
Cadiz a Londres
Galley Quay
Mr Nat Bramble

So these hard green pulses were raw qaveh - or coffy - beans. But who in Cadiz sent them to him, care of Galley Quay?

And yet there are these letters sent you from Spain, the Customer had said.

'Who do I know in Spain?' thought Nat. 'Did Anthony send this merchandise to discredit me in the Customer's eyes? If so, his plan worked, for the Customer never trusted me since. Did Thomas tell Anthony to do it? Maybe so. Where are these letters sent me from Spain?'

He searched beside the trunk. What he found there were not letters, but the last effects of Sir Thomas Sherley. It appeared that the Company had taken out an Act of Attainder on all of his possessions at the Brown Bull. Here was his straw-lined box of Baku lanterns. Nat shook each lantern in turn, but they had all been emptied. Under the box of Baku lanterns, the seditious libels were stacked as thick as the pile of outdated shipping manifests which once lined the floor of his pigeon house. There were perhaps about a hundred seditious broadsides all told, the whole batch fresh from the print and still tangy with printer's ink.

Babylon's New Slavemasters In The City Of London Discovered!

An Advertisement Touching The Levant Company's Trade In Christian Slaves.

Christ's Tears Over Galley Quay!

Tin goblets, Baku lanterns, broadsides, Nat put them all into the Cadiz trunk, shot and lot. Loose qaveh beans scurried inside the trunk as he tipped it onto the Beijderwellens' barrow.

He pushed the single-wheeled plank barrow out of the warehouse, onto Thames Street, past Romeland, up New Fish Street, and through potted, rutted Crooked Lane where the tin cups and pots clinked in the Spanish trunk. He passed St Michael's Church Of The Murdering Mayor, and hurried through the fetid fumes of Candlewick Street's soap-boilers and dyers. On Walbrook Street, between sandstone St Stephen's and the London Stone, he set down the barrow to rest his arms a moment.

A lonely Persian misfit, the unwieldy rump of the London Stone was the very opposite of prim, compact St Stephen's, where a fellow might pop in for a neat and tidy prayer to a convenient God, who fitted into the City. Not so the London Stone. The Stone was out of proportion and scale. Its shape and purpose in no way fitted in among straight roads and gable ends. This great boulder fastened with bars of iron was all that was left of the Fire Temple of Mithras that Persianized Romans had built on the east bank of the River Walbrook, which once flowed where the street now ran.

The empty street grew silent. Nat looked up and down. Suddenly there was no-one around. In the brief silence he heard a gurgling, trilling sound. Not Parboyl, no, but the sound of fresh water. Beneath the street the River Walbrook still flowed! The City of London, like ice, might silence the river's song for a season, but not forever.

I am the Walbrook,' sang the river.
The fire-breathing dragon fears fresh water,
And locks me underground.
But I come before and after him
And I'll see this dragon
Carried out on his shield to the Tideway
Along with the Exchange,
And the Levant Company's worshipful sharer,
For there are other powers than those that rule,
Untold types of commonwealth
Never seen on earth.

Listening to the River Walbrook's song, it struck him that the key to his future was sitting on his barrow. He could turn a penny from his barrow load of Spanish-Arab beans. He'd open London's only qaveh stall and sell hot cups of black elixir. He had, as yet, no idea how to roast the beans, but he could essay different roasts in the Seacole Lane scullery, until he concocted a brew which tasted as delicious as Kulsum's. He seized the barrow handles and bowled along Walbrook with the qaveh pots clanking.

'You sent a box of goods to snare me, Don Antonio,' he said out

loud, for he still believed it was he who sent the box as a sort of entrap-
ment. 'You chose these beans only for being the cheapest commodity to
fill a box, but from these qaveh beans you think so little of, like the oil you
never understood, I'll coin a fortune. I'm on my way!'

18

Nat and Miep opened London's first coffee stall in a sequestered nook off the West Nave Arcade of St Paul's Cathedral, London's busiest, noisiest building. Coffy, coffey or coffee they spelt it at different times upon the signboards of their stall. They decided to call it coffee because qaveh sounded too much like carvery and people turned up expecting a side of beef.

On seeing how people loved to drink coffee, Nat couldn't have been more proud if he had invented the drink. Not since selling oil with Darius on the maidan, had he experienced the success he now enjoyed selling coffee with Miep. He was elated. His hunch had been right. Their hard work had paid off. Londoners loved coffee. Some patrons took their coffee with expansive, lip-smacking '*aaahs*', others with a kind of grave, tightlipped, pensiveness, some leaned right into their cups to inhale the aroma, wafting the steam towards their noses to do so, others sat bolt upright, as wide-eyed as if someone under the table had put their feet in cold water. And they all came back for more.

The stall looked set to become a victim of its own popularity, however. Nat and Miep had gone through half the beans, and there were no more when these ran out. The coffee had peaked.

'I curse myself,' he told Miep, 'for all the beans we wasted in experiment.'

'Well, no-one's born knowing how to roast coffee beans. Who'd have thought the right answer was to char the beans brittle and smash them with a rawhide mallet!'

They were six feet off the ground and ten feet apart, each standing on the ledge of a pair of fluted pillars, affixing the stall's backdrop, the
Persian rug which had floored Sir Thomas's Brown Bull chamber. Nat
looped the rope around a painted wooden apostle's waist, and threw the
rope across to Miep's ledge.

'Half a bag wasted braising them in nut oil!'

'You could go to Cadiz for more,' she said.

'Cadiz,' he scoffed. 'I'll try blending the beans with toast or dandelion seeds first. A tad easier, methinks.'

Miep didn't exactly know what 'bitter tares' were in the Bible, but
she suspected they would taste like brewed dandelion.

'I speak enough Spanish to help you in Cadiz,' she said, roping a
painted apostle to look like a mountain guide.

'Oh, do you now?'

'Only we had best be quick about it.'

'Why?'

'It's the Moros who have the qaveh and they're being banished.'

'Since when?' Nat asked.

'Since Spain made peace with us.'

'With England?'

'With the Dutch. Now King Philip turns all his fury on the Moros.
It used to be that a *morisco* was safe so long as he converted to the Romish
church and made himself a Spanish Arab or Spanish Jew or Spanish Moro.
Not anymore. Conversion won't save them now. They can change their
name and Hail Mary all the livelong day, but it won't help them because
King Philip is a zealous demon bent on banishing every last convert.'

'It would be a sin,' Nat told her, 'to snaffle up the goods of exiles.'

'But if discarded cases are being left stranded on the wharf, 'twere a sin not to.'

They jumped down from their pedestals. Miep rubbed her hands on the thighs of her baggy black galligaskins, unwound a cord from the side of a stone pillar, and lowered the iron chandelier.

Nat took out the crooked dogleg key he wore around his neck, slotted it into a socket at the back of each Baku lantern, and turned the key a quarter turn. The lamps that brilliantly lit the stall were fuelled by ordinary rock oil now, instead of whatever mysterious mixture - part Baku, part gunpowder? - fuelled them before. Half the success of the stall owed to these oil lanterns as much as to the coffee. No wick lantern could ever be winched so high because it needed constant trimming. No spirit lamp or candle could ever blaze so brightly. The dazzling oil lanterns were a novelty that brought in the curious from Pauls' Walk in the Middle Aisle to the half a dozen tables made from beer kegs topped with slate.

'Hang out your light!' codded a few apprentices, mimicking the cry of the Night Constables as they hurried by to make mischief in the Walk.

And it was strange how, with its vaulted ceiling, shafts of light falling from on high, busy stalls and now these dazzling lamps, the West Nave reminded Nat of nowhere so much as the Isfahan bazaar.

'What if we went all the way to Spain only to find all the coffee gone?' he asked, lighting each lantern on the iron chandelier. 'I mean, if it's only the Moros who import it, then the coffee goes with them.'

Miep was vexed to see the return of Old Man Bramble. She spent her anger on hoisting the corona hand over hand high enough to illuminate the gaudy wooden dog roses at the fan vaulting's joints. Five glossy pink petals around a yellow stamen, the flowering bramble.

'Don't you want to keep this stall going?' she asked him.

'With all my heart,' said Nat, 'but they may soon let no stalls exist here anyways.'

Just this morning the Canon Chancellor had gone round handing an eviction notice to each and every stallholder. It was then that she'd
seen the shadow fall on him again. The first time she'd seen it since the
spectacular success of their coffee stall began, but now that it fell it fell
heavier than ever before. Nat's soul hung in the balance between hope and
despair. His sense that all was possible, his feelings of infinite capacity had
flowered here, but now the old man's face settled upon his features at the
mention of the threatened eviction. She was convinced that this was Nat's
last stand. Whichever way the wind now blew would set his face for life.
She wanted the ardent, keen-spirited, flowering Bramble, not the bitter
what's-the-point Bramble who would prefer to roast dandelions than to
sail to Spain. Except she knew it was out of her hands. It depended upon
the survival of London's only coffee stall.

Their stall hadn't wanted for luck so far. In fact they'd had the great
fortune to set up slap bang in the middle of a rage for all things Persian,
clothes, rugs, even hairstyles. The new fashion hairstyle was the Persian
lock, a long lock worn just off the crown. The Persians, it was popularly
believed, grew this single lock of hair in hopes of God lifting them by it to
heaven.

The Persian craze had to do with the innumerable travellers'
tales being sold out of Paul's Yard bookshops, with novel eastern imports,
with playhouse revivals of Christopher Marlowe's *Tamburlaine*, as well
as a hateful new play by John Day called *The Travails of the Three English
Brothers*, in which Sir Anthony Sherley and his brother Robert smote the
Christ-denying Shah Abbas in battle, in revenge for their brother Thomas's
imprisonment in the dungeons of the Shah's close ally, the Great Turkish
Sultan Ahmed - the battle lines between enemies and allies all wrong again,
just like those drawn between Nat and Thomas and the Levant Company.
Early one morning, when no-one was looking, Nat stuck a couple of Sir

Thomas's broadsides on the Nave Arcade's walls.

Babylon's New Slavemasters In The City Of London Discovered!

An Advertisement Touching The Levant Company's Trade In Christian Slaves.

London's only coffee stall soon filled with the usual morning crowd of Paul's Walkers, fashionable gallants hoping to see and be seen under the brilliant lanterns while sipping an Arab-East-African-drink in the belief that it was Persian. Then off they strolled, swinging their gorgeous Persian locks up and down the Nave's Middle Aisle, Paul's Walk, while swapping glances with the gangs of young women dangling a female version of the Persian lock, created by beribboning a topknot of hair from crown to end, and by wearing shorty waistcoats and baggy-arsed breeches in the Persian style.

By midday, just before the lunchtime rush, Nat was setting out more of the slate-topped kegs that served as tables when he looked up to see Miep returning from the direction of the Rose Window, that vast fireball in the east.

'What cheer?' he asked her.

'I've organised a meeting here at six against the planned eviction of stallholders, pedlars and tinkers from St Paul's.'

'Here? But we've only got one pot.'

19

'This being a free assembly of Paul's stallholders,' Nat announced at the meeting's commencement, 'coffee is served free to all.'

London's only coffee stall had never been so busy. There were upwards of sixty people. Nat brewed pot after pot, while Miep passed round tin goblets of steaming coffee to the assembly of pedlars, hawkers and traders whom she knew not by name but by the cries they barked.

'If we were to offer tithes,' said Hot Sheep's Feet, 'then the Church Warden would stay his hand and not put us out on the street. Tithes in kind, I mean. We should offer him a tenth of our produce.'

'That may serve you and your mutton trotters,' said Old Satin, Old Taffety, Old Velvet, 'but how many linen stomachers does the Church Warden want? How many yards of taffety petticoat is the Dean wearing?'

'Well, then we may pay him a part of our earnings in coin,' suggested Hot Sheep's Feet.

'That's all right for you fine burghers who hold stalls,' said New Brooms For Old Shoes, 'but it is death to us pedlars. The Canon Chancellor will set the rent beyond our means to pay. '

'Might we write a petition?' asked Fine Writing Ink, his funnel dangling at his side.

The echo of hooves reached them. The assembly looked round. In at the Ludgate entrance, a steaming mare pulled an onion wagon, the wagoner calling out,

'White onions, white St. Thomas onions!'

'Look at that!' said Spectacles To Read, who wore a dozen pairs of glasses all at once. Miep was entranced by this boggling array which gave him more eyes than a peacock's fan tail, each magnified eye identically appalled by what he now saw: 'An onion wagon in the side-aisle. I tell you it's wagoners, not Church Wardens, who've caused all our ache! I thought the new bye-law was supposed to have banned horses from inside the cathedral.'

'Too good a short cut, though,' said Strawberries Ripe, handing round a tray of cherries.

'Not when they lock the door against us it won't be,' said Spectacles To Read. Empty tray in hand, Miep herself addressed the meeting from the centre of the crowded assembly.

'What if we change the locks here ourselves,' she suggested, 'before the Dean has a chance to change them? Then we give him a present of one of our keys. So he can let himself in but nevermore lock us out.'

'The Dean will never agree to that, young maid,' said Fine Writing Ink. 'It would never work.'

'Oh, he'll be most agreeable,' said Old Satin, Old Taffety, Old Velvet, 'when he can't get in! Once we change the locks on the doors he'll agree to have a key all right!'

'It worked in Holland,' said Miep. 'When the Spaniards demanded keys to all the public buildings, we handed over the keys but changed the locks.'

'Well, we had better ask the Dean first, that's all I'm saying,' said Fine Writing Ink.

'And give him time to change the locks himself?' asked Ripe Cowcumbers, Ripe.

'Well, it is his church,' said Fine Writing Ink.

'Build it, did he?' asked Miep.

'If you think the Dean and Canon Chancellor are against us now,' said Old Cloaks, Gentlemen, Fine Felt Hats, 'just wait till you start forging your own keys!'

'No,' said Will Ye Buy Any Straw, 'they are the ones desecrating a customary usage of this cathedral that goes back long before King Richard's time.'

'And the Canon Chancellor's the one who started all this,' said Strawberries Ripe. 'He's the one who wants to end all indoor trade and honest business.'

'If we are agreed to change the locks,' said Nat, the coffee pot burbling and steaming being him, 'can it be done in deed? Does it not need a Guild of Locksmiths sort of fellow to change ancient locks that were fitted in Norman times?

'Well, can we, Alfred?' asked Ripe Cowcumbers, Ripe.

'Alfred?' Miep asked herself. 'Who's Alfred?' She looked around in confusion until a tinker stood up whom she knew as Brass Pot Or An Iron Pot To Mend.

'I can do all that those guilded fellows can do,' replied Alfred Brass Pot, 'and without the need of fancy badges and liveries neither, just so long as I have a subscription for the iron lock plates.'

'Can't we use old ones?' asked Nat.

'Aye, if you have 'em. If they're big enough.'

'I propose,' said Miep, 'we change the locks on all the small little doors round the back and sides of Paul's, perhaps half a dozen. A show of hands?' asked Miep. Almost all agreed.

'And I propose we let them hang the Dutch girl at the assizes,' joked Old Satin, 'for setting us on! For being the sole cause and instigator of our plot!'

'Seconded,' said Nat, a little too enthusiastically.

The meeting agreed to reconvene the following day when every-one would bring with them whatever old iron locks, lock plates and keys they had managed to find in the meantime.

'Any more of that black 'lixer?' asked Alfred. Miep gave him the last dregs, and then Nat was at her shoulder in his Old Man Bramble incarnation, mithering and fretting:

'Another meeting here tomorrow will rinse us. We're down to the last three bags.'

He lifted the hardwood lid, and scooped the last three bags from the bottom of the Cadiz trunk. As he did so, he noticed that one of the bags was much lighter than the others. He sat on the trunk and slit the bag open.

A few minutes later, Miep found Nat pressing a piece of embroidered silk to his heart, his eyes shining with joy. She sat beside him on the trunk and asked him what he held, but it seemed he had lost the power of speech.

'What's that scrap of cloth?' she asked again.

'A letter from Persia,' he replied, staring into the middle-distance.

'For you?'

'Yes.'

'Written on silk?' she asked.

'Yes.'

'In squiggles?'

'No, that's your Arab, Miep. Your Persian writes by embroidery.'

'They embroider the words?'

'Not words,' said Nat. 'Glyphs.'

'Show me!'

But Nat kept the silk clamped to his heart.

'It is a complicated alphabet,' he told her.

'Can you read it?' she asked.

Nat lifted the embroidered silk to his eyes.

> *'My dear friend Nat,*
>
> *I have taken to wife my raven-haired fiddle-playing Gol, and recommend marriage to you. I prosper as an oil factor in Tabriz. I counsel you, Nat-jan, to repose more trust in others, especially our old friend and benefactor Uruch Bey, who is a man to be trusted, after all. For he sent you this coffee, and will supply you with more, if and when you sail to Spain.*
>
> *Your loving friend,*
>
> *Darius Nouredini.'*

'He says all that on a little scrap of embroidered fabric?' asked Miep in wonder.

'Here, read it for yourself,' said Nat, and handed it to her.

Brilliant white silk flowed over Miep's hand and glowed in the West Nave Arcade's pall and gloom.

She ran her fingers along the intricate embroidery. The Persian way of writing was strange indeed, quite unlike any other. For it was written in an alphabet of tiny mirrors, paste pearls, sequins and coral tubes, all stitched together with silver thread.

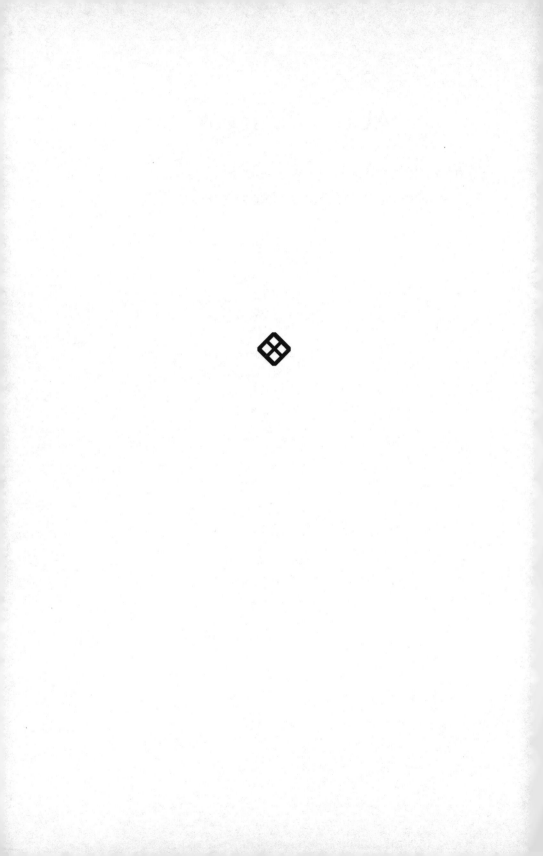

Acknowledgements

The author would like to thank the following people for their assistance in the creation of this book:

Mark Buckland
Alistair Braidwood
Craig Lamont
Anneliese Mackintosh
Karyn Dougan.

Ed Smith
Clare Alexander
Cassie Metcalf-Slovo
Mooness Davarian
Nargis Barahoi
Gunel Guliyeva
Drewery Dyke
Nick Hornby
Jeff Wood
John Gardiner
Ceri Jones
Nicky Fijalkowska
Adam Ma'anit
Esther Godfrey.

V&A and British Museum
Guildhall Library
Islington Library
British Library.